TOPOGRAPHIES OF FASCISM

Habitus, Space, and Writing in Twentieth-Century Spain

Topographies of Fascism

Habitus, Space, and Writing in Twentieth-Century Spain

NIL SANTIÁÑEZ

UNIVERSITY OF TORONTO PRESS
Toronto Buffalo London

ISBN 978-1-4426-4579-0

Printed on acid-free paper

Library and Archives Canada Cataloguing in Publication

Santiáñez-Tió, Nil
Topographies of fascism : habitus, space, and writing in
twentieth-century Spain / Nil Santiáñez.

(Toronto Iberic)
Includes bibliographical references and index.
ISBN 978-1-4426-4579-0

1. Spanish literature – 20th century – History and criticism.   2. Fascism
in literature.   3. Public spaces in literature.   4. Space (Architecture) in
literature.   5. Politics in literature.   6. Fascism – Spain – History – 20th
century.   7. Literature and society – Spain – History – 20th century.
I. Title.   II. Series: Toronto Iberic

PQ6073.F36S25 2013   860.9'3580904   C2012-908542-1

The University of Toronto Press acknowledges the financial assistance to
its publishing program of the Canada Council for the Arts and the Ontario
Arts Council.

University of Toronto Press acknowledges the financial support of the
Government of Canada through the Canada Book Fund for its publishing
activities.

To Marisol Barbón

Contents

Contents

Illustrations

Acknowledgments

This book grew out of the many conversations on fascism and the city that I had in Seattle, years ago, with Edward Baker. I owe him a debt of gratitude for his encouragement to pursue my investigations on fascism and for his comments on pieces that I wrote on the topic. For their unflinching support for this project, practically since its inception, I am also most grateful to Noël M. Valis and David T. Gies. Long in the making, these topographies of fascism have been written in Spain, Germany, and the United States. In Spain, José Luis Oyón and Carlos Sambricio provided me with substantial information on urban studies, fascist urban planning, and Falangist architecture. With Joan Gabriel López Guix I met often to talk about modern anti-Semitism. I would like to thank Facundo Tomás for his frank and judicious assessment of some of my ideas, Enric Ucelay-Da Cal for the very useful information he gave me concerning Spain's presence in Morocco, Enric Cucurella for encouraging me to delve further into the modern philosophical reflections on war and their connection with art and literature, Albert Freixa for always finding time to discuss right-wing politics, and Gonzalo Pontón Gijón (he knows why). In Germany, I felt warmly welcomed by colleagues and friends alike, most particularly Andrea and Wolfram Domke, Luis Muñiz, and Anastasia Telaak. Bernhard König, whose vast knowledge and savoir vivre is matched only by his generosity, was instrumental in making possible a three-month stay in Germany. José Antonio Barbón and Diana Auad offered me their house in Königswinter, their beautiful garden, their impressive library, their assistance, and their unconditional friendship; in their company I spent an unforgettable summer. In the United States, my sincerest gratitude goes to Michael Papio, Carlos Ramos, Enric Bou, Christina Karageorgou-Bastea, Fanny Rothschild, Travis Landry, Justin

Crumbaugh, John Wade, Steven E. Silvern, Suzanne H. Petersen, Rosa J. Bird, Alexander Hollmann, and Jean-Louis Pautrot. José Madiedo has spent many hours working on the illustrations; without him, this book would have none. I also wish to thank the two external anonymous readers of the manuscript for their meticulous reading, their judicious comments, and their extremely useful recommendations. I cannot forget the many ways in which the chair of my department, Anthony C. Daly, S.J. (with whom I have spent countless hours arguing about evil), has helped me; in him I have found nothing but friendship, understanding, and the fullest support.

I had the privilege to present my ideas as guest speaker at Yale University, Vanderbilt University, Brown University, and the Universidad Nacional de Tucumán. I am deeply grateful to my hosts for their kind invitation, and to the learned audiences of these institutions for their questions and remarks.

I would like to acknowledge the German Academic Exchange Service (DAAD), the Program for Cultural Cooperation between Spain's Ministry of Culture and United States' Universities, and the Mellon Faculty Development Grants for their generous funding of the research that I conducted in Europe. I am also very grateful to Saint Louis University for providing financial support for my project. Previous and revised versions of several sections contained in this book have appeared in journals or essay collections: "Habitus, Heterotopia and Endocolonialism in Early Spanish Literary Fascism," in *Studies in Twentieth and Twenty-First Century Literature* 33, no. 2 (2009): 248–74; "Mirada cartográfica y voluntad-de-arquitectura en la obra fascista de Ernesto Giménez Caballero," in *Bulletin of Spanish Studies* 84, no. 3 (2007): 325–47; "Cartografía crítica del fascismo español: *Checas de Madrid* de Tomás Borrás," in *Res publica* 13–14 (2004): 181–98; and "El fascista y la ciudad," which appeared as a chapter of *Madrid, de Fortunata a la M-40: Literatura y cultura urbanas*, edited by Edward Baker and Malcolm Compitello (Madrid: Alianza, 2003), 197–237. I thank their publishers and editors for allowing me to publish here substantially revised material from those works.

I was in the process of completing the book when my father passed away. He was not thrilled with my idea of writing on Spanish fascists: he knew them. Running for shelter in Barcelona during the aerial bombings routinely conducted by Italian squadrons and growing up in the early years of the Franco regime must have been on his mind when I told him about my research. I want to think that he would not disapprove of its outcome.

Being with someone who talks and writes about fascism is not always fun or easy. Marisol Barbón has never complained about that. Although her scholarly interests – colonial Peru – could hardly be further removed from mine, Marisol has devoted much of her time to my worries. She scrutinized every single draft of each chapter, and she made recommendations on the theoretical framework of the book. Conversations on European fascism and cultural geography have been, for a long time, the order of the day. I simply cannot imagine these topographies of fascism without her loving presence.

Note on Translations and Quoted Material

All translations of texts originally written in Spanish, French, Italian, and German are my own, except where otherwise noted.

All italics and capitalized words within quotations throughout the text appear in the original; when the emphasis is mine, I point it out in parenthesis.

TOPOGRAPHIES OF FASCISM

Habitus, Space, and Writing in Twentieth-Century Spain

Introduction

Before the passage of the Law of Historical Memory in the Spanish parliament on 31 October 2007, there still remained more than four hundred Francoist and fascist objects, such as busts, statues, inscriptions, the Falangist yoke and arrows, along with commemorative plaques in military installations, bases, and barracks across Spain.[1] Complying with one of the provisions of the law (Article 15.1), namely the elimination of Francoist symbols from public buildings and spaces, the Ministry of Defence instructed the armed forces to remove all residual objects of the dictatorship. Even though about 80% of those objects already had been taken away by the spring of 2010, the Ministry of Defence had yet to revise the names of buildings and sites belonging to the armed forces. A case in point is the name of the barracks of the Legion in Melilla: "Acuartelamiento Millán Astray." The barracks equestrian statue of Franco, the last of its kind to remain after the authorities of Santander had finally implemented the law by taking away the city's statue of Franco in 2008, would not be removed until August 2010. In addition to the places and spaces related in one way or the other to the armed forces, traces of fascism and the Franco regime are still everywhere to be seen on Spain's streets, squares, and buildings.[2]

Stubborn, pervasive, deeply rooted in certain strata of Spanish society and in the main conservative party, the Partido Popular (PP), the resistance against the erasure of these traces inscribed on space perpetuates and validates an authoritarian, and to a certain extent fascist, regime beyond its demise in 1977. In 2006, there were in Madrid no fewer than 350 streets with Francoist names. In 2009, the city hall of Gran Canaria changed the names of the streets "José Antonio Primo de Rivera," "General Millán Astray," and "General Queipo de Llano," among others. As

late as 2011 – that is, thirty-six years after Franco's death – Valladolid still
has an unabashed Francoist atmosphere. About 360 facades of buildings
displaying the Falangist yoke and arrows, neighbourhoods called "18 de
Julio" or "Girón," and streets bearing names such as "Primo de Rivera,"
punctuate the urban space; their presence thus provides a fascist and
Francoist meaning to Valladolid and frames the daily life of its citizens,
whose acting out of the urban grammar highlights and sanctions, whether they like it or not, this anti-democratic ideology stamped on the urban
landscape. There are many more cases, some of them disturbing indeed.
As I write these introductory pages in November 2011, there presides
over a square in downtown Granada a monolith in honour of José Antonio Primo de Rivera, co-founder of the fascist party Falange Española.[3]
Controlled by the Partido Popular, the city hall has refused to remove
this statue on account of its alleged artistic value. But perhaps the most
notorious instance of the survival of Francoism in space is the Valle de los
Caídos, this most blatant of fascist monuments in whose crypt the Bene-
dictine monks who administer this basilica and memorial celebrate mass
with mention of the "brother Francisco [Franco]." In its Article 16, the
Law of Historical Memory establishes (1) that the Valle de los Caídos will
be governed with the norms that apply to places of worship and public
cemeteries, and (2) that all political events and activities exalting the civil
war, its protagonists, and Francoism be prohibited. Despite these provisions, in the session of the senate on 22 September 2010, the PP was the
only party to vote against a motion urging the government to implement
the provisions of the Law of Historical Memory on the Valle de los Caídos.

Such resistance to remove the symbols of fascism and the Franco regime that are engraved on physical space correlates with the wish to hide,
to leave buried the deadly result of the systematic repression carried out
by the victors of the civil war. According to the most reliable sources,
between 1936 and 1945 there were about 130,000 "judicial" killings and
fifty thousand murders without the slightest pretence of a trial (Preston,
Spanish Civil War 302). Thousands of unidentified bodies lie in approximately 1,800 collective common graves across Spain. While the families
of the victims and the Associations for the Recovery of Historical Memory periodically request help in locating the remains of relatives, the
government has hitherto done little, if anything at all, to provide them
with adequate resources. The situation described by Preston in 2007 has
changed little in the past four years: "There is still no nationwide census
of the dead, no team of historians working on the problem, no funds for
DNA testing" (305). To do all this would amount to invoking the dead,

to bringing them back to social life, to conjuring up the spectres and thereby recovering the repressed. In order to keep the fascist and Francoist symbols in place, as well as the names of streets, it is necessary to hinder the exhumation of the remains of the disappeared, that is, of the victims of those whose names still decorate Spain's physical space. The invocation of the spectre would bring out the hidden meaning of those names or symbols, it would liberate what has been repressed, it would clean up, as it were, the dust covering monuments like the monolith in downtown Granada honouring Primo de Rivera.

The opposition to invoking the spectre explains in part the vicious reaction against Judge Baltasar Garzón, an investigating magistrate at the National Court in Madrid who on 16 October 2008 opened an investigation into crimes against humanity carried out by the Franco regime between 1936 and 1951. Garzón attributed to General Francisco Franco and thirty-four chiefs of the military rebellion of 17 July 1936 the organization of a systematic plan to exterminate their political enemies and a massive repression.[4] Among other things, the judge's decision called for the formation of a group of experts to determine the number, location, and identity of the victims murdered during that period, and authorized nineteen exhumations. Not surprisingly, Garzón's decision stirred a huge political, social, and juridical controversy. The office of the National Court's district attorney did not take long to appeal the decision. On 28 November 2008 the National Court's Civil Division decreed that Garzón lacked jurisdiction to investigate the disappearances. A few months later, Spain's Supreme Court granted the far-right union Manos Limpias, the rightist organization Libertad e Identidad, and the fascist party Falange Española de las JONS leave to file a lawsuit against Judge Baltasar Garzón on charges of distorting the law. After a highly politicized investigation of the case, on 12 May 2010 the Supreme Court's examining magistrate allowed the indictment of Judge Garzón to proceed. As a result, the General Council of the Judicial Power temporarily suspended the judge from office. On 7 September 2010 the Supreme Court validated the case against Garzón. Regardless of the judicial complexities and interpretations of this case, what matters here is that one of the main causes that prompted individuals, far-right organizations, and a fascist party to act against Garzón was the need literally to keep an unsavory past underground, to conceal the image of an insidious presence, to hold the spectre at bay.

The trace of Francoism and fascism in contemporary Spain consists therefore of a game of visibilities and invisibilities played out in social space. Although this phenomenon is not exclusive to fascist or far-right politics, it is consistent with the widespread interest that fascist politicians and intellectuals have always displayed for everything concerning space. The re-articulation of the nation and the body social under the guiding principle of organicism along with the structuring of the citizenry as an integral "people's community"; the tacit view of the state as a building; territorial expansionism; the undertaking of public works; the designing of plans to change the urban landscape; or the relevance given to architecture are but some of the most familiar indicators of the fascists' preoccupation with things spatial.

The observation of these and related phenomena led me to formulate the first proposition of this book on the topographies of fascism in Spain: *A proper understanding of fascism requires a proper understanding of how the fascists conceived of, used, and produced space.* Indeed, in fascist studies space has not been given its due. For the most part, space has been put aside in the interpretations of the nature of generic fascism and in general works on the topic,[5] in the comparative approaches to and histories of European fascism,[6] and in the histories and analyses of specific national fascisms.[7] Only in the works devoted to fascist architecture, urban planning,[8] and to public spectacles and rituals (e.g., political rallies, commemoration ceremonies, holiday festivities, parades)[9] do we get a glimpse of the fascists' deep, pervasive, all-encompassing interest in space.

Such critical preference and the generalized absence of a theoretical reflection on space have taken us one step forward and two steps backward: one step forward because our knowledge of fascism has been refined by the detailed studies of the centrality of rituals, geopolitics, architecture, and urban planning in fascism, and two steps backward because by treating atheoretically topics whose importance has been universally acknowledged, such scholarly works have consolidated a limited view of a multilayered phenomenon, precluding or at least making it difficult to conceive of space, in the context of fascism, as something more than buildings, roads, the urban landscape, or the occupation of foreign lands. In the otherwise vast field of fascist studies, there is thus something missing: a comprehensive exploration of the fascists' views, politics, and production of space. At the same time, in fascist studies the concept of space has been taken for granted. Tacitly, most scholarly works on spatial issues in fascism have embraced without any further scrutiny the otherwise predominant view of space in modern parlance as well as in most scholarship practised in the social sciences and the humanities: following a tradition born with Newton's theory of absolute space, space is considered as a container, a field, a universal receptacle of human agency and social action, in short, as a thing in itself.

My initial proposition was soon followed by a second one: in order to elaborate and prove the former, *it is essential to put aside the strongly entrenched concept of space as receptacle and apply in its stead a theoretical model built upon the recognition of the coexistence of different views (absolute and relative), categories (physical, mathematical, social, phenomenological, geographical, and the like), and dimensions (material, conceptual, experiential) of space.* Fortunately, there is no lack of scholarship proposing alternative theoretical models and analytical approaches. A number of cultural geographers, philosophers, sociologists, anthropologists, and historians have demonstrated that space should not be reduced to its absolute form or to its physicality. Thanks to the works of Gaston Bachelard, Michel de Certeau, Gilles Deleuze and Félix Guattari, Michel Foucault (*Dits; Punir*), David Harvey (*Condition; Cosmopolitanism; Spaces; Urban*), Henri Lefebvre (*Production; State; Writings*), Maurice Merleau-Ponty, Neil Smith, Edward W. Soja (*Postmodern; Thirdspace*), and Yi-Fu Tuan – to quote only some of the most influential – there is today a burgeoning field of spatial studies.[10] Although their reception in the social sciences and the humanities has been disparate (with some exceptions, historians and literary historians have been less receptive, for instance, than specialists in the disciplines of architecture and urban planning), these scholars and thinkers have provided us with theoretical models and analytical tools for the study of space in all its diversity, complexity, and multiple layers.

My third proposition, which underpins the analytical component of this book, condenses some fundamental presuppositions that underlie several of the above-mentioned works: *Space is both a product of social action and a determinant of human agency.*

Of the different available theoretical models, I have adopted, or to be more precise, adapted as the theoretical basis of my book, the most complete of them all. I am referring to the one put forth by Henri Lefebvre in his path-breaking and extremely influential *La Production de l'espace.*[11] Lefebvre, who has coined the expression *production of space*, argues for a unitary "science of space" that encompasses the physical, the mental, and the social. Concerned with "the logico-epistemological space, the space of social practice, [and] the space occupied by sensory phenomena" (*Production* 11–12), he puts forward two propositions: (1) space is a social product, and (2) new social relationships call for a new space, and vice versa. Hence each society has its own space. As he writes elsewhere,

"There is a production of space inherent to the mode of production, and ... this cannot be defined solely by class relations ... or by ideologies and forms of knowledge and culture ... but is also defined by this specific production" (*State* 234).

Lefebvre proposes a spatial triad to study space in all its dimensions: spatial practice, representation of space, and space of representation (*Production* 33, 38–9):

1 *Spatial practice* embraces the production process and the reproduc-tion of social relations of production while ensuring continuity and cohesion. This concept describes the physical, non-linguistic space in which flows of goods, human fluxes, personal activities and inter-personal relationships, exchanges, and the like occur. It refers to the world of the sensory perceptions and human actions. People live space through their senses. Their experience of space is defined and deter-mined by prohibitions and permissions, transportation and communi-cation systems, the relations between the country and the city, social networks, the laws regulating the property of the land, the state or the local administration of the territory, the articulation of the social and the private, and so forth. Considering the dynamics and nature of spatial practices, it follows that individuals have both a spatial com-petence (i.e., the acquired knowledge of the rules governing social space) and a spatial performance (i.e., the ability to properly use said space).

2 *Representation of space* is conceptualized space "established from objec-tive, practical, and scientific elements" (*State* 229). Tied to "the rela-tions of production and to the 'order' which those relations impose" (*Production* 33), representations of space encompass the signs, codes, knowledge, and language that enable us to understand, represent, and talk about spatial practices. This is the space of the engineers, ge-ographers, cartographers, scientists, urban planners, mathematicians, philosophers, and technocrats. Representations of space are abstract: think, for instance, of Newton's theory of space, Euclidean geometry, Einstein's theories of relativity, or Plato's, Aristotle's, Descartes's, and Kant's conceptions of space. This said, they have a practical impact and "intervene in and modify spatial textures which are informed by effective knowledge and ideology" (42).

3 *Space of representation* (a translation of the French *espace de représenta-tion* better than the one offered in the standing English translation: *representational space*) is the space lived directly through its associated

images and symbols. This kind of space "overlays physical space, making symbolic use of its objects" (*Production* 39). For Lefebvre, "the only products of spaces of representation are symbolic works" (42). Utopias, paintings, landscapes described in literature, poems, and spaces of ritual are instances of spaces of representations. Lefebvre relates this space to "the clandestine or underground side of social art as also to art" (33; see also 224, 232). Therefore, spaces of representation, which, unlike the representations of spaces, do not need to obey rules of coherence or consistency, can be described, in Harvey's words, as mental inventions "that imagine new meanings or possibilities for spatial practices" (*Condition* 218–19).[12]

The three spaces are connected dialectically, but they do not necessarily constitute a coherent whole. Each space contributes "in different ways to the production of space according to their qualities and attributes, according to the society or mode of production in question, and according to the historical period" (*Production* 46). In addition, the distinctions between the three dimensions, particularly between the representations of space and the spaces of representation, are not always clear, as Lefebvre himself avows. For instance, he contends that "today's practitioners have worked either for one side of it or the other, some developing spaces of representation and the remainder working out representations of space" (43); as an example, Lefebvre contrasts Frank Lloyd Wright's endorsement of a communitarian space with Le Corbusier's intellectualization of space (43). Sometimes, what truly matters are the gaps that separate those dimensions: thus, the work of artistic creation "occupies the interstices between representations of space and spaces of representation" (43).

I argue that fascism attempted to produce a fascist space at the three levels established by Lefebvre. Hence my fourth proposition: *The new social, cultural, economic, and political concepts and relationships brought about by the fascists implied new representations of space, new spaces of representations, and, once the fascists were in power, new material spatial practices.*[13] Naturally, the demise of Nazi Germany and Fascist Italy in 1945 halted *à jamais* the ongoing transformation of space in these two countries. Furthermore, for a Marxist like Lefebvre it would be hard, if not impossible, to conceive of a "fascist production of space," for fascism did not bring an end to the capitalist mode of production. But changes in the social fabric need not be driven solely by economics, as historians and sociologists have insisted since Max Weber. When we consider fascist ideas and actions, we have to give analytical preference to ideology, and most particularly habitus, for reasons that I hope will be clear throughout this book. Fascism did produce its own space. But it did not undertake such creation concurrently. The three spatial dimensions contributed differently to the fascists' production of space, depending on the circumstances. Thus material spatial practices were developed only when fascism attained uncontested political power, while fascist representations of space and spaces of representation produced a fascist conceptual and imaginary space prior to the consolidation of spatial practices. At the same time, the direct action carried out by political agents and paramilitary groups and, for instance, the habitus of the legionnaires posted in the Spanish protectorate of Morocco indicate by themselves the existence of incipient fascist spatial practices before the fascists' seizure of power.

Any analysis of the production of space has to take into account the connections between the spatial practices, the representations of space, and the spaces of representation. Considering that *production* means here, obviously, "production carried out by human action," human agency is at the core of the production of space. This is all the more evident in the specific case of the fascist production of space. As Paxton (*Anatomy* 15–23) and Mann (1–17) argue, fascism is better understood in terms of the actions performed by the fascists, for they saw politics "as unlimited activism to achieve moral absolutes" (Mann 8). In contrast to liberalism and Marxism, fascism lacks an elaborated philosophical system and political doctrine. Programs were vague and fluid in the extreme. Benito Mussolini, who boasted about his lack of a specific political program, expounded his own fascist doctrine ten years after he seized power in a piece co-written with Giovanni Gentile, published in 1932. The National Socialists' twenty-five-point political program, declared immutable at the party's Bamberg Conference on 14 February 1926, is not a model of coherence and clarity. Neither José Antonio Primo de Rivera nor Onésimo Redondo nor Julio Ruiz de Alda nor any other prominent Spanish fascist leader bothered to write a book elaborating his fascist politics and world view. Mann is right when he claims that fascism was much more than a group of persons with certain beliefs: "Fascism had a great impact on the world *only* because of its collective actions and its organizational forms" (12–13). While fascist ideology must be taken seriously, it must be done by considering it on its own terms. The prominence of action in fascist ideology and political practice (e.g., street violence, paramilitarism, warmongering) is yet another proof of the need to approach fascism topographically.

Given the prominence of action in fascism, I have prioritized the *habitus* over the *ideology* of fascism. This methodological procedure seems more productive than the examination of a fascist *mentality* or *ideology*; in my opinion these two concepts are not precise enough by themselves to explain the fascist performance of space, the appearance of fascism before the emergence of a full-fledged fascist political doctrine, or the presence of fascism in twenty-first-century political and social arenas. *Mentality* is not very operative on account of its psychological reading of complex social processes irreducible to mental structures, while *ideology* is problematic because of the widespread tendency to reduce *ideology* to *political ideology*. Moreover, in contrast to the abstractedness inherent in ideology, the habitus is deeply connected to the body, to human agency, and to the production of space. Pierre Bourdieu defines the concept as an acquired system of "long-lasting (rather than permanent) schemes or schemata or structures of perception, conception and action" ("Habitus" 43) produced by the conditioning factors associated with a particular class of conditions of existence.[14] By generating and organizing practices and representations, the habitus enables the production of individual and collective practices within the limits inherent in the specific conditions of such production. It is a net of acquired characteristics "which are the product of social conditions and which, for that reason, may be totally or partially common to people who have been the product of similar social conditions" (45). This habitus also can be modified through actions oriented by the individuals' intentions and consciousness. These generative schemata mean the internalization of social structures. The habitus of individuals inform their practices. As Judith Butler notes in her otherwise critical view of Bourdieu's concept, "The habitus is formed, but it is also *formative*" (*Excitable* 155). Performativity is thus at the core of the habitus. For this reason, the habitus should not be conceived of as an essence or as something previous to or independent from human agency.

The production of discourse, itself a manifestation of a habitus, played a substantial role in fascism. The pivotal function in fascist politics of rhetoric, symbology, rituals, artworks, literary texts, and propaganda material has been repeatedly noted.[15] Walter Benjamin famously referred to this phenomenon in his widely read piece on the work of art in the age of mechanical reproduction. According to Benjamin, fascism sees its salvation in giving the masses an opportunity to express themselves, but without modifying the property relations that those masses want to eliminate. By so doing, fascism introduces aesthetics into political life. In Benjamin's own words, "The violation of the masses, whom fascism, with its Führer cult, forces to their knees, has its counterpart in the violation of an apparatus which is pressed into the production of ritual values" (241). The culmination of these fascist efforts to aestheticize politics is, according to Benjamin, war (241–2). Seeking to mobilize the masses and impose a fascist habitus and ideology onto them, the fascists promoted an elaborated ritualism while disseminating discourse. In Mosse's view, "Aesthetics shaped the fascist view of man, of his surroundings and of politics. It was a cement which held fascism together" (*Fascist* 52). Furthermore, cultural products were of paramount importance to fascists, not only as a means of propaganda, but also as a way of inserting violence into language. By performing violence through words, fascist discourse refracted the physical violence routinely carried out by fascists in physical space. In her cogent study of masculinity in Italian Fascism, Spackman defines fascism as a "discursive regime" in which the relation between language and events is one in which language itself functions "as one of the realities of force and violence" (xv). In short, fascist discourse performs violence. Fascism put into practice a symbolic violence that functioned in tandem with the violence performed by individuals or paramilitary groups within material spatial practices.[16] Thus we may conclude that the violence inherent in the fascist habitus manifested itself through physical and symbolic actions that occurred across the three dimensions of the spatial triad alluded to earlier. Symbolic violence permeates fascist representations of space as well as spaces of representation. Fascist discourse was meant to express, shape, and impose a habitus onto others, to perform violence, and to contribute to the fascist production of space. Since the scholarship devoted to spatial issues in fascism has focused primarily on geopolitics, rituals, architecture, and urban planning, in this book the emphasis is placed on fascist written manifestations (e.g., essays, newspaper articles, political manifestos, novels, poetry) of representations of space and spaces of representation, without neglecting their relationship with material spatial practices.

The centrality of discourse in fascist movements and regimes is all the more evident in the case of Spanish fascism after the civil war of 1936–9. Within the Franco regime, the fascists enjoyed control over material spatial practices only between the outset of the new regime and the 1950s. Those were the years of the disastrous economic autarchy and of Spain's political isolation. Urban planners designed projects to alter the grammar of cities and towns across Spain after a fascist ideology, while architects built buildings and monuments based upon a fascist aesthetics. As of the early 1960s, though, the modernization of the industry, Spain's

economic growth, tourism, the country's integration in the networks of
international capitalism, and the migration from the countryside to cities
such as Barcelona and Madrid determined the urban planning as well as
the articulation of space and spatial relationships across the country. The
fascists' attempts to transform physical space and intervene in the urban
processes could not compete against capital.[17] In contrast to fascism's
partial failure to control spatial practices and transform non-linguistic
space in its image, Spanish fascists did succeed in developing a multifaceted discourse, born in the early 1920s, that moulded and taught a habitus
to the citizens (particularly through the educational system), expressed
a politics of space, and produced space according to the qualities and attributes of spaces of representation and representations of space.

My approach to the fascist production of space in Spain is topographical, for we are dealing with a constellation of fascist "localities" and "representations" of places and spaces. Here I use the word *topography* in two
different ways that correspond to the two clusters of meanings of the
word. First of all, *topography* is "the science or practice of describing a
place ... the accurate and detailed delineation and description of any
locality" (def. 1a) as well as "a detailed description or delineation of the
features of a locality" (def. 1b). Second, the word is defined as "localiza-
tion, local distribution; the study of this" (def. 1c) and as "the features
of a region or locality collectively" (def. 2). In the first set of definitions,
topography consists of the knowledge and writing about space; it is thus
a *representation*. In the second, it refers to the features of physical space.
Accordingly, by *topographies of fascism* I mean several things. On the one
hand, it has to be read as "topographies" of "fascism," that is, as the
fascists' knowledge and writing about space (e.g., works of art, literary
products, building programs, treatises on urban planning), and as the
features of the spaces and places that they themselves produced (e.g.,
roads, the urban landscape, the occupation and administration of foreign lands). On the other, the expression refers to my "topographies" of
fascism, to my knowledge and writing about the "topographies" of "fascism" in the two meanings just mentioned – in short, to the production
of my topographical discourse on fascist space.

In order to provide a more focused and nuanced "topography" of fascism, I investigate a specific national actualization of the fascist politics
and production of space: Spanish fascism from the late 1910s to the mid-
1950s. This is a territory that has been mapped unevenly.[18] To be sure,
historians, sociologists, and political scientists have produced important
scholarly work, quoted throughout the book, on the history and charac-

teristics of Spanish fascism. But few books have been written on Spanish literary fascism.[19] To an extent, it could be said that this marginality refracts the extraterritoriality of Spanish fascism within fascist studies. Due to the fact that Spanish fascism is a peripheral, lesser-known phenomenon with respect to National Socialism and Italian Fascism, I frequently compare the fascist politics and production of space in Spain with their counterparts in Germany, Italy, and, to a lesser degree, France. Accordingly, I analyse the corpus of Spanish texts in relation to works by, among others, Filippo Tommaso Marinetti, Curzio Malaparte, Louis-Ferdinand Céline, Robert Brasillach, Pierre Drieu la Rochelle, Ernst Jünger, Adolf Hitler, Albert Speer, and Joseph Goebbels. This book has therefore a comparative element. Still, there is another reason that has made it advisable to add a comparative dimension to my study of a specific case: the transnational nature of fascism.

In the last twenty years, the most prominent scholars in the field of fascist studies have argued for a theory of "generic fascism." Instead of producing grand, all-encompassing theories of fascism – as had been the tendency in the past among scholars, especially those of Marxist persuasion – they have centred their attention on establishing a "fascist minimum," that is to say, a set of characteristics common *to all fascisms*. Following the pioneering works of Juan Linz ("Some Notes") and George L. Mosse (*International Fascism*), these scholars (historians, sociologists, and political scientists for the most part) study the manifold ways and different degrees by which generic fascism manifests in specific fascisms within the historical period that typically covers the interwar years.[20] This is not to say that there are no significant differences in their methodology and approach. Some proceed deductively. Thus Roger Griffin starts with a theoretical model, in which fascism is conceived of as a genus of political ideology with a "mythic core" (characterized as a palingenetic form of populist ultra-nationalism). From this mythic core, Griffin derives the traits of generic fascism (e.g., anti-liberalism, anti-conservatism, tendency to operate as a charismatic form of politics, anti-rationalism, link to totalitarianism, racism, eclecticism) (Griffin, general introduction; *Nature*). Other scholars, in contrast, follow an inductive method. This is the case with Stanley G. Payne's theory of generic fascism. Payne builds his theory upon a previous historical account of fascism in Europe between the two world wars (*History* 3–19, 441–95; "Fascism" 82–8). In his work, empirical observation and the analysis of specific cases of fascism lead to the determination and description of the characteristics of generic fascism, which Payne groups under three categories: the fascist

negations (anti-liberalism, anti-communism, anti-conservatism), ideology and goals (creation of a new authoritarian state, corporativism, the
goal of empire, espousal of an idealist and voluntarist creed), and style
and organization (aesthetic structure of meetings, symbolism, and ritual;
attempted mass mobilization with militarization of political relationships
and style; positive evaluation of violence; stress on the masculine principle of male dominance; exaltation of youth; tendency towards an authoritarian, charismatic, personal leadership). Payne also distinguishes
among six varieties of fascism, one of them being Spanish Falangism
("Concept" 14–25). But regardless of the evident differences among
these and other scholars, what matters to us here is their development of
a theory of generic fascism.

In these topographies of fascism, Spanish fascism is understood as a
variant of generic fascism. Here, the view of fascism as a genus of particular cases, and consequently, as a transnational phenomenon, is
predicated on the notion that fascism is best understood from an anti-
foundationalist standpoint. Fascism lacks an essence, a defining feature;
it cannot be defined in terms of necessary and sufficient conditions; and
a nominalist approach (e.g., Allardyce) is equally unsatisfactory. The
things that we call "fascism" overlap and relate in different ways. One
may even say that fascism is a family-resemblance concept: what holds
it together is a complicated network of crisscrossing and overlapping
similarities.[21] The concept of generic fascism allows for the uncovering
of the crisscrossing of similarities and the presence of differences among
concrete instances of fascisms without losing sight of the fact that they all
belong to the same family. The varieties of fascism need to be placed in
conversation among themselves in order for the historian to determine
their common ground, because the roots, ideology, habitus, aims, political doctrine, style, and evolution of fascism, as well as the main traits of
the fascist movements (e.g., organizational structure, social composition,
tactics to attain political power) and regimes (e.g., tactics and strategies
of power) were shared in fundamental ways by all national realizations
of fascism – the Spanish case, of course, included. Hence the importance
of studying it within a comparative framework. As Iordachi points out,
"the comparative method is indispensable in fascist studies … in order
to capture the similarities and differences among historical examples of
fascism" ("Comparative" 4). This is precisely one of the methodological
presuppositions underlying this book. I have endeavoured to analyse in
depth little-known texts (even in Spain) in both their national and international contexts.

This book, whose organizing principle is space rather than time, itself approaches history through the lens of space. With the exception of the first chapter, each chapter is dedicated to several key places and spaces as represented and produced by the fascists at different or overlapping historical periods: Morocco in the first three decades of the twentieth century (chapter 2), the spatial myths of Castile, Rome, and the empire as envisioned by the fascists from the late 1910s until the mid-1940s (chapter 3), the city in the Second Republic and the civil war (chapter 4); and lastly Russia in the 1940s and 1950s (chapter 5). Without neglecting causal relations, I propose to study the history of the fascist production of space *geographically*, through the analysis of patterns, spaces, and spatial relationships vis-à-vis their variations within the different *durées* or time spans of fascism. While keeping in mind Spanish fascism's *longue durée* – a time span that reaches the present – my investigations have centred on the overlapping of two time spans: the conjunctural time span, which covers Spanish fascism from its beginnings until the beginning of the end of its hegemony in the Franco regime, and the short time span of, for example, the Rif War, the Blue Division's Russian campaign, and the Nationalists' victory parade in Madrid in 1939.

The first chapter is slightly different from the rest. While the remaining chapters centre on specific spaces, this one focuses on concepts of space as expressed in one generic instance of the spaces of representation and representations of space: fascist theoretical writing. It begins with a compact scrutiny of the fascist politics of space by contrasting the specific manner in which fascists in Spain, Germany, and Italy articulated three notions of space: the absolute, the relative, and the relational. The bulk of the chapter addresses the expression of this politics of space in three of the most influential fascist theoretical essays ever published in Spain: *Genio de España* (1932), *Arte y Estado* (1935), and *Roma madre* (1939), all written by Ernesto Giménez Caballero, one of the main ideologues of Spanish fascism in the 1930s. These books number among the most important manifestations of the fascist production of space through writing. Key elements are Giménez Caballero's tendency to represent the political, artistic, and literary space as architecture; his spatialization of discourse (e.g., preference for simultaneity, collage, and visual literature); and his cartographic approach to political, historical, cultural, and economic issues. Indeed, Giménez Caballero considered Spain's history as a "territory" defined by its own genius loci, one that had to be "mapped" before it could be understood. This chapter may be characterized as a point of departure for the examination of the fascist writing related in one way or the other to the fascist politics and production of space.

Chapter 2 is centred on the Spanish protectorate of Morocco (1912–56). After relating Spanish colonialism to fascism and framing the former in its historical context, I argue that the Spanish fascist habitus was forged in Morocco during the Rif War (1921–7). Works by Tomás Borrás, Francisco Franco, Ernesto Giménez Caballero, José Millán Astray, Luys Santa Marina, and Rafael Sánchez Mazas shaped this habitus in relation to the production of a colonial space and to an authoritarian view of Spain that was no less influential than the military successes on the battlefield, the creed and deeds of the Legion, and the administration of the protectorate itself. Published mostly in the 1920s, the texts studied in chapter 2 had a performative function: I claim that, in their own way, they made fascism. Particular emphasis has been placed in this second chapter on war writing and the role played by warfare in the production of space. Chapter 3 deals with the fascist reworking of three spatial myths that were of the utmost importance in Spanish fascism vis-à-vis the fascist habitus: Castile, Rome, and the empire – myths developed by a wide spectrum of fascists in journalistic articles, essays, books, poems, and novels. I consider Castile as the *ur-topia* of Spanish fascism and the point of departure for a new (fascist) production of space; Rome as the capital of Spanish fascism and the centre of a totalitarian production of space; and empire as both the control exerted over other countries and the colonial control of the state over its own citizens. Among other functions, within the fascist production of space the myths of Castile, Rome, and empire define and articulate the nation, insert the individual into a narrative presented as both original and constitutive, tint the nation with the intangibility and prestige of godlike essences superior to everything else, and impose a symbolic space that gives a ready-made meaning to the material spatial practices, thus restricting the individual's capacity to produce his or her own space. Chapter 4 explores the fascist urban writing as materialized in spaces of representation, representations of space, and, to a lesser extent, material spatial practices in the context of the violent struggle for hegemony during the 1930s. The rhetoric of walking and of mapping, as articulated in the fascist spaces of representation, is the central twofold theme of this chapter. I examine the representation/production of the city (Madrid in particular) in a number of representative fascist novels and essays by, among other authors, Tomás Borrás, Agustín de Foxá, Rafael García Serrano, Ernesto Giménez Caballero, José-Vicente Puente, and Felipe Ximénez de Sandoval – all of which were produced during the civil war or in its aftermath. In this chapter I also take up the rhetoric of war literature that was discussed in chapter 2, along with the theories on urbanism and architecture connected to the fascist politics of space analysed in chapter 1. Factually as well as symbolically, the war consisted of the defence/conquest of a topography. After their victory over the Republic, the Nationalists "rewrote" Spain by imposing an authoritarian administration and culture. The last section, devoted to the 1939 victory parade in Madrid, explores the rewriting of urban space at the level of material spatial practices. Finally, chapter 5 analyses the memoirs, diaries, poems, novels, and short stories written by veterans of the Spanish expeditionary force, known in Spain as *División Azul* or the Blue Division, sent by the Franco regime to fight as an autonomous unit of the Wehrmacht against the Soviet Union. I claim that the symbolic appropriation and conquest of space through writing is carried out from the experience of the spatial alienation felt by the fascist veterans disappointed with a regime that did not implement fascist policy. Another main focus lies in the consideration of a number of works as "spectral." I hope to show that writing constitutes, in these cases, the *house of the spectre*. Both the spatial alienation and the spectre are correlated with the political metamorphoses of the Franco regime, which distanced itself from Germany when it became clear, in the winter of 1942–3, that Hitler would lose the war. The withdrawal of the Blue Division corresponded thus to a new direction in Franco's foreign policy. To a certain extent, this was the beginning of the end of the fascists' hegemony within the Franco regime itself. But the marginalization of Falange from the power structures would be contested from different camps and by different agents, among them by the spectre returning from the Soviet Union in the form of those Falangist veterans of the Russian campaign who felt betrayed by the government. The Blue Division culture would come to represent both the bad conscience of the political establishment and the public display of such spectrality. In a sense, Spanish fascism became a spectral and somewhat embarrassing presence after the Second World War. Thereafter, the history of fascism in Spain is a ghost story of sorts, an unfinished tale of spectres haunting the land.

When I set out to design these topographies of fascism, I had to draw boundaries. A topographical approach to cultural phenomena may be defined as the self-conscious drawing of provisional boundaries to an amorphous locus. Like produced space, maps and writing are bounded territories. The act of producing space entails the construction of meaning by bounding space, or else by rearranging the existing limits that enclose a territory. Boundaries and meanings work hand in hand. "A boundary," writes Martin Heidegger, "is not that at which something stops … the boundary is that from which something *begins its presencing* … Space is in essence that for which room has been made, that which is let into its bounds" ("Building" 154). Borders thus are unstable entities immersed in a constant process of negotiation. In my previous scholarly work, the reality of everyday life affected little, if at all, the stability of the limits that I had put on my object of study. Not this time, for fascism has never left us. Rather, it has adopted altered shapes; it has infiltrated the functioning of democracy; it is alive in social space; it is part of the habitus of many. Walking in certain streets of cities and towns across Spain while I was doing research for this book was a painful reminder of the pervasiveness of fascism in social space. Staying in and crossing spaces stamped by fascist and Francoist traces, as well as learning through the media about political statements, activities, and social events that one could easily relate to fascism added a most unwanted, if not altogether unexpected pressure to change the horizons that I had chosen for this book – a pressure for writing, for instance, a sixth chapter on, say, the "Traces of Fascism in Twentieth-First-Century Spain's Social Space." But then I concluded that altering the boundaries of the map would blur the image that I intended to portray, as when one stretches a picture on a computer's desktop to make it fit the screen. I had to resist the craving for totality. My map had to be something different: a tale pointing to the present, the picture of an old relative, the representation of a land uncannily similar to our own.

Chapter One

A Politics of Space

Concepts of Space

A radical transformation of the social entails an equally radical modification of the material spatial practices, the representations of space, and the spaces of representation that delimit, structure, and perform the territory in which the revolution has taken place. The passage from one mode of production to another, a coup d'état that replaces polities, even the appearance of certain means of communication (e.g., the Internet) dramatically alter the perceived, conceived, and lived space. In the context that concerns us here, any political project that aims at modifying the social in its entirety – and fascism was one of them – must unavoidably address spatial issues. Within this schema, a revolution incapable of producing its own space has failed to achieve its essential objective, for instead of changing life itself, "[it] has merely changed ideological superstructures, institutions or political apparatuses" (Lefebvre, *Production* 54). A true revolution, holds Lefebvre, "must manifest a creative capacity in its effects on daily life, on language and on space" (54). Transformative politics comes from combining the different dimensions of space anew.[1] Since the state, itself a construed place,[2] has as its main business the demarcation, control, and administration of a territory through a complex of institutions, it follows that a revolutionary political project that aspires to take over and transform the state must at least (1) redefine and regulate the transport and system communications, the land uses, and the flows of goods and money that shape, articulate, and give meaning to a politically organized territory; (2) modify the laws, institutions, institutional relationships, and social conventions cemented by a rationality and shared values; (3) determine the spaces of representation that provide the codes and language that make the state and the national territory intelligible; and (4) affect as much as it can the mental inventions whereby individuals imagine the state and new possibilities for their experiential space. Hence, although revolutionary politics opens up new possibilities for space, thereby freeing places from old restraints and prohibitions, it also sets up the conditions of possibility for the new state's use of that space as a means of social control.[3]

Fascism developed and openly expressed a self-conscious and multifaceted politics of space. To many people, precisely the outcome of such politics of space is what first comes to mind when prompted to remember, imagine, or think about fascism. Countless documentaries, motion pictures, photographs, artworks, and printed material of all sorts devoted to Fascist Italy and Nazi Germany have represented and/or analysed spaces and places considered as emblems of these regimes, thereby stamping on everyone an image of fascism that is closely associated with a particular production of space. Crowded assembly halls and open-air stadiums, neoclassical monumental buildings, streets adorned with fascist insignia taken over by rowdy and bullying Brown or Black Shirts, smoky Bavarian beer halls engulfed in a conspiratorial atmosphere, roads filled with terrified civilians fleeing their homes before advancing German troops, territories crossed by train convoys transporting herded-in Jews to their death, the Nazi concentrationary universe: these are just some of the most representative places and spaces of a list as long as it is grim. After watching documentaries like Claude Lanzmann's *Shoa* (1985), with its unforgettable, disturbing portrayal of the railroad system so efficiently used by the administrators of the Holocaust, or the scene from Charlie Chaplin's *The Great Dictator* (1940) in which Adenoid Hinkel (Charlie Chaplin), dictator of Tomainia, plays with a large inflatable globe while dancing to the tune of Richard Wagner's *Lohengrin*, we are left with the impression that both Lanzmann and Chaplin underscore one of fascism's – to put it in metaphysical terms – "first principles": that of space.[4] The obvious link of these and other fascist spaces and places with a Weltanschauung dominated by a passion for the absolute as well as with an authoritarian conception of the political and the social should not lead us, however, to confine the fascist concept of space to one single way of understanding space and spatial relationships. Contrary to common belief, fascist ideology, political practices, social action, and cultural production show clearly that fascism held different concepts of space, at times intertwined, often overlapped, but always interconnected through a hierarchical relationship whose order changed, depending on the cir-

cumstances and political goals. As will be seen throughout this book, the
fascist politics of space articulated different views of space.

Using a model proposed by David Harvey, I will here differentiate between three ways of understanding space: absolute, relative, and relational.[5] By *absolute space*, we will understand a "preexisting, immovable,
continuous, and unchanging framework ... within which distinctive objects can be clearly identified and events and processes accurately described" (Harvey, *Cosmopolitanism* 134). In absolute space, people, objects,
and processes find their identity, uniqueness, and meaning in terms of
the fixed location that they occupy (134). A product of a geometrization
of space, absolute space is, in Lefebvre's words, "the true space, the space
of truth" (*Production* 236); it is located nowhere "because it embodies
all places" (236), and it comprehends and determines "the entire existence of the group concerned" (240). Prohibitions, threats, even physical violence regulate the places, networks, movements, and relationships
located within absolute space. In contrast to absolute space, *relative space*,
associated with non-Euclidean geometry and most particularly Albert
Einstein's theories of relativity, is a function of movement and behaviour. For this reason, it is more appropriate to denominate it as *relative
space-time*. In the relative space-time, the distance between places is measured in terms of the time needed to go from one location to the other.
Individuals link places in different manners and with different purposes, thereby providing those places with a diversity of interconnections,
meanings, and functions. The observer, who establishes perspectives and
therefore redistributes spatial relationships and temporal distances, creates maps of relative places and measures distances. Finally, there is the
Leibnizian view of space as relational. In Leibniz's philosophy of space,
distance, size, or *shape* matters less than *situation*. Opposing the concept of
space as an absolute entity, Leibniz viewed space as the order of relations
between coexistents, which unfold not as extended, but in extension.
Instead of conceiving of them as inert bodies extended in space, Leibniz
maintained that entities expand as one continuous whole. The nature of
a body "consists in nothing but the *dynamicon,* or the innate principle of
change and persistence" (Leibniz, *Philosophical Essays* 251). Subjects are
diffusely located, and "the diffusion of place forms space" (Leibniz, *Philosophical Papers* 2: 1011). In essence, relational space has to do with performativity. Human and social processes produce their own space and time.
In a certain way, they "do not exist in space-time" (Harvey, *Cosmopolitanism* 137). Instead, space and time are internalized within matter and process (137). Events and processes crystallize out of "a field of flows" (137).

Located in principle within absolute space (e.g., an assembly hall, a war room, a boardroom), individuals gathered there carry with themselves their own experiences, opinions, expectations, and agendas, which may be brought into the open during the discussion. As Harvey indicates, "Under the relational view disparate influences flow from everywhere to everywhere else" (137). Since time and space fuse in this kind of space, relational space is in fact *relational spacetime*. Dreams and memories are, according to Harvey (137), the stuff of this fusion. In its consubstantial instability, relational spacetime destabilizes identity and individuation. Moreover, it "generates entirely different understandings of the concept of 'place' compared to the territorial closures and exclusions that can so easily be manufactured out of absolute conceptions" (138).

Of these concepts of space, fascism prioritized absolute space over the other two, mainly because it found in that type of space a means to re-order the social under a set of hierarchical and static relationships. As envisioned by fascism, absolute space – the ultimate expression of un-contested hegemony – eliminates antagonisms, replaces the autonomy and dynamism of the subject with a static "people's community," shapes individual behaviour, and controls fluxes. Nevertheless, it must be em-phasized that under certain circumstances relative space-time and rela-tional spacetime became more dominant within the fascist politics of space. For the fascists, relative space-time was the space of the political tactics used to achieve specific goals, as well as of the strategic plans that were aimed, paradoxically, at the creation of absolute space.

During the "years of struggle" in Italy (1920–2), Germany (1920–33), and Spain (1933–9), the fascist parties in those countries understood space – perhaps inevitably – as mainly relative space-time. Those were years punctuated by the fascists' and their sympathizers' striving for po-litical hegemony. The design of strategic plans to gain political power and ultimately to take over the state and the nation, the dialogue with kindred political organizations, failed putsches, and the gradual consoli-dation of political positions within the party itself belong to the relative space-time of the fascists before their "conquest of the state" – to borrow the title of Curzio Malaparte's famous periodical. After the fascist take-over of the state (Italy, 1925; Germany, 1933; Spain, 1939), relative space-time would still play a dominant role in political practice, social life, and human agency. Think, for instance, of the redistribution of relationships within the political, economic, and cultural fields, the omnipresent geo-political considerations and warmongering, which prepared the path to war and to the National Socialists' building of a "new European order," the Falangists' project to expand Spain's "eternal values" (often grouped under the concept of *Hispanidad*) to Latin America, the German and Italian territorial expansion within Europe and Africa, or the train time-tables designed to deport the Jews and the so-called *Untermenschen*.

Relational spacetime was just as important. In fact, a fundamental family resemblance of fascism – its self-characterization as "movement" – constitutes a striking instance of relational spacetime.[6] In the context of fascism, "movement" is not only the motion of an entity in space, but also a set of ideas, beliefs, and habitus: a "place." Hence fascist "movements" may be considered as "places in motion." Heirs to the turn-of-the-century pan-movements (i.e., pan-Germanism, pan-Latinism), the Nationalsozialistische Deutsche Arbeiterpartei (NSDAP), the Partito Nazionale Fascista (PNF), and Falange Española y de las JONS (FE-JONS) presented themselves as the "third way," as "movements" altogether different from the party structures characteristic of parliamentary democracies. For Victor Klemperer, a professor of Romance Studies born to a Jewish family whose diary constitutes one of the most vivid and penetrating chronicles of everyday life in the Third Reich, *Bewegung* (movement) was "the quintessence, the unique quality, the very lifeblood of National Socialism which, after the *Aufbruch* [new departure] … would never be allowed to come to rest" (226). This statement may be applied mutatis mutandis to all fascist organizations. As movements, they set in motion a series of political, social, and cultural processes that created their own space and time. Some manifestations of the fascist generation of its own space and time through a never-ending movement are the National Socialists' *Gleichschaltung*, the elimination of political antagonism and otherness from the national territory, the control of the individual's dreams and desire, the manipulation of collective memory by rewriting national history, or the view of fascist society as an absolute break with the past. In this last case, there is a remarkable example of relational spacetime worth mentioning: the Italian Fascist calendar. Following the model of the Republican Calendar used in France from October 1793 until December 1804, the Fascists began counting the years starting with 28 October 1922 (the March on Rome) and designated the years with Roman numerals; thus, 1932 would be according to the Fascist calendar Anno X E.F. (year X of the Fascist Era). As Griffin explains, "The measure of time under Mussolini points to a profoundly mythic will to create a new type of State capable of realizing a new order in which *chronos* will be suspended and historical time will *literally* be made anew" (*Modernism* 223).[7] Furthermore, relational spacetime is closely linked to the fascist will-to-power. According to Klemperer, for the National Socialist, "the aim is not to let things dominate you, but to dominate ... one wants to be *dynamisch*" (226). In accordance with that dynamism and in contrast to the parties' programs that specified their political goals, fascist movements were deliberately vague when stating political objectives, thus allowing themselves to change course at will if circumstances demanded. Fascist organizations were always on the move – most particularly the NSDAP – their main practical goal being "to organize as many people as possible within its framework and to set and keep them in motion" (Arendt, *Origins* 326), placing them in a *perpetuum mobile* of sorts. The titles *Führer, Duce,* and *Caudillo* assumed by Hitler, Mussolini, and Franco respectively emblematize the fascist movement as relational spacetime.

In the history of Spanish fascism, there is a noteworthy instance of movement as relational spacetime. I am referring to the speech delivered at the Teatro de la Comedia in Madrid on 29 October 1933 by José Antonio Primo de Rivera, the dashing, refined, charismatic young lawyer destined to be, somehow incongruously, the uncontested Jefe Nacional (national chief) of FE-JONS between 1934 and 1936.[8] In characteristic fascist wording and tone, Primo de Rivera expressed a fundamental family resemblance of fascism when he declared to his enthralled audience: "Today's movement" is not a party, but a movement; it is a kind of "anti-party," neither right nor left (*Obras* 65).[9] Such movement has, he crucially added, a generative force: what "we" want is "today's movement" and "the state it may create" to be "the efficient, authoritarian tool for the service of an indisputable unity, the permanent unity, the irrevocable unity called Fatherland" (66). Thus, in the beginning was the movement. Nothing preceded it, not even the party: indeed, Falange Española would be founded after, and not before, "today's movement."[10] This phrase is crucial, for not only does it emphasize the absolute beginning of the movement; it also places this absolute beginning at the very moment ("today") that the "movement" was publicly declared to exist; in other words, it locates the origins of the movement in the language used to *utter it.* Not coincidentally, the rightist press, Payne reminds us, "generally described the event as the founding of a Spanish fascist movement" (*Fascism* 92). Movement and word have here – and thereafter – a symbiotic relationship. While the movement predated the fascist party in a sort of khoratic fashion,[11] the declaration of the existence of the movement *produced* the movement as a specific entity and put it in circulation. The movement became itself, thanks to the performativity of the word. Hence, to use freely an image from contemporary cosmology, the start of the Spanish fascist movement may be likened to the so-called big bang, for the big-bang model allows us to interpret the origin of the universe as an event that created space-time. Performed by speech, the movement generated a space and time of its own. It was, in short, relational spacetime. Other fascist texts would stress the relational nature of the movement. In the article "Estado e historia," published in *F.E.* on 25 January 1934, the anonymous author argues: "The national order cannot be static, it has to be dynamic, towards a supreme driving-force, towards a supreme reason that justifies the unitary, totalitarian, and authoritarian function" (1). For the author of "Noticiero de España" (*F.E.*, 7 December 1933), the "totalitarian state" is "a fatherland *that acts*" (4; my emphasis).

Considering the interconnection between movement and performative speech, Primo de Rivera's definition of the movement as a "poetic movement" (*Obras* 68–9) is far from arbitrary or naive.[12] "The peoples," Primo de Rivera claims, "have never been moved but by the poets" (68–9). Since prior to this statement he had defined the movement as a tool for the service of a future nation – conceived of as an absolute space – as well as the mechanism that would create the new state, it follows that movement and poetry, at least as regards their performativity, are one and the same thing. The movement is a performative speech act of sorts that, like poetry, brings into existence a space-time of its own. The movement and the word's performance of a party, a unified nation, and an absolute state – in short, the movement's self-definition and self-creation as relational spacetime – cohabit with the fascists' exalted defence of an absolute space (described in absolute terms with words such as *indisputable, permanent, irrevocable*) identified, in Primo de Rivera's speech, with the (fascist) state. This connection between movement and relational spacetime would be altered with the outbreak of the civil war. The Movimiento Nacional, as the movement was now called, had two different, albeit interrelated meanings. First, it denoted the conglomerate of hegemonic formations that participated in the military rebellion of 17 July 1936 against the Republic: Franco defined the Movimiento Nacional as a "communion of the Spanish people in the ideals that originated the Crusade" (qtd. in Sabín Rodríguez 23). Second, it referred to the only party that resulted from the unification decreed by Franco in April 1937 of the Carlists and the Falangists – the Falange Española Tradicionalista y de las JONS (FET de las JONS). By unifying these two parties with rather different programs and dissolving the other political organizations, Franco created a political space at once absolute and dynamic: absolute because in the political field there would be nothing else but the Movimiento

Nacional, and dynamic because it was envisioned as a process. As Franco himself stressed to the listeners of his radio address (19 April 1937) announcing the unification, "The movement that we lead today is just that: a movement more than a program. And as such it is in the process of development, subject to constant revision and improvement, to the degree that reality requires." This was to be indeed the fate of the Movimiento Nacional during the dictatorship.

In the context of fascism, the relative space-time and the relational spacetime were more often than not functions of absolute space, namely the space of truth where everybody and everything was located in and identified by fixed positions established by the fascist state. Under fascism, the national territory was seen as dominated space. In a passage from *Mein Kampf* (1925–7), Adolf Hitler depicts that subordination eloquently if awkwardly: "If ... we consider the question, what, in reality, are the state-forming or even state-preserving forces, we can sum them up under one single head: the ability and will of the individual to sacrifice himself in the totality" (152). "The Fatherland," categorically asserted Primo de Rivera, "is a total unity," a transcendent and indivisible synthesis (*Obras* 66). Earlier texts by Primo de Rivera and other prominent Spanish fascists already had put forth this most basic fascist principle. A civil servant, intellectually capable, published essayist and novelist, and voracious multilingual reader of philosophy, Ramiro Ledesma Ramos had written on 11 April 1931, "We want and demand the indisputable unification of the state" (*Escritos* 122); to this issue he devoted many pages (*Discurso* 234–8; *Escritos*).[13] Such a concept of national unity demanded as a matter of course the total subordination of the regions to the state.[14] Primo de Rivera's description of Castile, a region considered the embodiment of Spain's essence, is a clear instance of the fascist's defence of absolute space: "We have a lot to learn ... from Castile, ... the absolute land ... The land that is not ... the sum of several farms ... but the land [*sic*]; the land as the repository of ever-lasting values, the austerity of behaviour, ... the speech and the silence, the solidarity between ancestors and descendants ... And thus Castile, with the absolute land and the absolute sky looking at each other, has never been a region; it has had to aspire, always, to being an Empire" (*Obras* 189–90).

The evident tension between movement as relational spacetime and the nation as absolute space can be spotted easily in many texts, among them an article by Primo de Rivera entitled "Orientaciones: Hacia un nuevo Estado," published in *El Fascio* on 16 March 1933 (in *Obras* 37–40). Referring to the new state that he aspires to create, Primo de Rivera defines the fatherland as a "historical totality" (40). Aside from the fact that absolute space is here the substance of the fatherland, and relative space-time merely its attribute, the expression *historical totality* is a *contradictio in adjecto*, for a "totality" is an entity that ceases to be itself as soon as historical time swallows it up. The same could be said of Falange's view of Spain as a *unity of destiny in the universal*, a concept defined by Primo de Rivera in a somewhat self-contradictory fashion in his speech read at the Teatro de la Comedia: "Our total sense of the Fatherland" demands that "the peoples of Spain, regardless of their diversity, feel harmonized within an irrevocable unity of destiny" (*Obras* 66).[15] One could almost say that fascism staged a peculiar, rather improbable union of Euclidean geometry with Hegelian absolute idealism. Indeed, there were two basic inconsistencies underlying the fascist politics of space. First of all, absolute space (the state, the nation) was to be achieved through relational spacetime (the movement) and in relative space-time (the struggle for hegemony between fascism and other hegemonic formations). Second, the fascist drive to build an empire cannot be dissociated from the instability of relative space-time, that is, from the multiplicity of locations whose distance has to be measured by the units of time needed to go from one place to the other. Interestingly, in some instances fascist regimes acted out these concepts of space by following ideological and cultural preconceptions. Thus the Nazis' view of space vis-à-vis the countries conquered by Germany depended not only on military and political considerations, but also on ideology and cultural affinities. Whereas France was dealt with in terms of appropriated relative space-time, Poland and the Eastern Territories taken by the Wehrmacht suffered the imposition of a murderous absolute space. Again, the hierarchy among the three ways of understanding space depended on the situation.

Within the fascist politics of space, the main nexus of the three concepts of space examined thus far were the practice of and discourse on urban planning and architecture. To begin with, images from these two disciplines permeate and suture the fascist political discourse. Even a cursory reading of the fascists' written production reveals the extent and function of the use of spatial images. At a fundamental level, politics was considered by the fascist leadership and intelligentsia as the act of building a new organization of the social as well as an "edifice," a double meaning and a circular argument somehow reminiscent of the *natura naturans*, the nature that creates nature. In the preface to the first volume of *Mein Kampf*, Hitler characterized his book as the "foundation stones in our common edifice" (v); by "edifice" Hitler meant both the political doctrine laid out in his book and the movement of which he was part. In Spain, Primo de Rivera defined the task assigned to his generation as one of "building a new politics" (*Obras* 40) upon the fatherland's unity, or, as he put it elsewhere, of carrying out "*the building of the harmonious, whole Spain*" (692). In his above-mentioned speech of 29 October 1933, he talked about the new state that "we must strive to build" (*Obras* 67–8). For him, the movement's task lay in building, by violent means, a new way of doing politics. In a notorious and well-known passage, he encouraged his audience not to shrink from violence, for "there is no other admissible dialectics than the dialectics of fists and pistols" when either justice or the fatherland is offended (67–8). And this is precisely what he and his comrades thought about the new state (68). This connection between architecture and politics was further emphasized in an article published on 28 April 1934 (*Obras* 229–31), wherein Primo de Rivera explicitly opposed two political ideologies through the metaphoric use of the word *architecture.* "Revolution" (here a word connoting Marxism) entails disorderly behaviour and destruction; it is a "disorganized mutiny" (229). Since politics is "a great task of building," messing up the materials and throwing them around without a plan is not the best way of doing things. Whoever yearns for a true revolution must have imprinted in his soul "a new political architecture" (229), and in order to establish that political architecture, one must be in control of "all the instruments for building" (229). "The well-done revolution," in Primo de Rivera's opinion, "the one that truly subverts things, has as a formal characteristic 'the order'" (229).[16] Likewise, Ramiro Ledesma Ramos equated Spain's unity with a scaffolding: "Without the unity [Spain's] we Spaniards will always lack a steady scaffold upon which to build something serious" (*Discurso* 236). The "Falangist style" frequently alluded to (described by Primo de Rivera in *Obras* 217, 451–3) seems to refer, therefore, to a style based on principles related to architecture. We may conclude, thus, that in fascist political discourse the images "edifice" and "to build" condense the grammar and pragmatics of absolute space (the state, the nation, the party), function as instances of relational spacetime (the movement, in this context, is considered as both a "builder" and a "building"), and constitute places and actions located in relative space-time (the relative location of the nation-as-a-building-in-progress within a continuum formed by the nation's present state of disarray and the future attainment, through the act of building, of the organic and integral unity of the nation).

In regard to social practices, the profound, lasting, almost obsessive interest in architecture and urban planning shown by a vast number of fascist leaders, ideologues, and intellectuals manifested itself in fascist material spatial practices, representations of space, and spaces of representation. The fascist material spatial practices were predicated on the fascist drive to impose a physical absolute space. Hence, the German Autobahn system, the marginalization of the working class to the slums of the cities in Spain during the early Franco regime, and the construction in Fascist Italy of a transportation network that converged on Rome – thereby expressing at the material level the Fascists' concept of integral nation and of their consideration of Rome as the capital of a new Roman empire – are just a few cases of the imposition of codes and of a spatial grammar onto a non-linguistic, physical space. If we turn our attention to the fascist representations of space, we will notice that, at the most basic level, the function of urban planning and architecture resided in the elaboration of a new grammar and pragmatics of absolute spaces and places under the guidelines established by political power, frequently by the dictator of the fascist regime himself (Hitler is a widely known case in point). In difficult cohabitation with this political control of planning and building were the knowledge, theories, expectations, and professional ambitions of the architects and urban planners at the service of the fascist state – factors that introduced the instability characteristic of relational spacetime within the codes designed to understand, discipline, and impose absolute space on the population. Thus, the relational spacetime of processes could influence the outcome of discussions whose underlying assumption was basically the building up of absolute space. As regards the spaces of representation, they were meant to produce a symbolic absolute space. The new Reich Chancellery, the House of German Art, the never-finished Deutsches Stadion, Germany's Air Ministry, the Olympiastadion, the Nazi party's rally grounds in Nuremberg, the Casa del Fascio, the Italian Ministry of Foreign Affairs, the Esposizione Universale Roma complex, Spain's Ministry of the Air Force, and the Valle de los Caídos are some of the most emblematic fascist spaces of representation built in fascist Germany, Italy, and Spain. Monumental buildings had multiple functions, such as nationalistic self-assertion, political and social indoctrination, the assertion of the nation's greatness, political intimidation and social subjugation, the strengthening of the ties among the members of the "people's community," the stressing of the absolute pre-eminence of the party and the state, the will to leave an everlasting mark on history, the Leader's glorification, and the spatial expression of absolute power.[17] Many of the projected buildings and public works were never finished or even begun (most notably in Nazi Germany) for a variety of reasons, not least of them their economic unfeasibility and the outbreak of the war, which logically enough halted many projects. To a degree, such unfinishedness illustrates the tensions inherent in the production of absolute space in the modern era, the impossibility of attaining absolute power without fissures, and the difficulty experienced by the fascists in articulating without friction the representations of space, the spaces of representation, and material spatial practices.

A wide array of disciplines, technologies, materials, and tools were involved in the fascist politics and production of space. In addition to stone, brick, glass, cement, bombs, or tanks, words were fundamental tools for producing space, as we saw in the introduction. In effect, writing was a capital constituent of the fascist politics of space that greatly contributed to the fascists' production of space. The following sections of this chapter are devoted, precisely, to prove the centrality of writing in the politics of space sketched above. It is a centrality, I should like to add, underpinned by the topographical dimension of many written works produced by fascists. Indeed, a politics of space articulates the grammar, semantics, and pragmatics of fascist writing.

Writing – specifically writing putting forth a fascist politics of space – will be the first topography of fascism studied in this book. To make my point clearer, I will focus my analysis on three seminal essays, all of them produced by one of the founding fathers and main ideologues of Spanish fascism in the 1930s, Ernesto Giménez Caballero:[18] *Genio de España: Exaltaciones a una resurrección nacional. Y del mundo* (1932), *Arte y Estado* (1935), and *Roma madre* (1939; 1st ed. in Italian 1938). To be sure, several scholarly works have commented already on Giménez Caballero's profound, significant, idiosyncratic, long-lasting interest in architecture – a discipline that the writer considered the "supreme art" (*Arte* 245).[19] But it is equally true that those studies examine the issue exclusively at a thematic level – a methodological option that, in my opinion, has limited the scope of their conclusions. It has not been taken into account, for instance, that Giménez Caballero's high opinion of architecture in effect dominates his writing. Giménez Caballero's fascist writing, I should like to stress, goes far beyond the author's defence of the superiority of one art over the rest. As will be seen, the writing itself, impregnated by a fascist politics of space, *produces a fascist space*. The two driving forces of the production of space carried out in those three essays are the *cartographic gaze* and what I denominate as *will-to-architecture*. By *cartographic gaze*, I mean the series of operations carried out, in a deliberate and self-conscious fashion, to systematically produce the borders, grammar, con-

tents, and meaning of a particular space as well as the places enclosed in
it. With the expression *will-to-architecture*, I refer to the tendency to represent as architecture the national, historical, political, artistic, and literary
space. The cartographic gaze and the will-to-architecture complement
each other, and both constitute essential elements of the fascist politics
of space. Fascism concealed one of its fundamental operations: it hid the
fact that its "knowledge" (e.g., of the history of the nation) was in fact
and to a high degree a "doing." Like other fascist intellectuals, Giménez
Caballero produced the space that he claimed to be describing. Giménez Caballero *describes* and *writes* space. For this reason, his essays are
topographic in terms of the two clusters of meanings of the word *topography* mentioned in the introduction. Giménez Caballero's fascism provides such a double topography with an ideological direction. His essays
contain an evident propagandistic function; they aspire to modify the
"location" of the readers. The production of space is carried out, therefore, in the very act of enunciation: the author wants to engage the readers both with and within the topography described/written in his essays.
The basic questions to answer will be not so much what Giménez Caballero "says" about space, but rather how he "produces" the space that he
suggests he is "describing," and finally, how he "places" the reader in
that space. These two operations constitute fundamental techniques of
the fascist politics of space. The analysis of *Genio de España*, *Arte y Estado*,
and *Roma madre* will reveal the different ways by which absolute, relative,
and relational space permeate and articulate the structure, theoretical
framework, methodology, motifs, and main ideas of the writing devoted
to the propagation of fascism.

Mapping

Genio de España made a lasting impression on anti-Republican individuals looking for answers in the turbulent 1930s and shaped the thinking of the first generations of Spanish fascists (Selva 204–5).[20] Published
barely one year after the proclamation of the Second Republic, this provocative, exalted, and aggressive book – in fact the first long, detailed
exposition of a fascist doctrine ever published in Spain – represents an
outstanding instance of the fascist spatial view of and approach to political and cultural issues.[21] Giménez Caballero's low opinion of history is
the first sign of the constitutive spatiality of this seminal essay.

An unyielding self-conscious disregard for history saturates *Genio de España*. As if to set the record straight from the very beginning, the author

in the introduction avows that *Genio de España* was conceived of without "historical pretensions"; instead he claims to have written the book with the "wisdom of a poet who feels the mystical, mysterious, oracular truth of his people speaking through his mouth" (11). Thus Giménez Caballero's methodology consists of a poetic condensation. In contrast to historiography, poetry is better equipped, as the introduction suggests, to capture Spain's essence in an instant of mystical communion. "The task of feeling the meaning of a people," he remarks, does not lie in erudition, theory, or what he dismissively labels "intellectual snares," but rather "in the Prophecy, in the communion of a vigilant soul with the quiet genius of his people" (11). Moreover, he adds, "I know that my task has the shudder of the trance, of the sacred vision, of things religious. Oracular vision and words, where the oracle is what matters less, and what matters most: the Voice on behalf of whom the oracle talks. Genius of Spain" (12).[22] Indeed, *Genio de España* carries out the break with the lineal narrative that is implied in these claims. The work is divided into three loosely connected parts: the first is devoted to the decadence of Spain since the seventeenth century as well as the remedies applied to stop it; the second is a critique of José Ortega y Gasset's *España invertebrada* (1921) in counterpoint to Giménez Caballero's own ideas on the topics treated in that book; and the third expounds on the author's proposal for the "resurrection" of Spain from a fascist perspective. Far from elaborating his ideas in an organized and systematic fashion, Giménez Caballero presents them in an impressionistic language within a choppy *dispositio*.

The practice in *Genio de España* of what Joseph Frank (31–132) termed *spatial form* was nothing new in the works of Giménez Caballero. It can be found, in fact, in his avant-garde oeuvre of the 1920s. The collage, simultaneity, and visual literature articulating *Carteles* (1927), the dissolution of sequentiality in his surrealist novel *Yo, inspector de alcantarillas* (1928), as well as the application of a spatial analytic device called "ludigrama" (literally "ludigram") to the study of games in *Hércules jugando a los dados* (1928) share with *Genio de España* a characteristic modernist rejection of history.[23] The liquidation of history brought about by the Anglo-American and European modernism in the 1910s and 1920s challenged causation and chronology – two pillars of modern historiography and nineteenth-century realism – as valid means to articulate a narrative. Modernism prioritized space over time, or, to be more precise, it spatialized time, utilizing a procedure amply theorized in many avant-garde manifestos and theoretical pieces that, in effect, refracted radical changes in the conception and perception of time and space since the turn of the century.[24] Symptomatically, that theoretical positioning and literary practice would saturate fascist ideology as well as several artistic and literary artefacts connected in one way or the other to fascism. Fascism, Mosse reminds us, "considered itself as avant-garde: a group of men who were leading society into the post-liberal age" (*Fascist* 137). The apocalyptic tone, the wish to substitute "youthful vigor for old age" (138), the championing of modern industry and technology, the search for the "new man," and the dynamism of fascism are family resemblances of the avant-gardes.[25] According to Griffin, two elements of that kinship between fascism and modernism are, on the one hand, the fascist sense of beginning, of a complete, iconoclastic, definitive break with the past, and on the other, the mood of standing on the threshold of an altogether new world cemented by *Aufbruch,* or the "state of expectancy induced by the intuitive certainty that an entire phase of history is giving way to a new one" (Griffin, *Modernism* 9).[26] The penchant for violence and direct action, the contempt for bourgeois morality, and the exaltation of war are constituents of the fascist ideology and habitus as well as of the avant-gardes. Furthermore, in the literary field the Italian Futurism,[27] certain manifestations of Vorticism (most particularly Ezra Pound's and Wyndham Lewis's work)[28] and the avant-garde artefacts of Falangist authors (such as Tomás Borrás, Antonio de Obregón, Samuel Ros, and Felipe Ximénez de Sandoval)[29] constitute instances of the overlapping of fascism and modernism. *Genio de España* is perhaps the most complete and significant fusion of fascism and avant-gardism in Spain. Giménez Caballero expressed his fascist thinking and habitus through modernist techniques with which he was well acquainted; these techniques are characterized – let us insist on this – by a liquidation of history and spatial form. To put it with Hewitt's words apropos of the relationship between fascism and the avant-garde, "History has ceased, with the avant-garde, to function as a legitimating instance. One cannot simply return to a premodern linearity, either in theory or in practice…. Both politically and aesthetically, 'progress' and 'reaction' can no longer be fully disengaged as historical concepts. The stage is set for Fascist Modernism" (*Fascist Modernism* 47).

In *Genio de España*, the knowledge of the history and essence of Spain – two of the main topics of that book – can be attained only by an eidetic reduction of sorts. By this method, Giménez Caballero moves from consciousness to the trans-empirical realm of the essence of the nation and of the world. A "transcendental gaze" (66) transfers the contents of consciousness to the external world. The truth of the nation's history, claims

Giménez Caballero, resides in the depths of oneself because "oneself is a historical and national outcome" (66). By the same token, consciousness generates its own space and time. In this sense, at the metaphysical and epistemic levels *Genio de España* builds its ideas – among them a defence of absolute space – upon a relational spacetime. Since this is expressed through writing, the book itself may be viewed as an instance of relational spacetime – as a literary artefact that is the ultimate outcome of a transcendental consciousness generating its own space and time. The regeneration of Spain, the book's main goal, is the outcome of the same process: "It is something mystical (an inspiration, an intuition), what decides once and for all the solution to the radical problems of a country" (66). This *epoché* seems to be the most adequate way "to intuit the immanent generating genius where this contingent I [is] placed and rebound; namely, the *genius of a people*" (213). Consistent with this phenomenological reduction, Giménez Caballero repeatedly employs spatial images; words such as *assertion, intuition,* or *amalgamation* overlap with toponyms along with words that relate to space, such as *construction*; as he writes in the introduction to *Genio de España,* "The third part of this book is devoted to construction and to affirmations. To the immediate implementation of my radical intuition: of my melding with what I call the genius of Spain" (12). This is yet another instance of relational spacetime, of the generation by the consciousness of its own space and time by means of a transcendental gaze manifested through writing.

Giménez Caballero interprets the history of Spain as a process made up of two interrelated binary structures: emptiness/plenitude and dissolution/construction. Committed to a country conceived of as an integral, total, and organic unit, he manifests his fear of national dissolution, an otherwise central family resemblance of fascism studied by Theweleit, among others, in territorial terms.[30] The history of Spain has been tragically marked, according to Giménez Caballero (7–12), by thirteen "98s" (an allusion to 1898, the year in which Spain lost its last overseas dominions to the United States) or by losses of national territory that commenced with the Peace of Westphalia (1648) and extended to the proclamation of the Second Republic (1931), including milestones such as the treaties of Lisbon (1668), Utrecht (1713), and Paris (1898). The decadence of Spain and the slow but steady dissolution of the country's essence would reach its climax with the Second Republic since, according to the author, Spain ceased to be itself as soon as it was ruled by "un-Spanish" politicians who betrayed the nation (25, 64). Because of the Republic, Spain "is breaking up for good ... Catalonia's separation is accepted, the self-government of the regions, the restriction of Spain's unitary voice, the oxidation of the Sword, the marginalization of the Cross, and the kick on the Crown are being considered" (64). In contrast to these thirteen defining moments of its decadence, Spain had enjoyed a period of national plenitude. After a long process of national unification, Spain in the fifteenth century consolidated "its edification, its structure" (29). The crowning of that "edifice" – Spain's unity – was achieved by the Catholic Monarchs, "who had just bound the unity of Spain with their bundle or *fascio* of arrows under their symbolic yoke ... But that *linking together*, that concept of Spain would be ruined in thirteen falls" (30).

Such remarks, which would turn out to be capital topoi of the Spanish fascist discourse, indicate by themselves the author's topographical approach to history: in *Genio de España*, the "essence" of the nation is closely associated with a territory conceived both as a physical locus and a metaphysical ground. This is further emphasized by the "remedies" to such decadence that Giménez Caballero puts forth. Facing the decadence of Spain, he found the essence of his country's imperial past in Fascist Rome. Giménez Caballero did not think this reading of Rome was extemporaneous. In his opinion, Spain had once realized the ideals embodied in Rome. He stresses that in the sixteenth century Spain was "the national instrument of a universal idea, represented in the sphere of the temporal by a 'Caesar' and in the realm of the spirit by a 'God.' Such hierarchical subordination of things national to the Caesarean and of the Caesarean to the spiritual ecumenical realm – Rome – was the key of that Spanish greatness" (43). Yet for Giménez Caballero, Rome meant more than just the spiritual. In his work, the toponym *Rome* connoted empire, symbolized fascism, represented the total unity of the national territory, involved the social ("Rome" as the overcoming of the class struggle) as well as the spiritual ("Rome" as the synthesis of the Orient and Occident) (see 158, 206–10), and finally, it represented the model for the resurrection of a unified and imperial Spain (220–2). The rise of fascism in Italy meant the empirical realization of that idea of "Rome." The secret of fascism, according to Giménez Caballero, lives in Rome: "*Regarding the economic organization*, a *corporative, integrating* system, neither *left* nor *right. Capital and Work* united within a higher unity: the State" (208). Moreover, "Neither Europe nor the world will be able to live on the basis of *Exploiters* or on the basis of *Exploitees*. Neither the right nor the left. Neither *the Orient nor the Occident: Rome*. Sum and integration of the West and the Orient, of capitalism and Marxism: Rome" (208).

The core of Giménez Caballero's fascist politics of space resides in
the author's theory of the world's genii (182–210), along with the representation of these genii through a cartographic gaze. As a result of
its spatial connotations, the very concept of *genius* epitomizes the writer's cartographic consideration of political, social, and cultural issues.
In ancient Rome, the word *genius* had several meanings, which can be
grouped in three basic clusters: (1) an attendant spirit of a place (genius
loci), (2) the guardian spirit of an individual (the Greeks' *daimon*), and
(3) the masculine genesial force fulfilled by the paterfamilias and passed
on from father to son, thereby perpetuating a lineage. *Genio de España*
rewrites in a political tenor the concept of *genius* as it was conceived in
ancient Rome and in the Middle Ages. Two principles underlie Giménez
Caballero's view of the *genius*: the principle of identity and the principle
of reproduction. For him, each place and each nation has its own genius,
namely its essence as well as the capacity to reproduce and perpetuate
it. It is not for nothing that the author points out in a footnote that the
words *genius* and *nation* share the same "etymological substance: of what
has been engendered, of nativity (*genus, natio*)" (128). According to him,
for the sake of its progress and plenitude, it is imperative for a nation to
respect and act in conformity with its genius. When a nation betrays its
own genius, the identity and history of the nation fall out of joint. Such
is the case, argues Giménez Caballero, with Spain: by losing its essence
in a long process of territorial disintegration, the history of Spain has
been but a chronicle of its decadence. *Genio de España*'s undertaking is
precisely, as the subtitle of the book itself expresses, the "resurrection"
of Spain's genius. As a preliminary task for carrying out such a "resurrection," Giménez Caballero designs a map of what he refers to as the
"genial system of the world" (181–2).

A theory of the world's genii is a mythical theory of space and history
that presupposes at once the existence of an indeterminate number of
genii (every place has its own genius) as well as the possibility of its taxonomy and systematization. *Genio de España* classifies and analyses the genii through a cartographic gaze. Giménez Caballero already had applied
a spatial model to classify modern games in *Hércules jugando a los dados*
(1928): "armed," as he says, with a crayon and a blackboard – which he
calls "ludigrama" (ludigram) – he set the games in three groups or dimensions: a vertical, a horizontal, and a temporal one (*Hércules* 27–42).
In *Genio de España*, that "ludigram" turns into a map of the world modelled after the linguistic maps, a procedure that allows the author to sys-
temize and establish a typology of the great variety of genii. The choice

of the linguistic map is no coincidence, as it represents a connection between national territory and language established at the end of the eighteenth century and adopted by many scholars ever since. Herder claimed that each nation had its genius, which is linked to its specific language. In his view, the world comprises an indeterminate quantity of ethnic groups, each united by culture as well as by language, each of them articulated and governed by its own genius. Echoing a theory widely extended in German romanticism, Giménez Caballero maintains that if the different local genii "could be grouped as the philological phenomena of the world – the genii of speech – are, we would find out that such divine phalanxes are divided into three huge conglomerates, into a global triple partition, into three large chromatic patches" (182).

Considering the essence of its different territories, Giménez Caballero perceives then that the world can be reduced to three genii: the genius of the Orient (185–9), the genius of the Occident (190–6), and the genius of Christ (196–210). The first genius, located in Africa, Asia, and the Soviet Union, is described as the submission of the human being to an absolute authority; communism, Buddhism, and Islam are three of its most relevant manifestations. The genius of the Occident – the Western world – consists of just the opposite, since it confers an excessive importance on the individual, to whom everything, including God, is subordinated. Finally, the genius of Christ, which refers to those territories that, like Fascist Italy, have meant the resurrection of ancient Rome in both its Christian spirituality and imperial grandeur, is the dialectical synthesis of the other two: in this genius, the individual recovers a sense of transcendence without losing personal identity. This particular mapping of the world conveys the naming of places as well as the reordering of the relationships between territories. One has to bear in mind, in this respect, that the act of naming is a means of appropriation and control whereby differences are classified and organized according to a hierarchy of relations. The "proper name," Jacques Derrida has written, constitutes the "arch-violence, ... the original violence that has deprived the proper of its property" (*Grammatology* 111). The naming of a place – one of the most important performative speech acts, according to J. Hillis Miller (150) – is consubstantial to any production of space. Naming a place is a way of producing it. In the specific case of the three genii, giving them a name ("genius of the Orient," "genius of the Occident," and "genius of Christ") entails conferring a meaning to the space that they represent, since, as we have seen, a genius is the nomination of the limits and contents of a space. This means that genius and topography are intrinsically connected. One could even say that naming a territory is the same thing as naming a genius.

Giménez Caballero underscores this relationship between genius and topography in several passages of *Genio de España*. In one of them, for instance, he asks himself where the genius of the Occident "begins" and "where it ends" (191), and in another one he indicates that the genii of the Orient and Occident can be considered as "geographical symbols" (184). As a "cartographer," Giménez Caballero produces space by mapping the genii of the world, a production of space that translates as the disciplining of a territory by the imposition of power.[31] Giménez Caballero does not conceal his cartographic activity. On one occasion he even points it out in a self-referential passage wherein the reader witnesses the very moment in which the writer draws an aerial map: "What is the Occident? Let us dare – from our divining cockpit – to draw with a fundamental stroke (as we did for our vision of the Orient) the whole western sector" (190). Paradoxically, this reference to the act of drawing a map of the three world's genii reveals the ultimate impossibility of establishing an objective representation of space. Mapping is a performative activity. Hence Giménez Caballero stretches the spatial production realized by every cartographer, always conditioned by his ideology and relationship with political power. The purport of that cartographic appropriation of territory is all the more evident if compared with previous similar metaphysical readings of space in Spanish culture. At the turn of the century, there was much talk about Spain's *alma* (soul) (an important literary and artistic journal would be named, precisely, *Alma española* [1903–4]).[32] Later, in several *glosas* or short essays collected in *¿Qué hace la historia?* (1929), Eugenio d'Ors, a prominent Catalan writer, art critic, thinker, and theorist of culture who was destined to become one of the leading Falangist intellectuals since the late 1930s, differentiated between six supranational "spirits" (*Nuevo glosario* 2: 468). Alluding to the League of Nations, the spirit of Geneva comprehends liberalism, democracy, and plutocracy (2: 469–71, 711–12); the spirit of Paris refers to the cultural hegemony exerted by France since the twelfth century (2: 476–9); the spirit of Moscow synthesizes Bolshevism and Soviet culture (2: 474–6); the spirit of Salzburg is the symbol of the rival of the spirit of Paris (2: 479–80); the spirit of Salamanca means the cultural unity of all the Spanish-speaking countries (2: 480–1); and finally, the spirit of Rome, described by Ors in rather favourable terms, alludes to Fascist Italy (2: 471–4, 711–12). Aside from the points in common between the "soul" of Spain, Ors's transnational spirits, and Giménez Caballero's

three genii, there is a substantial difference in the three approaches to
national and supranational phenomena: the concepts of *soul* and *spirit*
name the immaterial essence, the animating or vital principle of a being,
irrespective of its location, whereas that of *genius* implies a territory. As
used by Giménez Caballero, the *genius* conveys a cartography, that is, the
symbolic appropriation of space.

Employing a literary device already present in Marinetti's Futurist verse
novel *Le Monoplan du Pape* (1912), in which the Italian Peninsula is portrayed by the poetic voice from an imaginary airplane, Giménez Caballero projects his cartographic gaze from the air, describing the location
and characteristics of the three genii of the world as a pilot would aboard
his plane. By drawing the map of the three genii of the world from an
airplane, the writer becomes a literary "winged mapper," to freely use
Wilford's expression to portray the cartographers who produce maps
from aerial photographs (268–79).[33] The intertextuality with Italian Futurism could hardly be more evident. Indeed, the image of the airplane
and aviation in general are at the core of the Futurist poetics and literary
practice. Soon after Marinetti's second Futurist proclamation "Tuons le
clair de lune!" (1909) and *La Bataille de Tripoli (26 Octobre 1911)* (1912),
the airplane and a particular interpretation of its cultural meaning, military function, and socio-political purport would pervade Futurist literary
and artistic works. The Futurists' fascination with speed and aviation,
which led to the creation of major expressions of Futurism such as the
aeromusica, the aeropoesia, and the aeropittura,[34] refracted not only the
popular interest in airplanes in Italy in the 1910s and 1920s,[35] but also,
and more importantly, the Fascists' attraction towards aviation, "a symbol of visionary leadership and military prowess" (Poggi 254). As Mosse
points out in the context of Fascist Italy and Nazi Germany, the airplane
illustrates the relationship between fascism and some avant-gardes (i.e.,
Expressionism and Italian Futurism), "for here the new frontiers of technology and time became a new elitism, the search for a new man at the
same time eternal and modern" (*Fascist* 138; see also 138–40). Futurists and Fascists alike developed a cult of flight,[36] whose semantic field
contained, among others, the following traits and associations: warfare
and violence, speed, exaltation of military power, elitism, the aviator as
a leader and the new warrior, omniscient perspective and threatening
gaze, military prowess, exhilaration, and an admiration for the beauty
of the machine. In *Genio de España*, the airplane has precisely these connotations. Like the Futurists, Giménez Caballero likens himself to a pilot
aboard his airplane, divinely dominating the skies, threateningly flying

over the land. From the skies, Giménez Caballero possesses a pilot's eye, an all-encompassing view of the "genial or divine system of the world" (214).[37] The pilot's gaze reorders the plurality into patterns and creates new areas of experience. It is, to borrow an expression by Virilio, a "watching machine" (*War and Cinema* 3).[38] The perspective adopted by Giménez Caballero is therefore consistent with his fascist ideology.

Giménez Caballero involves his readers in his aerial reconnaissance of the world's genii by inviting them to climb into the cockpit of his airplane and by appealing directly to them. Thanks to its aerial cartography, the cartographic gaze allows the reader to comprehend from a global perspective the distinctive traits of each genius as well as the relationships that they maintain among themselves. This is, however, a manipulative technique, for the reader's point of view is directed and limited by the author, as reflected in his recurrent use of the imperative mood for the verbs *to see* (185, 186, 189, 192), *to contemplate* (189), and *to look* (191), his anaphoric repetition "there you have" (187, 188) or the expression "if we look at" (188). Needless to say, the imperative is consistent with *Genio de España*'s intended perlocutionary effect, for it replicates, on a minor scale, Giménez Caballero's imposition of an ideological map (i.e., the map of the world's genii) onto his readers. This undisguised ideological coercion is even more evident when it is carried out through the dynamic image of the plane: "If, after we look to the *right* – the *Orient* – and contemplate that immense global space where God is above the *man*, where the *man* is a concept absolutely 'dependent' upon *God*, we turn our gaze towards the *left*, what will we see on our world map? Well, we see a reddish patch, much smaller than that of the right or Oriental: a vibrant sector, dynamic and mysterious called *Occident*" (190).

One might argue that the verbs *to look* and *to contemplate* demand from readers a passivity consistent with the self-conscious projection of a pattern onto a place through the cartographic gaze. In fact, the aerial cartography of the world's genii and its correlative imposition, through comments of the author-as-aviator, of a single perspective to be unquestionably adopted by the reader turn the cartographic gaze into a totalitarian one. In effect, this is one of the meanings that aviation had for the Futurists and the fascists. Indeed, fascist politics and political discourse reproduced the relationship of equivalence between the aerial cartographic gaze (as realized by fascist writers like Giménez Caballero) and the totalitarian gaze. We can see such interconnections, for example, in several speeches of Primo de Rivera. In one delivered on 30 May 1935, the Jefe Nacional of FE-JONS proposes a totalitarian gaze

altogether different from the partial, incomplete gaze of the rest of the
political parties, which see the country from a single point of view (leftist
or rightist) rather than in its entirety, thereby missing Spain's "harmonious integrity." They thus do not desire the "total interest of Spain" (*Obras*
583). Consequently, the "total" interest of Spain can be achieved only by
a total, all-encompassing gaze. In a speech read on 22 July 1934, Primo
de Rivera opposed the political parties' "point of view" in favour of a
totalitarian gaze, complaining about the otherwise constitutive limitations of the former. According to him, Spain lost its style and personality
when the political parties were born, for they view Spain from a single
perspective instead of "taking it in totally and absolutely" (*Obras* 289–90).
As he had maintained in the "Puntos iniciales," published anonymously
on 7 December 1933 in the first issue of *F.E.*, the fatherland must not
be looked at from either the left or the right – standpoints that he calls
"*partial*" – but instead from "a *total* point of view … that by taking [the
fatherland] in as a whole *corrects* our defects of vision" (4). The Jefe Nacional of FE-JONS would insist on the totalitarian cartographic gaze in a
keynote address in the Segundo Consejo Nacional de Falange delivered
on 17 November 1935: "The best of our youth had to enlist in the right
or in the left, some as a reaction against the insolence and others out
of disgust for the mediocrity; but by turning on both … they had to
subject their soul to a mutilation, they had to resign themselves to seeing a slanted Spain … with one eye, as if their soul were one-eyed. In
the youth from the right and the left burns … the eagerness for finding
the harmonious and whole vision of a Spain that is not properly seen if
looked at from only one side, that can be understood only by looking at
it face-to-face" (*Obras* 713–14).

The technique of placing the cartographic gaze on an airplane underscores a fundamental aspect of *Genio de España*'s production of space: the
spatialization of history. The mythical cartography of the world represents
the three genii in their static distribution as well as in the changes that
they have undergone in the course of a historical sequence over two mil-
lennia. These changes do not alter the essence of the genius, but they do
add to it new content and modes of expression. Space becomes history,
or, to be more specific, space acquires a temporal meaning, whereas history becomes a geometry of sorts, thereby ceasing to be a mere aggregate
of past events arranged in their chronological order. To accuse Giménez
Caballero of practising an ahistorical discourse would be therefore unjust. His "spatial history" resembles to some extent the spatial history
that Kristin Ross (75–99) ascribes to the European expansionist imperi-

alism of the last three decades of the nineteenth century. According to Ross, "the privileged and exclusive status of space as a natural referent corresponds to the needs of Western colonialism" (87); European colonialism, as Ross explains, demanded "a certain production of space that Vidalian academic geography was to help provide: natural, which is to say, non-historical" (87). For Paul Vidal de la Blanche and his followers, geography was the science of landscape; consequently the geographical study of a country was limited to the description of its regions, and thus its social and economic contradictions remained hidden. However, in the case of Giménez Caballero one has to proceed with caution, since his cartographic performance contains a strong historiographic element. In *Genio de España* there is no repression of history, but rather a systematic production of a space/time structured around the figure of the genius. In this sense, the genius may be considered as a chronotope. The space described in this section of the book is thus a relational spacetime.

The aerial survey of the world conveys that fusion between space and time. As Marinetti and eight fellow Futurists had remarked in their "Manifesto della aeropittura" (1929), the speed of airplanes pulverizes both time and space, "the earth disappears at high speed under the immobile airplane" (Marinetti, *Teoria* 199–200). With the airplane's speed, in his aerial reconnaissance of the three genii Giménez Caballero eliminates the distinctiveness of the objects, generates space and time, and like other modernists, most particularly the Futurists, provides a new perspective from which to understand history. Seen from the airplane, space seems to be on the move; at the same time, the mobility of the airplane refracts the historical changes that have taken place in the world. Thus, the genius of the Occident, far from being a static and passive demarcation of its contents, has its origin in the "Caucasus region" of the Aryans, who, in turn, expanded or settled down among the Balts, Iranians, Hindis, Slavs, Germanics, Greeks, and Celts (191). It moves from Greece to Rome, surviving in Plotinus, Augustine, Thomas Aquinas, and the Hispanicized Jews and Arabs (194), and reaches its second dawn during the Renaissance (194). The Reformation, the rationalist philosophy, and the French Revolution are further milestones of the genius of the Occident's historical evolution. The genius of the Occident covers a broad period that extends to the Bolshevik Revolution. The genius of Christ, in turn, is a dialectical synthesis of both genii, since it is born in the Orient and consolidated in the Occident. Christ settles in neither Moscow nor Paris nor Mecca, but in Rome, which is understood as the spiritual and material "confluence" of the Occident and the Orient (200–1).

Aerial photography can have either a military or a civilian purpose.[39] Both are simultaneously present in *Genio de España*. It is worth remembering here that aerial photography is an offspring of the First World War. In 1915, the French military produced the first cameras designed for aerial reconnaissance. Having reformulated the meaning of aerial perspective, "warfare had led," in Piper's words, "to the establishment of an industry that saw its subjects as hostile, dehumanized, and disorganized. Indeed, territory could only be correctly and safely interpreted during war through the view from above" (68). For Virilio, alongside the war machine there always has existed "an ocular ... 'watching machine' capable of providing soldiers, and particularly commanders, with a visual perspective on the military action under way" (*War and Cinema* 3). In the Great War, claims Virilio, reconnaissance aircraft had replaced the original watchtower and its successor, the anchored balloon (3). Reconnaissance airplanes became "the eyes of the high command, a vital prosthesis for the headquarters strategists, illuminating a terrain that was constantly being turned upside down by high explosives" (70). Flying turned out to be the ultimate way of seeing (17).

In *Genio de España*, the aerial reconnaissance of the topography of the world's genii generates a spacetime with the intention of reinterpreting the history of the world. But this spatialization of history through a cartographic gaze is also part of a military project. The map of the world drawn by the author through a cartographic gaze from the air is presented as a tool and as an incentive for future combats. Giménez Caballero designed a map of the three genii in their space-time in order to make his readers understand the necessity of resuscitating, by all necessary means, the genius of Spain. It is therefore a propagandistic map whose ultimate goal is to influence the readers so that they will join the ranks of fascism. Cartography constitutes in *Genio de España* a topographical description/production, the imposition of an absolute world view, and the attempt to affect the emotions and thinking of its readers so as to prepare them for a battle. Like its aggressive language and illocutionary force, *Genio de España*'s cartographic imagery is for the service of war. "This book offers battle," Giménez Caballero avows, "and shoots, without batting an eyelash, against three centuries of Spanish bastardies, of Spain's imperial and moral failures" (10). Hence the map of the world's genii plays a function similar to that of military maps, for both provide extremely detailed knowledge of the territory in which the battles will be fought.[40] As anti-Republican organizations and the Catholic Church did in the political and social fields, so Giménez Caballero prepared the path to the Spanish Civil War.

The "battle" offered by the author would indeed take place. Without the map of the genii, the civil war would lack an important symbolic mainstay. Since *Genio de España* is an essay, we are talking, of course, about a battle of ideas. However, we should not forget that *Genio de España* established basic ideas of Spanish fascism and that it had a powerful influence on people who did not hesitate to take up arms four years after the appearance of the first edition of the book. In the prologue to the third edition (1938), Giménez Caballero himself summarized, with characteristic hyperbole, the function, meaning, and effect of his book: in *Genio de España* one can find sketched nearly the whole *"terminological and conceptual matériel of our Movement.* To the point that this book has been considered … as the *spiritual justification of our Cause"* ("Nota" xv–xvi). *Genio de España* is thus a space of representation that to a certain extent conditioned the production of new material practices; to put it differently, it contributed symbolically to the conquest of physical space: the national territory administered by the republican state. The bellicosity of the book, manifested specially through its violent language, culminates in the last pages with a passionate call for a coup d'état addressed to the social nuclei that truly feel and share the genius of Spain (260–5). Giménez Caballero heralds a unified Spain, an absolute space led by a new Caesar condensed in Rome and politically represented by a fascist organization. The map of the world's genii has taught the reader to understand space-time; with this knowledge the author is finally capable of contributing to the regeneration of Spain. The book is concluded. The map has been read and understood. Now it is the reader's turn.

Giménez Caballero's call for a coup d'état is the logical outcome of the genesial meaning of *genius*, present above all in the last section of *Genio de España*, entitled "Exaltación final sobre el monte de El Pardo" (254–65). In that symbolically charged place, the author synthesizes his ideal of a fascist resurrection of the imperial essence of Spain. He relates that one evening at dusk in Corpus Christy he was on Mount El Pardo, from where he contemplated the Royal Palace of El Pardo, built by "the Hispanic Caesar Charles V" (255). El Pardo, claims the author, is the mount where Spain's monarchy and empire came about, and he considers the Royal Palace of El Pardo the forerunner of El Escorial (255). In El Pardo, Giménez Caballero has the prophetic vision of the arrival of a Hitler-like Charles V "fighting for the Cross" (256) and for the subsequent resurrection of the genius of Spain (265). It is evident that in El Pardo his irrationalist techniques are in sync with the spatial symbolization of his ideology.

Within Giménez Caballero's ideology, El Pardo is a trace of an irretrievable past. What seems to be present in all its plenitude is paradoxically the provisional outcome of a free play of absences. As a trace, El Pardo is the physical reminder of a grandeur that was once "here" and is now "somewhere else." The author aspires that El Pardo, as a mediator between the present and the absent, transforms into the pure presence of the genius-like essence of Spain. But that is impossible, as becomes apparent in the book itself. Giménez Caballero's irrationalist method and cartographic gaze ought to be understood in their relationship to the acknowledgment of the impossibility of all plenitude. He renounces referential language and historical rigour in favour of a phenomenological reduction of sorts, a poetic language, and the actualization of a topographical view of the world and of history. The epoché, the poetry, and the prophecy, along with the cartographic gaze, seem more appropriate for the apprehension of a presence whose existence is deduced by the interpretation of a trace of Spain's imperial past. In Giménez Caballero's mythical cartography, the most important element is absent. As a play of oppositions and differences, every map is the tacit recognition that there can be only traces of what is constantly somewhere else. In other words, a map consists of the semiotic systematization of a series of traces, and it is itself the trace of the totality of the space that it represents. The desire to actualize what the trace hints at cannot be satisfied. The prophetic and utopian gesture of *Genio de España* is but the recognition of this impossibility. A few years after the publication of the book, the death of José Antonio Primo de Rivera in November 1936 would mark decisively the history of this impotence: with the "absence" of the leader of FE-JONS and Nazi Germany's defeat in 1945, the future of Spanish fascism became a trace of what could have been, of the "pending revolution" that never came. From then on, Falangism would be the desolate cartography of an empty space.

Planning

Arte y Estado (1935) has no equal.[41] Not only is this essay the most extensive, thorough, original, and formally innovative exposition of fascist aesthetics and poetics in Spain. In addition, it had a huge influence on art theorists and literary critics of the 1940s and early 1950s. One might go further to argue that neither the literary criticism and theory nor the theory of art during the early Franco regime can be comprehended without knowing *Arte y Estado*.[42] Giménez Caballero's conception of the arts and literature as tools in service of the fascist state, as mystical revelation, and as propaganda opened up the path followed by Francoist criticism on art and literature, while also establishing the foundations of the meaning and ideological direction of artworks and literary artefacts.[43] For instance, his seminal interpretation of the Royal Monastery of San Lorenzo de El Escorial forms the core of one trend of fascist architecture as well as the literature produced after the civil war. Amidst the many instances of the *escorialismo* initiated by *Arte y Estado*, the cultural journal *Escorial* (1940–50) stands out; its notion of literature, art, politics, and cultural mission, stated in the "Manifiesto editorial" published in the first issue of the journal (November 1940), stems from Giménez Caballero's reading of El Escorial.[44] As mentioned earlier, the reception of *Arte y Estado*, as well as some important issues and topics from that book, have merited scholarly attention. Nevertheless, two aspects closely related to the fascist politics of space remain to be properly examined. I am referring to the thread linking the structure, theoretical ground, and perlocution of the book on the one hand and to the cartographic gaze that, driven by a will-to-architecture, underlies *Arte y Estado* on the other.

Whereas *Genio de España* forms a textual map, *Arte y Estado* can be likened to the plan of a building as well as to an edifice. To his cartographic gaze, the writer adds a will-to-architecture. To begin with, Giménez Caballero's cartographic gaze articulates the author's reading of the history of art. In keeping with his cartographic classification of genii, Giménez Caballero groups artworks into three different modes or styles: Oriental romanticism, Occidental romanticism, and Christian classicism (*Arte* 24–26). The first includes Chinese, Muslim, Hindu, and Aztec art, representing "a world where Nature predominates over everything human … pantheism over Christianity, the mass over the individual" (24). The second refers to a type of art predominant in the Western world since ancient Greece, representing the "yearning to create a world at least equal to the divine. To match or to surpass Nature.... Satanic, Promethean, defiant urge" (35). Finally, Christian classicism is the synthesis of Oriental romanticism's determinism and Occidental romanticism's free will (25). These three modes of art are specific manifestations of the genius of the Orient, Occident, and Christ respectively, so much so that one could even say that *Genio de España* is the condition of possibility for *Arte y Estado*. The author's reading of his coetaneous artistic field reinforces such an interpretation. For him, both the art of the twentieth century (which he identifies for the most part with the avant-gardes) and the world lack equilibrium; each is out of joint (26). Thus, the crisis in the artistic and

literary fields refracts the all-encompassing crisis of the genius of the
Occident. The solution to the former – Christian classicism – is just one
part of the answer that will solve all the problems: the genius of Christ.
However, there is an important difference between *Genio de España* and
Arte y Estado. In the latter, Giménez Caballero proceeds not as a cartographer but as an architect. This self-conscious approach, as well as the
will-to-architecture that defines *Arte y Estado*, emerges at the beginning
of the book. As he had done in the preliminary pages of *Genio de España*,
the author reveals at the outset the rules of the game, namely the constitutive spatiality of *Arte y Estado*. Accordingly, in the preface to *Arte y Estado*
(9–13) Giménez Caballero describes his essay as a "vast plan," adding
that such architectonic view of writing is indebted to his long conversations on architecture with an architect and member of the GATEPAC
(an avant-garde group of Spanish architects), José María Aizpurúa (12).
Arte y Estado is thus portrayed as an edifice planned and built by a cartographic gaze and in turn driven by a will-to-architecture. In this context,
the three parts of the book ("Arte, realidad y Estado," "Las artes y el
Estado," and "El artista y el Estado"), which Giménez Caballero tellingly
denominates as "sectors," are meant to be the "structure" – in the architectonic sense of the word – of *Arte y Estado*.[45]

In analogous fashion to *Genio de España*, there is a tension in *Arte y
Estado* between an irrationalist methodology and the concept of art as
action on the one hand and the will-to-architecture on the other. Giménez Caballero's approach to art and literature follows the irrationalist
methodology set up in *Genio de España*. He claims to have written *Arte y
Estado* "starting from hunches, fits of faith, courageous gazes ... Then, I
have tried to document those starting points as best as I could. Method
of mystic, and not of didactic philosopher" (12). In the closing section
of the book, he summarizes his methodology so as to make it clearer to
the reader: the "suggestion" is always a "vivid method to give sense to
reality: to materialize it, to live it up" (223). Further on, Giménez Caballero acknowledges having skipped a definition of the state. This is no
accident, for he has preferred to insinuate its character, to allude to it
indirectly rather than openly establishing its parameters (224). This literary technique is of the greatest importance, for it shows that an irrationalist methodology and the will-to-architecture can coexist in harmony:
"I have ... left in the utmost vagueness the concept of *state* ... making
the reader ... see in the concept ... what my incitement and his imagination suggested to him: a mountain, a kingdom of seraphs, a dragon, a
monstrous palace, an angel ... There are *concepts-cloud* that without being

delimited themselves work as delimitations for bringing out the profile of a landscape. One of such concepts is, undoubtedly, that of *state*" (224).

Giménez Caballero practises in *Arte y Estado* a kind of writing at once totalitarian (the attempt to control the reader by prescribing formulae to understand and practise art) and violent (the illocutionary force of the discourse of the book). *Arte y Estado* is passionately geared towards manipulating its readers. For Giménez Caballero, art is a form of action, a "human activity," "an active dimension ... of life" (17), but it is also a product of that activity. The etymological roots of the word *art* lie, as he explains, "in the action, in the Doing, in the Active," in "facing up, in a certain way, to the Reality of the world" (17). Art and the arts are "ways to fight ... instruments for waging war ... swords" (86), or, as the author writes in chapter 1 of the "Second Sector," a "technique of conquest" (91).[46] Furthermore, the artist is a soldier whose orders are "to kill or to take prisoners" (87), by which Giménez Caballero understands "to win over souls" and "to catechize hearts" (87). Interestingly, this concept of art as a function of fascist discourse is expressed through an avant-gardist language, as witnessed in several passages of the book, most particularly in the closure of the section titled "Propaganda y arte," in which Giménez Caballero uses the anaphoric, programmatic, *épatant*, and aggressive language and rhetoric of the avant-garde manifestos to defend a constituent of fascist aesthetics – art as propaganda (86–8). Crucially, the artistic action that Giménez Caballero talks about, which may be viewed as a discursive refraction of the direct action practised by fascists, finds in architecture its ultimate expression. In *Arte y Estado*, propagandistic art is viewed as an artistic action consisting of the imposition on the reader of a static place, a "building," an absolute space. For not only does architecture express the will and nature of the totalitarian fascist state; the outcome of its action – buildings – is considered the only acceptable space for the citizen, or, to be more precise, for the member of the "people's community." The movement of the individual – a metaphor of free, autonomous thinking – must be replaced by stasis, by a *pensée unique*.

The key to understanding *Arte y Estado*'s spatiality lies in the last two chapters of the "First Sector," "La 'Nueva Arquitectura' (o la revolución fracasada)" (51–62) and "El expediente Le Corbusier" (63–72), where Giménez Caballero expounds his ideas on architecture. This was not the first time that he wrote about the topic, nor would it be the last.[47] Architecture had always been an art of great interest to him since the late 1920s.[48] As the director of *La Gaceta Literaria* (1927–32), he had devoted an entire issue of the journal (no. 32, April 1928) to modern architecture. Aside from articles by Paul Valéry, José Ortega y Gasset, Le Corbusier, Jacobus Oud, August Perret, and other renowned figures, the issue included answers from writers and architects to a survey prepared by the noted architect Fernando García Mercadal. Furthermore, essays on the new trends in architecture appeared regularly in *La Gaceta Literaria*.[49] After his conversion to fascism, Giménez Caballero distanced himself from the rationalist architecture that he had championed. As a result, he produced two articles, "Disgusto por la arquitectura nueva" (1931) and "Posibilidad de una arquitectura nuestra" (1932), which marked his break with rationalism and laid out his new views on the topic. In these two pieces he sharply criticizes what he considers the false modernity of the rationalism practised in northern Europe, arguing for a Mediterranean-style architecture, which he deems the most adequate architectonic expression of both the essence and the climate of Spain. To be sure, this was not a new proposal. In the late 1920s, Mercadal had already written a series of articles praising traditional Mediterranean architecture. What sets Giménez Caballero apart from Mercadal is, as Carlos Ramos (137) has rightly observed, his radicalism, sectarianism, vehemence, and, I should like to add, his extreme nationalism. Such positioning vis-à-vis modern architecture would reach its climax in the above-mentioned chapters of *Arte y Estado*.

In *Arte y Estado*, Giménez Caballero rejects the International Style, whose main principles (rationality, social equality, internationalism, and utilitarianism) were diametrically opposed to some tenets of his fascist ideology (irrationalism, totalitarianism, anti-liberalism, nationalism, and anti-materialism) (59–60). After reviewing the history and main characteristics of the International Style that was predominant at the time (53–60), he notes that in Nazi Germany as well as in Bolshevik Russia that kind of architecture has been forsaken after discovering that the only fundamental law of architecture is the climate (60–1), that is, the interconnections between the topography, climatic conditions, and characteristics of a nation on the one hand, and the materials and style of buildings on the other (63–6). According to Giménez Caballero, the only "salvation" for the new architecture is to "expiate its sins" by "peregrinating" to Rome (61–2). To exemplify both the insufficiencies of the International Style and the search for new architectonic forms, he focuses on Le Corbusier. Without giving specifics, apart from quoting a statement by the Swiss architect ("a social truth: Rome" [67]), Giménez Caballero claims that Le Corbusier has found his path of "contrition and recreation" after discovering "Rome's majesty ... the architecture of the peoples ... Of the State" (67). Indeed, the great Swiss architect had visited Rome in 1934 by invitation of Mussolini. A man whose ideas on urban planning and architecture were greatly admired by Georges Valois and other French fascists, Le Corbusier had moved increasingly to the political right since the end of the 1920s. While not a fascist himself, Le Corbusier had contacts with fascism and the extreme right in France. After 1925 he participated in Ernest Mercier's organization Redressement français and gave lectures at fascist rallies. In the 1930s he went out of his way to meet Mussolini, endorsed a brand of regional syndicalism associated with Hubert Lagardelle (a future Vichy minister), and gave his support to Italy's invasion of Ethiopia.[50] As for his conception and practice of architecture, his support of regional syndicalism "led him to repudiate his rationalist modernism in favor of architectural forms whose curvilinear structure exemplified Lagardelle's 'corporativist' and 'organic' definition of the nation state" (Antliff 119).

Giménez Caballero's choice of Le Corbusier as an example was thus far from arbitrary. From Giménez Caballero's standpoint, Le Corbusier was at the time renouncing rationalism in favour of a humanization of architecture born out of the architect's contact with Rome (66–7). Commenting on a statement made by the architect,[51] Giménez Caballero argues that Le Corbusier's new aesthetics balances the collective and the individual in an attempt to rescue human beings from their servitude to the machine. The equilibrium between the community and the individual present in Le Corbusier's new architecture is precisely, according to Giménez Caballero, a fascist formula that deals with both the social and the political (68). These remarks on Le Corbusier frame the exposition of one of the main ideas underpinning *Arte y Estado*: the interrelations between the fascist state, architecture, and absolute space: "*To structure, to build, to order* are the verbs of the State. Architectonic verbs. Any resurrection in history of 'what belongs or relates to the State' means a resurrection of 'architectonic things.' Supremacy of the State; precedence of the Architecture. Architecture: art of the State, function of the State, essence of the State. The time of a new architecture, of a new style of building has come. Because the time of a new State – genius of Rome, hierarchical, provider of an order – has come to the world. Let the other arts ... be disciplined and ready to take their combat range [*sic*] ... Architecture has a command post. The State. Rome" (71–2; see also 67, 77, 81).[52]

Giménez Caballero's view of the state, the nation, and the political as architecture materializes in two loci: the "casa sindical" or central office of a trade union (209–19) and the Royal Monastery of San Lorenzo de

El Escorial (233–40). The former is the prescribed locus of the fascist artist, while the latter represents the totalitarian state. Giménez Caballero claims that the "casa sindical" – also called "refugio gremial" (a labour union shelter) – is the most appropriate place for the new (fascist) artist.[53] Societies of artists like the "Gu" in San Sebastian are instances, according to him, of labour union shelters.[54] A "casa sindical" (the members of the "Gu" typically met and exhibited in their own headquarters) is radically different from the typical milieu of "individualistic art" – the exhibition halls (211–12). The unions mean "determined affirmations against that myth, failed and tragic, of the solitary artist" (214). Artists cannot live alone because deep down they are members of a brotherhood in the monastic and professional sense of the concept (214). After reviewing several experiments in artistic communes across Europe (e.g., the Group Porza), Giménez Caballero asserts, "Both the artist and the intellectual already feel the anguish ... of their straying, of the breaking up of their brotherhood" (215); this anguish has caused the emergence of such "casas sindicales," in which he envisions the fascist dirigisme of art and cultural production in general, the dissolution of individual identity into the "people's community," and the metamorphosis of the individualist artist into a mere member of a guild. Above all, what really matters is the subordination of the artist to the state (215). "The union principle," writes Giménez Caballero, "tends to pick up the artist from his peripheral position and ... to bind him to the life of the nation" (218).[55]

The architectural model favoured by Giménez Caballero was the Royal Monastery of San Lorenzo de El Escorial, the greatest symbol, according to him, of the future state (233–6).[56] He opposes Ortega y Gasset's interpretation of the monastery as a "treatise of the pure effort," as an enormous endeavour without an object, symbolizing Spain's poverty of ideas and its abnormality in relation to the other European nations.[57] For him, El Escorial represents simultaneously the "supreme state" achieved at the peak of Spain's world hegemony, the imperial essence of Spain, and the ideal of a hierarchical, static, trans-temporal, totalitarian state. Yet El Escorial also contains an affective force since, by its simple presence, it calls for the restoration and implementation of the state that it symbolizes: sunken in the depths of time, the bells, towers, crosses, and domes of El Escorial "speak to us ... so that a titanic Spanish generation brings it out again" (233). Hence it could be said that El Escorial is conceived of as both an absolute locus and an instance of relational spacetime. El Escorial, he writes further, is the most sublime image of what Spain "*wanted to be, was, and would like to be again*" (235).[58] The essence of Spain "*stopped being what it was* to roll away down the Guadarrama's ravine like yet another stone, drowned, crushed by bourgeois and democratic chalets ... Because it stopped wanting that *state*. Because *its will to be El Escorial* weakened" (235). The will-to-architecture produces a building, controls nature, imposes a political system and a Weltanschauung, projects a drive for imperial domination, and presents itself as an aesthetic and political model. As he writes in a crucial passage,

> El Escorial is first and foremost Architecture ... It is construction. It is measurement.... It is conquest – before the surrounding nature – of a mathematic formula for building. Its stones are pieces from the neighboring mounts.... But man's hand, his will, has thrust those stones in order, phalanx, and cross ... All of it [El Escorial]: hierarchy, harmony. Spain's "First Cause." The *King* subjected to *God* ... *Nature* ... subjected to *Man* ... And as the landscape around El Escorial – subdued by the architectonic hand in gardening and in the forest arts [*sic*] – so in all the other *arts*. What a hierarchy, what an order, what a discipline for all the arts! (236–7)[59]

This concept of El Escorial, which – as mentioned earlier – left a mark on a whole generation of Falangists, may seem at first sight to contradict Giménez Caballero's irrationalist methodology. To be sure, El Escorial's balanced and austere classicism has little in common with Giménez Caballero's expressionism, vehemence, and irrational exaltation. Nevertheless, a closer inspection reveals the writer's coherence and consistency in his symbolic use of the monastery. Giménez Caballero does not develop his concept of art and state in a rigorous way and with a denotative language. Rather, in keeping with his contempt of historiographical approaches and his use of a mystical and poetic language, he resorts to the symbol in order to present his aesthetics and political model, a method to which he refers on several occasions (e.g., 223–5). "El Escorial" is therefore the result of a complex process of symbolic condensation; in this sense, it has to be considered as the epitome of the author's irrationalist method as well as the refraction of the will-to-architecture underpinning the book's structure, content, and discourse. One has to distinguish between El Escorial as the building located in the outskirts of a Castilian village and "El Escorial" as the discursive symbolic construct realized by Giménez Caballero. This distinction resolves the apparent incongruence of putting forward a classicist building as an aesthetic and political model in a book whose language seems to contradict that model. When Giménez Caballero writes that there is no example "that better summarizes the whole book than ... El Escorial" (236), he is undoubtedly referring to the political message of *Arte y Estado* as well as to his defence of a specific architectural model. But he is alluding as well to the exalted kind of writing practised in *Arte y Estado* and its will-to-architecture. To put it differently, *Arte y Estado* may be characterized as a discursive "Escorial." Indeed, the book presents itself as a building constructed after a "plan" and made up of three "sectors." Moreover, it houses and prescribes – like El Escorial – both an aesthetics and a type of state. For these reasons, one could apply to *Arte y Estado* the following depiction of El Escorial: "Hierarchy and ordering and synthesis of a whole world, of an entire epoch. Perfect style of a whole creation. All the arts hierarchized, disciplined by a supreme will to attain what it already was: to achieve Spain's unity, not only in politics, but with *matter to service* the monastery's great harmony and *great State*" (238). Ultimately, El Escorial and *Arte y Estado*-as-an-Escorial (a drawing of Juan de Herrera's building, I should like to add, was printed on the cover of the first edition) may be viewed as two "houses" of Spanish fascism: the former would be the home of the Falangist conception of Spain and the state, whereas the latter would be inhabited by all those who found in Giménez Caballero's book the main source for basic ideas on fascist aesthetics and poetics. Inhabiting any of those places would not be an easy task, for to be able to do so one had to follow the rules governing their grammar. Shortly after the civil war, Sánchez Mazas put it in succinct, clear, and somewhat ominous words: El Escorial is a building infinitely hospitable and immensely inhabitable because, while it welcomes everyone, "it will let itself be inhabited only by those who can rule the universe" ("Textos" 20–1), that is to say: by the new masters of Spain.

Ordering

If architecture was for fascist intellectuals the ultimate expression of an imperial past and of the new state's atemporal greatness, as well as the best symbolic means to manipulate and unite a national community, it is only logical that fascist writing itself attempts to metamorphose into a building, into an absolute place. In Giménez Caballero's work, this conception of writing as a building reaches its climax in a book neglected by scholars: *Roma madre* (1939), whose Italian version was awarded in 1937 the Premio Internazionale di San Remo, granted by the Reale Accademia d'Italia. This book may be read as the ultimate manifestation of the cartographic gaze and the will-to-architecture of *Genio de España* and *Arte y Estado.*

To understand the book fully, it is indispensable to be aware of a crucial fact: *Roma madre* consists of a collage of articles, prologues, fragments of books (e.g., *Hércules jugando a los dados, Circuito imperial, Genio de España, Manuel Azaña, La Nueva Catolicidad, El Belén de Salzillo en Murcia, Arte y Estado, Exaltación del matrimonio*), and unpublished lectures written before 1937. Therefore, one could presume that *Roma madre* does not add anything new and consequently lacks any interest whatsoever for readers and critics alike. But this is not so: its importance lies precisely in the collage-style composition of the book, for *Roma madre* is not an arbitrary collection of previous essays. On the contrary: it is a deliberate imposition of a structure on most of Giménez Caballero's previous works. Giménez Caballero himself points this out repeatedly. *Roma madre* "was made by the systematic accumulation of many fighting days, of many books of mine, and it is therefore 'my true anthology.' My *opera omnia*" (*Roma madre* xxxi). Such *opera omnia*, Giménez Caballero stresses, should be understood as an edifice. In the prologue, he indicates the relation between the book's architectonic structure and its metaphysical and political aims: "This book is the organic and systematized summary of a ten-year-long task to bring out the resurrection of Rome in Spain, and in other countries" (2). Similar to previous essays that obey a "unitary and systematic conception of the present-day resurrection of Rome in the world," *Roma madre* "is passionately structured and woven together … it is built, constructed" (2). The author characterizes his book as a house of sorts. In fact, the very structure of the book is described explicitly in architectonic terms: "This book has been built with a *Central section* flanked by two lateral wings. This Central section (the Second part) is elaborated upon the *Genius of Rome* … The first lateral wing, or *First part* is glassware and terraces, viewpoints over the whole of Italy. The final wing or *Third part* is like the key to or secret motor of the entire building: the *present Duce of Rome*" (2). Following this identification of the book with a house, Giménez Caballero considers his prologue as a "plan," a word he had used already to characterize the prologue to *Arte y Estado.*

Roma madre is divided into three parts preceded by an introduction titled "Roma, resurgida del mundo. Un español ante Italia." Both the first ("Mi marcha sobre Roma") and the third part ("'El Duce' de Roma") converge into the second ("Fascismo, genio de Italia"), the centre and conceptual heart of the book whose importance is underscored by its extension, for it has 146 pages while the other two parts have only 53 and 21 pages respectively. In the introduction, Giménez Caballero tells us about his epiphanic discovery of Rome. The territorial organization and the cities of Italy are at the centre of the first part; its last chapter, "Rome," functions as a transition to the second part, which is devoted to the central topic of *Roma madre*: fascism. In that part, Giménez Caballero analyses the religious foundations (61–78) and the stoic roots (79–89) of fascism, presents the fascist view of Europe (90–121), elaborates on the concepts of resurrection and rebirth from a fascist perspective (121–30), studies the links between art, literature, and fascism (130–76), and describes the economic organization, rural life, and public works in Fascist Italy (176–203). The third part focuses almost exclusively on Mussolini, and ends up in a climatic section titled "La resurrección de Roma en la juventud del mundo" (228–9), a summary of the entire book and a tacit call to its readers: "Rome has re-emerged! And Rome will make today's world, old and faded, resurrect. Oh Rome, Rome! Motherhood of the world! And its salvation. Oh, *Mother Rome*!" (229).

Given the ideology that underpins *Roma madre*, the imposition of a structure onto an amorphous set of essays and passages from other books has to be read as an attempt to coerce the reader. Instead of hiding the book's authoritarian stance towards the reader, Giménez Caballero underscores it from the outset by reflecting on *Roma madre*'s ideal reader. Thus the book "wants readers-tenants who dwell and live, enjoy and suffer this building. It does not want banal passers-by" (2). Here, the concept of "readers-tenants" refers to "passive readers," while the image of the "passers-by" connotes the kind of readers who are actively involved in the hermeneutics of the book; the ability of these readers to contradict and subvert *Roma madre*'s political message makes them suspect and dangerous. The ideal reader demanded by Giménez Caballero in *Roma madre* must not leave the interior spaces of a "book-house," nor question its foundations or its grammar. A "reader-tenant" is a domesticated reader, someone lacking a strong, independent will defined, in spatial terms, by intellectual stasis. In some passages, Giménez Caballero even displays his contempt for the "quick reader, degenerated by a culture composed of short, comfortable books … by books with no solid architecture" (121). Considering that El Escorial was to Giménez Caballero the ideal building and the model of the new state, we could argue that *Roma madre* eliminates the diversity of the possible. As happens in functionalist architecture, in which "the habitat capitalizes the habitudes" (Virilio, *L'Insécurité* 198) and thereby intervenes in the inhabitant's affective space, the architectonics and functionality of *Roma madre* as-a-building does not allow its tenants to take over their places; quite the opposite: the rules of the locus possess the inhabitants.

As just seen, *Roma madre* is a summa that provides an architectonic unity and a meaning to the whole oeuvre of Giménez Caballero. It is thus an absolute place. On the other hand, the implied immobility overlaps with a dynamic dimension. "This book," warns the writer, "goes after something more difficult and ambitious: to look for the secret of all these works. This book lands in Rome. And in Rome it sinks its arm, searching for the entrails of that City ... in search of the new life that is reborn to save the world" (7). The first part of the book tells the story of the author's search for and epiphanic finding of truth, and teaches the reader to recognize, learn, and interiorize such truth. That movement is framed within a discursive space whose architectonic immobility represents absolute truth. In other words, the absolute space represented in the "book-house" determines the relative space-time in which the search for truth has been undertaken. The cartographic gaze and the will-to-architecture are the tools used to produce and combine these two types of space.

The cartographic gaze articulates the first part of the book, in which the author explores and describes the topography of Italy and the genii of its cities. This gaze follows a movement that ends in Rome. After expressing his thoughts on the borders separating Italy from its neighbouring countries (chapter 1), the writer proceeds to talk about Genoa, Turin, Milan (chapter 2), Venice, Naples (chapter 3), and Florence (chapter 4), to end with his arrival in Rome (chapter 5, the last one of this part). With this type of movement, the author aspires to be true to the centralist territorial and administrative structure of Mussolini's Italy (11). In Giménez Caballero's judgment, it is crucial to understand this organization in order to capture the essence of Italy: "Whoever considers and visits and tries to romantically, inorganically understand Rome ... won't be able to grasp anything at all of the new Italy, stacked up, compact, unitarian, full of one meaning only" (11). Once again, the reader faces an absolute truth (i.e., fascism) embodied in absolute space (i.e., Italy and Rome). The second part of the book provides a detailed description of this absolute truth/space. Thus the movement converging in Rome that is realized in the relative space-time leads to the ideological core of the book: fascism as absolute space. One could therefore argue that the second part is the structural and ideological "Rome" of *Roma madre*.

True to his customary cartographic approach, Giménez Caballero represents his turning away from and repudiation of liberalism and democracy with spatial images. For a time, says the author, he was under the spell of a series of "liberal prejudices," of "idols" that "could be reduced to a few names of cities or civilizations: Paris, London, Moscow" (3). The "eyes" of an Italian woman (his future wife Edith Sironi Negri) led him to Italy, to his original fatherland, Rome: "They took me to the motherly home of my Spain, to the people who founded my soul" (6). An emotion – instead of a careful intellectual consideration of political doctrines – thus would be the factor that determined his embrace of fascism. The discovery of the absolute truth of fascism in a place conceived as absolute (Rome) occurred thanks to an "amorous gaze."

Several interrelated spatial elements articulate the first part of *Roma madre*: the limit, the *fasces lictoriae* (bundles of the lictors), the portal, and the threshold. As in Spain, the "limits" or "borders" of Italy provide, in Giménez Caballero's opinion, a rigid separation between the interior and the exterior. "Whereas there are countries with loose limits (Switzerland, Belgium, Poland) … there are others where the borders squeak like drawbridges" (8–9). Spain and Italy belong to the latter category; they are countries "with gates, with sally ports" (8–9). A place exists because limits were previously imposed upon an amorphous space. Every place or space exists and has a meaning, thanks to its limits. On the other hand, a boundary connects spaces. Giménez Caballero affirms that the boundaries of Spain and Italy isolate their respective genii.

Now, these limits have vanishing points, which he calls "portals." Italy's portals are grouped into two main sets: portals to the Occident and portals to the Orient. In chapter 2, he describes the Italian portals to the Occident (Genoa, 11–17; Turin, 17–19; Milan, 19–26), and in chapter 3 the Italian portals to the Orient (Venice, 27–39; Naples, 36–42). Like the limit, the portal is an ambiguous locus, since it separates as well as joins spaces. Such ambiguity is consubstantial to what the author calls "portalidad" (literally "portality"). Sometimes, the intrusion carries danger (as happens with the penetration of the Orient through Venice), while on other occasions it enriches the space that it penetrates. In his description of Milan, Giménez Caballero specifies what he understands by *portality*. Again, it is a description characteristic of the author's cartographic gaze: "Milan is … a prime portal to Italian life … What in Milan gives you the feeling of 'Italianity' is its conception of the portal. Hence its immense train station…. The whole Milan is a gate. Latin door without hinges, triumphal arch for people just passing through. The northern civilization, liberal and mechanical, enters and leaves through it. The sentimental and millenarian reaction from the South leaves and goes through it as well" (21).

For Giménez Caballero, Italy's gates to the exterior allow for both a centripetal (penetration of the Orient through Venice) and centrifugal movement (Genoa as the point of departure for Italian expansionism). Both gates lead to Rome: "*Today Rome is Italy. And the rest: Gates to Rome, meaningful transit towards Rome*" (11). In order to capture the meaning of Rome, it is imperative, according to Giménez Caballero, to understand Italy's gates. The centre is defined by the periphery: "Whoever wishes truly to reach Rome must pass through all its Italian gates and read on their thresholds the secret therein engraved ... Only thus does Rome reveal its entrails. Only thus will Rome tell us all about what Italy means nowadays in the world" (11). Notice the language employed by the writer: he suggests the reader to "read" the "thresholds" of Italy's gates, for there he will find an engraved "secret." In this passage, the hermeneutics of space is identified with the act of reading. Space and the text overlap to such an extent that one may be tempted to describe them as one and the same thing. Since writing constitutes itself as a map/plan, the reader reads the text as a topographical account. The decoding of that space/text leads the reader to discover the "entrails" of Rome, namely fascism's absolute truth and absolute space. As readers, we are still at the "gates" of the book (i.e., the first part). Only if the secret of these "liminal" chapters is grasped can we gain access to the structural "Rome" of the book, that is, to the second part, in which the author elaborates fascism's absolute truth, symbolically embodied in "Rome."

But there is still a semantic component of "Rome" to be considered: the "ordering." "Ordering" holds a meaning similar to that of the other semantic components already explored – especially those of "synthesis" and "unity" – and yet it contains an illocutionary force that is lacking in them. For Giménez Caballero, fascist Rome is a space that irradiates an order – understood as a certain way of organizing life – to the rest of the world. But in its ecumenical and imperialistic drive, Rome irradiates that order in an imperative fashion: "Rome's eternal mission ... To be like Rome! *Because Rome is the origin of all ordering....* To attain a universality, a common homeland for the people, a catholicity. Dream of Europe ever since Rome was born to the world" (60–1). At its deepest, Rome consists of what we could call an *order to order* the world. In other words, *Roma madre* describes an order *and* demands this order of all the citizens. Rome interpellates everyone and commands a habitus. Everything and everyone must be like Rome. *Roma madre* does not exclude itself from that demand and realizes the imperative of being Rome. First of all, the entire book is the verbal expression of an order, at both the thematic (i.e., a synthesis of fascism) and rhetoric levels (i.e., the book as an *opera omnia* and a "house" resulting from a cartographic gaze driven by a will-to-architecture). Second, this verbal expression functions as a command in itself, a fact made evident by the book's propagandistic component. Hence "Rome" condenses the grammar, semantics, and pragmatics of the essay. One might even argue that *Roma madre* is Rome itself. Giménez Caballero's writing is therefore consistent with its ideological proposi-tions. The illocutionary speech act (*to order*) is born from the integration of "Rome" into the production of discourse. "Rome" is a doing, the ulti-mate actualization of the *haz* (fasces) as theorized by the editors of the journal *El Fascio*, for whom the word *haz* (which besides referring to the Roman fasces is the imperative of the Spanish verb *hacer*, that is, "to do") means the grouping of all genuine Spaniards against the enemies of the fatherland as well as the imperative addressed to the Spanish people: "the imperative mood of 'to do.' Do!" ("El Fascio" 1). Something simi-lar could be said of *Genio de España* and *Arte y Estado*. El Escorial in *Arte y Estado* and El Pardo in *Genio de España* are, like Rome in *Roma madre*, absolute spaces in action: they prescribe to the reader a set of beliefs and norms of behaviour.

A few years after the publication of *Roma madre*, Rafael Sánchez Mazas would use the concept of *order* in a similar fashion. In his 1942 program-matic article "Textos sobre una política de arte," Sánchez Mazas exhorts the artists to work according to the "total order" emanating from the new regime. The arts cannot be indifferent to the "order of the father-land" (10). "I'll tell you something," Sánchez Mazas writes. "You shall win victories in the canvases if you paint according to the ideas and methods that have won in the battlefield, if you serve the total order … The State can tell you now, like never before: 'In the struggle for the country's order, I am your big brother'" (15–16). Describing himself as someone who builds bridges between political power and the artistic field, Sán-chez Mazas writes a text with a clear illocutionary force, for it does what it says: it dictates an absolute order to the artists, who in their turn must produce works articulated by that order. In Sánchez Mazas's text, *Roma madre*'s *order to order* is transferred into the political and artistic fields.

The analysis of *Roma madre* shows that Giménez Caballero's fascist writ-ing is better understood if one considers it as space. The cartographic gaze and the will-to-architecture of his fascist essays mean a continuity with the spatial form of his avant-garde works in the 1920s. Giménez Ca-ballero politicizes his avant-gardism right after his "discovery" of Rome. An analysis of the space in his fascist essays reveals, in this sense, the ideological ambiguity inherent among the avant-gardes as well as their links to fascism. Moreover, the study of the cartographic gaze and the will-to-architecture in *Genio de España, Arte y Estado,* and *Roma madre* provides strong evidence that fascist writing itself produces space according to the spatial principles that it defends. Writing incorporates in its texture the fascist politics of space, thereby refracting essential spatial practices characteristic of fascism while carrying out – ultimately – the will-to-power in which fascism finds its raison d'être. The books by Giménez Caballero explored in this chapter constitute much more than three crucial foundations of the fascist ideology and aesthetics in Spain: they are some of the most significant instances of the fascist production of space through writing. While none of those books should be seen as the "origin" of the fascist production of space realized through written spaces of representation and representations of space, they may be considered as a conceptual framework of the copious fascist literature related to space.

Chapter Two

Morocco: The Forging of a Habitus

Colonial Space and Fascism

In his prologue to the 1956 edition of Francisco Franco's *Marruecos: Diario de una Bandera* (1922), Manuel Aznar Zubigaray narrates a recent trip to Morocco with a touch of nostalgia. A fascist journalist and the author of the massive three-volume *Historia militar de la guerra de España* (1964; 1st ed. 1940), Aznar writes that a few months earlier "I peregrinated, again, in Morocco. Interesting and moving experience, that of contemplating once more ... the landscapes where our youth got excited" (16–17). To Aznar, that "pilgrimage" meant returning to a place where some seeds of the Franco regime had been sowed. There, "on the ... shady spot, on that valley's hollow, on the stones of the green hillock ... the lights of glory for one of the best generations ever born in Spain lit up" (17). It was in Morocco, rather than in the Peninsula, where the regeneration of a country adrift brewed: "There, Spain was rescued from past errors in Europe and the Americas; there, the inextinguishable flame of the Spanish soul was called to be revived, and a decisive fork in the road was presented to us so that we could choose who would lead our people to the salvation of its historic being and its fate" (19). The armed forces posted in the Spanish protectorate of Morocco (1912–56), viewed in characteristic fascist fashion as the strongest and fullest collective expression of the people as well as the most perfect bearer of the nation's soul (22), were destined to rescue Spain from its decadence. It is far from accidental that the introduction was signed on the twentieth anniversary of the armed rebellion against the Second Republic, and that it described the very land where the rebellion commenced. But in this narrative of origins that pays homage to the master and celebrates the insurrection, there is also the tacit recognition of the profound interconnectedness between colonialism, war, and fascism.[1]

The creation of the Spanish protectorate of Morocco in November 1912 represented a turning point in Spain's modern colonialism, and it laid out the conditions for the forging of a fascist habitus.[2] Spain had meddled with Moroccan affairs for centuries. From the end of the fifteenth century until the first half of the nineteenth, Spain's presence in the Maghreb had been limited to a handful of enclaves on Morocco's northern coastline; broadly speaking, these fortified settlements had been built to protect maritime trade from piracy and the Peninsula from possible military incursions. The French invasion of Algeria in 1830 would trigger a new vision of what the Spanish role in Morocco should be. The proximity of French troops to a territory to which Spain believed it had "historical rights" greatly alarmed Spanish politicians, intellectuals, and the military.[3] Antonio Madera y Vivero, Donoso Cortés, Serafín Estébanez Calderón, and Antonio Cánovas del Castillo – to mention only a few – wrote essays and delivered lectures demanding from the government a complete reassessment of its relationship with Morocco. Echoing opinions phrased one year earlier by Manuel Malo de Molina in *Viaje a la Argelia: Descripción geográfica y estadística del África francesa, del desierto y de los árabes, con sus usos, costumbres, religión y literatura* (1852), Crispín Ximénez de Sandoval and Antonio Madera y Vivero stated in their *Memorias sobre la Argelia* (1853) that events in the Maghreb were a cause for concern among farsighted Spaniards; considering their connection with European politics and the Peninsula's geographical position, "it is essential," conclude the two authors, "to acknowledge that Africa offers some glory and interest for the future of our Fatherland" (9). These thoughts underlie, too, Serafín Estébanez Calderón's *Manual del oficial en Marruecos: Cuadro geográfico, estadístico, histórico, político y militar de aquel imperio* (1844), a book written, as the author avows, to provide the Spanish people with information about the economy, politics, and geography of Morocco, and to set up the guidelines for political and military action (331). As Pedro Mata flatly claims in the prologue to his novel *Los moros del Riff o el presidiario de Alhucemas* (1856), northern Morocco "belongs to us," and for this reason "it is only fair to conquer the Rif" (3).

The Spanish-Moroccan War (1859–60) – known in Spain under the somewhat pompous name of *Guerra de África* – gave a new direction to modern Spanish colonialism.[4] The declaration of war in the fall of 1859, the military campaign, and the victorious entrance of the expeditionary troops in Tétouan on 6 February 1860 not only awoke amongst many

Spaniards a dormant patriotic enthusiasm, but also originated a considerable number of poems, musical pieces, plays, articles, and books of all sorts.[5] While the country faced the disintegration of its squalid overseas empire, there emerged in Spain a modern colonialist mentality focused on the Maghreb. In 1876 the Real Sociedad Geográfica de Madrid was founded, followed by the Sociedad Española de Africanistas y Colonialistas in 1884, a learned society that would urge politicians and the government alike to carry out a more assertive politics of intervention in Morocco. These were not the only geographic learned societies interested in northern Africa: in 1877 the Asociación Española para la Exploración del África was created, in 1885 the Sociedad de Africanistas de Sevilla, and in 1886 the Centro hispano-mauritano de Ceuta.[6] Several phenomena helped shape an incipient, tottering, but altogether lasting *africanismo* (literally "Africanism") that would prove decisive in the formation and structure of Spanish fascism: the coeval publication of essays on Morocco, such as Manuel Pablo Castellanos's *Descripción histórica de Marruecos y breve reseña de sus dinastías, o apuntes para servir a la historia del Magreb* (1878), Manuel González Llana and Tirso Rodrigáñez's *El Imperio de Marruecos* (1879), and Julio Cervera Baviera's *Expedición geográfico-militar al interior y costas de Marruecos* (1885); the topographic studies and maps drawn by the Comisión del Estado Mayor del Ejército en Marruecos as of 1881; the pioneering development of Arabic Studies at the University of Madrid in 1843–68 vis-à-vis Spain's "civilizing mission" in Morocco; the Mudejar-style architecture of the Elizabethan period; and finally, the fin-de-siècle literary orientalism.

Spain's interventionism in Moroccan affairs increased exponentially after the country's loss of its last colonies in 1898, an event that led to a reappraisal of Spain's foreign policy. A feeling of strategic weakness in relation to France, the United Kingdom, and Germany, the profound, pervasive, and lasting resentment in the military for the humiliating defeats suffered in Cuba and the Philippines, certain tendencies of the so-called *pensamiento regeneracionista* (voiced, for instance, in Ángel Ganivet's *Idearium español* [1897]), as well as the avidity of some mining companies were factors that determined the course of Spanish ambitions in the Maghreb, which eventually led to the creation of the Spanish protectorate of Morocco, a nation that lost its sovereignty to France and Spain. Much smaller and much less profitable from an economic standpoint than the territory under French control, the Spanish protectorate of Morocco extended over 23,000 square kilometres that comprised the Rif, Jibala, Gomara, the area of the Loukkos River, and the plains of the Kert River. With Tétouan as the capital, at first Spain parcelled out the protectorate via three military commands (Ceuta, Melilla, Larache), but as of 1918 the protectorate would be divided into west and east sectors under the authority of the military commands of Ceuta and Melilla respectively (see figure 2.1).

In order to better understand the fascist writing and habitus forged in Morocco, we have to keep in mind that any protectorate presupposes a double process of de-territorialization and re-territorialization. The net of circuits linking places, the human fluxes, the trade relations, the regulation of property, and the local administration are de-territorialized; they are forced "to abandon" their usual modus operandi. At the same time, they are re-territorialized because the protecting state regulates the daily life of the local population, administers the territory, exploits local resources, controls the trade and the tax system, and arrogates for itself the right to interfere in the protected country's foreign policy, thereby re-codifying the grammar of a territory that has been annexed de facto by the protecting state. Held previously by a delicate balance between regions, each controlled by its respective Kabyles (Berber tribes), in 1912 the totality of the Moroccan territory was compartmentalized arbitrarily into two zones under foreign rule.

As in similar cases, the de-territorialization and re-territorialization of Morocco were achieved by what I denominate as a *technology of striation*, that is, a set of applied rationalities whose end resides in the organization of a smooth space according to principles and objectives stemming from the state, which here is the state of a foreign country (Spain). In Deleuze and Guattari's definition of the term, the *smooth space* characteristic of nomads lacks homogeneity; it is a heterogeneous field linked to rhizomatic multiplicities without a centre, conduits, or channels (371). One mission of the state is the striation of the space under its control (384). In the state there is a need to set up paths, establish well-defined directions, regulate traffic, measure in detail the movements of subjects and objects (386). The space striated and instituted by the state (474) produces order and a succession of forms (478). In the specific case of Morocco, whose rural population was made up of farmers and nomadic shepherds, the smooth space was a mixed space inhabited by nomadic and sedentary people articulated by a constellation of fluid rules lacking a common regulating principle. The colonial administration of Morocco was carried out by a technology of striation built upon a series of cultural, ideological, epistemological, and strategic assumptions. The duality of smooth space/striated space will help us to understand the forging of the fascist habitus through material (e.g., military action) and symbolic practices.

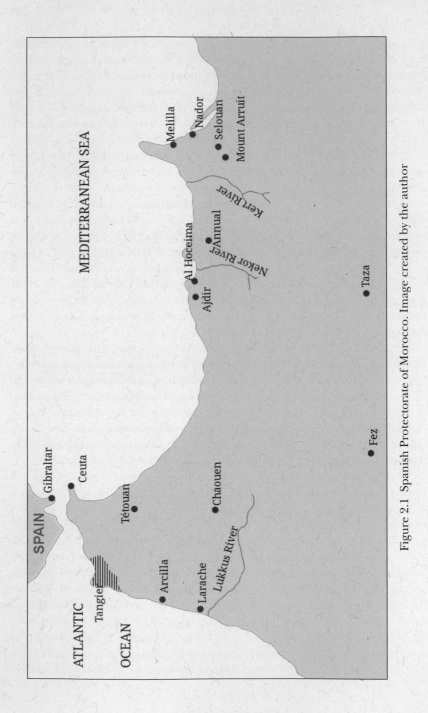

Figure 2.1 Spanish Protectorate of Morocco. Image created by the author

In the next sections, I will explore the interconnection between Spanish colonialism and fascism by analysing material spatial practices and spaces of representation. Four propositions underlie the analytic component of this chapter. According to the first, the earliest Spanish fascist works were written in the 1920s apropos of the Rif War (1921–7), with most of them being examples of war writing.[7] According to the second, which refers to the textuality of fascist literary works, the fascist dimension of a particular text lies not only at the semantic level, namely the political and social thinking expressed by the implied author; it also can be found in the discursive strategies that articulate such thinking. The emphasis on ideology by scholars of Spanish literary fascism and the epistemological difficulty that many experience in considering as "fascist" those cultural artefacts produced before the creation of fascist organizations, the emergence of a full-fledged fascist political ideology, and the circulation of the words *fascista* and *fascismo* in Spain have left out a corpus of works that in fact belong to fascism because of their rhetoric and language.[8] Few literary critics consider that fascism was a cultural phenomenon before it became a political force, as Sternhell has demonstrated in *The Birth of Fascist Ideology*, which deals with the creation of the conceptual framework of fascism in France and Italy between the turn of the century and the First World War. "The cultural revolt," argues Sternhell, "preceded the political" (3). The third proposition has to do with the relationship between linguistic expression and the non-linguistic world. As in the rest of the book, this chapter considers the act of writing not as a mere representation of a non-linguistic reality, but rather as an instance of what Stanley Cavell (153–91) terms *passionate utterance*, defined as a perlocutionary act produced to have consequential effects on the listener's or reader's feelings, thoughts, and actions. This model is particularly useful to the study of fascist literature, for "texts with moral designs upon their readers ask to be treated" as passionate utterances (Cavell 186). The absorption in the Peninsula of the Legion's mythology created by the vast literature devoted to this corps of the Spanish army, as well as the enlistment of young men in it, are two effects of the Africanist writing's perlocution. In both cases, actions were affected by speech. Together with this perlocution, fascist works in the 1920s carried a performative element: in their own way, they made fascism; thus their production of fascism was no less important than the one carried out by the colonial army. Such performativity cannot be understood as separated from the decisive significance of language in war. Wars begin and are maintained and remembered through a proliferation of language. The declaration of war, proclamations, speeches, hymns, songs, journal articles – to mention just a few – have to be considered as actively participating in the war effort. As Dawes says, "Wars are born and sustained in rivers of language about what it means to serve the cause, to kill the enemy, and to die with dignity; and they are reintegrated into a collective historical self-understanding through a ritualistic surplus of the language of commemoration" (15). Finally, the fourth proposition is the cement holding together the other three: in Morocco, during the 1920s, a fascist habitus was forged in relation to the conceptualization of Morocco as a heterotopia of Spain by a heterogeneous group of writers, intellectuals, politicians, and military personnel who defended an authoritarian concept of nation as a model for the political organization of Spain as well as a colonialist gaze and stance towards their own country.[9] This proposition takes into account a crucial factor in war and its language: space. The army creates space before, during, and after a war (e.g., in erecting walls and bastions, building fortresses, bunkers, and nuclear shelters, setting up defensive positions along the borders of a country, and creating military bases at home and abroad). Hence one could talk of the existence of a "military space."[10]

The fascist habitus emerged from the interstices of what I will call *dual space*, constituted, on the one hand, by Morocco's topography and its heterotopic function, and, on the other, by the re-territorialization of Morocco into a military geometry (e.g., the division of the Spanish protectorate of Morocco into two military commands, the construction of blockhouses, the erection of encampments, and the laying out of roads and supply lines between the front and rearguard positions).[11] Born in the dual space, Africanist war writing not only duplicated – through its discursive appropriation of Moroccan territory – the material spatial practices carried out by the army and the civilian administration of the protectorate. It certainly did so, but more decisively Africanist war writing brought to the Peninsula (making intelligible while at the same time modifying) the dual space, the actions that defined that space, and the fascist habitus. This double "translation" ultimately would take to the homeland an endo-colonial project that was initiated in the protectorate, a phenomenon that I will discuss at the end of this chapter.

Technologies of Tropological Striation

As is well known, any colonial power requires a "narrative," a constellation of texts whereby the colonizers institute and reaffirm their common identity, legitimate their right to exploit the colonized land, establish the net of regulations to subjugate the colonized people, and organize the administration of the territory.[12] Therefore one could argue that colonial centres deploy what I have elsewhere termed *technologies of tropological striation*, namely rhetorical and linguistic tools whose main function is the symbolic domination of a determinate territory.[13] My concept of *tropological striation* is predicated upon Paul Ricœur's *metaphoric enunciation*. Moving beyond the usual theoretical accounts of the metaphor, which typically take either the word or the sentence as their basic analytic unit, Ricœur suggests instead to focus on the discourse. He is less concerned with the form and meaning of the metaphor than with the "reference of the metaphoric enunciation as the capacity to 'rewrite' reality" (Ricœur 10). Based on a split referentiality and equipped with a realist intentionality, the metaphoric enunciation is a way to access the non-linguistic reality that exceeds the linguistic, rhetorical, and epistemological patterns underlying the mimetic representations of the world.

Like Ricœur's metaphoric enunciation, a tropological striation plays a valuable cognitive role by expressing the unknown or relatively unknown through its superposition of two levels of signification: the literal and the figurative. By so doing, it performs a conquest of sorts, a naturalization of the terra incognita that it produces/refers to. The cognition intrinsic to a tropological striation contains a performative force, for it produces the territory to which it refers. A technology of tropological striation forces a symbolic space upon a physical territory, in a performance analogous to the technology of striation carried out by colonial armies and administrations. Troops and tropes have interdependent objectives, and in fact they need each other: the former attempts to conquer a territory while the latter takes it over symbolically. The tropological striation presupposes a military control and allows for the cognition of a foreign territory. It must therefore be considered a discursive strategy of colonial conquest and domination. In the Spanish protectorate of Morocco, the fascist habitus would be the ultimate articulation of that complex technology of striation. In the 1930s the Catholic Church, anti-Republican political organizations, and some factions of the army would displace the point of application of the technologies of material and tropological striations from the protectorate to the Peninsula. A defining characteristic of the fascist attitude toward the nation, this displacement would be crucial in establishing the path that led to the civil war of 1936–9. Two works, both of them produced by writers who shortly thereafter would join FE-JONS, have been chosen to explore the links between the technologies of tropological striation and the fascist habitus: Tomás Borrás's novel *La pared de tela de araña* (1924) and Ernesto Giménez Caballero's memoirs on his military service in Morocco, *Notas marruecas de un soldado* (1923).

Tomás Borrás, a journalist, novelist, playwright, and poet of note who played an active role in FE-JONS in the 1930s and early 1940s, worked in Morocco between 1920 and 1921 as the war correspondent for *El Sol*.[14] His well-documented fascination with violence, cruelty, and abjection grew out of his experience as a war correspondent covering the Great War for the daily *La Tribuna* and especially out of his professional sojourn in Morocco. Written in 1920 but published four years later, *La pared de tela de araña* expresses in 1924 fundamental components of the author's fascism as displayed in his future political activism and literary practice, and it constitutes an instance of the connection between the incipient fascist habitus and the technology of tropological striation.[15]

La pared de tela de araña, narrated by a Spanish officer posted in the protectorate's west sector in 1920, is built upon a systematic technology of tropological striation, which mirrors the campaign undertaken in March 1919 by General Dámaso Berenguer to eliminate guerrilla resistance in the zone. The narrator striates space by providing it with meaning: the narrative voice imposes a symbolic order upon a land repeatedly portrayed as lacking a rational organization. As perceived by the implied author, Morocco is a smooth space. The narrator's trip from Tétouan to the front refracts the troops' movements as well as the conquest and occupation of Chaouen – in which the narrator participates – thereby carrying out a multiple striation of the territory. Significantly, *to striate* implies here "to populate" an empty, dead territory. At the level of the story, this is shown in the narrator's trip to join Berenguer's troops, which are ready to attack Chaouen. The territory that he crosses is silent, dry, with no vegetation or villages (107); it looks like a "lunar landscape. Coldness, harshness of lines, bitterness, sterility. An immobile silence. Not even one hut, not even one bird, not even a haven of sweetness" (108). In contrast to such lifeless landscape, the army camp looks like a city as a result of the military striation of the land. The Spanish army has imposed an urban structure onto a desolate territory.[16] In the narrator's words, "Each camp astonished me. A few thousand men had arrived. They halted there, and suddenly, an unexpected city emerged" (111–12). "There is an enterprise to undertake," writes the narrator, "and everyone works in the interstices of Nature in order to level it out. Lanes for the automobiles are being built; telephone lines are being hung; one is on the watch; one carries; one piles up in an orderly fashion" (113). To use a term of Deleuze and Guattari, the state's "war machine" has striated a smooth space. The army has appropriated that smooth space by imposing a new grammar based upon modern technology. To populate, observes the narrator, is "to make sounds, and all camps and trucks begin to acquire the pitch of civilization's noise. Most especially that energetic pounding of the automobiles' motors ... And the air itself ... with the enormous bumblebee of the airplanes' motors" (112, see also 129).[17]

Borrás's novel populates that very space with words.[18] On the level of discourse, the narrator provides both an ideological direction and a semantic hierarchy to a purportedly chaotic, irrational land. Aside from the plot, carefully organized in three interconnected parts (each devoted to one space: Tétouan, Chaouen, and the Jibala), there is a fundamental technology of tropological striation, consisting in the cognition of the customs, traditions, people, and territory of Morocco by the emplotment of the novel through three literary subgenres from the European cultural archive: the Orientalist romance, the novel of adventures, and the authoritarian fiction. Borrás employs the romance in the first part, in which the narrator tells an ill-fated love story between two Arab characters. In this part, the diversity of the Moroccan "other" is eliminated, thanks to the framing of the story within the conventions of the Orientalist romance: the Moroccans are reduced to the stereotypical, Orientalized image of the Moor created and developed in some European countries – Spain in particular.[19] By employing this major strategy of colonial discourse, Borrás dominates the colonial "other."[20] In the second part of the novel, the story is narrated according to the conventions of the adventure novel. While in the first the "other" is conquered by imposing the generic rules and rhetorical conventions of a specific literary subgenre, in the second the *friction* of war, to borrow Clausewitz's celebrated concept, is reined in by a particular point of view – that of the officer's – as well as by the subgenre that encapsulates it. Finally, the logic of the authoritarian fiction articulates the third and last part; through the authoritarian fiction, the implied author confronts Spanish colonialism against some tribes' recalcitrant resistance, obstinate in their desire to remain in a state of barbarism and ignorance.[21] Thus Borrás erases ideological nuances and subordinates the multiplicity of human relationships to a binomial structure constituted by representatives of the colonial power (i.e., the narrator and his fellow officers) and the colonized subjects (i.e., the Berbers from the Jebala region and the Arabs living in Tétouan, some of whom have accepted Spanish rule).

La pared de tela de araña eliminates the otherness of the "other" by assimilating Moroccan places into Spanish towns. This technology of tropological striation, otherwise common in colonial literature since Columbus's *Diaries* and the *Crónicas de Indias*, has here an additional function not always apparent in that tradition, for its purpose consists not only in the familiarization of the reader with unknown territories; it also carries a strong colonialist direction. This colonialist rhetorical device is based on the paradigmatic substitution of one place for another. The narrator repeatedly identifies Moroccan places with Spanish towns. Chaouen, for instance, is not a Moroccan town (132–47): "It is an Andalusian town and not a Moroccan town proper. It is an Andalusian town of the Arabized kind" (131). Further on, the narrator elaborates on his spatial substitution: Chaouen "is a Spanish town surrounded by a wall still not demolished by the city hall in whose main square, or square of the Constitution, there must be a gazebo for the garrison's band to play music every Thursday" (132). The citizens of Chaouen who welcome the Spanish troops are in fact, according to the narrator, the Moors expelled from Cordova. Whereas the outward appearance of Chaouen identifies this town as an Andalusian city, its streets and houses are identical to those in Toledo. Such is the impression the narrator has of the house where he lodges: "As soon as I shut the front door ... one can have no doubts whatsoever: this is indeed a house from Toledo" (147).[22] The paradigmatic substitution determines the meaning of the novel's syntagmatic relationships. By revealing the Spanishness of Moroccan towns, Borrás redirects the relationship of alterity between Morocco and Spain.[23] With this discursive strategy, Borrás lets the reader assume that the Spanish army is not conquering and occupying a foreign land. On the contrary: it is reconquering "Spanish" territory "occupied" by Moroccans.

For Borrás, as well as for other fascist intellectuals, Morocco constituted a heterotopia, an absolutely other place, which related to the rest of the places in the Peninsula in such a way that it questioned, represented, and reversed the totality of relationships designated or reflected in and by Morocco. The colonial space is, in *La pared de tela de araña* as well as in coetaneous and subsequent fascist texts, a constellation of other places that reproduces places located in the Peninsula, represents a set of relationships marked by a military conflict that reflects the social and political tensions in Spain in the 1920s, and sets up a "purifying" space from which Spain, a country deemed "decadent," could be regenerated.[24] Indeed, heterotopias have the capacity to be regenerative spaces, as David Harvey maintains in his incisive analysis of the concept. For Harvey, there are many spaces in which "'otherness,' alterity, and, hence, alternatives might be explored not as mere figments of the imagination but rather through contact with social processes that already exist. It is within these spaces that alternatives can take shape and from these spaces that a critique of existing norms and processes can be mounted most effectively. The history of such spaces ... shows us how and in what ways spatial forms might connect to radically different social processes and so disrupt the homogeneity to which society ... typically clings" (*Spaces* 184). Harvey, however, does not mention that these alternatives and disruptions of homogeneity also may be associated with authoritarian political projects whose goal paradoxically lies in the elimination of differences. And this is the case with Spanish Africanism, especially from the 1920s onwards. To some individuals, Morocco seemed to offer a possibility for change, and in fact ended up being literally so, for, as mentioned earlier, the civil war started in the protectorate on 17 July 1936. By hispanicizing Morocco, Tomás Borrás gave a new nuance to the otherwise *longue-durée* relation of alterity between Spain and Morocco.[25] The close connection between Moroccan territory and national identity in *La pared de tela de araña* on the one hand, and the emergence of a fascist habitus in the dual space on the other allow us to infer the heterotopic nature and function that Morocco held for some nationalists and fascists.

Years later, a whole generation of leading fascist theoreticians of empire and *africanistas* expanded Borrás's and other coeval intellectuals' position on Morocco. Thus in 1941 José María Cordero Torres categorically declared Morocco to be a divine gift to Spain: God has expressed his will "by establishing permanent bonds between the Iberian Peninsula and Barbary, specially on its western side ... the human crossovers have never been interrupted throughout the centuries" (*La misión* 63). In 1942, Rodolfo Gil Benumeya (pen name of Rodolfo Gil Torres) would condense that perception, so common in Spanish fascism, in a book whose peremptory, statement-like title speaks volumes: *Marruecos andaluz*. For Gil Benumeya, Andalusia and northern Morocco are one and the same land, for they share the same topography, the same flora, the same kind of people, the same history, but with one important qualification: despite the fact that Morocco "is the root of the leafy tree of the Spanish race, for the origin of life in the Peninsula lies in those Moroccans known as Iberians" (7), northern Morocco is an extension of Andalusia – and not the other way around – as eloquently shown in several of the maps inserted in the book, such as the one bearing the header "Dialecto árabe andaluz en Marruecos" (see figure 2.2).

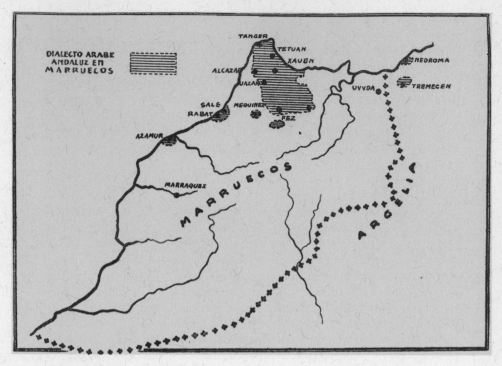

Figure 2.2 "Andalusian Arabic dialect in Morocco." From Rodolfo Gil
Benumeya, *Marruecos andaluz,*1942

To prove this view, he focuses on what he calls the "Andalusian Empire in Morocco," created and administered by the Umayyad dynasty.
Not only did the Umayyads represent the "Cordovan supremacy in Morocco" (94–8). In addition, "The Umayyads were also the ones to create a concept of unity, greatness, and freedom of Spain. A Peninsular
patriotism more complete than the Visigoths', based upon segregation
between races. The Ummayyadism defended the merge of all races …
in order to unify Spain. With only one type of Spaniard. That Spain is
based on Andalusia, and not on Castile, as present-day Spain. But Spain,
nonetheless" (97–8; see also 122). Hence the Umayyads anticipated the
fascist view of empire and of the nation. Further in the book, Gil Benumeya devotes an entire chapter to the "Andalusian colonies in Morocco"
(139–76), thereby elaborating a heterotopic reading of Morocco present
in Borrás's *La pared de tela de araña.*

A discursive strategy related to *La pared de tela de araña*'s technologies of tropological striation resides in the novel's symbolic violence.[26] An undisguised bellicose spirit underlies the book, as indicated by the explicit authorial support of the war and by the author's fascination with military violence and the Moroccans' death drive. The space striated by the Spanish military, for instance, is the point of departure for a combat mission described in terms very common in fascist literature. In chapter 2 of part 2, the narrator writes, "Everyone has taken his position. A united and disinterested will moves all those men to where they may die" (115). An admiring exclamation by the narrator apropos of the troops about to attack condenses the novel's bellicosity: "The spectacle would make a child happy" (124). The military discipline, the loss of the soldier's individuality, the common objective, the "altruism" of the "civilizing" mission, the colonial striation of space, and the violent imposition of an absolute model for human relationships are elements belonging to the fascist habitus. The army's violence and the narrator's bellicosity refract the Moroccans' violent behaviour, unleashed in war and acted out in the Dionysian-like carnival described in chapter 2 of the first part (11–18).[27] The scene, which anticipates Borrás's fascination with sheer, unrestrained violence, represents a carnival in Tétouan. The reader learns about men eating raw meat, devouring lambs, eating living poisonous snakes or straw with delight, swallowing balls made of mud and trash, and spitting foaming drool amidst a frenzied, fanatic mob (14–15). In this carnival of violence, the Moroccans "danced, groped each other lasciviously.... The square was like a great boiling lake" (18). As part of the axiology underpinning the novel, that carnival as well as other equally brutal scenes (e.g., third part, chapter 5) demonize the Moroccans. This colonialist discursive strategy is decisive, for it justifies Spain's right to conquer, its moral obligation to civilize. The Spaniards are in Morocco to civilize these barbarians. From that perspective, their colonialism is a beneficial undertaking.

As can be seen, the fascist habitus was forged in a heterotopic space and within a military geometry. Such habitus underpinned the view of Morocco as an "other space," an act that was performed simultaneously with the production of a neocolonial concept of Spain by some key Africanists. Borrás's novel is a literary map that, through the narrator's cartographic gaze, creates an imagined geography that tropologically produces and controls a sector of the protectorate. Novels like *La pared de tela de araña* have as their ultimate goal the symbolic appropriation of space; therefore, they refract the fascists' determination to take over, mould, and police the totality of spatial practices. At the same time, they intend to perform certain effects on their readers. As a space of representation, Borrás's novel cannot be dissociated from the colonial undertaking, part of which consists of the de-territorialization and re-territorialization of Spanish Morocco.

In the 1930s and 1940s some fascist writers – among them Borrás himself – would use technologies of tropological striation to write about Republican Spain and the Republicans. They adapted, for example, the negative image of the Moor to describe the Spanish working class and the Republicans in general. Giménez Caballero is a case in point. In *Genio de España*, he repeatedly establishes a synonymy between the Moors and the communists. In his view, communism in Spain "would mean a return of the Moors" (181, see especially 244–6). Establishing a striking connection between the proletariat and the colonized, Giménez Caballero views the communist leaders and Mahomet in the same place: in "Barbary," which is where all the *colonized* and *exploited* live (245–6). Several factors underpin this synonymy: both the Moors and the communists are "foreign" to Spanish culture, both represent the exploited people, both threaten to invade the country.[28] The Spanish Civil War, as is well known, meant for rebel intellectuals the "recuperation" of a territory "occupied" by the Republicans, who were perceived as "foreigners." The fascist literature written during the war, which was conducted by the rebels as if it were a colonial campaign,[29] applied to the Peninsula technologies of tropological striation already present in some works on Morocco written in the 1920s.

Spatial History and Tropological Striation

Embedded in a rich, albeit barely explored tradition of chronicles, diaries, and memoirs set in Morocco,[30] Ernesto Giménez Caballero's *Notas marruecas de un soldado* (1923) belongs to the group of articles, essays, and novels produced in response to the so-called Disaster of Annual (21 July–9 August 1921) and its profound reverberations in Spain's political arena.[31] This book, based on the author's military service in the protectorate (summer 1921 to fall 1922) and extremely well-received at the time by critics and readers alike, brought Giménez Caballero face-to-face with the army. Zealously protecting its good standing, the army did not welcome the young writer's sharp critique of the military forces posted in the protectorate – so much so that a military court sentenced Giménez Caballero to eighteen years in prison, commuted by General Primo de

Rivera shortly after his coup d'état in September 1923. *Notas marruecas de un soldado* applies a technology of tropological striation to the Moroccan territory oriented by a colonial stance, tinted, as the closure of the book unveils, by a fascist habitus. For all Giménez Caballero's critical comments on the colonial army, one can find a strong militaristic discourse underlying this *opera prima*.[32]

While the events of the author's military service are laid out in chronological order, *Notas marruecas de un soldado* breaks up the story's linearity once and again. Giménez Caballero does not even bother to date the narrated episodes. In this mixture of diary – the book was originally written during the author's military service – and memoir, actions and things seem to float in atemporality. In his very first book, Giménez Caballero opts for a literary strategy that would be used prominently in his subsequent essays and literary works: the practice of spatial history. As happens in *Carteles*, *Genio de España*, and *Arte y Estado*, in *Notas marruecas de un soldado* the spatialization of time is a way of writing history, a technique that attempts, in a seeming paradox, to demonstrate Morocco's purported lack of historical past. The structure of the book mirrors the author's spatial history. Giménez Caballero groups his "notes" – in most cases vignettes describing local customs and places – into six parts, each titled after a place: "Notas de un campamento," "Notas de hospital," "Un viaje en el *Giralda*," "Notas de Tetuán," "La judería," and "Notas de otros lugares." But these are not the only places described in *Notas marruecas de un soldado*. There are depictions of a camp's mess hall (21–6), a hospital (39–40), the Martin River (61), the Rif's coast (66), Melilla's old quarter (70–2), Mount Gurugú (73–4), Nador (75–7), Málaga (81–3), Tétouan's streets, neighbourhoods, buildings, domestic interiors, and Jewish quarter (89–91, 96–7, 103–4, 112, 117–20, 125–7, 129–45), Ceuta (149–58), Chaouen (159–66), Tangier (166–75), and Gibraltar (177–82).

Oddly enough in a soldier's memoir, action is practically nonexistent; there are no war scenes, and rather than the soldier's notes they resemble observations of a tourist travelling in a country at war without realizing it. By contrast, Giménez Caballero favours the picturesque, a kind of evocation described thus: "Pleasant and surprising to the eyes, 'picturesque' is what one would like to save from time and space.... Nowadays it would be more fitting to say 'Kodak-like' or worthy of being photographed. Those landscapes or scenes that in a moment during our journey pass by quick and beautiful can be saved thanks to the magical palette of a snapshot. Here in Africa, with the arrival of recruits, there is a squander of Kodak" (96).

It could be said that the overwhelming predominance of the "descriptive" over the "narrative" deliberately hides the social contradictions and complexities that unquestionably underlie the relationships between the people and places portrayed in the book. In accordance with his colonialist-oriented spatial history, Giménez Caballero deploys in his descriptions a technology of tropological striation consisting in gazing upon and describing a place from above. His avowed preference for going to such places ("from them ... one understands the fundamental character of the town on view" [89]) to better contemplate an area is far from accidental. To a certain extent, his descriptions of Tétouan from the city's citadel (89–91) and of Ceuta from Mount Hacho (152–3) may be considered as meta-literary, for they point out the *intentio textis*: the symbolic colonial domination of Morocco by means of a cartographic gaze.

Needless to say, applying a cartographic gaze from an elevated place was not a new device in 1923. Two of the most basic techniques of nineteenth-century realism consist of the description of the social in all its complexities and the unification of the multiple into one single tale. Frollo's contemplation of Paris from one of Notre Dame's towers in Victor Hugo's *Notre Dame de Paris* (1831) and Fermín de Pas's analogous glancing over Vetusta from one of the towers of the town's cathedral in Leopoldo Alas's *La Regenta* (1884) thematize those two pillars of classic realism. The difference between the technique as it was used in nineteenth-century realism and in *Notas marruecas de un soldado* resides in the fact that Giménez Caballero's cartographic gaze from an elevated point is at the service of a colonial enterprise and a nascent fascist habitus. In other words, "seeing from above" belongs here to the modern colonialism's repertoire of technologies of domination. As Bhabha has pointed out, "In order to conceive of the colonial subject as the effect of power that is productive ... one has to see the *surveillance* of colonial power as functioning in relation to the regime of the *scopic drive* ... the drive that represents the pleasure in 'seeing'" (*Location* 76).

Notwithstanding the lack of war stories in *Notas marruecas de un soldado*, war pervades the book's discourse. Moreover, a militaristic attitude underpins the book. In "Diana" (13–14), the author reveals his aesthetic sensitivity and enthusiasm for the reveille, "admirable and beautiful" in its warrior-like essence, clear, lively, triumphal (13–14). In a way, the narrator's ecstatic, almost poetic rendering of the sounding of the morning bugle could serve as *Notas marruecas de un soldado*'s own reveille: after two introductory vignettes, "Diana" is the first one devoted specifically to the author's stay in Morocco, and it is also the first instance of *Notas marrue-*

cas de un soldado's militaristic and bellicose stand. Giménez Caballero is here awakened both as a soldier (level of the story) and as a writer (level of the discourse).[33] Not unlike Ernst Jünger, who thought of "combat" as an "inner experience,"[34] Giménez Caballero's view of war is nothing short of a "mystical thing that stirs up the essence of humans" (21). His remembrance of a trip by van carrying him and other comrades-in-arms leads him to exalt army life: "There are chaps who do not want or do not know how to take some enjoyments, rather simple, of military life. Not everything consists of humiliations and suffering" (61); to travel sitting on a truck's roof rack "with the prospects of a picturesque trip, in which one will have to do small jobs, cross a piece of the Mediterranean and examine closely the high little world of the military [*sic*], are things that ... cheerfully lighten up my spirits" (61).[35] In the military hospital, he had "a very good time" with several legionnaires (48). A cliché in many narratives on the Legion, each legionnaire carries within himself "a more or less complicated novel ... Having lived all their lives in a haphazard fashion ... to end working out their butts off in the Rif ... makes up a whole program that prompts to take those men seriously" (48).

Giménez Caballero's militarism, evinced in these and other passages, intertwines with a no less evident colonialist stance and the use of technologies of tropological striation. One of the most striking links between these three elements is the author's emphasis on an almost obsessive passion for photography amidst the soldiers. Giménez Caballero seems to be perfectly aware of the function of representation in the war effort and the colonial enterprise.[36] In Morocco, officers and privates take many pictures (96). Thus the military shoot bullets *as well as* pictures. In the context of an ongoing war, shooting with a Kodak or with a Mauser are two acts working in tandem: the former symbolically "kills" places, objects, and/or people by freezing them into a two-dimensional image, whereas the latter physically kills or harms people. This complementarity of the Kodak and the Mauser is a well-known one, particularly by military commanders, always wary about filtering information on the campaign to the civilians. Moreover, the snapshot constitutes an effective teaching mechanism.Overlapping militarism, colonialism, and symbolic domination, Giménez Caballero points out that as soon as the campaign is over, "the fatherland will know for the first time about the geography of its Moroccan zone" (96). Interestingly, he has chosen for his *Notas marruecas de un soldado* a descriptive modality akin to the snapshot: the vignette. *Notas marruecas de un soldado*'s vignettes – literary snapshots of sorts – discursively refract the military's shots of pictures and bullets. For this reason, we could conclude that in Giménez Caballero's *opera prima* the vignette is a fundamentally violent technology of tropological striation. The alternation of vignettes of motifs and places related to the army with orientalist vignettes written on local traditions and places underscores the otherwise obvious impossibility of separating a colonial project from military action and domination. The former is not feasible without the latter, which is routinely justified as an indispensable if regrettable tool for "civilizing" a local population that resists assimilating – something that could only be beneficial to their country.

Giménez Caballero's technology of tropological striation is most evident in vignettes like "Cogiendo higos" (16–17), in which the narrator establishes a metaphoric connection between the fig tree – the Semitic tree par excellence, according to the author – and the "genius of Morocco."[37] To describe its fruits amounts to describing and thereby knowing the genius of the country: "On the outside a sober covering of folds, a little wretched and mysterious. But in the inside syrup and fire. Smiles, salaams, genuflections, arch-polite formulae. Sugariness, sickly sweetness. And deep down a flavor and an ardent, passionate, turbulent outcome" (17). The genius of Morocco "unveiled" by the metaphoric reading of the fig tree reveals the ambivalence at the core of any stereotype of the colonized "other" which always vacillates "between what is … already known and something that must be anxiously repeated" (Bhabha, *Location* 66). One vignette, "Kif y cigarrillos" (18–20), underscores the force of that ambivalence by juxtaposing this stereotype of the "Moor" with an equally stereotypical image of the colonizer through metaphoric enunciation: the comparison of the kef with the cigarette differentiates the Moor from the Westerner.[38] In this vignette, kef and tobacco function as metaphors of two habitus. Sitting on the beach near a group of Moroccans, Giménez Caballero counteracted the "strange and unpleasant [smell] of the kef" enveloping him by lighting up a "nice English honey-smelling cigarette" (18). A duel between "both scents and both lights" (18) ensued. For Giménez Caballero, the kef is "instantaneous and out of proportion" (19), the "oasis where the Oriental man unloads the weight and gravity of his life, waiting for nothing else … it belongs to those men from a world closed up in a dogma" (19). By contrast, the cigarette's smoke represents lyricism" (18) and is a "philosophical quid consumed with critical eagerness" that fosters human effort (19). While the kef's scent "brings to mind the scorched lands, with prickly pears, with measly rivers, with reptiles, with immense skies and an infinite desolation," as well as "the attic of the Moorish villages, dark and repulsive" (19), the tobacco smoke evokes "the electric lights of a parlor ... rainy days, the wide armchair next to the fireplace ... the crowd in a boulevard full of radiant shop windows ... The music-hall and its shining bars" (19–20). At the close of the vignette, the narrator culminates his stereotyping of the Moors by reifying them: the Moroccans have now put away their pipes, yet they "stay on, immobile, like things, before the incessant murmur of the sea" (20). Indeed, such statuary, hieratic pose forms a leitmotif (see 63, 91, 96–7, 114–15) that highlights the Moroccans' supposed cultural backwardness and their recalcitrant resistance to any modification of their lifestyle. As in *La pared de tela de araña*, the Moroccans' immobilism and savagery serve to justify Spain's civilizing mission in the protectorate. Apropos of the dance of the Hamachas, Giménez Caballero states that "it resembled a nightmare. One felt a violent wish to intervene, to finish it, to complain ... Why should one respect them? Let the French respect them" (106–7).

The metaphoric enunciation, the reification of the Moroccans, and the spatialization of time are three pervasive tools of the tropological striation carried out in *Notas marruecas de un soldado*. Connecting the material and the tropological, Giménez Caballero on more than one occasion refers to the military, administrative, and economic striation of the protectorate. "Travesía a Melilla" (64–7) is a case in point. Spain's task in Morocco, according to Giménez Caballero, is not an easy one, particularly in areas like the rugged Rif, with "its coasts ... with no vegetation, unpleasant, with no natural bays" (66). But despite the problems caused by the local topography, there have been cases of successful striation, enthusiastically reported about by Giménez Caballero, who considers the material striation of space as an activity intrinsic to any colonial endeavour. A town near the Martín River is accordingly portrayed as an exemplary case of successful colonization through the striation of physical space: "I think it is the best model, if not the only one, of a modern colony [in the Spanish protectorate] ... White houses, clean, well built, of indigenous style, with terrace roofs ... Straight streets, perfectly drawn. Bars where soldiers drink and play. The church, very small.... The school ... whitewashed and elegant ... The whistle of a steam engine.... Every now and then, from some house, comes out an Andalusian chant. And some pretty brunette, with a geranium in her hair" (63). Similarly, the archaeological excavation in Tamuda is "one of the triumphs of our protectorate ... Not everything is a work of destruction in our Moroccan zone. Tamuda proves that we are also capable of other kinds of work – brickwork" (108). Unfortunately, thinks the author, the colonial enterprise has lacked continuity. In "Noche de luna" (27–8), Giménez Caballero censures the incompetence of the colonial army and administration of the protectorate, and contrasts the administrators' slackness in the implementation of colonial policy with what should have been done. Again, the writer's words reflect the close link between colonization and striation: "I think very frequently about what ... more than a thousand men, subject to a severe discipline such as the military one, could do here. By the river, on a meadow, near the sea. With the clay soil, we could almost have a small village completely built ... An aqueduct to solve the water problem ... We could have cultivated this fertile meadow. Channelled the river in certain profitable places. The Moors would look at us with absorbed attention, they would see the superior man that builds, that transforms. Sadly, we do nothing worthwhile" (28). Giménez Caballero presents the actual or potential progress of Spain's colonial enterprise in the protectorate through description of striated physical space.[39] Likewise, his criticisms of the colonial army and administration of the protectorate are conveyed by a harsh appraisal of their material spatial practices. Thus his description (68–9) of the ruinous state of the theatre of Alcántara – the residence of the high commissioner – represents an indirect albeit clear way to denounce the deficiencies of the protectorate's administration. A similar conclusion could be drawn from Giménez Caballero's depiction of the army's bureau that holds General Picasso's files on the debacle of Annual, "forgotten" on a shelf "to the mercy of any gust of wind": "What negligence for a thing as serious as a set of responsibilities [referring to the officers' and high command's incompetent performance during the rout]! But in the end everything has to be like this. Should there have been no negligence, Annual's defences would have withstood [the attack]" (112).

Giménez Caballero's colonialist and militaristic stand, as well as his employment of technologies of tropological striation, are functions of a fascist habitus brought to the surface in the closing section of the book, "Nota final en Madrid" (183–7), where the author underscores the illocutionary force and intended perlocutionary effect of *Notas marruecas de un soldado*.[40] His intention in writing the book, avows Giménez Caballero, consists of "bearing witness that among the generations of Spanish youth who have been there [Morocco], there is someone speaking up," of inquiring about what has been and must be done (185), "of contributing to clearing the national public opinion on Morocco based on our stories and judgments" (186), and of "intervene[ing] in the determination of guilt" in the debacle of Annual (186). *Notas marruecas de un soldado* vindicates Spain's colonizing mission not only because of the alleged welfare it will bring to the Moroccans, but also as a way to overcome the political divisions and regional tensions in Spain that, should they persist, will likely end in a civil war. This call for the unity of all Spaniards uttered in 1923 by a man who just a few years later would become a prominent member of FE-JONS, as well as its wording, has an undeniable fascist flavour: "Let us unite in *fasces*! [Let us unite] in something, Basque, Catalan, Galician, Asturians, Andalusians … Castilians, *all those who like us have … lived up to the name of 'Spaniards' and have … looked at each other as brothers.* If we abandon ourselves to the fate losing all hope of a *new shared and national enterprise, falling back on the particularisms of our regions,* it is possible, certain, that that misfortune will put us tomorrow face-to-face, looking at each other with hostility." (187).

The last part of the book is crucial because it puts on display both the ideology and the habitus underpinning *Notas marruecas de un soldado*'s militarism, colonialism, and symbolic appropriation of space. If it has been said that *À la Recherche du temps perdu*'s raison d'être and real beginning lie at the end of the seventh and last volume of the novel, we could equally argue that *Notas marruecas de un soldado*'s ending is both its foundation and its beginning. Hence the book's efficient cause is a nascent fascist habitus, while its militarism, colonialism, and tropological striation work as functions of that habitus shaped in the protectorate by many agents and forces, most particularly by the military.

The Legion: A Pedagogy of the Habitus

Spain's erratic, inconsistent, and unimpressive administration of the protectorate, along with the deadly, poorly managed, and very unpopular war in Morocco, catalyzed four interlocked processes: the end of the Restoration's formal democracy (1875–23) as a result of General Miguel Primo de Rivera's coup d'état in September 1923; the ensuing eight-year dictatorship (1923–31), considered by Ben-Ami as the forerunner of the fascist regimes established in the Balkans years later;[41] the professionalization of the colonial army and the brutalization of the Rif War; and finally, the forging of a fascist habitus in the dual space of which I spoke earlier. In each of them, the armed forces played a crucial role. The armed forces, understood here as a *field,* namely as a space of forces and determinations made up by a closely woven net of tensions and contradictions wherein its agents position themselves, propelled by their own dispositions and predispositions (Bourdieu, "Habitus" 47),[42] were at the time composed of several castes and factions.

Two basic antagonisms dominated the field. First, within the colonial army there was tension between a "progressive" faction (respectful towards the autochthonous population, in favour of a pacific penetration in Moroccan society by subordinating military action to political dialogue and peaceful agreements with the Kabyles) and the Africanists (strongly favourable to the military expansion into and domination over the entire protectorate, imbued by an authoritarian nationalism, racism, a mystique of force, an intolerance for civilian society, and an elitist concept of the army, regarded as the sole bearer of Spain's essence). Second, there was the antagonism between the so-called *junteros* (members of the Juntas Informativas de Defensa, whose two main objectives lay in eliminating the salary inequalities between the military posted in the protectorate and those who had remained in the Peninsula, and in the creation of a promotion system based on seniority in place of a mention in dispatches) and the two factions of the colonial army (opposed or reluctant to accept the two proposals put forth by the *junteros*).[43] The problematic relationships within the military field on the one hand, and the tensions between the military field, the social field, and the field of power on the other were conditions of possibility for the emergence of a fascist habitus within the colonial army.[44]

The campaign undertaken after the Disaster of the Barranco del Lobo (27 July 1909) provided a new colonial identity for the veterans of previous conflicts (particularly the Spanish-American War) as well as for the junior officers (Balfour 65). Among other determinants, the territory in which the campaign was fought greatly contributed to the emergence of a new habitus in the colonial army. According to Balfour (65), the Rif's rugged landscape, the harsh conditions of the campaign, and the bloody battles created among the officers a feeling of not belonging to the culture characteristic of garrison life, dominated by routine and bureaucracy; on the contrary, their culture was defined by their elitism, their scorn for the softness of civilian life, and their growing disdain of a government led by civilians. This incipient new identity grew slowly but steadily, reaching maturity after the Disaster of Annual. Resenting the otherwise well-grounded condemnation of the defective strategy and incompetent tactics that led to the debacle of Annual, high-ranking Africanist officers felt misunderstood and unfairly treated by the press, the political caste, the population at large, and those who questioned the army's performance and presence in Morocco. Their feeling of alienation translated into an increasing antagonism toward democracy, enhanced their view of Spain as a decadent country, and reinforced the belief, so characteristic of the Spanish army since the nineteenth century, of being the institution that incarnates the so-called *esencias patrias*.

The colonial army was formed mostly by poorly trained, insufficiently equipped, and little-motivated conscripts. With the aim to fight the enemy more efficiently and decisively, in January 1920 the Spanish government created (on the basis of a project drafted by Lieutenant Colonel José Millán Astray) a professional Infantry unit made up entirely by Spanish and foreign volunteers: the Tercio de Extranjeros, later to be known as La Legión.[45] The Legion, whose basic function consisted in fighting as the foremost unit of the army and carrying out the most dangerous and difficult missions, altered positions within the military field, contributed to the brutalization of the war, and shaped and put into practice a habitus that can be perfectly characterized as fascist (e.g., cult of death and the fallen; exaltation of the hero; war as an activity that regenerates the individual and the nation; ritualism; vitalism; absolute hegemony of the values and the behaviour commonly associated with the male principle of domination; rhetoric of glorious violence and death in combat; anti-intellectualism and anti-subjectivism; unquestioning discipline and spirit of sacrifice; the view of the warrior as the highest mode of being).[46]

While the Legion's history, organization, function, deeds, daily life, and weaponry have been examined already by scholars, the literary artefacts produced about the Legion have merited barely any attention.[47] This fact, though consistent with the lack of scholarship on the literature devoted to or produced apropos of Morocco and the Rif War, is all the more striking if we consider the function and perlocution operated by the corpus of literature on the Legion. Indeed, the image that Spaniards had of the Legion in the 1920s and 1930s was mediated by a rich literary, journalistic, and even cinematic production.[48] Some works portrayed the Legion in negative terms (e.g., Fermín Galán's 1931 *La barbarie organizada*), but those written in praise of its values and deeds would create a romanticized image of the legionnaire,[49] as well as play a significant role in forging and spreading a habitus born and put into practice in Morocco. Novels such as Julián Fernández Piñero's (pseud. "Juan Ferragut") *Memorias de un legionario* (1921–2), Carlos Micó España's *El camillero de la Legión* (1922), Luys Santa Marina's masterful *Tras el águila del César: Elegía del Tercio, 1921–1922* (1924), José María Carretero's (pseud. "El Caballero Audaz") *El héroe de la Legión* (circa 1930), José Asenjo Alonso's *¡¡¡Los que fuimos al Tercio!!!* (1932), or Juan B. Ros Andreu's *La conquista de Alhucemas o en el Tercio está el amor* (1932); memoirs and war diaries like Carlos Micó España's *Los Caballeros de la Legión (El libro del Tercio de Extranjeros)*

(1922) and Francisco Franco's *Marruecos: Diario de una Bandera* (1922); or books describing the characteristics and narrating the history of the unit such as José Millán Astray's *La Legión* (1923) constructed all together, alongside the Legion's deeds and rituals, a fascist habitus related to a totalitarian nationalism and a virulent patriotism. Of all of them Millán Astray's and Franco's just-mentioned books stand out, not only on account of their intrinsic qualities, but also because both authors were the most prominent figures of the Legion. To these works we must turn our attention in order to better understand the forging of the fascist habitus by the colonial army.

Millán Astray's *La Legión* brings out the formation, conditioning elements, liminal phase, and structure of the Legion's fascist habitus.[50] Millán Astray includes most of the important aspects of the habitus: its historical, sociological, and human determinants, its forging through physical and symbolic action, its acquisition, and its actualization. *La Legión*'s opening provides general information about the origins of the Legion (1–9), in order to then turn directly to establishing the conditioning elements of the legionnaire's habitus, with special emphasis on the constituents derived from the biography as well as from the psychological and moral makeup of the volunteers. Millán Astray characterizes the legionnaires as lifelong fighters, adventurers, desperados hoping for the best who enlist "because of the human complexity": "Because of the passions ... the vices, the social alienation, the thirst for glory, the zest for life or the desire to die, the past search for means to sustain themselves, finding nothingness ... desperation, hunger. Love! Also love. Let them be left with that romantic consolation!... And afterward, the prosaic: food, salary, a home.... Far away from Justice, so hard in its ways, and, finally, those major factors – money and alcohol" (11–12).

Despite the variety of types ("from the mystic to the wicked"), the future legionnaires share an "eagerness to fight, aggressiveness, uneasiness, horror of quiet" (106); danger appeals to them, "suffering emboldens them," "fighting is their happiness" (106).[51] In the Legion, no documentation or even their real names are required from those cast-out violent men enveloped by a romantic aura (11–12). In this sense, the legionnaires lack history: since their enrolment in the Legion, only the present exists for them. The untold – and to a degree unmentionable – past makes the legionnaire a being without origin, a newborn individual whose only fate is war. As if to stress this point, the next section of *La Legión*, dedicated to the military instruction received by the volunteers, bears the title "Riffien: La cuna de la Legión" (19–20). Indeed, at a denotative level the title refers to the Legion's base camp at Dar Riffien, located not far from Ceuta. But in addition, it connotes the first place of all humans: the cradle. To that very notion Francisco Franco had referred a year earlier in a passage of his war diary devoted to the trip from Algeciras to Ceuta by the first group of volunteers. "In the boat," evokes Franco, "jokes and entertainment begin, the men gather in a ring ... soon Spaniards and foreigners jump and laugh, their previous lives forgotten. It seems that they return to being children ... These are the future legionnaires" (*Diario* 39).

From this standpoint, the training camp is a "liminal" space, that is, the locus of what Arnold van Gennep has termed as the *liminal phase* of a rite of passage. All rites of passage, according to van Gennep, follow a three-phase process: separation, margin or *limen*, and aggregation.[52] While the volunteers aboard the ship taking them from Algeciras to Ceuta are in the phase of separation – detachment from the earlier position within the social – as soon as they cross the camp's "threshold" they enter into the liminal phase proper. There, they become neophytes who possess nothing; they are liminal *personae*, entities "necessarily ambiguous since this condition and these persons elude or slip through the network of classifications that normally locate states and positions in cultural space" (Turner 95). In the liminal phase, the ritual subject has been stripped of his identity without yet having acquired a new one. In the camp at Dar Riffien, the future legionnaire receives much more than conventional military instruction; his training is above all psychological and moral, as pointed out by Millán Astray in "La instrucción moral" (23–9). In that section, the author reproduces the legionnaire's creed, penned by Millán Astray himself "in a moment of exaltation of enthusiasm and faith [*sic*]" without "the slightest literary embellishment" (23–4). A fundamental element of the legionnaire's liminality consists in his full internalization of the way of being and acting prescribed in the creed. The liminal dimension of Riffien and the sui-generis application of the structure birth/birthplace/education reveal a seminal moment in the acquisition of the habitus. The volunteer's social marginality and predisposition towards violence are determinants of a being who, once in the Legion's cradle or liminal place, will internalize a new habitus through military training, drill, and ideological indoctrination.[53]

The literature devoted to the Legion highlights this liminal process. A "school of stoics" (Asenjo Alonso 73–4), the Legion brings an end to the disoriented lives of the volunteers by channelling their predispositions into military discipline and ideological indoctrination at the base camp of Dar Riffien. Several novels and short stories narrate in detail this ritual process (e.g., Asenjo Alonso 68–85; Ros Andreu 23–32; from a critical standpoint, Galán 37–44). In the words of Micó España, the volunteers "arrived … a little disconcerted and grumbling about Spain, until there was someone who told them what camaraderie, duty, glory and the Fatherland are" (*Los Caballeros* 251). If the drills for shooting practice and the use of the bayonet mean the reorientation of the volunteers' aggressive impulses, the creed and the constant boisterous recitations record in their minds a mentality and a style of life. Both forms of instruction lead to the internalization of the fascist habitus, maintained to the letter by the threat of exceedingly severe punishments. A radical break with the past, the Legion collects the "dregs of society," educates them, and returns them "purified by the melting pot of discipline and love for the country" (64). "By the magical force of an ideal," writes Micó España, "one can channel a defect, a bad condition, or a terrible instinct and turn it in a useful force and a good quality; it is the transfiguration of the feelings that engenders moral values" (40–1).

Several scholars have already explored the Legion's creed distributed to all volunteers, a crucial text in the configuration of the legionnaire's fascist habitus.[54] Here I call attention only to the elements belonging to the fascist habitus that are present in it: the exaltation of violence, the legionnaire's spirit of sacrifice and obedience, brutality as a norm of conduct, the cult of death, irrationalism, the dissolution of personal identity for the sake of the community, and, lastly, the use of a vehement and aggressive language.

The words preceding the reproduction of the creed in *La Legión* (23–8) are most revealing: "The Legion," writes Millán Astray, "is also religion, and [the creed] comprehends its prayers, the prayers of valour, companionship, friendship, unity and assistance, marching, suffering, enduring fatigue, camaraderie under fire, and the cardinal virtues: Discipline, Combat, Death, and Love for the Flag" (23–4). The creed, which consists of twelve rules or "spirits," is saturated with violence. The "spirit of the legionnaire" – his essential trait – "*is unique and without equal* [*sic*], *it is of blind and ferocious aggressiveness, of looking always to shorten the distance to the enemy and arrive at the bayonet*" (23). After this primordial spirit, the Legion's creed follows an order in crescendo. The next three spirits to be interiorized by the legionnaires are the spirits of camaraderie, friendship, and then unity and mutual assistance. Thus the legionnaire is shown to belong to a compact group of comrades-in-arms supportive in solidarity who will never leave a man behind. Setting these spirits at the beginning of the creed is rhetorically necessary in order to make the following ones more palatable: the "spirit of marching" (*"Never will a legionnaire say that he is tired until he collapses, he will be the fastest Body"* [25]), the "spirit of suffering and hardship" (*"He will never complain of fatigue, nor of pain, nor from hunger, nor from thirst, nor from lack of sleep; he will do all jobs: he will dig, drag cannons, carts, he will be assigned to whatever is necessary, convoys; he will do whatever is ordered of him"* [25]), and the "spirit to come to fire" (*"The Legion, from the man alone to the entire Legion, will always come to wherever fire is heard, day, night, always, always, even if there is no order to do so"* [25]). The "spirit of discipline" ("He will complete his duty, he will obey until death" [25]) comes next as the culmination of that series of spirits. Naturally, this spirit is consubstantial to every army, though most particularly to units that, like the Legion, impose extremely harsh combat conditions on the troops. Further, in a chapter titled "La disciplina y la obediencia" (33–4), Millán Astray claims that discipline "is the fatherland's health, it is synonymous with the army and with the troops, it is the foundation of the military edifice; sustained by it, dependent on it, it is, simply, *everything*" (33), thereby proposing a militarization of the social – a characteristic component, let us add, of fascist thought. Discipline demands obedience to authority. This alienation of the self for the sake of dutiful obedience – extended to a determined concept of nation – brings with it purification (34). Two spirits clearly related to the fascist habitus close the Legion's creed: the will to fight ("spirit of combat") and the cult of death ("spirit of death").[55] The former is addressed to the Legion, whereas the latter refers not to the legionnaires but rather to death itself (*"To die in combat is the greatest honor. No one dies more than once. Death comes without pain and to die is not as horrible as it seems. The most horrible thing is to live as a coward"* [26]).

The creed thus begins by synthesizing essential traits of the legionnaire and ends by summarizing the essence of death. By means of its *dispositio*, the creed therefore associates the essence of the legionnaire with death. The legionnaire, a subject without past or name, reborn in a liminal space that makes out of brutality a modus vivendi, finds his precarious and paradoxical ontological structure in limitless violence, in the dissolution of his own self, in placing himself in the ever-present possibility of dying. Such a being – who from a Heideggerian standpoint might be considered as a Dasein at its most essential, for the legionnaire has fully assumed his being-to-death – this "betrothed of death" (*novio de la muerte*) whose battle call, "Long live the death!" condenses his existence, floats in a medium underpinned by an erotics and aesthetics of death.

Death, in Millán Astray's view, is something beautiful, something to be cherished. "Let us talk about death to the soldiers," writes the founder of the Legion, "let us remove the horror from their minds. Be death not the fearful Fury, enshrouded and sinister, that frightens them with her scythe. Let us show her to be young and beautiful, kissing the hero's forehead and throwing flowers about him. So that it might be for the soldier the guardian angel carrying him to heaven" (26).

In the section "El holocausto" (109–11), Millán Astray embellishes the legionnaire's death and burial: "The Legion has a special rite of burial for its children. No one may touch their bodies apart from their fellow legionnaires. Only they can proceed with them, after having covered them with flowers and branches, wrapped in the flag of Spain. They lower them to the grave, and following a brief and pious prayer, let out with true fervour their lively 'Long live Spain! Long live the king! Long live the Legion!' so as to say farewell forever. Soon thereafter, fanatically, with alacrity, they throw holy earth, crowned with stones that each one brings, raising quickly a simple tumult that instantly becomes a verdant garden covered in crowns and branches" (111).[56] After the reproduction of the creed, the author refers to the flag of the Legion (26), the bravery of the legionnaires (27), and the tripartite "Long live!" of the legionnaires (to Spain, the king, and the Legion), all of them, explains Millán Astray, "cries of combat and death" (28).[57]

It is important to remark that the fascist constituents of the Legion's habitus are expressed in a text whose rhetoric and language strongly evoke in the reader the manifestos of the artistic and literary avantgardes. Its preamble ("And we dictate"), the anaphoric style (each trait of the Legion or demand of the legionnaire is preceded by the phrase "The spirit of"), the programmatic tone and aggressive language, irrationalism, anti-subjectivism, exaltation of war, and parody (to a certain extent the creed is a parodic inversion of the Christian creed and catechism, since what it preaches is not *caritas*, but rather the homicidal violence against one's fellow man) are each a characteristic component of the avant-garde manifestos, which in turn relate to the cultural and political currents at the time in which "the military values and virtues had enormous importance" (Togores 165). Without dismissing in any way its relation to the Bushido,[58] the Legion's creed can indeed be read as an avant-garde manifesto of sorts addressed not to artists, writers, or people interested in literature and the arts, but rather to the members of an elite military unit created to fight in vanguard positions.[59] Millán Astray carries Italian Futurism's call to violence to its ultimate consequences.

It must be remembered that in the 1909 "Manifesto del Futurismo" Marinetti affirmed that "we want to sing the love of danger, about the use of energy and recklessness.... We intend to glorify aggressive action ... There is no longer any beauty except the struggle." Moreover, "We want to glorify war – the sole cleanser of the world – militarism, patriotism, the destructive act of the libertarian" (Marinetti, *Critical Writings* 13–14), this last idea developed at length in the pamphlet *Guerra sola igiene del mondo* (1915), whose central tenet Marinetti summarizes as follows: "We consider the hypothesis of the friendly unification of peoples to be outmoded and utterly dispensable, and we see for the world only one form of purgation, and that is war" (*Critical Writings* 53). Futurism, Marinetti would say in an interview published in *L'avvenire* on 23 February 1915, brings with it the "militarization of innovative artists" (*Critical Writings* 239). The repudiation of tradition, exaltation of violence, aggressive tone, nationalism, and eradication of self expressed by Marinetti in "Manifesto tecnico della letteratura futurista" (1912) and in "Imagination sans fils et les mots en liberté" (1913), and, lastly, the fascistization of the Futurists in the 1920s bears resemblance to the Legion's values, function, and creed.

Armed with pens and guns respectively, the Italian Futurists and the legionnaires participated decisively in forging the fascist habitus. This association of a literary avant-garde and a military elite unit at the vanguard of the army illuminates the nature of both and their common ties to the ideology and political praxis of fascism. In the same way that the Futurists exalted war, the instructors of a military unit indoctrinated their soldiers with a text that evoked the avant-garde manifestos. In other words, not only do some avant-garde movements have affinities with the army; in its turn, the army displays a resemblance to the artistic avant-gardes. If for the Futurists war was much more than literature or art, for the legionnaires fighting implied at once the use of weapons and words.

Indeed, the Legion never concealed the discursivity of war, nor its fictional dimension. The history of war, Virilio has written (*War and Cinema* 7), is basically the history of radical changes of perception. For Virilio, the purpose of war resides in producing spectacle; without representation and psychological mystification, there can be no war (5). In all wars there is a "dissolution," a "derealization of language" present, for instance in military strategy, verbal alliances, briefings, daily conversations, reporting on combats, or the history of war itself (Scarry 133–9). The fictional, writes Scarry, is a major attribute of the language of and about war: "The lies, fictions, falsification, within war ... together collectively objectify and extend the formal fact of what war is, the suspension of the reality of constructs, the systematic retraction of all benign forms of substance from the artefacts of civilization, *and simultaneously*, the mining of the ultimate substance, the ultimate source of substantiation, the extraction of the physical basis of reality" (137). The battlefield itself contains elements that can seem unreal to those unfamiliar with combat. Clausewitz (113–14) has vividly shown the de-realizing effect of war with a description of a soldier's baptism of fire: approaching the front line, the soldier hears with growing intensity the discharge of cannons and the whistle of the bullets; lacking experience, he perceives combat as a hallucination, as if it were something theatrical rather than real and life-threatening; consequentially, the soldier loses the usual points of reference and finds himself at a level of reality with rules and a rationality of its own. The Legion's high command stressed war's fictional quality, in part for propagandistic purposes. The journalist and legionnaire Carlos Micó España put it this way: the enthusiasm for the Legion is transmitted "through the word" (*Los Caballeros* 56). Myriad written artefacts were produced to communicate that enthusiasm, such as recruitment posters, war diaries, memoirs, newspaper articles, documentaries, and fiction. Millán Astray knew the key function of language in war and military instruction; as he writes in *La Legión,* "There can be no soldier without the 'long lives!' etched on his soul. The 'long lives!' will be what pushes them, they are the motors of the will, the spirit, the encouragement, the cry of war, of salute, of death, of happiness, of farewell, and of pain.... The 'long lives!' are the soul sketched on matter" (54). Similarly, literary writing is indispensable for the dissemination of the Legion's feats and for gaining the support of the Spanish people, as explicitly stated in *La Legión* (81–3); official propaganda, although indispensable, is not enough: "It is cold; its voice does not resound or have an echo; it needs heat and resonance and only literary propaganda provides these elements. [Literary propaganda] will be the one to make the [Legion's] legend through highly patriotic lyric poetry; with epic songs of glorious deeds; searching for the romantic side of military exploits and painting soldierly life with vibrant and bright colours. The patrician pens are in charge of writing all this" (82–3).

Aware of what he owes to journalism, literature, and cinema, Millán Astray does not hesitate to express his gratitude to "all those who, moved by such patriotic and noble wishes, sang to the legionnaires, hyperbolized their feats, and made their legend. To them, the legend is owed" (83). Notice that Millán Astray does not hide the fact that representations of the Legion have exaggerated its feats. Reality, on the one hand, must be transformed into an epic song, and brutal actions of war (decapitation of corpses, mutilation of enemy bodies, raping, punitive expeditions, and the like) must acquire an aesthetic category. On the other hand, opinions critical of the Legion have a positive value. In truth, what really matters is the constant production and circulation of cultural artefacts on the Legion: "It is so vital," avows Millán Astray, "and of imperious necessity for the life of the Legion that people talk about it, know about it ... that even *negative* propaganda is acceptable" (*La Legión* 82–3).

Francisco Franco's *Marruecos: Diario de una Bandera* (1922) was part of that effort to create and circulate the "legend" of the Legion that Millán Astray spoke of.[60] Like *La Legión, Diario* may be considered as a passionate utterance, a work with an intended perlocutionary effect. First of all, it attempts to persuade readers of the need to fight on in Morocco. Second, it tries to stamp on them a fascist habitus played out by a unit of the Spanish Army. Franco, a major of the army in 1922 promoted to lieutenant colonel on 31 January 1923 and chief of the Legion as of 8 June that year, offers a detailed account of the Legion's fascist habitus in a book articulated by technologies of tropological striation that are closely related to that habitus. In a sense, *Diario* may be seen as a topographic approach to the war deeds of the brigade (or *bandera*, as brigades are officially called in the Legion) commanded by Franco, for topography is the book's principal building block and thematic axis.

Diario follows a linear chronology that runs from October 1920 through May 1922. That said, Franco does not structure his diary in units of time, as is often the case in most journals. Instead, priority is given to space, at both the thematic and discursive levels. The organization of the book is a clear indicator of that precedence of space over time, given that it is divided in two parts, each dedicated to a particular territory. In the first part ("El territorio de Tetuán"), Franco recounts the already-mentioned campaign in the west sector of the protectorate that was initiated in March 1919 and led by General Berenguer, and closes with the sudden, urgent dispatch of Franco's brigade, in the early morning of 22 July 1921, from its Ceuta camp to Melilla by foot, train, and boat in order to defend the city and participate in the counteroffensive to regain the territory in the east sector that had been conquered by the harkas (Moroccan irregular troops) commanded by Abd el-Krim. The second part ("En territorio de Melilla") narrates the counteroffensive.[61] Thus *Diario* reproduces structurally the two-sector division of the Spanish protectorate.

Despite the inevitable temporal references – in *Diario* always a function of military operations – space enjoys the leading role. To be sure,
such prevalence pervades war writing. In war journals, memoirs, fiction,
or motion pictures, the soldiers seem to be buried, to quote from Henri
Barbusse's *Le Feu* (1916), in the bottom of an ever-lasting battlefield
(11). In the trenches of the Great War, for instance, the soldiers lost
track of time. "Time went by," recalls Edmund Blunden in his war memoirs *Undertones of War* (1928), "but no one felt the passage of it, for the
shadow of death lay over the dial" (169). This defence mechanism can
also lend itself to the evocation of the living conditions of war. Ten years
after the Armistice, Blunden acknowledges the difficulty of determining
the exact sequence of the events that had occurred during the war. Chronology "atrophies" (133), while the topographical impressions remain
vivid. In war writing, the soldier is portrayed in a constant spatial tension
between front line and rearguard positions, between the battlefield and
home. An acute experience of space compensates for the soldier's radical fracture with his past – superbly captured by Remarque in *Im Westen
nichts Neues* (1929) – and a future overshadowed by the omnipresence of
death. Soldiers look at and live out space. To know the terrain, to be able
to orient oneself efficiently so as to determine which are the dangerous
areas are decisive for the soldier's survival. To lose oneself in space can
mean to lose oneself absolutely.[62] Considering all this, the prominence
of space in Franco's *Diario* must be framed within the context of the war
experience, its recollection, its writing. What differentiates *Diario* from
the aforementioned books resides in the fact that its symbolic treatment
of space contains an illocutionary force that refracts the troops' movements, one that is closely linked to the spatial determinants of the nascent fascist habitus as manifested in and actualized by the Legion.

In *Diario*, there is no shortage of descriptions of places (e.g., Rincón,
Tétouan, Chaouen, Mount Arruit) and landscapes, or of the itineraries
followed by Franco's troops. Places and itineraries carve out spaces of
violence – which is fully enjoyed by the legionnaires and Franco himself.
While the places are more often than not the object of military destruction, the brigade's itineraries imply a constant deadly threat to Moroccan
villages. With regard to the production of space, Franco's deployment of
a technology of tropological striation mimics the army's material spatial
practice. As Viscarri has argued, in *Diario* "there is an accumulative effect
of territorial acquisition in the name of the metropolis accentuated by
the list of toponyms" (*Nacionalismo* 87). Certainly, the act of naming is,
in general terms, a means of appropriation and control. The recursive

naming of places in *Diario* should be understood in that performative sense, for in addition to describing places, *Diario* names them, or, if you will, *writes* them. Most descriptions are rather conventional and usually portray places in a pseudo-impressionistic fashion. Franco employs techniques of dated impressionism that naturalize, in ways similar to the ones already seen in Borrás and Giménez Caballero, an "other" territory by means of images from the European cultural archive. Take, for instance, the author's portrayal of Tétouan. From the distanced point of view adopted by Franco, "the silhouettes of the towers are drawn against the horizon, and the confusion of voices runs through the lines [of the brigade]; at the farthest end of the gardens, majestic and white, rises the city; ... at its foot [the fort's], like clothing hung out to dry, the graves and decorative stones of the cemetery fade" (47). The range of bright colours used to describe Tétouan sharply contrasts with the external appearance of the inhabitants of the city, "dirty and dishevelled Moorish women ... little Moorish boys with dirty faces" (48). Hence the tropological striation of the country extends to the Moroccans by underscoring one single trait: dirtiness. In the area surrounding Tétouan, Franco's brigade sights a "reduced and picturesque little valley flanked by a long, outstretched beach"; on the seashore "the boats of fishermen rock" (50). Further, he dabs again with the impressionist palette to describe a landscape: "Toward the beach, the green shade of the bushes surrounding the Bedouin camps gives a note of colour to the monotony of the cultivated lands" (53). En route to Chaouen, Franco and his legionnaires contemplate "lively and picturesque hamlets hanging, like eagle nests, on the crags" (70). Chaouen is a "mysterious" city, one "quite like other Maghrebi villages" (73); its wall gives Chaouen "the look of our picturesque Andalusian towns" (73). Franco's lack of literary talent intensifies, paradoxically, the performative force of the descriptions, given that they reduce the complexity of the "other" to a handful of overworked conventions. In that same description of Chaouen, he writes, "To the south of the city, the Barrio de los Molinos constitutes one of the prettiest corners. The river jumps among the cliffs moving millstones and, in the middle of verdant, flowing trees, runs the crystalline water from the city through the exposed canals" (74). Like Borrás in *La pared de tela de araña*, Franco transforms Chaouen into a heterotopic space by conceiving of this holy Moroccan city as a degraded version of a Spanish town (74).

Not only does the violence underpinning *Diario*'s tropological striation duplicate the violence of war. More importantly, it is the literary refraction of the violence in which the legionnaires find the fullest real-

ization of their being. An erotics of violence permeates *Diario*'s discourse
and story. This is patent even in the most insignificant episodes, as, for
instance, in the passage on a support mission executed by the brigade
just before its baptism of fire. Such is the pleasure felt by the legionnaires
in that mission that several give themselves to dancing while they come
under enemy fire (76). But that is not enough, for the legionnaires yearn
to see real action; they feel a "healthy envy" upon seeing the Regulars
deployed to go to combat, while they do not move from their positions
(76). The legionnaires, notes Franco, "grow impatient with so much in-
activity" and feel annoyed when they are not sent to the front line (82).
To the "betrothed of death," fighting is a celebration. Thus an American
legionnaire "fights in a festive way" (159) and his comrades enjoy themselves "each time they 'hunt' an enemy sniper," pursuing with "shouts
and hurrahs" because, adds Franco, "the 'hunt' for the sniper is so fun!"
(172).

A similar phenomenon complements this erotics of violence: the aesthetics of violence. The advance of the Regulars towards the ridges of
Ismoar, for instance, "turned out precious" (109), as "precious" as was
the taking of Dar Quebdani (206). In the Larache area, writes Franco in
his diary, "the column halts upon nearing the ridges that rim the plain to
the right, and then we sight one of the most beautiful movements of the
cavalry ... the riders circle around and shoot their weapons ... and it is
then when we see Moorish horses that, in a fast gallop, advance along the
flank towards the enemy.... Throughout the entire afternoon this grandiose spectacle of that resolute cavalry squadron stays before us, which
puts the prettiest note on the advance" (90).

In contrast to the erotics and the aesthetics of violence, Franco shows
indifference and even coldness before the pain and death of his comrades-in-arms, of which he tends to speak tersely, without emotion. A
scene as tremendous as the death of the Lieutenant Penche is told by
Franco in this fashion: "Lieutenant Penche ... took a shot in the head.
He was found dead; only a trickle of blood flowed from his forehead:
his thoughts were carried out" (126). And Franco recounts Lieutenant
Ochoa's death thus: "An enemy bullet had wounded him in the heart.
Poor little Ochoa, gloriously dead in the prime of youth!" (142). The
language used in his account of the death of his aide-de-camp does not
persuade the reader of the sorrow that he claims to feel: "Now my faithful aide-de-camp falls with his head pierced through; the enemy lead has
mortally wounded him; from the fray two soldiers carry his inanimate
body, and with pain I see my faithful and beloved comrade baron of

Misena separated forever from my side" (150). In an equally succinct manner he describes the body of a dead soldier ("A stretcher with a dead soldier arrives at the small plaza-like area of the base camp. His head pierced through" [195]), and the death of a commissioned officer ("in the heat of the combat, Second Lieutenant Llaneza, from the 13th, receives glorious death" [203]).

While evincing Franco's notorious coldness before other people's deaths, his indifference and partial concealment of the outcome of combat are intrinsic to the structure of war. This last point is important to keep in mind in order to place *Diario* within the genre of war writing, as well as to interpret the discursive strategies used to mould a fascist habitus that made war one of its essential constituents. In Franco's book, one can detect an ambiguity characteristic of war writing and fascist discourse: both of them exhibit and conceal – depending on the circumstances – the result of violent action. According to Elaine Scarry, war pertains to two broad categories of human experience: injuring and struggle. "It is in the relation of these two rather than in either individually that the nature of war resides" (63). With respect to the first category, Scarry points out that the structure of war requires the act of injuring to remain partially eclipsed by one or another constellation of motives (64). She analyses two techniques in the formal and informal accounts of war that make the act of injuring invisible: the omission and the re-description of the event (66–72). Since total invisibility cannot always be maintained, the act of injuring is relegated to a visible but marginal position. There are four way to put aside from our view the act of injuring: (1) to affirm that the injuries and the death are secondary consequences unfortunately inevitable (72–4); (2) to identify the injury as an unforeseeable interruption of a process aiming to achieve a given objective (74–5); (3) to assure that the injuries are the inevitable cost of achieving some objectives (75–7); and (4) to distance the act of injuring by transforming the act of injuring into the continuation of something different, benign in itself (77–8), as, for example, the victory over Nazism, or, in the case of Morocco, the pacification of the protectorate, the modernization of the country, and the "civilization" of its inhabitants. In all of these cases, through the disappearance or attenuation of the centrality of the act of injuring, "the centrality of the human body [is] disowned" (80).

To a degree, Franco follows in his war diary a common practice in the official war writing – to omit or to attenuate the injuries caused by the Spanish army. Franco regulates the information given to the reader on the damage done to the enemy by his brigade. At the same time, he brings to the fore the cruel, inhuman behaviour of the Moroccan fighters in their routing of the Spanish colonial army in the summer of 1921 (142–3, 155–6, 193). Neither the unabashed exaltation of death and killing, nor the degree-zero narrative of the punitive operations ordered by Franco himself (110, 112), nor the expressionistic descriptions of face-to-face combat (149, 158) is an omission of the outcome of war. But within the logic of *Diario*, the only item that needs to be omitted or downplayed is the Spanish casualties suffered during the counteroffensive initiated on 17 September 1921 to regain the territory taken over by the harkas (i.e., the entire east sector with the exception of Melilla).

Franco's fascination with death may be interpreted as an ambivalent literary technique in the book's relegation of the act of hurting to a marginal position. Instead of referring to dead bodies, Franco emphasizes the heroic dimension of death on the battlefield. Recalling a situation in which a lieutenant gathers his troops to ask for volunteers to break the enemy's siege of Blocao Mezquita, Franco notes, "All the soldiers fight with one another over who is going," even though they know perfectly well "that they are going to die" (119). The mission fails to achieve its objective, but the legionnaires die as real heroes: "The Moors had drawn their cannons closer and furiously bombarded the blockhouse; shortly afterwards 'The Evil One' [the blockhouse's nickname] had disappeared, and its defenders remained buried under the rubble ... That's how one defends a position! That's how legionnaires die for Spain!" (119). "La canción del legionario" transcribed in *Diario* (166–8), considered by Franco to be "inspired" and "one of the prettiest chants devoted to the Legion" (166), underlines the cult of violence and the exaltation of death expressed throughout the book. Some of the song's lines condense the topics studied thus far:

> When they advance thirsty for the fight
> There is no force able to stop them,
> Since they destroy, burn, and kill
> As if possessed by an infernal fury.
> Harvesters of lives they are called;
> Each legionnaire resembles a Titan,
> And joyful, they use the machete
> Like a sharp, steel dagger.   (167, lines 26–35)

In the last chapter the glorification of death reaches its climax. Titled "Infantes heroicos" (218–20), it is an homage "to those gloriously fallen in the heroic defence of the positions" (218). The book's closure could hardly be more expressive of the basis of the fascist habitus articulated in the diary: "Hail, heroic defenders of Igueriben; hail, glorious Infantry soldiers. The horror of the disaster [of Annual] will never be able to cloud your glory" (220). By ending his war diary with this passage, Franco emphasizes the cult of death and war that underlies the entire book.

Like other Africanist officers, Franco resented the political and popular indifference towards the protectorate as well as the pent-up critical attitude toward the colonial army. In the Peninsula, according to Franco, people look at "the action and the sacrifice of the army with indifference" (77). Reflections upon the country's "insensitivity" (78) and the "extremely dangerous decadence of the military spirit" (78) led him to draft an article for the journal published by the army. Significantly, he inserted that text in *Diario* under the title of "El mérito en campaña" (78–81). It is a defensive text, attempting to vindicate, but also expressing a messianic conception of the colonial army with respect to the political situation of the Peninsula. Referring to the large number of officers "who gloriously died for the Fatherland," he exclaims, "They are the ones who make the Fatherland!" (79). The deaths of the colonial army's officers *perform*, therefore, the fatherland itself. The troops, wrote Carlos Micó España in a book published in the same year as Franco's, "are the walking symbol of the fatherland, the *walking fatherland*" (*Los Caballeros* 21; my emphasis), thereby emphasizing the fusion of army and nation on the one hand, and the performing quality that both achieved through movement, on the other. Franco conceives of the campaign of Morocco as the best training school of the army, where "positive values and merits are confirmed" (79–80). The officer's corps of the colonial army, concludes Franco, "must be someday the nerve and soul of the Peninsular army" (79–80), in an affirmation that provides direction to the habitus described in the story of the book and practised at the level of its discourse.

Places of Radical Evil

In 1924 the press of Paulus Bernsteini published a disturbing novel devoted entirely to the Legion, *Tras el águila del César: Elegía del Tercio, 1921–1922,* by the Falangist-to-be Luys Santa Marina (pen name of Luis Narciso Gregorio Gutiérrez Santa Marina).[63] This *opera prima* would be followed by *Tetramorfos (Memorias de César Gustavo Giménez)* (1927), yet another novel dedicated, if only partially, to the Moroccan conflict; essays; poetry books (e.g., *Primavera en Chinchilla* [1939]); as well as biographies (e.g., *Cisneros* [1933] and *Hacia José Antonio* [1958]). The high literary quality of Santa Marina's work has made him not only one of the foremost Falangist writers, but also one whom contemporary readers may enjoy reading regardless of their political inclinations. Santa Marina's novel *Tras el águila del César* was an almost instant success, crowned paradoxically if not altogether surprisingly by the seizure by the police of unsold copies at the request of General Primo de Rivera's censors. In 1939, Editorial Yunque would issue the second edition; on that occasion the reception would be rather limited because another general's censor (Franco's) acted swiftly, confiscating all copies shortly after the book's publication. An expressionist ode to unrestricted violence – a positive portrayal of the Legion's frequent criminal behaviour with the Moroccans – Santa Marina's novel exceeded the prejudices of two military dictatorships eager to uphold the reputation of the armed forces at all costs.[64]

In contrast with most fiction on the Legion, *Tras el águila del César* is a modernist work characterized by experimental language, poetic prose, the dissolution of the subject, spatial form, a distancing from the communicative function of language, a mixing of genres, the alternation of prose and poetry, simultaneity, and – among other modernist traits – a transgression of temporal boundaries. Narrated by a Spanish legionnaire, Santa Marina's novel is divided into seven parts, each composed of very short lyrical vignettes. The novel's modernist plotlessness refracts the seemingly chaotic nature of war (e.g., the changes in strategic planning, the sudden modification of military tactics, the unpredictable behaviour of the troops and officers in the battlefield, the friction of war, and the like) while mimicking at the level of discourse the deconstruction of ethical behaviour, the human body, the subject, and space that was undertaken in the novel.

To a degree, one could even affirm that the plotlessness of Santa Marina's narrative actualizes what Maurice Blanchot has called *the writing of disaster*. For Blanchot, the disaster is a break with any form of totality that means the "ruin of the word" and entails the dissolution of the unity of the subject who has lived it (67). It is not, according to Blanchot, a name or a verb, but rather a reminder that "would cross out through invisibility and illegibility all that shows itself and all that is said" (68–9). Hence the disaster "un-writes"; it limits and erodes the individual's ability to understand and express it through language. In Blanchot's view, the disaster seems to tell us that "there is no law, prohibition ... but transgression without prohibition that ultimately congeals into law, into a principle of meaning" (121).

In the historical context of *Tras el águila del César*, the First World War generated literary and artistic representations criss-crossed by the writing of disaster. A "crisis of meaning" arose as an aftershock of the Great War (Dawes 131). The solidity of the nineteenth-century mainstays (liberalism, the unitary self, reason, representational language, belief in the progress of humankind) melted in the mud of the trenches. Profoundly baffled and traumatized by the magnitude of the tragedy as well as by the mechanized and industrial dimension of the war, European and American writers and artists had to figure out how to represent an experience lived and perceived as indescribable and incommunicable. Their response is well known: the dismantling of the myths of nineteenth-century Western society had its literary and artistic correlate in the practice of an experimental, fragmentary, playful, illogical, oneiric language.[65]

Like the artistic avant-gardes and the Anglo-American modernism related to the Great War, *Tras el águila del César* may be viewed as a novel whose modernist language and rhetoric are closely linked to the effects of modern warfare on psychology, ethics, and language.[66] An exploration of the multiple deconstruction carried out in *Tras el águila del César* through a writing of disaster sustained by an ethics and aesthetics of evil provides, I believe, a new perspective on the forging of the fascist habitus within the interstices of the dual space.

In Santa Marina's *Tras el águila del César*, Morocco is conceived of as a heterotopia of Spain, but with an element not openly present in *La pared de tela de araña* or *Notas marruecas de un soldado*. I am referring to the idea of nation defended in key passages of this novel. In his foreword to the 1939 edition of the novel, Santa Marina states that the Rif War brought minimal gains to Spain, considering the courage that it demanded. All Spain received were "burnt pieces of land" (13). That notwithstanding, on the spiritual level, "the booty was splendorous: the reconquest of the Spanish soul, its return to the path of Don Quixote ... without those fierce flags, our victorious flags [by this image the author means Franco's army] would have been impossible" (13). If we are to follow the logic of *Tras el águila del César*, this "re-conquest of the Spanish soul" – clearly seen as a spiritual good – was achieved through the practice of evil. Furthermore, the legionnaires' evil behaviour opened up space for the good, a space articulated by the norms of coexistence (e.g., political organization, economic order, articulation of the network of cultural and symbolic products) imposed years later by the Franco regime. As

Santa Marina's novel insinuates, a new Spain would emerge in the space opened up by the systematic practice of evil.

The legionnaires' evil in *Tras el águila del César* is an actualization of radical evil – a concept that needs some clarification before proceeding any further. The term *radical evil* was coined by Immanuel Kant in the first part of *Die Religion innerhalb der Grenzen der blossen Vernunft* (1793). Kant does not use this term in reference to a type of evil nor to an inconceivable one, but rather to the propensity (i.e., the subjective principle of the possibility of an inclination, such as concupiscence) of the person to deviate from the moral law; radical evil is thus the subordination of the moral law to selfish interests. For Kant, the statement that "someone is evil" means that the individual is aware of the moral law, in spite of which he has incorporated in his maxims a deviation from such law. "Radical" therefore does not mean a "degree" of evil, but rather that evil lies at the "root" of human nature. Although that propensity is rooted in human nature, the individual is morally responsible for all his acts: the individual does not choose his predispositions, but he does choose the importance he gives them in relation with his duty. Kant argues that the subordination of selfish interests to evil would not be human, but diabolic; accordingly, for Kant there can be no diabolical evil, namely, people who practise evil qua evil; in such cases, the human actions would present the formal criteria of an ethical act.

Hannah Arendt pushed the Kantian sense of radical evil beyond Kant by assuming the real possibility of a diabolical evil, considered by Kant as not-human. Thus in the last phase of totalitarianism, which Arendt locates in the Nazi extermination camps and in the Gulag, there appears an *absolute evil*, a concept that alternates with *radical evil* in Arendt's *The Origins of Totalitarianism* (viii–ix, 437–59). For Arendt, this evil is "absolute" because it cannot be deduced from motives humanly comprehensible such as selfish interest, cowardice, the will to power or *ressentiment*, unless one would ground it in the undeniable idealism of many Nazis willing to sacrifice everything, including themselves, for the sake of their ideas (*Origins* 307–8, 322). In Arendt's own words, "The disturbing factor in the success of totalitarianism is rather the true selflessness of its adherents" (307). This disposition to self-sacrifice makes absolute evil a most perturbing phenomenon, for it transforms evil behaviour into an ethical act. This is crucial to the adequate understanding of fascism and literary artefacts like *Tras el águila del César*.[67]

Referring to this very problem in his *Tarrying with the Negative* (95–101), Slavoj Žižek remarks that in his refusal of the hypothesis of a diabolical evil Kant withdraws from the basic paradox of radical evil, of the possibility of human acts that, though evil in their content, fulfil the formal criteria of an ethical act. Such acts, claims Žižek, are not motivated, as Kant would say, by pathological considerations; their "sole motivating ground is Evil as principle, which is why they can involve the radical abrogation of one's pathological interests, up to the sacrifice of one's life" (95). To prove his point, Žižek analyses Mozart's *Don Giovanni* (95–6). The story is well known: Don Giovanni persists in his libertine attitude, even when his own life is at stake at the end of the opera. He refuses to repent, and by so doing – Žižek argues, quite rightly – Don Giovanni does something that can be properly designated only as a "radical ethical stance" (95–6). One could say that Don Giovanni inverts the example given by Kant himself in his *Kritik der praktischen Vernunft* (1788), according to which a libertine renounces the fulfillment of his passions at the very moment that he realizes that his licentiousness can lead him to the "gallows." Far from giving it up, Don Giovanni persists in his licentiousness when he knows that what awaits him are precisely those "gallows" of which Kant spoke.

To return to Žižek, by taking as a point of reference his pathological interests, what Don Giovanni should do is show repentance, even if that were a provisional, formal gesture; by so doing, he would lose nothing. On the contrary, he would end up winning, since he could resume his libertine life in due time; that is, he could continue fulfilling his passions outside the moral law. And yet, and – more importantly – by principle, Don Giovanni chooses to persist in his defiant attitude: he takes the arduous, non-selfish path. As Žižek concludes, "How can one avoid experiencing Don Giovanni's unyielding 'No!' to the statue, to this living dead, as the model of an intransigent *ethical* attitude, notwithstanding its 'evil' content?" (96). Don Giovanni does not subordinate his predispositions to the moral law, but rather to evil as the only principle of all of his acts; for this higher principle – evil – he is willing to sacrifice, if necessary, his own life. According to Žižek, "If we accept the possibility of such an evil ethical act ... one is compelled to conceive of radical Evil as something that ontologically precedes Good by way of opening up the space for it" (96). Choosing between good and evil is not, in a way, the original choice. The first real choice is choosing between the pathological inclinations and the radical evil – an act of suicidal egoism that opens up the space for the good (96–7). The good, as a mask of radical evil, is an attempt, ontologically secondary, to re-establish the lost balance; its ultimate paradigm is the corporatist project to build a harmonious, organic, non-antagonistic society (97). Although Žižek does not say it, fascism is a case in point of such a paradigm.

The evil of the legionnaires consists in the transgression of the forbidden, in the playful and unconstrained violence performed on the "other" body beyond any law that regulates individual and collective life. Their practice of violence is a modus vivendi that asserts the supreme freedom of the body from communal values in a fashion not unlike the marquis de Sade's ecstatic embracing of desire in all its manifestations. In Morocco, the legionnaires perform violence with joy, putting themselves in harm's way for the sake of an erotics of violence; they are therefore "evil" in the sense of the word that we have just seen. The legionnaires' propensity for violence appears from the very beginning, in the chapter that narrates the trip from New York to Spain of ninety-six volunteers. Although all of them – except the narrator – travel in third class, they are masters of the ship (21). "We organized boxing matches, fights, and steeplechases; we climbed the masts, gave speeches, formed choruses"; in sum: it looked like "a pirate ship" (21). As was to be expected, they also fought with the passengers: "So hard did we beat up one Greek who teased us that he ended up with all his bones broken. Rare was the day without trouble and without the shining of jackknives" (21).

Once in Morocco, the legionnaires live out violence gleefully. In one of the first vignettes of the novel, they jubilantly welcome the order for a bayonet assault (29). "Even the bayonets seemed to jump for joy … Poor things, they are thirsty" (29). During the assault, one of the legionnaires exclaims, "Life in the Legion is excellent! Let's be glad for having been born!" (29). The narrator summarizes the ensuing hand-to-hand combat: "The bayonets were really thirsty, and it took some time to quench that thirst" (29). During the fight, a gigantic black legionnaire stabs the Moors while joyfully singing (29).[68] Bayonet assaults, commonplace in the coetaneous literature devoted to the Legion, abound in *Tras el águila del César*.[69] The first vignette of the second part of the novel, "El choque," narrates a bayonet assault in Esponja Alta de Taxuda: "When we assaulted the hill, they were waiting for us hidden between the stones.… It was then the bayonets' turn. Those of us with experience stabbed them on the neck or the chest, so that we could pull out the knife quickly; the rest, for the certain hit – in the stomach: it is deadly and [the bayonet] enters easily" (27); at the end of the fight, there were only fifteen legionnaires left. "We finished off the wounded Moors, and because they pretended to be dead, so as to avoid oversights we stabbed them all. It was over. Some beheaded the fallen; others cleaned the blood from the bayonets by using their djellabas" (27).

Santa Marina's novel evinces the fetishistic perception and function of the bayonet, particularly in the vignette "¡Oh, los cuchillos de los mosquetones!" "Those who had one," writes the narrator, "took care of it as if it were a talisman, which, if handled coldly, deadly, saved one's life. Oh muskets' knives! Pale, white, forty-centimetre blades; rifle's spike, your blows were quick, precise. Oh muskets' knives! In the clashes, the Moroccan daggers fell away, while the bayonets tattooed strange drawings on chests and stomachs" (164). The phallic symbolism of the bayonet is evident in "La morilla burlada" (37–8). In a ruined hovel, several legionnaires find a sixteen-year-old Moroccan woman with a rifle next to her, still hot. "She could not escape ... The whole Company first and later the whole Regiment stabbed her, and pretty soon the bayonets hit in already inflicted wounds ... And they cut off fingers and ears, covetous of her rings and beautiful earrings" (37). Bayonet assaults like this one (see also 36, 72) usually end with the beheading of the enemy, with the mutilation of corpses (28, 42, 50, 128), or with lynching (42).

Sometimes, the severed heads are used in macabre games, as happens in a scene ironically titled "Apreciaciones" (36). In a fortified encampment the legionnaires come up with different ways to use the heads. In a chilling vignette, "¡Sandías, sandías!" (36), several legionnaires go through the streets of Melilla hawking watermelons, and, when a housemaid asks about them, they take a Moor's head by the hair (34). In the following vignette, "La última copa de un mojamed" (35), one legionnaire enters a canteen and orders two drinks from the waitress, one for himself and the other one for his friend. He puts aside his djellaba, and, taking out the head of a Moor, puts it on the zinc counter. The legionnaire encourages his "friend" to drink: "Drink, drink, Moor, for this is your last drink, and you will pay for it with your head" (35).[70]

As performed by the legionnaires, evil is a rapturous way of being that subverts any rational behaviour based upon personal interest and communal values. It does not take only the Moroccans as its victims. If that were the case, the legionnaires' conduct might be explained in functionalist terms, and it would be a simple outcome of the brutalization of wars in which the enemy is, to paraphrase Carl Schmitt, an "absolute enemy," a less-than-human outlaw who must be pitilessly annihilated at all costs.[71] What distinguishes the legionnaires, as depicted by Santa Marina, is their excess in the battlefield and on the home front.[72] The vignette "Noche de aguiluchos" (114–17), centred on the visit of four legionnaires to a brothel, is perhaps the most disturbing instance of the legionnaires' evil as actualized on the home front.[73] The violence begins with no warning as soon as the leader enters the brothel: "And with his long glove he slapped her head [the madame's] as with a whip" (114). Perceiving the prostitutes' nervousness, one legionnaire tries to calm them by announcing that the "foxtrot" will start soon: "He pointed the gun at the whore and shot: the bullet scorched her hair" (115). Cursing, the legionnaires go room to room whipping, shooting, throwing out of windows those who try to defend themselves (115). They drink without measure (115), take drugs, and force the prostitutes to do the same (116). The vignette's closure underscores the gratuitousness of the legionnaires' evil: "When he was about to leave, he heard someone sobbing in a bed.... 'Good-bye, pretty lady' [in English in the original]. And he shot towards the place from which the sobbing was coming. No one answered" (117). The degree zero, the stylistic terseness, and the use of ellipses enhance the climate of violence in a scene in which both assassination and mistreatment are correlates of sexual intercourse. The battlefield and the bed merge beyond recognition; in both spaces the result is just the same: the wounding or the destruction of the "other's" body.

In their torture and dismembering of the human body, the legionnaires place their victims beyond their symbolic capacity to represent the world. In the suffering of torture, reality is experienced without transcendence, without language, because extreme physical pain cannot be grasped by words. It is for this reason that Elaine Scarry has considered torture as an "unmaking of the world." And this is precisely what the legionnaires do with their victims: they "unmake" their world. As practised by the legionnaires, evil subverts all rational conduct based on interest and coexistence. The legionnaire does not incarnate any viable alternative to a world governed by rationality. From this perspective, one has to consider the legionnaires as *sadists* in the sense given the word by Bataille (77–96), as individuals who, in their radical negation of social conventions and the "other's" right to existence, proceed towards the destruction of human beings and the world.[74]

In view of their notorious reputation among the civilian population, the indifference and sometimes hostility with which they are received in the city does not come as any surprise ("El Tercio en la ciudad" 167–73; see also "Desaliento" 154–5). The fifth part of the novel, "Elegías de Cantabria," centres on the return home of the narrator and stresses through a spatial contrast the hiatus between the veteran and the civilians. His native region's landscape seems to him depressing, cold, unpleasant (179). There, the narrator is a *dépaysé* who misses the land where he has fought (184). This contact between the soldier and the civilian, as well as the former's surprise upon realizing that, at the home front, life goes on as usual, generates a deep resentment and feelings of alienation. Santa Marina follows here a commonplace of modern war literature (coeval examples are Henri Barbusse's *Le Feu (Journal d'une escouade)* [1916], Rebecca West's *The Return of the Soldier* [1918], Erich Maria Remarque's *Im Westen nichts Neues* [1929] and *Der Weg zurück* [1931], and Siegfried Sassoon's *Memoirs of an Infantry Officer* [1930]). In *Tras el águila del César*, the legionnaires' evil – actualized as a radical freedom of the body, unrestrained violence, torture, and destruction of the "other" – contrasts with order and money, values that Bataille ascribes to the Good in *La Littérature et le mal*. The patriotism of the legionnaires has not been rewarded by the population: those who came "in a generous impulse to save the Fatherland" were despised as pariahs (154). "All the anguish," complains the narrator, "all the pain that we suffered: we kept suffering them as a martyrdom only for Spain" (157). Note the lack of a solid connection between the discouragement, patriotism, and resentment toward the civilian population in these last chapters and the experience of evil in previous chapters of the novel. This change in the legionnaires' attitude has to do mostly with a worsening of the conditions at the front and with their visit to the city. At the closing of his novel (199–202), Santa Marina warns of the possible consequences of the legionnaires' resented patriotism. The narrator decides to leave his hometown, where he has returned after his service in the Rif War. "I left through the door of contempt.... And those who were the first to benefit from our sacrifice ... raised their shrill, conceited voices to vilify us" (201). If we take into account the subsequent history of Spain, the complaint that closes the novel is ominous: "We are fed up with calumnies! The Tercio is not a band of *condottieri*.... It was formed almost exclusively by Spaniards ... who loved Spain over everything" (202).[75] The constant performance of evil deeds establishes, thanks to the legionnaires' patriotism in the last vignettes of the novel, the condition of possibility for opening up a space for the good. The resentment towards civilian society is a seed sown precisely in that space out of which may germinate, as the novel subtly hints at the end, a new type of society. This indirect allusion to a new organization of the social is better understood if we compare *Tras el águila del César*'s political subtext with the political discourse underlying other legionary novels. Consider, for instance, Asenjo Alonso's 1932 *¡¡¡Los que fuimos al Tercio!!!* and Ros Andreu's 1932 *La conquista de Alhucemas*, two novels in which the legionnaires' practice of violence shores up not only their patriotism, but also an anti-communist ideology. The

latter phenomenon is most symptomatic, for it links the Legion with
right-wing, anti-democratic, and fascist organizations.

In Asenjo Alonso's novel, a legionnaire named Otto infiltrates a group
of German, Polish, and Russian volunteers suspected to have plotted,
alongside "some Moors," against the Legion and Spain's interests in Morocco; he informs his superiors that they are dealing with a plot "of a
communist sort, with touches of Islamic vindications" (321). Noteworthy
is the perceived close connection between communism and Islamism,
both of them taken in opposition to Spain's (Christian) essence. As happens in fascist texts, in this novel the communist and the Moor incarnate
Spain's threatening otherness. Ros Andreu's *La conquista de Alhucemas*
manifests a similar but more interesting anti-communist discourse. First,
one legionnaire, Lisandro, sets himself to thwart the sabotage planned
by Russian and German legionnaires, thought to be Soviet spies aiming to commit crimes against Spain. Second, Lisandro's anti-communist
activities continue in the Peninsula after he is discharged from the Legion. In Spain, he commits himself to anti-communist propaganda with
his comrade-in-arms Teodorino. Thus the conflict between communism
and anti-communism moves out from the protectorate to the metropolis.
The novel ends with a passage revealing the continuity between the Rif
War and Spain's convulsed political life: Lisandro and Teodorino – who
dedicate all their energy to anti-communist propaganda – and the communist ex-legionnaires whom they met in Morocco stroll through the
same Spanish and European streets; there, "like in the Tercio, the fierce
struggle to death between them continues" (328). The anti-communism
beneath Ros Andreu's and Asenjo Alonso's novels is consubstantial to
the fascist habitus forged within the interstices of the dual space.[76] *¡¡¡Los
que fuimos al Tercio!!!* and *La conquista de Alhucemas* supplement *Tras al
águila del César*'s political discourse.

Consistent with its lyricism and its emphasis on radical evil, Santa
Marina's novel does not openly address these political issues; rather it
insinuates them while relating politics and evil. *Tras el águila del César*
does not intend to provide any sense to the legionnaires' evil. Such evil
is simply the manifestation of a habitus. The legionnaires' murderous
drive is located beyond any explanatory frame of reference; it constitutes
what Clifford Geertz has called, in his description of evil, "a problem of
meaning" (105–9, 131, 140, 172). Paradoxically, in this unsayability of
the legionnaires' evil, in this malignant silence of the narrator an empty
space opens up, a space filled later with an ethical and political choice
vaguely alluded to at the end of the novel. If the written or spoken word

requires silence as its condition of possibility, the construction of the ethics and the political thought of fascism had in the ontological empti-ness of malignity one of its foundational moments. The fascist habitus of the legionnaires provided, with the unsayable evil that underpinned it, a legacy that was later adopted in the Peninsula. The theory of fascism, the direct action performed by the Falangists in the streets of Spain in the 1930s, the tactics and strategy followed by the high command of Fran-co's army during the civil war, and finally, the repressive organization of the Francoist state together actualized the legionnaires' fascist habitus, which was spread, and more importantly, discursively modified by a lit-erature favourable to the Legion that took up the mission of bringing the Rif War into the Peninsula's bookstores. In its paradoxical mission to express with words the unsayable malignance of the legionnaires, *Tras el águila del César*'s perlocutionary speech act would effect, along with other texts devoted to the Legion, the internalization among Spaniards of the legionnaires' fascist habitus and its projection to the specific political life in the Peninsula.

Warmongering and the Colonization of Spain

One of the most fascinating and complex literary artefacts that forged the fascist habitus is a practically unknown work (treated only in pass-ing in Carbajosa and Carbajosa 32–3) of Rafael Sánchez Mazas. I am referring to the series of fifty-three articles titled "La campaña de África" and the eleven war dispatches (usually under the headlines "Impresión de nuestro enviado en Melilla" or "Impresión de Sánchez Mazas") that he wrote between 14 September and 23 December 1921 as the foreign correspondent for *El pueblo vasco* in the east sector of the protectorate. For his chronicles on the campaign undertaken to recover all the terri-tory lost to the Moroccan harkas during the Disaster of Annual, Sánchez Mazas would be awarded the Premio Nacional de Crónicas de Guerra Fundación de Chirel in 1922. Even though the readers of *El pueblo vasco* could learn through these articles about the taking of souk El Arbaa, Na-dor, Selouan, Atlaten, Mount Arruit, Uixam, Ras Medua, and Taxarurt, a striking characteristic of the chronicles lies in the scarcity of specific factual information on the ongoing military operations. In place of re-porting the facts, Sánchez Mazas opted to offer his readers abundant reflections on war and politics. In this deliberate move, neglecting to adequately fulfil the task he had been assigned by the Basque newspa-per, resides a key to understanding his chronicles. On the one side, "La campaña de África" deliberately forged by symbolic means, along with other cultural artefacts, a fascist habitus. On the other, it is a passionate utterance whose main purpose consisted of etching that habitus on the readers.

To begin with, Sánchez Mazas conceives of war as a spectacle of great beauty ("Bajo" 1; "Desde Segangan" 1; "Impresión" [18 September] 5; "La toma" 1; "Telegrama" 1), as an activity closely related to the arts. Like music, war always contains a scherzo, an andante, and an allegro ("Antes" 1; see also "Los instantes" [4 November] 1), while military strategy resembles instrumental music: "The *crescendo* is the victory, and the *diminuendo* is the withdrawal" ("Antes" 1). It is also a form of cinema and fiction ("Hacia Atlaten" 1; "Desde Segangan" 1) as well as of painting ("Hacia Atlaten" 1). The aesthetic dimension of war does not conceal its horror. In "La campaña de África," there is no trace of the scrupulous concealment of the "original ludic and aesthetic trait of the warlike values" distinctive, according to Sánchez Ferlosio, of what he calls "ideology of war" (341–5). Quite the contrary, these values are put on display.

In a manner reminiscent of Ernst Jünger's *In Stahlgewittern* (1920), *Der Kampf als inneres Erlebnis* (1922) and *Feuer und Blut* (1925), as well as of "classics" of *Freikorps* literature such as Peter von Heydebreck's *Wir Wehr-Wölfe: Erinnerungen eines Freikorps-Führers* (1931), Sánchez Mazas does not hide his admiration for war and violent action, or his profound contempt for pacifism and democracy. Africa and the war have for him a "profound charm," for both constitute "a liberation from a thousand trifles of the civilian order." Likewise, the climate and the frenzy of military operations are a tonic that has produced "a marvellous effect on my health, not because of the things that I do or the country where I live, but rather because of the number of insipid … things that I don't see, or hear, or do, and because of the splendid inhibition that one feels" ("Bajo" 1). Near the front line he feels a pleasant, reassuring peace of mind ("Hacia Atlaten II" 1). For Sánchez Mazas, the attraction of war thus is something "profoundly humane," the "quenching of a mysterious thirst" ("Vuelven" 1). War, he claims, has a positive effect on the soldier; it purifies the race and regenerates the country. It constitutes, in sum, a "spiritual benefit, a lesson, an open-air and powder cure" for both the troops and Spain ("En la posición" 1). To set on fire, to destroy, to raid are not only natural, but also necessary activities in warfare ("Algunas" 1; see also "Hacia Atlaten III" 1). Sánchez Mazas's exaltation in violence and the cult of death ("Algunas" 1; "Examen" 1; "Hacia Atlaten" 1; "Sensibilidad" 1) need to be understood vis-à-vis that conception of war.

Beneath the writer's virulent warmongering and view of war as a purifying force lies a fear of cowardice. Sánchez Mazas himself acknowledges this otherwise characteristic trait of some manifestations of fascism in a chronicle unambiguously titled "Examen de conciencia del cobarde" (1). His cowardice, confesses the author, resides at two different levels. First, he is a coward for having asked other people whether he should join the colonial army, knowing all too well he would be told that he would serve the country better as a journalist than as a soldier. "The brave ones," says Sánchez Mazas, "do not consult their decision to take risks" ("Examen" 1). Second, his cowardice consists in looking for "compensation and consolation" in the practice of journalism, for that is precisely the aim of those who have failed in "matters of bravery." This double cowardice has decisive consequences in the shaping of the individual's personality because shrinking from fighting in a war is "a cowardly act that will stamp a character for the rest of his life." He adds that if he does not get cured of this, his cowardly reaction will be repeated "on all the fronts" (notice the use of military language) he will go to in times of peace. Pusillanimity entails corruptibility in the same way that heroism and violent action keep men in a certain state of incorruptibility. The fascist's will to violence can therefore overlap with a fear of what Sánchez Mazas calls, in another article, "the contagion of effeminacy" ("El contagio" 1).

Sánchez Mazas's fear of effeminacy reveals a vague awareness of the ambiguity inherent in the fascist cult of violence. Theodor W. Adorno reflected on this issue in *Minima Moralia* (71–3). Thinking of the National Socialists, "tough babies" (as Adorno calls them) are, in effect, effeminated individuals "who need the weaklings as their victims in order not to admit that they are like them" (73). In totalitarian societies, the "strong man" negates everything that is not of his own kind. "The opposites of the strong man and the submissive youth," writes Adorno perceptively, "conflate in an order that asserts unalloyed the male principle of domination" (73). By transforming everything – even the supposed "subjects" – into "objects," such a principle turns into something passive, effectively effeminated. For this reason, Adorno believes totalitarianism and homosexuality to be closely associated – a thesis to a certain extent shared by Jean-Paul Sartre, who in his 1945 article "Qu'est-ce qu'un *collaborateur*?" (in *Situations III* 43–61) saw homosexual tendencies in French fascists.[77] Curzio Malaparte, a conspicuous Fascist until his repudiation of fascism in the early 1940s, shrewdly notes in his novel *Kaputt* (1944) that Nazis "kill and destroy out of fear … they are afraid of all that is living, of all that is living outside of themselves and of all that is different from them" (12); they fear the defenceless, the weak, the sick, the oppressed, women, Jews (91); what drives the Germans to cruelty in Poland, writes Malaparte, "to deeds most coldly, methodically and scientifically cruel, is fear," whose nature, adds Mapalarte, is "feminine" (91). From very different angles and personal backgrounds, Adorno and Malaparte reached similar conclusions, which, mutatis mutandis, apply to Rafael Sánchez Mazas.

As pointed out earlier, Sánchez Mazas argues that war has a positive effect on the "race" and the "fatherland." A case in point is "Bienvenida a los de Garellano" (1), a harangue of sorts delivered to the Battalion of Garellano that intends to inculcate a fascist habitus in the soldiers just arrived in Morocco *and* in the readers of *El pueblo vasco*. Similar to other works explored in this chapter, "La campaña de África" not only represents the forging of a habitus. A habitus is a condition of possibility of human behaviour, but at the same time human actions such as writing have the power to shape it. In this sense, "Bienvenida a los de Garellano" is a meta-literary comment on that transformational capacity. At the end of the article, Sánchez Mazas proclaims that Morocco is a "necessary battlefield to test the men; for the race it is a battlefield for the renovation of virile virtues, an opportunity to show the strength of which we are capable" ("Bienvenida" 1). It is essential to cleanse – so the author writes – the pettiness, cowardice, vile passions, acts of treason, and sins that try to tear the fatherland apart. After passing through the battlefields, "thousands of men can return to Spain turned into thousands of courageous men, into thousands of men who fulfil their duty, into thousands of good and strong men, into thousands of men who will revitalize history and the future" ("Bienvenida" 1). Furthermore, he views the Rif War as a great opportunity to regenerate the country, a "measure of our strength" at home and abroad. For all these reasons, it would be a pity if war, with all its cruelty, were to disappear ("En la posición" 1). In consequence with such a notion of war, Sánchez Mazas viciously attacks those journalists who spread humanitarian and pacifist ideals, which are, in his view, by-products of Marxism ("Sensibilidad" 1). What pacifism strives for is nothing else than "a banal world, a world without free will, a world without punishment and rewards, a world without pain and, ultimately, a world without finality" (1). By contrast, the Christian theory of war is "more spiritual, more ennobling of humankind" (1).[78]

The purification of the race and the regeneration of the fatherland take place in a territory that has in Sánchez Mazas's chronicles the same ambiguity that we have seen in other texts explored in this chapter. Morocco is both a foreign and national territory. "One of the most profound and reaffirmed feelings that I have in the Rif," says the writer, "is that this land – with its Moors and Berber villages – looks just like any other province of the kingdom [Spain] ... A sort of recondite voice tells me that all this can belong only to Spain" ("Vuelven I" 1). But Sánchez Mazas does not limit himself to interpreting the purifying function of the heterotopic space in his articles. In addition, he inscribes this function into the very fabric of the text at two different levels. First of all, his provocative, quarrelsome, insulting language brings the war and its purifying force to the written discourse.[79] In the second place, Sánchez Mazas's violent text transfers the brutality of the battlefield to the intellectual and political life of the Peninsula, thus performing an action akin to the brutalization of German politics after the First World War.[80] His vicious attack against Spanish intellectuals and writers is one example among many ("Intermedio" 1). For him, the silence of some writers is much worse than some intellectuals' opposition to the war. He finds it rather odd that writers who fight each other for literary matters, "musical fussing," or "literary whims" now keep quiet. For this reason, they make up a useless, invalid squad. "When an organization of cultural implements is of no use for all the occasions of the national life," points out the author rather ominously, one has to conclude that it is "something useless, a waste" ("Intermedio" 1).

A fundamental element of this discursive strategy resides in the unconditional and virulent defence of the military and its performance during the Disaster of Annual (he even exonerates General Berenguer, high commissioner of Spain in the protectorate and commander-in-chief of the colonial army in 1921, of any responsibility in the debacle ["La impresión genuina" 1; "La toma de Atlaten" 1]).[81] Most politicians, "the Republicans, socialists or whatever they are," have no idea whatsoever about colonial issues; they cannot pass judgment because they lack knowledge and experience ("La furia" 1). The lowest-ranking staff officer has a better discernment of the war than any of "those unintelligent and plebeian bellowers" who criticize from the parliament or the press the way the army is conducting the war (1). The loss of lives on the battlefield is not the result of wrong military tactics, or of a lack of strategic planning. "What causes more loss of lives ... is the cowardice ... the doubting and hesitation of those who are above and below" ("Empezamos" 1). The troops have been wounded "from behind, wounded by Spaniards, wounded by treachery perpetrated by imbecile tongues"

("La sed" 1). All the attacks against the army's performance are no more than deliberate calumnies and distortions ("La sed" 1), and the campaign would run much more smoothly "if it were not ruined from the social and political cowardice and treachery coming from the Peninsula" ("Intermedio" 1). With these statements, Sánchez Mazas reiterates what constituted a central topos of the Nazi propaganda: the *Dolchstoßlegende* (myth of the stab in the back).

In "La campaña de África," Sánchez Mazas, who repeatedly boasts of his preference for dictatorial regimes (e.g., "Interrogaciones" 1; "María" 1), proposes a very specific program of endo-colonial action: the projection of the war and the colonization of Morocco into the Peninsula in order to "regenerate" Spain. According to him, it is necessary to organize "to the finish" a sanitary moral front in charge of keeping watch on "all the opinions that might cause damage [to Spain]" ("La Legión" 1) as well as to create a spiritual army that will go back to Spain to annihilate the traitors and the cowards ("Hacia Atlaten" 1).[82] Morocco plays a crucial role in the formation of this spiritual army. There, the soldiers learn the "beautiful technique of pacifying the roads and sweeping the mountains with fire," a technique that needs to be applied later to the Peninsula without leniency ("Hacia Atlaten" 1). The colonizing enterprise should have two objectives: first to colonize Morocco, and then to colonize Spain. Sánchez Mazas, who on several occasions praises civil wars (e.g., "Los que se van" 1), articulates this double operation through a trope: the comparison between the harkas of the Berber tribes and what he calls in several of his articles the parliamentary, journalistic, and working-class harkas, which are parts of the "uncivilized" front. In his chronicle "Empezamos o acabamos," he expresses this idea with the utmost clarity. It is worthwhile quoting this paragraph at length because of the reverberations from it on the subsequent history of Spain:

> This rebel parliamentary and journalistic harka is very similar to the harkas of the tribes of Beni Urriaguel and Gomara.... The harkas resemble each other in every aspect. They are both cruel enemies who martyr [others], profane the unburied dead, are ready to flee ... one moment [they are] unified, the next they are shooting at each other for the First or the Second International. It is a bad idea to wound or to corner them, just as it is with the Moors. It is better to build for them a 'silver bridge ...' Sometimes I wonder if in Spain they are not an African backwardness of our race that brings to the moral world the same tactics used by the snipers in the rugged Rif. (1)

Both the parliament and the editorial departments of the newspapers are full of moral and political harkas, banditry, and piracy. Sánchez Mazas concludes that in Spain there is only one civil war, which extends from the shores of the Nervión to the shores of the Muluya ("Una mañana" 1). He even considers that instead of focusing first on the Moroccans, it would be better to begin with the Spanish politicians opposed to the war, "to colonize them" and establish "a protectorate controlling their Kabyle of dumbness in order to free them from their confusion and lack of education" ("La furia" 1). In another chronicle, Sánchez Mazas pens the following sinister paragraph: "In the Rif we will learn how to sweep the harka. We are already being successful thanks to the new machine guns. Let's see if we are as successful with our old brooms in the second phase. And those of us who have not been courageous enough to join the Foreign Legion will perform an act of bravery with regard to the rubbish that is threatening Spain. And leaving behind the words that we have loved all our lives, we will make a special sacrifice of the stomach, we will have to come together as a legion of hygiene, as voluntary road sweepers of the rabble" ("Interrogaciones" 1).

And he (accurately) predicts,

It is likely that in view of the unpopularity that has been created in certain places towards the campaign, in view of the continuing presence of thousands of bourgeois young men in Africa, and in view of the leftist activity that courts fear … the tension of certain conservative classes will give in, the Spanish environment will demoralize, the economic situation will worsen. Then working-class harkas, the opposition, pacifists, revolutionaries will rise in the capitals of the provinces and in the Puerta del Sol … Then they will loudly demand an arrangement. Thousands of those seeking only their own interests will emerge … And they will ask for Berengueres and for personal powers and dictatorship, as always … We could follow such a path that moves the African front to the Royal Palace. ("Interrogaciones" 1)

To a certain extent, one could argue that Sánchez Mazas is anticipating a phenomenon that, according to Paul Virilio, took place in advanced societies after the Second World War. For Virilio, the growing influence of the military in civil society has to be understood in conjunction with the decolonization that began after the war. According to Virilio, without a place for manoeuvring both their equipment and their whole apparatus, "the military disseminated into the civil state until it captured it entirely, thus recreating at home the para-civilian conditions characteristic of colonial society" (*L'Insécurité* 154).[83] Spain, the first modern imperial country to lose its empire, was also the first to convert its colonialism into an endo-colonial military and political praxis. Some sectors of the hegemonic class and of the military redirected their tactics and strategies of colonial control towards the civil society of the Peninsula. In due time, this new direction produced new spatial relationships and meanings. Sánchez Mazas's chronicles calling for the military, moral, and political colonization of Spain have to be understood within this context. "La campaña de África" is, most certainly, a tropological striation of Morocco and the expression of a fascist habitus forged within the interstices of the dual space, constituted by a heterotopic territory and a military geometry. It is, too, a passionate utterance produced to affect the feelings, thoughts, and actions of its readers. But we also have to see Sánchez Mazas's forging of a fascist habitus as well as his endo-colonial attitude as primitive discursive forerunners to a wider, more threatening, and immediate phenomenon – a phenomenon of which Dwight D. Eisenhower warned in his final televised Address to the Nation (17 January 1961) as president of the United States: the political and economic hegemony of the military-industrial complex in the civilian life of advanced societies.

Chapter Three

Spatial Myths

Fascist Journeys

Six months after his return from Morocco, Rafael Sánchez Mazas set off for Italy as the foreign correspondent for *ABC* in Rome. His career as journalist seemed to be on the right track. To work for *ABC*, a prestigious conservative newspaper with one of the highest circulations in Spain, represented a conspicuous recognition of his literary talent, while the assignment enhanced the young writer's visibility within the Spanish literary field. Perhaps more decisively, it put him in close contact with events, ideas, people, and places that greatly contributed to the ripening of his ideology. Appointed cultural attaché to the Spanish Embassy after his arrival in Rome, through his diplomatic position Sánchez Mazas would have the chance to meet Italian diplomats, politicians, and intellectuals. The seven years spent in Italy (in 1929 Sánchez Mazas returned to Spain, where he wrote chronicles for *ABC*, *El Sol*, and *El pueblo vasco*) proved to be decisive in his life. In a sense, he was the right man in the right place at the right time twice over. First, reporting from Melilla on a brutalized colonial war configured his fascist habitus. Second, the seven-year sojourn in Italy contributed to the full maturity of that habitus by providing it with an articulated, self-conscious intellectual foundation. Between 1922 and 1929, Sánchez Mazas witnessed events that reverberated throughout Europe: the Fascists' March on Rome in late October 1922 (only four months after his arrival in Italy), the Matteotti Crisis of June 1924 to January 1925, which ended when Mussolini peremptorily announced the dictatorship to the Chamber of Deputies on 3 January 1925, the steady consolidation of Fascist rule and culture, and the Fascist production of places and spatial relationships through rituals and public works. He did not take long to fall under the spell of Fascism, some of whose tenets coincided with ideas that he had vigorously expressed in his series "La campaña de África": an unforgiving opposition to Marxism, liberalism, and parliamentary democracy; an imperialist drive; a radical authoritarian nationalism; a discourse on national regeneration and on the "people's community"; a political dynamism and existential vitalism; and the consideration of war as a cleansing experience for both the individual and the nation. He familiarized readers of *ABC* with Fascist politics, ideas, and actions through articles such as "Roma la vieja y Castilla la Nueva" (21 June 1922), "La victoria fascista y la marcha sobre Roma" (15 November 1922), "El Imperio o la muerte" (30 June 1923), "El Directorio militar a la luz romana" (10 October 1923), and "Maura, el fascismo y la ilusión nacional" (25 December 1925). Sánchez Mazas did not completely stay out of the upheavals. His professional obligations and diplomatic status helped him get acquainted with leading fascist politicians. Among Sánchez Mazas's ties with Italy's political elite stands out his friendship with Luigi Federzoni, founder of the Associazione Nazionalista Italiana, journalist, novelist, art critic, three-time minister of Mussolini's government between 1923 and 1928, director of the journal *L'idea nazionale,* member of the Grand Council, and one of the leaders of the "moderate" wing of the Partito Nazionale Fascista in spite of his virulent, almost genocidal racism.[1] Back in Madrid in 1929, Sánchez Mazas was a new man.[2]

Ernesto Giménez Caballero undertook an uncannily similar journey of self-discovery. As will be remembered, he had absorbed a fascist habitus during his military service in Morocco. Shortly after the 1923 military coup d'état led by General Primo de Rivera, Giménez Caballero went off to the University of Strasbourg as a reader in Spanish language and literature, a consequential move in his life, for in Strasbourg he would meet his future wife, the Italian consul's sister, Edith Sironi Negri, a young lady who introduced Giménez Caballero to Italy's cultural and political circles. Already a writer and active cultural impresario of note, notwithstanding his youth, in 1928 Giménez Caballero upon invitation toured several European universities, a professional trip that crucially ended in Rome. Like Sánchez Mazas's stay in Rome, Giménez Caballero's visit to the Eternal City would be a momentous event, as the writer himself acknowledged in *Circuito imperial* (1929) and, further, in *Genio de España* (1932).[3] By the end of the 1920s, the Fascists had attained not only complete political control of Italy; they also had carried out policies that seemed to have unified and reinvigorated a politically divided

country demoralized by the Great War and its outcome (e.g., the huge
human cost of a war conducted with criminal incompetence, skyrocket-
ing unemployment, strikes, social unrest, peasant seizure of land, factory
occupations by workers). The overbearing, omnipresent, always-right
Duce implemented social and economic reforms under the opportunistic, approving gaze of industrialists and landowners and undertook
public works on a great scale; in doing so, he had apparently accomplished what no other Italian leader had hitherto been able to do. Not a
few foreign politicians, intellectuals, journalists, businessmen, and social
observers hailed the Duce's energetic, expeditious, decisive way of doing politics. Arriving in a city revitalized so as to make it the centre of a
new Roman Empire after years of being second to buoyant, modern, industrial urban centres like Milan and Turin (Bosworth 14–17) made an
impression on Giménez Caballero. In Italy he befriended, among other
prominent Fascist intellectuals, Giuseppe Bottai (an occasional poet regarded as the "intellectual" of the movement, founding editor of the
journal *Critica fascista*, and deputy secretary of the Corporations), Curzio
Malaparte (a self-consciously eccentric theoretician of Fascist activism
who cut a dashing figure, editor of the journal *La Conquista dello Stato*,
and one of the most brilliant, controversial, fascinating Fascist writers),
and Massimo Bontempelli (an influential poet, novelist, and critic, for a
time secretary of the Fascist Writers' Union).

From the brutalized Rif War to Italy's booming Fascism, from the rugged northern Maghreb to modern and cosmopolitan Rome, from a colonial territory impregnated by a murderous military ethos and a fascist
habitus to the first country ruled by fascism: these are the points of departure and arrival of what to Sánchez Mazas and Giménez Caballero constituted a fascist journey that would have an impact on Spanish culture
and politics, for both personal trips ushered in a fascist topography in
the two senses of the word analysed in the introduction and in chapter 1.
Their stay in Morocco and Italy ultimately entailed transferal of the fascist
ideology and habitus into Spain through symbolic products (journalistic
articles, lectures, books of essays) and their political activism as first-hour
members of Falange Española. To phrase it differently, a personal, formative voyage abroad meant bringing home a habitus and an ideology as
well as the purpose to impose them onto Spanish political, cultural, and
social life. A trip – this most basic technology for the production of space
– effected the objective to produce space on a national scale.

To be sure, Sánchez Mazas and Giménez Caballero did not act alone in
the task of circulating the fascist ideology in Spain during the 1920s. On

7 November 1922, José María Salaverría had already published in *ABC* "El fascio y España," in 1923 appeared Vicente Clavel's *El fascismo: Ideario de Benito Mussolini*, and one year later Francesc Cambó, the tycoon of Catalan right-wing nationalism, published a collection of journalistic articles under the title *Entorn del feixisme italià: Meditacions i comentaris sobre problemes de política contemporània* (Spanish trans.: *En torno al fascismo italiano* [1925]). Cambó's book became as influential as Juan Chabás's *Italia fascista (Política y cultura)* (1928).[4] But more decisive than this otherwise necessary circulation of ideas, let us insist, would be Sánchez Mazas and Giménez Caballero's itinerary and the subsequent involvement of both intellectuals in the adaptation of Italian Fascism into the Spanish political, social, and cultural arena. From the early 1930s onwards, Giménez Caballero, Sánchez Mazas, as well as other leading intellectuals and politicians, such as Ramiro Ledesma Ramos, Onésimo Redondo, José Antonio Primo de Rivera, Julio Ruiz de Alda, Eugenio Montes, Agustín de Foxá, José María Alfaro, Luys Santa Marina, and Dionisio Ridruejo endeavoured to elaborate a *mythology of space* with the aim of prescribing a fascist habitus and ideology.[5]

The fascist habitus forged in Morocco, embodied by the Legion, but shared also by some intellectuals, colonial administrators, and politicians, together with the divulgation in the Peninsula of Italian Fascism during the same years and, of course, a set of local political, economic, and social determinants brought about the conditions of possibility for the appearance of the first fascist organizations in Spain. In early 1931, Ramiro Ledesma Ramos, alongside Giménez Caballero and a handful of collaborators, launched La Conquista del Estado, the first fascist organization proper, in addition to a boisterous weekly named after the organization.[6] A political manifesto, "Nuestro manifiesto político," appeared in the first issue of *La Conquista del Estado* (14 March 1931) with an evident fascist flavor, propounding the absolute supremacy of the state, elitism, the provinces as the country's prime reality, the creation of civilian militias, direct action as the most effective way to take over the state, and the embrace of politics with a "military sense of responsibility and struggle" (Ledesma Ramos, *Escritos* 45–8). In the summer of 1931, with a few friends and supporters, Onésimo Redondo, a civil servant, tireless reader like Ledesma Ramos, devoted Catholic, and notorious anti-Semite created in Valladolid a racist and radical nationalist weekly called somewhat incongruously *Libertad*, its first issue appearing on 13 June 1931.[7] In August, they founded the Juntas Castellanas de Actuación Hispánica.[8] Both La Conquista del Estado and the Juntas Castellanas de Actuación Hispánica were tiny, virtually insignificant groups, when compared with the rest of the political parties in Spain. For this reason, in October 1931 they merged into a new organization, the Juntas de Ofensiva Nacional-Sindicalista (JONS).[9] Two years later, Manuel Delgado Barreto edited *El Fascio: Haz Hispano*, featuring articles by Ramiro Ledesma, José Antonio Primo de Rivera, Ernesto Giménez Caballero, Rafael Sánchez Mazas, and Juan Aparicio. The first issue (16 March 1933) would also be the last: the Republican government confiscated all copies and prohibited its further publication; nevertheless, *El Fascio* enjoyed a remarkable press run.

In the summer of 1933, Primo de Rivera, Julio Ruiz de Alda, and Alfonso García Valdecasas founded the Movimiento Sindicalista Español (MES), and a few months later they launched a new party. To introduce the new political project to the public with flair, they organized a public event – to which the *jonsistas*, or members of the JONS, were invited – at the Teatro de la Comedia in Madrid on 29 October 1933. Well-organized, strategically scheduled for a Sunday, broadcast over the radio, the foundational act of the new party turned out to be a huge success (the organizers having assembled a full house of two thousand people) that soon would acquire a mythical aura within fascist circles. On 2 November 1933, the movement was given a suitable name, Falange Española (FE). One month later, on 7 December 1933, FE published the first issue of its mouthpiece, the weekly *F.E.* The JONS, burdened with a very low membership and limited funding – when existent – called a meeting of its Consejo Nacional to consider the merger with Falange Española, which took place on 11 February 1934. Predictably, both movements fused, thereby creating the political party Falange Española de las Juntas de Ofensiva Nacional-Sindicalista (FE de las JONS), whose political doctrine would be condensed in "Los 27 puntos del Programa de Falange Española de las JONS." Until the civil war, FE-JONS would never enjoy a large membership nor have a significant role in Spanish politics. At the end of 1934, it had around five thousand members, and in the general elections of February 1936 it garnered forty thousand votes, that is, a sorry 0.7% of the popular vote. Had it not been for the war, Falange might have plunged into oblivion. The civil war affected FE-JONS in the same way that the aftershock of the 1929 crash did – as Evans argues in *The Coming of the Third Reich* – the National Socialists: it became the catalyst for acquiring prominence and, ultimately, hegemony.

The constellation of forces that determined the apparition of fascist political organizations in Spain, as well as FE-JONS's foundation, doc-

trine, political activities, practice of direct action, and involvement in
the civil war of 1936–9 have been widely studied.[10] Less attention has
been paid to a capital factor underpinning the ideology and habitus of
FE-JONS: the production of a mythology of space. There is little mention
of spatial myths in the few studies on the role played by myths in Spanish
fascism and in Francoism.[11] Although the scarcity of works devoted to
the fascist myths in Spain is consistent with the critical prioritization of
time over space, it is nonetheless surprising if one considers that the relevance of the myth in fascism has been frequently pointed out and studied by scholars specialized in other national fascisms.[12] In effect, one of
the most influential and innovative scholars in the field of fascist studies,
Robert Griffin, bases his own theory of fascism not on a common ideological component, but on a shared mythic core. In Griffin's definition,
"Fascism is a genus of political ideology whose mythic core in its various
permutations is a palingenetic form of populist ultra-nationalism" (*Nature* 26). As he writes elsewhere, this mythic core consists of the "vision
of the (perceived) crisis of the nation as betokening the birth-pangs of a
new order" (general introduction 3).

  In the following sections, I will focus on the fascist mythology of space
from the late 1910s through the 1950s. A crucial dynamo of the fascist
production of space, the mythology of space formed a grammar that,
underpinned by a politics of space, allowed for the production of space
in close association with the moulding, description, and prescription of
a habitus. As repeatedly observed, a habitus cannot be dissociated from
space. Lifestyles are rooted in specific loci, such as hometowns, regions,
countries, and institutions. A habitus may be described as the acting out
of the rules implied in a certain territory. As Bourdieu has observed, the
habitus is a network of acquired characteristics "which are the product
of social conditions and which, for that reason, may be totally or partially
common to people who have been the product of similar social conditions" ("Habitus" 45). Therefore, a spatial myth goes alongside a habitus.

  The myth and the processes that constructed it belong to a technology
of power and to the fascist aestheticization of politics. In the context of
fascism, myths have a variety of functions. They define and articulate the
history of a one-dimensional national community; insert the individual
into a narrative presented as both original and constitutive; underscore
fascism's anti-materialism and anti-rationalism; tint the nation with the
intangibility and prestige of god-like essences superior to everything
else; replace reason and analytic thinking with emotion and ritualism;
mobilize the citizens and turn them into mere members of a unified,

compact community;[13] help to formulate a nebulous political program; function as technologies of tropological striation; defend the interests and aspirations of the dominant classes; and impose a symbolic space that gives a ready-made meaning to material spatial practices, thereby limiting the individual's capacity to produce his or her own space. In Harvey's reading of the connections between myth, space, and politics, "The intangibles of myth and memory, morality, ethics, and rights, of affective loyalties to imagined communities and to places, do a great deal of work with far-reaching objective consequences in the dynamics of political struggle. Conceptual political battles fought in this immaterial realm become crucial" (*Cosmopolitanism* 163).[14]

In this chapter, I will explore three of the most important spatial myths of Spanish fascism: Castile, considered as the *ur-topia* of Spanish fascism and the point of departure for a new production of space; Rome, capital of Spanish fascism and centre of a totalitarian production of space; and the empire, understood mainly in two senses: what I call *endo-empire*, or the hegemonic power's empire over its own country, and *exo-empire*, that is to say, the imperial control, empiric and/or symbolic, over a network of foreign territories. As relational spaces that construe a space and time of their own in order to impose an absolute space (i.e., the "real" Spain), the three spatial myths are here considered as discrete entities that nonetheless acquire full meaning through their mutual relationships. In order to better understand these myths, it is important to analyse first the fascist habitus in the 1930s. Although the capacity of the habitus to produce space should not be overemphasized, its role within the production of space is significant nonetheless. David Harvey is basically right in his criticism of Lefebvre's interpretation of the connections between the three dimensions of the spatial triad. To argue, as Lefebvre does, that they are dialectical and not causally linked begs for clarity. Harvey claims that the habitus – as the human capacity limited by social and political constraints to engender products – constitutes the mediating link between the material spatial practices, the representations of spaces, and the spaces of representation (*Condition* 219). In this sense, the habitus may be considered the cement that binds the spatial myths of Castile, Rome, and the empire.

Habitus and Myth

To a degree, early fascism was a modus vivendi. Take, for instance, the Italian *fasci* between 1919 and 1922. To unify into a single, neat narrative the motives that led Roberto Farinacci, Italo Balbo, Dino Grandi, or the notorious thug Amerigo Dumini into becoming fascists is no easy task. Following a circuitous route, these men – destined to play a prominent role in Italian Fascism – opted at the beginning of their political careers "for a 'new politics' before that politics acquired the name Fascism" (Bosworth 143). Earnest ideals, as Bosworth (143) underscores, coexisted unproblematically with personal self-interest and a fondness for bullying and murder.[15] A similar story could be told about the members of the *Freikorps* and the first-hour Nazis studied in Theweleit's influential book. Not unlike the legionnaires in Spanish Morocco and the writers who praised the Legion's ethos, deeds, and creed, their lack of a coherent, articulated ideology was compensated largely by a common fascist habitus. In a book written shortly after being expelled from FE-JONS, Ledesma Ramos shrewdly noted, "The real mechanics of today's socio-political fights makes fascism the banner of a very complex net of unsatisfied, marginalized, and discontented people. Hence the multiform origin of its quotas, otherwise unanimous in their manifestation of a fighting spirit … which reveals that they are not life's residues, but rather fertile and very valuable groups" (*¿Fascismo?* 54).[16] These attitudes, ideas and objectives floated in the political atmosphere not only in connection with political organizations and parties; they were also ready to be picked up by any organization and individual; in Ledesma Ramos's own words, "Not only are there fascist individuals, groups, and organizations, but also, and perhaps to a greater degree, *fascistized* individuals, groups, and organizations" (55).[17] In the 1930s, together with the moulding and acting out of this habitus, the ideologues of La Conquista del Estado, JONS, the Juntas Castellanas de Actuación Hispánica, and FE-JONS set out to give shape to and spread the political doctrine associated with the label *fascism*.

The fascist habitus forged in Morocco lacked a specific political program. In order to effect change on the political and spatial practices, it required a self-conscious theoretical elaboration of the set of ideas and beliefs that reflected understandings of the social, cultural, economic, and political world. Without such theoretical formulation, at a fundamental level the legionnaire habitus is not substantially different from the habitus manifested by military personnel – and policymakers for that matter – who consider the inhabitants of occupied foreign territory as *Untermenschen* that can be kept in jail, tortured, or murdered at will. For this very reason, not only can the social analyst denominate as "fascist" the legionnaire habitus of the 1920s before the emergence of fascist parties. In addition, it is legitimate to consider as "fascist" the habitus acted out by armies occupying foreign countries *after* the demise of fascist regimes in 1945. While habitus are not necessarily associated with specific political programs, any habitus whose implicit purpose resides in the modification of social, political, and spatial relationships within a politically organized territory requires some sort of organization. None other than Adolf Hitler insisted on this phenomenon in the pages devoted in *Mein Kampf* to the *völkisch* movements. In Hitler's opinion, those movements needed to merge into a single political party if they wished to realize their ideals. The problem did not lie, therefore, in the ideology underpinning the *völkisch* habitus, but in the latter's lack of an adequate, effective political direction. This task was to be undertaken by the Nazi party, as Hitler himself asserted in *Mein Kampf* (362–3, 378–85).

In Spain, the relationship between habitus, ideology, and a totalitarian production of space was laid down by the first fascist political manifestos. Like other revolutionary movements (e.g., Bolshevism), La Conquista del Estado, the Juntas Castellanas de Actuación Hispánica, the JONS, and FE-JONS set out to alter spatial networks and connections by refining and trying to impose onto other citizens an existing habitus. Ramiro Ledesma Ramos, whose philosophical knowledge would never be matched by any other Spanish fascist during the 1930s, devoted considerable attention in his weekly *La Conquista del Estado* to the prescription of crucial characteristics of the fascist habitus, such as the discipline, courage, disposition to violent action, military ethos, and renunciation of one's own individuality. The pages of "En esta hora, decimos" (25 April 1931), "El individuo ha muerto" (23 May 1931), "Nuestras consignas: La movilización armada" (27 June 1931), and "Las Juntas de Ofensiva Nacional-Sindicalista: Nuestras consignas" (24 October 1931) attempt less to indoctrinate readers by providing them with a set of logically argued ideas than to prescribe a way of being and acting whose ultimate goal consists of the empirical realization of a particular notion of Spain. In the ephemeral *El Fascio: Haz Hispano* appeared "Conjunción y organización: Cómo ha de formarse el núcleo inicial del fascismo," devoted to the fascist habitus; it argues for the militarization of politics, elaborates on the discipline expected from the fascist, and displays an anti-individualist stance (5). In the same journal, Sánchez Mazas encourages readers to embrace "a discipline, a behaviour, a style, rather than a politics" ("Haz y yugo" 8). Similar sketchy descriptions/prescriptions of the fascist habitus can be found in articles published in *Libertad* by members of the Juntas Castellanas de Actuación Hispánica, such as Luciano de la Calzada's "Hacia la nueva España" (27 June 1931) and the anonymous "La conquista del Estado" (20 May 1935).

The most complete description of the fascist habitus would be formulated nonetheless by FE-JONS. Primo de Rivera's foundational speech of 29 October 1933 established, on the one hand, the tone further used by Falange and, on the other, the relationship between the overarching purpose to produce a new space, the elaboration of a mythology of space, and the constitution of a fascist habitus. For Primo de Rivera, the fatherland consists of a "total unity" in which all individuals, social classes, and groups are integrated (*Obras* 66). In order to achieve this ideal nation, the movement needs to create a "new man." "Our movement," Primo de Rivera stresses, would not be properly understood if it were perceived merely as a "way of thinking" (68). It is not, he categorically asserts, a way of thinking, but rather "a way of being." Consequently, "We must not only endeavour the construction of a political architecture. We must adopt, before the whole life, in each of our acts, a humane, profound, complete attitude. This attitude is the spirit of service and self-sacrifice, the aesthetic and military sense of life" (68). Displaying a characteristic fascist attitude, Primo de Rivera contemptuously looks down on the intellect while giving priority to the habitus, defined as the fusion of ascetics and militarism (68). Hence the "fascist man," a mixture of "monk and soldier," re-enacts the habitus of the religious military orders of the Middle Ages.[18] The pseudo-poetic language and style employed by Primo de Rivera to formulate the fascist habitus would be Falange's favoured means to prescribe it. The first-hour Falangists chose this means to affect people's thinking and actions. In part, this preference was due to the fact that some of Primo de Rivera's closest associates were writers (e.g., Eugenio Montes, Agustín de Foxá, Ernesto Giménez Caballero, Rafael Sánchez Mazas, Dionisio Ridruejo, José María Alfaro, Luys Santa Marina).[19]

In Falange Española's first political manifesto, the "Puntos iniciales" (*F.E.* [7 December 1933]; in Primo de Rivera, *Obras* 85–93), presumably drafted by Primo de Rivera himself, the fascist habitus is described systematically. Divided into nine sections, the manifesto starts with a definition of what Falange understood by "Spain" and ends up by specifying, in the section titled "La conducta," the path to be followed in order to realize the Falangists' notion of Spain. Thus the myth of Spain and the fascist habitus (the *conducta*) frame Falange's political doctrine. As stated in the "Puntos iniciales," Spain is not a mere empirical territory, or a sum of men and women, or a language, but a "unity of destiny in the universal," the basic goals of which consist of the permanence of its unity, the re-emergence of its inner vitality, and the participation with a pre-eminent voice in the world's spiritual enterprises ("Puntos" 6). Presupposing a totalitarian concept of both the nation and the state, the author proclaims the freedom of the individual, "bearer of eternal values," to be a function of the "basis for the people's coexistence" (6). True freedom can be reached only by people belonging to a strong, free nation built upon authority, hierarchy, and order. Accordingly, the individual's political status is justified inasmuch as he fulfils his function in the nation. Those willing to participate in the "crusade" to "re-conquer" Spain must be ready to serve and sacrifice themselves for the cause; they will have to consider life as "military service, discipline, and danger, self-denial and renunciation of all vanity, laziness, and slander. At the same time they will serve in a cheerful and sporting fashion" (7).[20]

The relevance given to topography for the consideration of political issues is further emphasized by the publication of three ideological maps of Spain in the same issue of *F.E.*, illustrating the essential interconnection between space and habitus on which the "Puntos iniciales" builds (see figure 3.1). These maps visualize the fundamental differences between three political models for Spain as well as the contrasts among the habitus underlying them. The first two maps portray what the Second Republic has allegedly brought to the country. In the first of them, the reader learns that Marxism has chained and blackened Spain, thus transforming the country into a wasteland. Marxism's allegedly inherent materialism and absolute lack of spirituality are represented in the muscled, bare-chested body of the man who symbolizes Marxism. The second map depicts one of the weaknesses attributed to liberalism, namely its support for the Catalan and Basque demands for political autonomy, perceived by the fascists as leading to secessionism and therefore to the "disintegration" of the country, a spatial myth, let us add, still employed in present-day Spanish right-wing politics (a more complete picture of the supposed causes of such "disintegration" in figure 3.2). Notice that on the second map, Catalonia and the Basque Country begin to rot as soon as they move away from Spain, as the black spots on the two regions seem to indicate. While the symbol of Marxism points to its "materialism," the bespectacled man reading a book *outside* the country's borders alludes to the prominence of intellectuals in the origin and development of the Republic, to their importation of "foreign" ideas, and finally, to the intellectuals' lack of real interest in the problems affecting Spain, thereby underscoring the fascist view of them as "foreign-

Figure 3.1 Spain according to Falange Española de las JONS. *F.E.*, 7 December 1933

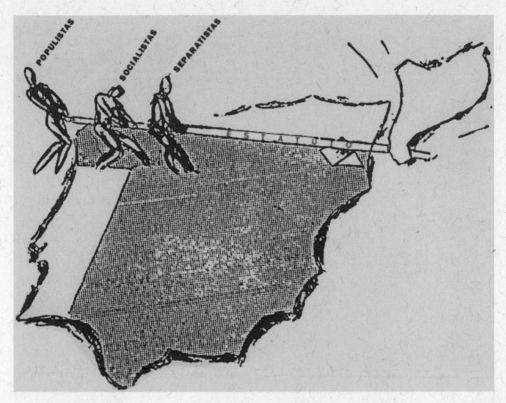

Figure 3.2 "Populists, socialists, separatists." *F.E.*, 5 July 1934

ers." In contrast with the first two maps, the third one represents the
idea of Spain defended by Falange Española in the "Puntos iniciales"
as well as the role prescribed for its citizens. Here, the man is neither
above (map 1) nor outside (map 2) Spain. By placing the body of this
fascist *behind* the country, the draftsman emphasizes the prescribed subordination of citizens to the nation and their equally prescribed support
of the objectives set by the state. The acronym *FE* on the background
conveys the idea that only one party can unite and articulate the country, thus representing the totalitarian, anti-democratic polity defended
by Falange, while the two only visible parts of the man's body represent
both the fascist ideology (the head) and habitus (the muscular arm ex-
ecuting the Roman salute).[21]

Two months after the founding of Falange Española, an anonymous article significantly titled "Hábito y estilo" was published in the third issue of *F.E.* (18 January 1934). From the outset, the new party took on the description and prescription of the fascist habitus, which, according to the author, entails two types of performativity. On the one hand, joining Falange Española ("our ranks," to quote the article's military language) means above all "to assert a way of being," and on the other, to give one's existence to the essence ("Hábito" 6). "To assert" implies "asserting the habitus," while "to give" conveys the phenomenological move of this habitus, that is to say, the bracketing of the natural world by the consciousness so as to directly and reflectively engage with and subordinate itself to the "essence." In the author's view, the subordination of the existence to the essence, to "the idea," demands a style, which is "acquired through a habit, an imitation, and a rhythm. This imitation and this rhythm ... tend to incessantly create and set a rite, a liturgy" (6). Four commands follow: (1) to subordinate the "way of living" to the "way of being" – to self-sacrifice; (2) to be in shape bodily and ethically, which means "to live in the religious ascesis of patriotism"; (3) to acquire "habits" through imitation of the best models; and (4) to convince oneself that a "grand style" can be achieved only "by force of renunciations" (6). "Individual style," however, does not suffice, for style, in its noblest, most civilized, and universal sense does not belong to the individual, but to the community (6–7). The author's call to his readers is consequential with this subordination of the habitus to the fatherland: "Engrave in yourselves in the same image of indescribable beauty: the Fatherland's face" (7). By being aware of this subordination as well as of the country's decadence, the individual will help Spain regain "its way of being, its grand style ... our whole movement must be a way of being, the style of future Spain, the perfect, legitimate, unmistakable homogeneous evolution of a great Spain" (Hábito" 7); such "style of the nation" is composed of a religious and patriotic spirit on the one hand, and of a military order on the other.

The FE-JONS political program, written immediately after the first Consejo Nacional de Falange Española (4–6 October 1934), expands upon those ideas on the nation and the habitus, with the addition of a few nuances. As stated in the program, individual and class interests must "inexorably yield" to the nation's strengthening and greater glory ("Los 27 puntos" 3), separatism is a crime (4), Falange has a "will-to-empire" (4), the state is a totalitarian tool at the service of the fatherland's integrity (5), true freedom exists only insofar as the individual belongs to a strong nation (5), a strict discipline will hinder "any attempt to poison, to divide the Spaniards, or to influence them against the Fatherland's destiny" (5), discipline will be attained though education (10), and finally, FE-JONS "wants a new order.... Its style will prefer what is direct, passionate, and combative. Life is military service, and must be lived with a true spirit of service and self-sacrifice" (11). In addition to "Los 27 puntos" and the previously studied manifestos and programmatic texts, some articles deal with specific components of the fascist habitus. Keen as always to describe the "new man," *F.E.* published several journalistic pieces on the topic: "Sacrificio" (11 January 1934: on the fascist's self-sacrifice and renunciation to his personal freedom), "Dar" (8 February 1934: on the individual's abnegation to the cause), "Compostura y orgullo" (8 February 1934: on the fascist's military stance), "Renunciar" (8 February 1934: on the individual's renunciation of superfluous matters for the sake of the fatherland), "Sobriedad" (8 February 1934: on the personal sobriety in deeds and words), "Disciplina" (18 January 1934: on the fascist's discipline to the party), and "Moral de la falange clásica" (25 January 1934: on order, discipline, and prompt action).[22] An anonymous article titled "Reconquista" published in *Libertad* on 6 May 1935 condenses the close link between fascist habitus and space: "Whatever does not further the ceaseless struggle for a resolutely intransigent reconquest of a free Spain," claims the author, "lives with the Nation's enemies and consolidates its ruin" (6). In this new "War of Reconquest," not only must "the noxious freedom of the inner enemies die, but also … the freedom of the new soldier. Those who enlist in the campaign to free the Fatherland … must voluntarily put their freedom at the service of Spain. In this voluntary immolation of freedom, of one's self … lies what is distinctive about the new politics … The conqueror of our time … must offer his life to the nation" (6). This was the habitus that articulated the different levels of the production of space and its elements, among them the spatial myths.[23]

Castile, or the Ur-topia

Castile, a myth cherished by some sectors of Spanish fascism, was understood by many fascists as the cradle of the conquest of the Americas as well as the repository of Spain's "essence." The fascists did not invent the myth of Castile. Similarly to the National Socialists' adoption of the pre-existing *völkisch* ideals and the Fascists' use of the *romanità*, they shaped a vision of Castile developed by the nineteenth-century nationalistic historiography and consolidated by prominent turn-of-the-century writers.[24]

Although Sánchez Mazas already had written on the subject of Castile with fascist undertones in "Roma la vieja y Castilla la Nueva" (*ABC* [21 June 1922]), the fascist version of the myth originates in the writings of Onésimo Redondo and his group of collaborators. Born in 1905 in Quintanilla de Abajo – a small town near Valladolid – to a conservative Catholic family of small landowners, Onésimo Redondo received his law degree in 1926 and worked as secretary of the Sindicato de Cultivadores de Remolacha de Castilla la Vieja in 1928. Cardinal points of Redondo's ideology are a radical nationalism, an uncompromising defence of rural society, an ethical and metaphysical approach to economic issues, and a strict Catholicism. An event in his life greatly contributed to configure these elements into a fascist ideology and habitus: his sojourn in Mannheim, where he worked as an assistant in Spanish language courses in the School of Commerce at the University of Mannheim between June 1927 and August 1928. A man of his strong nationalistic convictions could not fail to observe the growth of the NSDAP, whose membership increased exponentially during 1925–9 from 25,000 to 180,000 while its organizational system of district leaders spread steadily throughout Germany. The second volume of Hitler's *Mein Kampf* appeared in 1927. Furthermore, the twenty-five-point program of the NSDAP publicly presented on 24 February 1920 was declared immutable at the party's Bamberg Conference on 14 February 1926. In this conference, Hitler imposed his claim to the absolute leadership of the NSDAP over strongmen of the party, particularly Gregor Strasser – eventually murdered on 30 June 1934 under Hitler's order in the Röhm purge. Of the different tenets of the NSDAP's doctrine, its *völkisch* component, discussed by Hitler himself in *Mein Kampf* (362–3, 378–85, 383, 448, 452–3, 458, 460–2), probably left the deepest imprint on Redondo's thinking. Certainly, the Nazis were not alone in defending *völkisch* ideas; they simply gave political expression to a world view deeply ingrained in large segments of German society. Impelled by a "hunger for wholeness,"[25] the conservative Deutschnationale Volkspartei, veterans' organizations such as the Stahlhelm, the white-collar union Deutschnationale Handelsgehilfen Verband, and student associations (the *Bünde*) all shared a *völkisch* thinking voiced time and again in newspapers, essays, and books published in the 1920s.[26] Redondo might have read or been acquainted with known representatives of *völkisch* literature, like Paul Bang's *Judas Schuldbuch* (1919), Arthur Moeller van den Bruck's *Das Dritte Reich* (1923), and Hans Grimm's novel *Volk ohne Raum* (1926). Back in Spain, Redondo would soon conflate the myth of Castile with the *völkisch* philosophy. *Völkisch* beliefs, such as the *Volk* as the union of a group of people with a transcendental essence; the intimate correspondence between the individual, the native soil, the *Volk*, and the universe; the spirit as an entity superior to the matter; the nature and soul of the *Volk* as determined by the native landscape; the struggle for national unity; the priority given to the state; and finally anti-materialism, anti-Semitism, and the rejection of modern civilization would mould and give new sense to the myth of Castile. The fusion of the myth and the *völkisch* ideals would turn the myth of Castile into a fascist myth. Redondo's trip to and stay in Germany constituted therefore yet another fascist journey.

Immediately after launching *Libertad*, Redondo and the Juntas Castellanas de Actuación Hispánica initiated an agrarian, folkish fascism in Spain.[27] Eventually, this modality of fascism would form an integral part of the FE-JONS program. On a general level, one priority of the Juntas Castellanas de Actuación Hispánica was its opposition to the Agrarian Reform Law (Ley de Bases de la Reforma Agraria) promulgated on 9 September 1932 and suppressed by the conservative government that ruled in 1934–6. The Valladolid group exhibited a classic fascist defence of the small landowner in the articles published in *Libertad*. For Redondo, the Republican agrarian reform means no less than the "persecution" of the landowners and, worst of all, the death of agriculture itself ("La agresión socialista a la agricultura" [13 July 1931]). The class struggle in Castile's towns, complains Redondo, represents a "crime" against the farmers' interests. In "La tierra" (10 December 1934), he mounts a harsh attack against the agrarian policies of what he contemptuously calls "social-communism." The territorial and agrarian problems are understood as a "historic mandate" for their generation to produce the "national soil" anew. This attack mounted against the Second Republic's Agrarian Reform Law follows the fault lines of a folkish defence of the moral, purifying virtues of the land in contrast to the city – the headquarters of all the evils brought about by modernity. This attitude is similar to the response to the "hunger for wholeness" in Germany in the 1920s. According to Peter Gay, these reactions turned out to be a great regression born from a great fear – the fear of modernity: "The hunger for wholeness," concludes Gay, "was awash with hate; the political ... world of its chief spokesmen was a paranoid world, filled with enemies: the dehumanizing machine, capitalist materialism, godless rationalism, rootless society, cosmopolitan Jews, and that great-devouring monster, the city" (93). The opposition between the city and the countryside is further conveyed in Javier M. de Bedoya's "Miremos hacia el campo" (16 April

1934). A view to which many Nazis would subscribe is Bedoya's belief that cities are both Marxist *and* capitalist loci. The city – corrupted, frivolous, materialistic, desired by many for its material comforts – has been incapable of teaching the people to "feel" the fatherland; in the cities, "the love of Spain" (*el españolismo*) does not beat vigorously. For Bedoya, the members of FE-JONS have not succumbed to the charms and unholy idols of the cities, which conceal "all kinds of putrefaction and destitution." Longing for a "great Spain," the fascists place themselves at the service of Castile and its peasants. Everything hated by the fascists – liberalism, parliamentary democracy, capitalism – merits the applause of the cities. At the same time, all they love and admire – austerity, discipline, small capital, temperance, and sense of honour – "lives and has value in the country." In conclusion, "The Castilian peasants' moral fortitude is nowadays the only thing that can save our Fatherland. The revolutionary energy needed to build a new Spain will not be found in city dwellers. Rather, it will be found in the towns of Castile." For this reason, the "national" youth looks only at the countryside, the rural life – Castile. An even starker negative portrayal of the cities' evils resides in another *Libertad* folkish article, Nemesio García Pérez's "Contra la ciudad" (11 March 1935). Urban life, maintains the author, "corrupts the race's vitality with the poison emanating from easy culture … or from nihilism." In contrast to such corruption, the countryside purifies life, which it keeps free from any foreign barbarian mixture by means of faith, work, personal sacrifice, and Spain's "eternal spirit." Worthy of notice is the author's fear of contamination. Alien invading elements are pernicious for the "people's community" and must therefore be eliminated, lest the nation's eternal essence be degraded. This fear applies to the cultural and literary life, too. Tacitly claiming that modern literature must be avoided, García Pérez asserts in quite a folkish tone, "For the good ordering of life, our sayings' honest and heartfelt philosophy suffices us … as concerns literature, we have the old wives' tales … and regarding the aesthetic feelings, there is the beauty emanating from our folk songs … and all this together with the fields' solemnity, a reflection of God's marvellous immensity." Spain lies here, not in the cities.[28]

The fear of the "weaker 'other'" lurking everywhere in readiness to contaminate and ultimately destroy Spain's essence and territorial unity is related to the anti-Semitism of several members of the Juntas Castellanas de Actuación Hispánica, above all Onésimo Redondo.[29] Many of Redondo's articles exude anti-Semitism.[30] In February–July 1932, he published in *Libertad* a serialized abridged Spanish translation of Roger de Lambelin's French version of the *Protocols of the Learned Men of Zion*. In 1934, that translation would be reissued as a short book.[31] Redondo's anti-Semitism should be understood as a tool to oppose what Redondo and many fascists considered the evils par excellence threatening the very existence of Spain: Marxism, liberalism, and capitalism. Considering the acknowledged absence of Jews in Spain at the time (one even wonders how many Jews Redondo ever came across), his anti-Semitism may appear to be a nonsensical stance; yet the Jew does make sense in Redondo's fascism, for he represents the altogether "other" who embodies a race, a religious belief, but more decisively, everything alien to the "people's community." For Redondo, the Jew symbolizes any enemy of Spain.

This was a view shared by many coeval Spanish rightists. Laid down in modern times by the count of Gobineau, Édouard Drumont, Houston Stewart Chamberlain, and turn-of-the-century Austrian and German intellectual quacks like Guido von List, Lanz von Liebenfels, and Arthur Trebitsch, the myth of the "Jew" as the embodiment of the enemy found a politically organized framework in the 1930s. During the Second Republic, most of the anti-democratic political forces circulated anti-Semitic propaganda as part of the vicious campaign launched by the Catholic Church, some sectors of the armed forces, and right-wing political parties against the Republican government. "Theorists of the extermination" – in Preston's graphic words (*Spanish Holocaust* 34–51) – like the priest Juan Tusquets, Father Aniceto de Castro Albarrán and the lay theologian Marcial Solana wrote books, articles and sermons that disseminated the idea that there was a Jewish-Masonic-Bolshevik plot to destroy Spain and the rest of the Christian world. The political left had thus to be annihilated at all costs. Notwithstanding the lack of a significant Jewish population in Spain, everyone was familiar with the popular image of the Jew as the killer of God, as a sinister, demonic figure who represented the epitome of evil and the so-called anti-Spain. "For the Spanish extreme right," says Preston, "the Second Republic was an outpost of the Elders of Zion" (*Spanish Holocaust* 42).

Onésimo Redondo's anti-Semitism is at the core of his folkish fascism. "The survival of Spain as a nation," affirms Redondo, "is seriously threatened by the foreign press, published in the Republic's territory … the publications of a Jewish kind share the task by dividing it into two activities. One tends to inflame a civil war with its campaigns of extreme political hatred. The other wants to destroy the youth by making it a victim of stupefying pornography" ("Los enemigos de España" [27 June 1931]).

Again, the answer lies in the countryside, or, to be precise, in Castile. As he says further, Castile "is destined to rise up, on the Fatherland's behalf, against that invasion … clandestinely organized with foreign money." In "La revolución hispánica" (13 July 1931), he explains why the Spanish people are, together with the Japanese, the only ones who can oppose the hegemony of capitalism and communism. The Spanish people conform to a cultivated community that is not intoxicated by the "Jewish" ideas disseminated in Western civilization. In Redondo's opinion, being paradoxically the most Semite people in Europe enables the Spaniards to reject and expel the Jewish ideas and mentality that have eaten up their country. Both capitalism and Marxism belong to that group: "The great figures of capitalism and socialism are Jews." But in order to purify the country from these excrescences, the "people's community" needs a leading figure, a leader capable of taking up the "collective ideal dwelling in our people's subconsciousness." Equally fundamental is the undertaking of a crusade with the ultimate goal of giving Spain a leading role "in the spiritual forces defending the Mediterranean culture." One sentence condenses the fascist's fear of the weakling as well as the unforgiving violence needed for his extermination: "If it is necessary to do it, we will crush the weak, the timorous, and the traitors."

Focusing on Castile once and again from a folkish stance, these writings produced a space of spaces, or, to be more precise, what I call *ur-topia*, that is, an originary utopia out of which other utopias spring. In Spanish fascism, Castile constitutes a mythical source, an overarching mythical space that to a great extent underpins the fascist myths of Rome and the empire. The mythologization of Imperial Rome and the Spanish empire in the Americas, the Philippines, and several European territories would make little sense without Castile. The Juntas Castellanas de Actuación Hispánica's pervasive insistence in Castile as the point of departure for a "Hispanic" fascist world view and revolution – which is precisely one of the meanings of the expression "actuación hispánica" – points in this direction. Onésimo Redondo was adamant about the ur-topian nature of Castile. In this respect, of his articles published in *Libertad* stand out "La misión de Castilla" (3 August 1931), "¡Castilla, salva a España!" (10 August 1931), and "A España, por Castilla" (20 November 1933). While Catalonia's goal – so proclaims Redondo in "La misión de Castilla" – resides in achieving its independence, Castile is the only region that feels "responsibility" towards Spain. Basing his discourse on a rather pervasive antagonism, Redondo argues with a barely veiled threat against Catalans' presumed separatism, which, if successful, will amount, according to him, to the destruction of Spain's unity. If Catalonia is granted a Statute of Autonomy, Castile will have no other option than to take up arms against the politicians who have made that "historic crime" possible, namely those who support a referendum in Catalonia that would "break up" Spain (Redondo, "La misión de Castilla"). In sum, Castile's mission is to save Spain and "to drown all the traitors, regardless of whether they are journalists, members of the parliament, kings, or ministers."[32] Likewise, "¡Castilla, salva a España!" is a folkish manifesto encouraging Castilians to rebel against "socialist parliamentarianism." The article "A España, por Castilla" expands upon precisely that idea. The "masonic-Marxist" revolution is addressed, so believes the author, against Castile. If Castile dies, so does Spain. The immanent and necessary source of Spanishness resides in Castile: to redeem Castile amounts "to defend[ing] the Spanish people." The redemption must be first of all economic, basically because "Castile's economic servitude is the necessary cause of its spirit's decadence."[33]

In a country predominantly agrarian, as Spain was in the 1930s, it was only logical that FE-JONS sought the support of peasants and farmers, an attitude visible in essays published in *El Fascio* as well as in the main Falangist periodicals.[34] When just a few weeks after the foundation of Falange Española Primo de Rivera declared that the "real" Spain did not lie in parliament but in the "crags and rough terrain," he was thinking primarily in tactical terms. "We will go," Primo de Rivera maintains, "to those fields and towns of Spain to transform their desperation into an impetus. To incorporate them to an enterprise that belongs to everyone" (*Obras* 97). His speech of 30 May 1935 in Campo de Criptana is yet another instance of this tactical support of Castilian peasantry and of his embrace of the folkish ideals expressed in *Libertad* (in *Obras* 583–94). In a seminal speech delivered at the Teatro Calderón in Valladolid on 4 March 1934, quoted in chapter 1, Primo de Rivera had described Castile as an "absolute land" (*Obras* 189–90). For him, Castile's spatial absoluteness is the house of Spain's absolute being. Always more to the point and with characteristic logic, Ledesma Ramos already had written in the political manifesto in the first issue of *La Conquista del Estado*, "The foremost Spanish reality is the provinces, not Madrid" ("Nuestro manifiesto político" [14 March 1931]; in Ledesma Ramos, *Escritos* 46–7). Consequently, their first priority must be to unite and articulate them, "discovering its myths and sending them [the provinces] towards its conquest [of the myths]" (46–7). Notice Ledesma Ramos's awareness of the important role played by the myth in the articulation of political discourse and the manipulation of potential supporters. First, argues Ledesma Ramos, one has to find out the "myths" of the peasants, and only then proceed to their "conquest."[35] As he would claim two months later in "El Bloque Social Campesino" (*La Conquista del Estado* [13 June 1931], in *Escritos* 214–15), "It is necessary to mobilize, in a revolutionary fashion, the Spaniards from the countryside. To inject in them the notion of an armed protest, an eagerness for violence" (214).[36] Julio Ruiz de Alda, another of the founding fathers of Falange Española, thought along the same lines (e.g., "Tierra," *Arriba* [18 April 1935]). In José Simón Valdivieso's candid avowal, "If the peasant doesn't join our ranks, the national revolution won't be possible" ("El campesino de España estará con nosotros," *F.E.* [7 December 1933]).

On these grounds, it is no coincidence that six out of the twenty-seven points of Falange's program are devoted to land reform. And yet, there is little trace in them of a folkish ideology; instead, the authors focus on economic issues. Far more interesting are two articles that appeared anonymously in two periodicals of FE-JONS: "Agrarios" (*F.E.* [25 January 1934]) and "Esquema de una política de aldea" (*Arriba* [25 April 1935]). The first of them reveals Falange's assumption of the Juntas Castellanas de Actuación Hispánica's folkish ideology. In the anonymous author's opinion, the expression *agrarian issues* refers not only to the land proper. There is also a peasant culture and civilization that the party wishes to promote: "The essences of that great sense of family, religion ... and hierarchy upon which Europe's civilized order had its pillars have been corrupted by the cities." The countryside is what gives back to the nations "history's poetic intelligence, its great baptismal innocence for setting out again." The essay "Esquema de una política de aldea" assumes the Juntas Castellanas de Actuación Hispánica's folkish ideology while at the same time indicating the approach to follow in order to establish that world view in Spain. A "black colony" of the city, the land is a victim of urban and banking "gamblers" (1). Going beyond the economic criteria laid out in "Los 27 puntos," "Esquema" argues that "the unity of destiny joined by the peasantry is not limited to technical, administrative, or financial problems" (1). Five steps ought to be taken in order to create a folkish state: (1) religious, moral, and spiritual reform of the peasantry; the parish must be the spiritual centre of the village, "the supreme organ of its morality," so much so that parishes will be given higher priority than universities; (2) educational reform; (3) military training of the peasantry; (4) unionization of the peasants; and (5) "politics of infancy," which consists basically in health-care improvements. The author's conclusion frames what he calls "Falange's village" within a totalitarian and imperialistic state, ending his article with a revelatory diagram: "Small village {Religion, Culture, Militia, Work, Health} Imperio." The points of departure (the small village) and arrival (the empire) condense the ur-topic dimension of the myth of Castile in relation to the other two spatial myths that I am focusing on in this chapter: Rome and the empire.

The Telluric Being

Folkish habitus and ideology are predicated on an anthropology centred on what could be called *telluric being*. By this expression, I am referring to the ontological structure of those individuals who for complex social, cultural, psychological, and political reasons explicitly forsake the urban forms of life and the "urban fabric" studied by Lefebvre (*Urban* 3–4; *Writings* 71–4) so as to return to the native land, conceived of in metaphysical terms as the spatial embodiment of a lost wholeness. A consubstantial element of the structure country/city since the consolidation of modernity, the telluric being acquired a new physiognomy through fascism. In folkish thinking, the ideal man resides in the telluric being.

This myth pervades not a few literary works produced in France, Italy, Germany, and Spain. In his treatment of the alienation felt by men in cities, the French fascist Robert Brasillach praises in his novel *Le Marchand d'oiseaux* (1931) the communion of peasant and nature, which he contrasts with the city's vagabonds. Similarly, Italian fascists revitalized an opposition otherwise common in Italian society between the rural world and industrial centres: such are the cases of Lucio D'Ambra's *Il guscio e il mondo* (1931) and Gian Paolo Callegari's *La terra e il sangue* (1938). Among the numerous examples that could be drawn from German fascist literature it is worth mentioning the successful novel by Hans Grimm *Volk ohne Raum* (1926). The second remarkable example that I am thinking of is the only known literary work by Joseph Goebbels, *Michael: Ein deutsches Schicksal in Tagebuchblättern* (1929). A Bildungsroman narrated by its main character in the form of diary entries, it tells the story of Michael, a Great War veteran and a student during the Weimar Republic who, through his readings and conversations with friends, develops an ideology characterized by anti-intellectualism, anti-Marxism, the idealization of the countryside, a wish for a stronger Germany, and the belief that a Christ-like figure, a *Führer*, might lead the country to redemption and bring about a "Greater Germany." Believing that the best way to contribute to a Greater Germany resides in working rather than in studying, Michael quits everything and decides to work in a mine – in the depths of the German soil. In Goebbels's novel, the protagonist strives to become a telluric being, a goal he achieves when he accidentally dies in the mine. In the depths of the mine, his being becomes absolutely telluric. Thus the land, through its fusion of soil and the (telluric) man, forms the basis for the regeneration of Germany. *Michael* thereby demonstrates with absolute clarity the links between *völkisch* ideals, fascist habitus, and a fascist political project.

Leoncio Pancorbo (1942), the only novel ever written by José María Alfaro, belongs to this folkish literary tradition.[37] Alfaro's Bildungsroman constitutes perhaps the most complete novelistic adaptation of the ideas put forth by Onésimo Redondo and his collaborators in Valladolid. A member of FET-JONS National and Central Committees, director of prominent Falangist periodicals, enthusiastic supporter of the Nazis during the Second World War, a chameleonic man of the Franco regime who managed to present himself as a "liberal" after the dictator's death, this author of a scarce, largely forgotten literary production wrote a folkish novel that somehow betrays his Castilian origins (he was a native of Burgos), notwithstanding the fact that he was a man of the world, a true cosmopolitan who felt at home in big, modern cities.

Alfaro's novel builds upon two different literary traditions. On the one hand, it relates intertextually to the folkish works already mentioned. On the other, *Leoncio Pancorbo* is a fascist Bildungsroman akin to Pierre Drieu La Rochelle's *Gilles* (1942), Robert Brasillach's *Les Sept couleurs* (1939), Ramiro Ledesma Ramos's *El sello de la muerte* (1924), and Gonzalo Torrente Ballester's *Javier Mariño: Historia de una conversión* (1943). Alfaro articulates the two groups of intertexts through the chronotopos of the round-trip journey (town-city-town). At the formal level it refracts the overarching technology of striation underpinning the central tenet of the novel: the need to impose onto Spain a folkish conception of space. Furthermore, it articulates the two principal loci: the main character's mind and the space resulting from the dialectical relationship between Pancorbo's Castilian hometown and Madrid. The relevance of dual structures manifests itself in the novel's plot and discourse. *Leoncio Pancorbo* is divided into two parts framed by a dual paratext consisting of a prologue and an epilogue; the discourse alternates between two narrative voices (an extradiegetic narrator in the first part, Pancorbo's intradiegetic voice in the second); and the novel combines two subgenres: the psychological novel and the epistolary narrative. In the first part of the novel, the narrator relates Pancorbo's life and thoughts in Madrid during his university years, from his arrival in the city in the fall of 192... (*sic*) until his return to his Castilian hometown, Dueñas de Campos, while the second consists of a series of letters written by Pancorbo from his hometown to a friend in Madrid. The counterpoint technique extends to the organization of the chapters. Thus in part 1 the chapters focusing on different components of Pancorbo's personality are followed by chapters on his ideas on a diversity of topics, while chapters devoted to the character's tendency to melancholy and seclusion alternate with chapters on Pancorbo's support of political engagement and direct action. Through this technique, Alfaro stresses the protagonist's contradictions and unstable personality – a common feature, let us add, in fascist decadent heroes.[38] Pancorbo's indecisiveness about whether he should stay in Madrid or go back to Dueñas del Campo parallels a crucial spatial conflict during the civil war: the spatial conflict between on the one hand the fascist zone, made of small, rural towns, and on the other the Republican zone, which included the richest, most modern, and advanced cities in Spain.[39] The wholeness of being will be attained by the return of the native via a dialectical path comprising a thesis (Pancorbo's family roots in Castile, a locus where beings live in communion with the land), an antithesis (Pancorbo's apprenticeship in Madrid), and a synthesis (an ideologically self-conscious return to the hometown by which Pancorbo overcomes his dilemmas).

Pancorbo's roots lie in Castile at the crossroads of spaces and family origins. From the father's side, the family comes from the Alto Ebro, while the mother's native region is the bank of the Douro River. Belonging to a family of prosperous merchants, the father studied law in Valladolid and was later employed by the state administration, and the mother, coming from an *hidalga* (lower rank of the nobility) family of farmers and small landowners, brought to the marriage a house and estate "buried deep in the heart of Dueñas [del Campo]" (27). Pancorbo was born at the centre of Castile, "on the edge of the roads of Burgos and Palencia, Valladolid and Salamanca" (27), from the merging of merchants and small landowners. Having enjoyed a happy, protected life in the benign world of deep Spain, Pancorbo does never feel at home in Madrid, the city that he perceives as the buzzing locus of struggle, of limitless and unsatisfied ambition and desire, as a place lacking unity and wholeness (45–6). Unsurprisingly forlorn and alienated in Madrid (e.g., 93–8, 99), Pancorbo suffers a spiritual crisis (61–6). As the novel's story advances, so does Pancorbo's sense of existential failure, made plain in chapter 19

of the first part (99–105): "A moral abandonment … enveloped him …
If life itself … would decide at every turn the course of his steps, what was
the purpose of fighting?" (104). Since he seemed doomed to be an au-
tomaton, the best course of action was to let himself be ruled by instinc-
tual drives (104). Adjusting to this new life is a rather problematic task.
His nostalgia for the slow-paced life of Tierra de Campos destabilizes his
thoughts and feelings, placing him in an emotional no-man's-land of
sorts in which Leoncio alternates moments of activity and an impulse to
fight on with a "crashing quietism" (47), thereby refracting the duality of
city (activity) and country (stasis).

A melancholy, nostalgic Pancorbo entertains the possibility of leaving
Madrid and going back home to immerse himself "in the arable land as
a root … in order to live in it" (47–8). This notwithstanding, without his
formative years spent in Madrid, Alfaro's hero most likely would have
ended up as a farmer, a landowner, or a provincial civil servant with few,
if any, intellectual preoccupations. Reading, studying, going to class, and
talking to people interested in things intellectual refine a country habitus
and transform it into a folkish, fascist one. Pancorbo admires the hero
figure, considered in his double capacity of self-sacrifice (22–3, 134–7)
and preaching "with the dialectics of the facts" – a statement evocative
of Primo de Rivera's famous dictum on the dialectics of the fists and the
pistols (*Obras* 67–8); he defends violence and war as valid ways of doing
politics (43–4; see also 125–8, 129–33); he has an instinctive fear of the
masses, which he compensates with an urge to study and conquer them
(86–92); and he asserts that men must be the agents of history, regardless of the consequences (131–2). Neither personal maturity nor true
knowledge thus can be attained in the city. Despite the decisive function
it plays in Pancorbo's *Bildung*, the city – a locus dominated by centrifugal
forces, fragile interpersonal relationships, threatening vectorialities of
the masses invading the downtown, as well as inauthenticity and anomie
– cannot be a propitious place for solid learning – for learning beyond
transient, contingent truths.

Pancorbo's realization of something in fact intuited at the very beginning of the novel but never taken beyond the realm of intermittent
considerations comes suddenly, as an epiphany of sorts, in an event most
fascists were attracted to: death, here the death of the father. An absolute, irrevocable passing leads to the comprehension that truth resides
in an absolute world, his native rural Castile. His father, Pancorbo understands – as if hit by an obvious but long-neglected fact – all along had
been to him "a plenitude of continuity and shelter, the certainty of an

affective maturity above all contingencies. And from that absolute world
he had lived distant, almost forgetting it" (106). Pancorbo perceives now
with clarity his own anomie, "the empty despair of his aimless combats"
(107). For to live is much more than being always on the move in a world
of representations surrounding him in the city (109). His father's death
shows him the path to follow: in Dueñas de Campos, Pancorbo would
see the days slip by in a permanent dialogue "with the earth and the sky"
(110). He set out "as a visionary in order to integrate himself within the
fences of his estate and see the ripe grains grow, the wind blow, and the
inexorable passage of time" (110).

Unlike other "returns of the native" (take, for instance, Lucien
Chardon's in *Illusions perdues* [1837–43], Frédéric Moreau and Charles
Deslauriers's in *L'Éducation sentimentale* [1870], Pedro's in *Pedro Sánchez*
[1885], or Clement (Clym) Yeobright's in Thomas Hardy's *The Return
of the Native* [1878]), Leoncio Pancorbo's does not end in tragedy or
disappointment. On the contrary, it leads to the full assumption of a
folkish fascist ideology gestated in the city. Four techniques underline
Pancorbo's awareness of the relationship between the final stage in the
development of his political ideology, deeply linked to telluric forces,
and the opposition of this ideology to the political left: (1) the shift of
the narrative voice from a third-person narrator to Pancorbo's; (2) the
presence of a narratee, a friend of Pancorbo's living in Madrid identified
with left-wing politics; (3) Pancorbo's growing aggressiveness towards his
friend's ideas; and (4) the fact that the epistolary exchange is one-sided:
in this second part there are no letters from his friend (even his name
is silenced by Pancorbo), thereby underscoring the fascist's intolerance
for political dialogue and its constitutive totalitarian approach to political practice.

In the fifteen letters written by Pancorbo between 21 May 1934 and
30 April 1936 there are two dominating motifs: the myth of the telluric
being and the dissolution of the subject through its fusion with nature
and ultimately with the soil. Echoing the Juntas Castellanas de Actuación Hispánica's folkish ideas about the land and national regeneration
through violent means, Pancorbo claims to have understood his mission
to change Spain: in the Castilian countryside he has been able "to get a
glimpse of my mission and become aware of myself so as to get ready for
the big battle" (132–3). This comprehension of the metaphysical connection between man and land, threateningly expressed by Pancorbo to
his friend, comes from a character whose death drive, implicit in his fascination with the dissolution of individuality amidst the masses, overlaps

with his anti-intellectualism and irrational attitude, both closely related to Pancorbo's need to overcome the internal contradictions born out of his alienation in the city as well as his continuous contemplations on himself and the world. A whole letter is devoted to develop such anti-intellectualism (145–9). In it, Pancorbo states emphatically that the act of reasoning empties the world of its "mysteries." By a "failed intellec- tualism," writes Pancorbo to his friend, "you get the wrong end of the stick, of the human vocation for knowledge" (146). Reason leads only to a deadlock (147). Pancorbo proposes to his friend a folkish solution: "to discover man as man, and the land as mother" (148). Consequent with his irrationalism, Pancorbo confesses that he can think well only by means of the "dialectics of my actions," which he considers, in a fascist fashion, as "the best of them all" (148). To this it follows the clearest definition of the myth of the telluric being as manifested in the novel: "I have discovered in myself … the telluric man … by pointing it out thus I think of the impossibility of falling into … representations of landscape of any kind … I think of that man whose blood seems to circulate, indif- ferent, through his veins, or through the rivers or by the mountains … that man … who has to throw himself into his own being in order to feel the pulse of the earth, the movement of the planet" (148). This telluric man, he adds, cannot be reduced to statistics or to a laboratory file, for he is a soldier, a priest, a farmer, a father, a mountain, a storm (149). In this crucial passage, the folkish habitus takes the individual towards his self-destruction.

Pancorbo has worked out his contradictions by *disappearing* into his native land. The country constitutes the answer, therefore, but at the cost of the subject's specificity. In other words, the folkish solution resides in the dissolution of the individual. Certainly a classic element of fascism, such a folkish answer to the problem of subjectivity is akin to other fas- cist disintegrations of the person's individuality. Consider, for instance, the military discipline, the required blind obedience to the party and the state, and the total subjection of the individual to the fascist spatial practices imposed by the state. In *Leoncio Pancorbo*, Alfaro makes explicit the close link between the dissolution of the individual's subjectivity as a sine qua non of fascism and the fascist production of space. The indi- vidual disappears into a space conceived of as mythos, as a non-empiric locus where the seeds of a "national revolution" have been sown. Castile, the ur-topia and epicentre of the "real" Spain, is hence the source of au- thenticity as well as the point of departure for both personal and nation- al redemption. Conceived of as a spatial entity affected by geographic forces, the telluric being is not, strictly speaking, a being-in-space, but rather a being-as-space. A fascist politics of space therefore articulates Alfaro's novel. Pancorbo's project to marry a local woman is associated by Pancorbo himself with space. As he writes to his addressee, "Of my mental deliquiums of other times remains nothing but a fossilized ... remembrance. The pass of time ... the absoluteness of the land, and the wind's tireless gusting have given birth in me a furious hunger for continuity ... I have decided to be an upright man, with my own home" (165).

The second part of the novel ends with Pancorbo's announcement of the date of his wedding: 8 September 1936. But in the epilogue, the reader learns from the extradiegetic narrator that Pancorbo never married (171). His spatial project was interrupted by the outbreak of the civil war three weeks before the wedding. "The bugle call of light that inflamed Spain," the narrator clarifies, "took him shoulder-high ... He fought valiantly ... with the dream of an everlasting Spanish spring fixed on his chest" (171). Pancorbo died in January 1937 at the Madrid front, falling "with the sober and concise posture of someone who has done his duty" (172). Pancorbo has returned to Madrid; but while the first time he went there to study, now he goes to participate in its military conquest. And to conquer means in this context the imposition onto the city, and by extension onto the rest of Spain, of a folkish world view. The epitaph at the end of the novel to honour Leoncio Pancorbo, "Chief of Centuria [local section of a Falange's militia] of the 3rd Bandera [battalion] of Castile," reflects the definitive, absolute disintegration of the individual, a disintegration that began in his communion with the land, continued in the discipline and obedience expected from a soldier, and completed with his death in combat. The ideal has been achieved. But as soon as this happens, writing must also cease. Pancorbo's death drive and anti-intellectualism find in war the perfect field of action. The wholeness of being is attained through war. Better than any other expressive means, silence represents the dissolution of the subject. In the context of fascism, the purification of the self requires the supreme sacrifice of its own destruction. The highest degree of self-reflection coincides, paradoxically, with the dissolution of individuality. *Leoncio Pancorbo*'s closure is very similar to the end of Brasillach's *Les Sept couleurs* (part 7), Drieu la Rochelle's *Gilles* (613–87), and Torrente Ballester's *Javier Mariño* (595–6), whose main characters end up joining Franco's army. There has been real learning. The fascist *Bildung* consists in assuming violence as the means to achieve the transformation of the social. Pancorbo's fascist *Bildung* necessarily requires taking a decisive step: to replace the automatic rifle for the word. On the battlefield, the individuality of Alfaro's hero dissolves into the anonymous, automatized behaviour of the soldier, into the acceptance of hierarchy, and most important, it fuses with the soil. Pancorbo's folkish fascism finds in death the complete realization of a habitus based on violent action. Significantly, the novel ends at the very moment of the self's dissolution. Writing ceases as soon as the self dies. Hence *Leoncio Pancorbo* presents two parallel processes. The death of writing reproduces at the discursive level the death of the self. The telluric being is beyond representation.

Rome, Epicentre of a Totalitarian Production of Space

In many respects, Rome is one of the most pervasive myths of Western civilization. By *Rome* I am referring not only to the artistic, cultural, political, and legal legacy of ancient Rome,[40] but also to Rome as a city, as the urban centre and embodiment of that legacy, as spatial synthesis of its empire, and as the ensemble of rules whereby a particular type of production of space was realized. The references to the ancient city of Rome are many and diverse from the Middle Ages to the present, as multiple and manifold are the narratives produced to interpret its meaning. Ever since Rome's demise, Europeans and – centuries later – Americans fascinated by Rome have written about the spatiality of the empire and its capital. In modernity, the myth of Rome has been revisited by, for example, Edward Gibbon, the French revolutionaries, the Founding Fathers of the United States, Napoleon Bonaparte, Victorian novelists, Jean Moréas and his turn-of-the-century École Romane, the Italian cinema of the 1910s, Gabriele D'Annunzio, and, of course, the fascists.[41]

As is well known, Rome played a pivotal role in interwar Italian Fascism and to a lesser degree in Nazi Germany. In Italy, "Fascist Rome" constituted a potent, extremely visible reinterpretation of the city. Under Fascist rule, the new Rome embodied the self-image of the "revolution" realized by the Fascists as well as two crucial components, not always easy to reconcile, of their ideology: the endeavour to modernize the country and the purpose to create a new Roman Empire. Rome had to be, as Mussolini envisioned it, the heart of Fascist Italy, the capital of a new "Roman Empire," a site of renewed grandeur. "The new Rome," stresses Painter, "its streets, buildings, exhibits, and spectacles would proclaim all the essential messages of fascism" (6). To put it in Mussolini's words, "Rome is our point of departure and reference. It is our symbol or, if you wish, *our myth*. We dream of a Roman Italy, that is to say wise, strong, disciplined, and imperial. Much of that which was the immortal spirit of Rome rises again in Fascism" (qtd. in Painter 3; my emphasis).[42]

In Nazi Germany the myth of Rome was not uncritically assumed by everyone, particularly by party ideologues like Alfred Rosenberg. The guardians of the Arian race's purity did not welcome with enthusiasm the prominence of neoclassic constructions within the German urban landscape. Paradoxically, National Socialism would have had an altogether different grammar without its reflection on classical antiquity – Rome and Sparta in particular. This is so due to a great extent to Hitler's profound attraction to the Roman Empire, its politics, and its monumental architecture and public works. Hitler's interpretation of Rome propelled the vision of Rome held by the Nazis. To Hitler, Rome meant internal order, model community, world domination, architectural and political inspiration, and racial immortality through lasting, monumental constructions. His conception of power and his view of historical processes were based on a consideration of world empires, particularly Rome's. "The Roman Empire," remarked Hitler during one of his table talks, "never had its like. To have succeeded in completely ruling the world! And no empire has spread its civilization as Rome did" (*Hitler's Table Talk* 111). Hitler admired Roman monumental state art and public works, constant sources of inspiration for his totalitarian production of space. In fact, "Rome was," Spotts reminds us, "the only city that he truly admired and that he felt challenged to surpass" (322). In contrast to the most important modern German cities, "nearly every one [ancient city] possessed a special monument in which it took pride," writes Hitler in *Mein Kampf* (264). "The characteristic aspect of the ancient city did not lie in private buildings," claims Hitler, "but in the community monuments that seemed made, not for the moment, but for eternity" (264). In a crucial passage, Hitler affirms, "The few still towering colossuses that we admire in the ruins and wreckage of the ancient world are … temples and state structures; in other words, works whose owner was the community" (265). In Nazi Germany, as well as in Fascist Italy, the new Rome would be the outcome as well as the symbol and epicentre of a totalitarian production of space.[43]

While it is true that Spanish fascism of the 1930s drew elements of its *romanidad* from the Fascist *romanità*,[44] one should pay attention to the hardly mentioned fact that the fundamental elements of the former's conception of Rome were conceived of *before* or *simultaneously* with the rise of Italian Fascism. This is most important because such precedence over or simultaneity with the Fascist moulding of *romanità* demonstrates that the notion of "Rome" shared by Spanish fascists was to a certain degree non-derivative. In Spain, the origins of a novel interpretation of Rome are to be found in the circle of friends who in the second half of the 1910s met periodically in the Café Lyon d'Or in Bilbao and gathered around the slightly snobbish Basque journal *Hermes*. Falangists-to-be Rafael Sánchez Mazas and Pedro Mourlane Michelena, as well as José María Salaverría, Julián de Zugazagoitia, Pedro Eguillor y Atteridge, and José Félix de Lequerica were members of this literary circle, named Escuela Romana del Pirineo by its leading figure, Ramón de Basterra.[45] Although this name refers to the École Romane founded by Jean Moréas in 1891, it would be erroneous to interpret the literary and journalistic products of the Escuela Romana del Pirineo as a mere replay of the poetics and nationalistic doctrines put forth and applied by Moréas, Charles Maurras, Maurice de Plessys, Ernest Raynaud, and other writers of the École Romane (e.g., vindication of the Greco-Roman legacy, neoclassic idea of beauty, poetic use of classical forms, classical sources of inspiration, themes from ancient Rome and Greece). Rather, the Escuela Romana del Pirineo ought to be placed within the orbit of fascism. The writings of Ramón de Basterra and Rafael Sánchez Mazas from 1917 onwards are two cases in point.

Having passed the official examination of admission to the diplomatic corps with flying colours, Basterra picked Rome as his first diplomatic post.[46] This was a momentous decision because he would find in Rome a source of poetic inspiration and a path that would provide him with a philosophical and political ground for his growing nationalism. Basterra's soul experienced in Rome a spiritual conversion. In his direct contact with Rome's legacy, Basterra found the supreme form of social harmony. Shortly after his return to Bilbao in 1917, he published in *Hermes* seminal poems on Rome and Italy, comprising four series of poems under the general title of "Paseos romanos" (June 1917, July 1917, December 1917, February 1918; reprinted in Basterra, *Poesía* 2: 117–49) and the poem "Heros: Llegada a la isla de Capri" (15 July 1919). *Las ubres luminosas*, a book that includes most of his poems on Rome, would see the light of day in 1923, while in 1971 Guillermo Díaz-Plaja edited an unpublished book of poems titled *Llama romance*, the second part of which contains eleven poems devoted to Rome. The themes and the production of space performed by Basterra's poetry anticipate both the representation and the function of Rome in the Falangist discourse of the 1930s and 1940s.

At the most basic, the poet insists on several interconnected characteristics of Rome: Rome as order and discipline ("Voces en la fronda," lines 11–12, 60–4, 139–40; "Foro Trajano" 46–8), as "building centre" ("Voces en la fronda" 71), as "the mother of all cities" ("Roma" 1, in *Las ubres* 5), and finally, as the spatial embodiment of "Canon and Law" ("Roma" 8, in *Las ubres* 5). The ravages of time brought to the buildings notwithstanding, these distinguishing features cannot be destroyed, not only because they are still visible in the ruins ("Rincón del Foro" 13–16) but also because Rome's law and order persist in people's minds ("El Foro ideal" 37–40, in *Las ubres* 39). More revealing, nonetheless, are the poetic voice's remarks on Rome's production of space by military action, and its perception of Rome as the centre par excellence. Hence Rome's production of space was a civilizing force to the barbarian lands – among them the Iberian Peninsula – conquered by Rome. In "Los silencios del Foro," Basterra writes, "Universal roads that went to the peoples, / Carrying, like irrigation ditches, waves of thought! / Among the barbarian tribes, under black branches, / The city emerged" (46–9, in *Las ubres* 26). The poet repeatedly stresses the positive effects of Rome's production of space ("Escuchando a la eterna ciudad" 13–15, in *Las ubres* 7; see also "Paseos romanos: Otro rincón del Foro" 44–53). In accordance with the folkish conception of the countryside as the essence and beginning of both the authentic man and the fatherland, Basterra claims that Rome's capacity for creating space grew out of the "meadows," of the land itself ("Paseos romanos: Ponte Mole" 38–40). Like other fascists, Basterra conceived of spatial order and space ordering as two phenomena rooted in the soil of the "people's community." To put it in Aristotelian terms, the Roman meadows have the potentiality (capacity, *dynamis*) to *produce ordered space*; the actualization (realization, *energeia*) comes about with *human action*. Basterra's association of spatial ordering and a totalitarian production of space pervades several of his poems, particularly "Paseos romanos: Templo de Augusto" and "El homenaje a Augusto" (*Las ubres* 21–3). For Basterra, the Temple of Augustus represents the first step towards the imposition of an ordered space as well as the projection of such order to other lands through their military conquest and occupation. Although he does not specifically address the issue of empire in this poem, Basterra expresses nonetheless a view of Rome and its mission not unlike the one held by Italian Fascists a few years later. Mussolini's reordering of the city of Rome as well as his regime's imperialistic drive (e.g., the Italian invasion of Ethiopia in October 1935) were seen by the Fascists as two types of actions that reproduced and modernized the empire of Augustus.[47] Lines 13–15 from "Templo de Augusto" point in this direction: "Here the man would order / In well-tamed stones / The noble soul / That set in the

legions a drive to invade." In "El homenaje a Augusto," the validity of
Rome's order and the need to project it into twentieth-century Spain
are underscored: Rome constitutes the model for the political and spatial reorganization of modern Spain (50–6, in *Las ubres* 22). In more
than one sense, Basterra's hope anticipates FE-JONS and Franco's production of Spain. Basterra relates Rome's unification of Hispania with
an endo-imperial project, that is, with Spain's empire over itself. In its
way back from the Palatine Hill, the poetic voice dreams of a new Roman Empire for Spain:

> That fine freshness in which was brought up
> Our law and the people's destiny!
> … I understand you, original joys
> Caused by the gradual discovery of the Order, because today
> I am discovering the Law, the eternal Law,
> Newest Man.
> … Empire's organized dream,
> Of power's core.
> The hustle of swords that set out
> From this hill that milked the spirit,
> Paved Spain, binding in speech
> Its barbarian races.
> The races that have chanted the benefit
> Through the centuries, in expressive voices,
> In the east and the south, in the north and the west
> Of the Peninsula.
> … I am going with the heart that found the Order
> Jumping from joy within.
> ("Paseos romanos: Monte Palatino" 17–18, 33–6, 43–52, 59–60)

The poetic voice longs for the totalitarian production of space, for
the imposition of "Rome" onto Spain. Somehow foretelling events, some
poems establish a connection between Roman order and a possible civil
war in Spain (see, for instance, "Paseos romanos: Foro Trajano" 49–54).
The fact that these poems were written in the late 1910s and early 1920s
shows the extent and depth of the fascists' commitment to impose their
political project. Worrying about the present chaos in Spain, the poetic
voice in "Paseos romanos: La campiña en tren" displays its disposition
to fight liberalism – the main cause of that chaos, in its view – with the
production of spatial order and unity:

Spain and its Bilbao, which a new chaos devastates,
I left with my longing only,
An adventurer of the soul, beggar of an Order.
Hail, oh liberalism, with equality and trains,
I am your scion. Congratulations!
Whistle, cheerful … with your barbarian whistle!
But the land passing by these windows,
Paved the two Castiles,
In speech, which later ties the Americas.
Constant virile determination, oh Roman, oh modern man,
Worthy of him, let us *innerly*
Fight for the Order and the Unity in us!   (17–27; my emphasis)

Such a reordering of Spain can be achieved only through civil war. In "El sacrificador de sí mismo," Basterra writes, "I defend, inwardly, against enemy winds, / The flame lit by Rome on my land, / And there, giving its aroma to the Fatherland's air, / Holocaust sheep, I burn my thoughts" (33–6, in *Las ubres* 4). He wants to borrow from Rome the sacred fire in order to win the fight against the barbarian within ("Los silencios del Foro," 52–5, in *Las ubres* 26; see also lines 55–68). As expressed in "El Foro ideal," there are two imperial productions of space: first, the one projected from Rome to Hispania, and second the one imposed by Spain to the Americas. Interestingly, both types of production of space are presented vis-à-vis present-day Spain, immersed, according to Basterra, in anarchy. The country thus lacks an otherwise much-missed political and territorial unity (21–6; in *Las ubres* 38–39).

It is important to keep in mind that aside from writing about the production of space, Ramón de Basterra writes space; in other words, the poet produces a new, fascist Rome using several technologies for the production of space. First of all, Basterra performed material spatial practices that actualized both his perception and assimilation of Rome. His material spatial practices could be reduced to a structure made up of three elements: the peregrination to the origins, the daily walks of (self-) discovery, and the return home. Omitting the real, more banal cause for his trip to Rome, the young poet and diplomat claims that he went in pilgrimage to the Eternal City, especially for the order it represents. Apropos of Trajan's Column, the poetic voice confesses, "Here is what I loved, alone, there in my home, / Brave rough stones, towards you I set off, / And towards that Order that has regulated your pillars" ("Paseos romanos: Foro Trajano" 25–7). Once there, the poet's walking in Rome

– not for nothing is *paseos* the title's first word of a significant number of poems – reconfigures the city in a particular way. The act of walking, for many a refraction of the act of thinking, is a process of topographical appropriation as much as the acting-out of the rules of the place. In "Voces en la fronda," Basterra hints at both the act of walking and his intimate rapport with the city: "Oh Rome, Rome, the loving passer-by / Of all the roads ending / In your bosom, has one which is yours / And under your patrician laurel branches / Its cordial adhesion, like a cord, / Oh Rome, Rome, it binds you to his land!" (87–92). Feeling himself to be a simple villager in Rome, the poet believes his own country to be within himself; this means that in his walking through the city there is a communion of two lands ("Paseos romanos: A un gallo en el Palatino" 4–7). In sum, Basterra's poetry articulates the structure pilgrimage/walking/return home, provides a vocabulary and a set of codes that would enable future fascists to talk about Rome, and imagines new meanings for the myth of Rome. Just like Sánchez Mazas's and Giménez Caballero's wanderings through and writings on Rome, Basterra's conjunction of material spatial practices and spaces of representation laid down the path subsequently trod by the Falangists, who would adopt Rome as the capital of Spanish fascism.

A fellow regular at the literary gatherings at the Café Lyon d'Or, Rafael Sánchez Mazas exhibited very early in his career a conception of Rome that was closely associated with his dreamed totalitarian, imperial Spain.[48] To Rome he dedicated one of his earlier articles, "La excursión por el Gurugú y la excursión por la Historia" (16 October 1921), part of the series "La campaña de África." Interestingly, his consideration of Rome as a model for Spain's polity and this country's territorial expansion was developed before his trip to Italy. "La excursión" sketches out several guiding ideas of the myth of Rome as it would be later conceived by Italian and Spanish fascism, one of them being the synonymy between Imperial Rome and Spain. This sameness is implied in the historical parallelism established by Sánchez Mazas between the Moroccan armed resistance to Spain's colonial presence and the fierce, non-negotiable resistance of the inhabitants of Numantia (a Celtiberian town near modern Soria) to the Roman troops led by Scipio Africanus the Younger, who blockaded and unmercifully starved out Numantia in an eight-month siege. Such a remarkable reversal of roles (to a degree a logical move, given the fact that a colonial power always identifies with another colonial power, regardless of whether they are friends or enemies), cannot be dissociated from the technology of striation articulated in "La excursión." For Sánchez Mazas, true freedom does not reside in Numantia's opposition to Roman domination. On the contrary, the Romans bestowed freedom on "us," thanks to the transmission of their language, laws, spirit – in short, their civilization. Hence Spain's mythic roots lie not in Numantia, nor, for that matter in the Iberians, Celts, and the Kingdom of Tartessus, as several generations of nationalist historians have maintained.[49] Instead, in the values of Imperial Rome are to be found both the origin of Spain and its "national essence": "Our present national freedom," claims Sánchez Mazas, "is Roman and Christian – twice Roman – rather than Numantian and idolatrous." In a barely disguised critical allusion to Catalan and Basque nationalisms, Numantia and the Rif personify a negative "nationalistic spirit of freedom," while Rome and Spain embody a "statist spirit of freedom." In the view of Sánchez Mazas, nationalism represents an imperfect stage of civilization. Paradoxically, "in history the capability for independence has been gradually won by means of dependence." The myth of Rome condenses and underpins a fascist political program for a totalitarian production of national space and the state's aggressive drive to territorial expansionism: "Rome did with Numantia what we are doing with the Rif.... With the Rif War, one feels that that great Roman occasion is happening again in miniature." Imperialism is seen as a necessity, for "no civilized nation could do without the inevitable burden of dominating and saving the rebellious neighbour from his state of barbarism." Those nations that "stop giving their law, their culture, their language, and their blood to others" halt their mission in history.

In "Roma la vieja y Castilla la Nueva" (*ABC* [21 June 1921]), Sánchez Mazas refined his identification of ancient Rome with his ideal Spain. On this occasion, he discerns an otherwise counterintuitive spatial similitude between Rome and New Castile. His remarks make sense insofar as the traditional view of Castile as the locus of Spain's essence is taken into consideration. The significance of this article does not reside, however, in the repetition of such a commonplace, but in its reinterpretation. No longer the arid, depopulated, monotonous land, New Castile shares a significant family resemblance with ancient Rome. The Rome enclosed within the Palatinate, the Capitol, the Theatre of Marcellus, and the Piazza Fontana is more reminiscent of New Castile than of Madrid (2). The Castilian passer-by, maintains Sánchez Mazas, "goes through this poor and lively part of Rome as if through his village in Castile, illustrious and wretched, golden and rundown. Here he finds again the heart made of decayed luxury, disappointments, penury, pride, but also of simplicity" (2). This similitude leads the author to a crucial historical reading that views Spain's empire in the Americas as a sort of continuation of the Roman Empire. In his words, "Eventually, Old Rome was New Castile. With skills of old, we spread an empire ... Thus did we have the ephemeral illusion of being Rome. Thus this old Rome – like old Spain for the young Americas – is for us a motherly gallery of moving archetypes.... Castile, thrice Roman by paganism, Christianity, and the Renaissance, knew how to spread the legacy of its language, faith, and style. The New Castilians went [to the Americas] like Old Romans" (3).[50]

Rome, Capital of Spanish Fascism

A decade after Basterra and Sánchez Mazas laid down the conception of Rome as the epicentre of a totalitarian production of space, Spanish fascism would make the myth of Rome much more than a pivotal element of its mythology of space. With Falange, Rome became the capital of Spanish fascism, the central metaphysical locus of fascist discourse. It provided Spanish fascists with a mythic past, a political and ethical model, a language, an ensemble of symbols, even the tools for the reconstruction of a new Spanish empire. The Spanish fascists never concealed this phenomenon, even when for tactical reasons the leaders of FE-JONS tried to play down the party's obvious ties to Italian Fascism.[51] Discussions on Rome were a consubstantial part of fascist discourse from the very beginning.

Consider *El Fascio: Haz Hispano*'s editorial (16 March 1933). Reflecting on the spatial concepts of *fascio* and *haz* that comprise the title of the journal, its authors justify their adoption of the Italian word (*fascio*) on several grounds. First, for being the most commonly used and for its universal nature. Second, because it emblematizes the kind of imperial, totalitarian production of space the fascists would like to carry out: "The 'fascio,'" the authors note, "is the bundle of sticks with an ax used by Rome to gradually found and consolidate its 'Pax Romana,' the 'orbis romanus,' the first united and civilized Europe of our history" ("El Fascio" 1). Furthermore, the word contains the potentiality to influence other people. As seen in chapter 1, the word *fascio*, when uttered, has an illocutionary force akin to the *order of an order* to which Giménez Caballero's work can be reduced in terms of speech-act theory. For *haz* is not only a noun, but also the second person of the imperative of *hacer* or "to do." Hence *haz* constitutes fascism's imperative to the Spanish people: "the imperative mood of 'to do.' Do!" ("El Fascio" 1). As if to underscore the performativity of *haz*, the journal published an illustration that de-

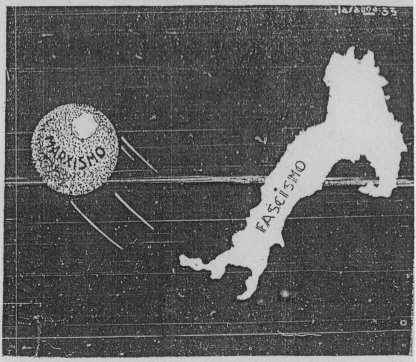

Figure 3.3 "As you can see, to throw that 'ball' away from Spain we needed only that kind of boot." *El Fascio: Haz Hispano,* 16 March 1933

picts the Italian Peninsula, here a symbol of fascism, kicking away a ball representing Marxism (figure 3.3).

The map portrays the struggle between two ways of producing space. On the one hand, Marxism has an agenda of world conquest (the ball seems to represent the Earth). On the other, fascism produces space via violent means while saving the world from Marxism. The obvious consequence of fascism kicking Marxism is the latter's expulsion from the map and therefore from all possible representation. And this is what has to be done in Spain: "As you can see, " the caption states, "to throw that 'ball' away from Spain, we needed only that kind of boot." Hence the

Figure 3.4 "Whereas the communist destroys, the fascist builds up his house, bombproof and fireproof." *El Fascio: Haz Hispano*, 16 March 1933

performativity of *haz* (*haz* as a command to act) is a spatial gesture that produces space by expelling the enemy from the fatherland. At home, the outcome of expelling Marxism is the production of a hierarchically organized space built and menacingly defended by fascism (see figure 3.4).

In this figure, the triumphal arch represents the genealogy of fascism, the violence by which the fascist control of domestic politics has been achieved, and the imposition of a static spatiality onto the citizens. Like-wise, the authors of *El Fascio*'s political manifesto reiterate the meaning of the synonymy of Rome/Spain, concluding that Spain "will be able to work only for the Roman idea, which is the Catholic and universal idea, for which it has been fighting [throughout its history] [*sic*]. Today, fascism is the world's new catholicity. And Spain must be again ... the right hand of that human, justice-seeking, and universal ideal" ("Puntos" 3).

On 19 October 1933, Primo de Rivera had a high-profile thirty-minute interview with Mussolini at the Palazzo Venezia in Rome, a visit he described shortly afterwards in his preface to the Duce's *El Fascismo* (*Obras* 53–5). Back in Spain, Primo de Rivera responded to José María Gil-Robles's portrayal of fascism as a "passing fad" ("Al volver: ¿Moda extranjera el fascismo?" *La Nación* [23 October 1933]). According to Primo de Rivera, fascism is not only an Italian movement, but also a total, universal "meaning of life," adding, "No one can reasonably confuse the 'racist' German movement (and hence 'anti-universal') with the Mussolinian movement, which is, like Rome – like Imperial Rome and the Rome of the popes – universal by definition; that is, 'Catholic.'" Primo de Rivera goes on to argue that "Spain" (meaning Hispania) played an important role in the Roman Empire. "Spaniards" such as Trajan, Seneca, Martial "and so many others" occupy a pre-eminent place in history.[52] Why does Mussolini – asks Primo de Rivera – talk about the Roman Empire? In the answer to his own question, Primo de Rivera provides a ground – or so he believes – for the interconnections between Rome, fascism, and Spain. Taking into account the proximity in time of his foundational speech of 29 October 1933, the following words sound like a premonition: "[Mussolini] talks about the Roman Empire because he wants to find in it the traditional vein of Italy's spirit. Therefore, fascism is 'essentially traditionalist.' In Italy, it searches the tradition of Empire. In Spain it will look for the tradition of our Empire.... With a fascist spirit, the Italians have found Italy. The Spaniards, with the same spirit, will find Spain."

In a speech delivered at the Teatro Calderón in Valladolid on 3 March 1935 (*Obras* 421–7), Primo de Rivera compares the barbarian invasion of Rome with Spain's lack of political and social unity, a situation caused by the "barbarians" leading Spanish politics. In this context, the Falangists constitute an army, the mission of which is to force a new order upon Spain (421). The different ages of history can be classified as "classical" or "middle": the distinguishing trait of the "middle" ages is the search for unity, whereas the classical ages already have found that unity. For Primo de Rivera, Falange's main goal is the establishment of an order similar to that of ancient Rome (425; see also 425–7). As Maeztu had stated one year earlier, Spain had learnt from Rome the language that allows its tribes to understand each other "and the organizing ability to make them co-exist within the framework of the law. In the language from the Latium, [Spain] receives Christianity, and along with Christianity, the ideal" (*Defensa* 11).

In the topographical analysis in chapter 1 of Ernesto Giménez Caballero's production of space in *Genio de España* (1932, 1934), *Arte y Estado*
(1935), and *Roma madre* (1938), I focused on the author's cartographic
gaze and will-to-architecture, paying some attention to the function of
"Rome" within Giménez Caballero's topographical approach to and conception of fascism. As mentioned earlier, those texts, particularly *Genio
de España* and *Arte y Estado*, were very influential, and they stamped on
some readers a conception of fascism articulated by key concepts like,
for instance, "Rome." Giménez Caballero's vision of Rome would not
have been so influential, however, had it not provided an ensemble of
codes and signs allowing for material spatial practices to be understood
and talked about. Nor would it have been so quickly assimilated by a
younger generation of fascists without the existence of a constellation of
coetaneous fascist essays on the Eternal City – in other words, without a
complex web of texts producing the rules governing the fascist discourse
on Rome. Hence the need to explore other works by Giménez Caballero devoted to this topic. In addition to the pages on Rome in *Circuito
imperial* and *Genio de España*, Giménez Caballero published nine articles
under the generic title of "España y Roma" in *F.E.* between 11 January
and 19 April 1934. This series represents the first work of Giménez Caballero devoted entirely to the subject of Rome.[53] It belongs, therefore,
to the group of texts that configured in Spain the fascist perception and
refashioning of Rome.

In the introductory article, the author sets up the plan and spells out
the aim of his series. Rather revealingly, Giménez Caballero links his
analysis of Rome with political ideology and direct action. He sees as his
duty the task of searching for the Spanish soul by analysing the decisive
contribution of "Spain" to the Roman Empire, a remarkable piece of
acrobatics for its reversal of roles: in these articles, "Spain" is never seen
as simple colony of Rome, but rather as a partner in the construction
and administration of its empire (Introducción 10). His focus does not
reside, asserts Giménez Caballero in "Roma y la España antigua," in going through Rome's legacy to Spain. On the contrary, he will concentrate on Spain's contribution to Rome's greatness at the cultural, literary,
philosophical, social, and religious levels. Keeping in mind the underlying political goal of these articles, it is only logical that Giménez Caballero begins his study of the "Spanish" contribution to Rome with Seneca,
considered as the philosopher who established the stoic foundations of
fascism ("Séneca" 9). This article centres on the foundation of the fascist
doctrine from a pseudo-philosophical standpoint, and aspires to set up

for Spain a "profound, intimate, and original current called today 'fascist,' albeit for us it is as old as our Christian *senequismo*" (8). In Seneca, he argues, one can find the foundation of a philosophy of the will, of the pagan virtue, of the hero, and the grounds for a doctrine of resignation (9). In Giménez Caballero's opinion, fascism contains an ample Senecan basis (9). First, one of fascism's main characteristics lies in its anti-democratic ideology, which is, so he claims, linked to Seneca's philosophy. Second, fascism views life as a struggle, an attitude closely associated with the practical and ethical dimension of life discussed by Seneca. And finally, "where Seneca writes 'the wise man,' 'the strong man,' one must write today the 'Duce,' the 'Führer,' the 'hero.' Much earlier than Nietzsche, Seneca is the great forger of the *will to power*" (9; see also 10).

While Seneca's philosophy projects itself towards a fascist future, the other intellectual figures from Hispania studied by Giménez Caballero are mostly considered vis-à-vis their contributions to Imperial Rome. Thus the poet Lucan provided Rome with the first essay of "imperial mystique" ("Romance" 9). To Marcial, Rome owes the "salvation of its intimate life, of its unspeakable secrets"; Quintilian brought to the Caesarean world the art of being a politician, Columella thought of returning Rome to its rural tradition, which Giménez Caballero explicitly relates to folkish fascism ("Foro" 11), and Pomponius Mela represented the Roman world ("Orbe" 14). The concluding observations in the article "Orbe y pueblo" round out the supposedly pivotal contribution of "Spain" to Rome with a spatial image indicative not only of Giménez Caballero's topographical writing, but also of his view of Rome and Spain as two intersecting spaces, thereby producing a new space that consists of the overlapping of two countries as well as two epochs. The last three articles of the series explore Hispania's role in the development of early Christianity. For Giménez Caballero, there are three traditions in Spain's early Christianity: Saint James, Our Lady of the Pillar, and Saint Paul ("La primera" 9). More significant in regard to the connections between Rome, Spain, and fascism are the writer's observations on the persecution of Christians and the Christian martyrs, whom Giménez Caballero likens to the Falangists killed in Spain's streets, thereby linking the fascist cult of the dead with Christian martyrdom ("La primera" 9).

None of the authors studied thus far intersected their poetic (Basterra), impressionistic (Sánchez Mazas), political (Primo de Rivera), or – so to speak – "historical" (Giménez Caballero) ruminations on Rome with comments about the important events taking place in the Eternal City, starting with the Fascist takeover of the country's political institutions in January 1925. The main purpose of their works, which in spatial terms have been considered as both spaces of representation and representations of space, consisted of the production of a place viewed as the metaphysic capital of a future fascist Spain. Rome, Spain's "mother," was seen as the foundation and centre upon which a unified and totalitarian state might be built. By means of different modalities, these works prioritize ancient Rome over the present-day city, and their images and language lack a solid representational power.

A more realistic approach would be furnished by Vicente Gay – a university professor, convinced anti-Semite, and great admirer of National Socialism who had authored *El Nacionalsocialismo y el nuevo Derecho* (1933), *Qué es el socialismo. Qué es el marxismo. Qué es el fascismo: La lucha de las tres doctrinas* (1933), and *La revolución nacional-socialista* (1934) – in his 1935 travelogue *Madre Roma*. Expenses defrayed by the Italian government, Gay's trip to and sojourn in Italy was, like Basterra's and Giménez Caballero's, a discovery of sorts. Gay travelled to Italy already biased towards Italian Fascism. Prompted by the chaotic, "revolutionary," political state of affairs in his country since the proclamation of the Second Republic, he was heading to a "haven of peace" in the hope of finding the revelation of a "redeeming truth" (xiii). Gay arrived in Italy "thirsty," and soon he came upon a "belief" (the fascist ideology) and a "creation" (the Fascist state) that, as the book makes evident, he felt must be put into practice in Spain.

In contrast to the goals of the authors analysed above, who made Rome a mythical place, Gay's main objectives reside in observing Italy's political situation and cultural life (xiv). As announced by the title, his view of Rome is mythical too, but the myth of Rome is based here upon a detailed observation of the city, in particular of the archaeological works and urban changes brought about by the Fascists (e.g., 25–9). Thus *Madre Roma*'s metaphysical discourse – Rome as an exemplary spatial myth – is grounded in the description of the material spatial practices that have brought back to life ancient Rome, as well as in the association of ancient Rome with the Italian Fascist doctrine and "revolution." According to Gay, the Fascist revolution has led to the restoration of monuments and the excavations in Rome. It is thus Mussolini's Rome (22). The multiple archaeological excavations undertaken by the Fascists have meant the resurgence, in both a literal and figurative sense, of Imperial Rome (26). The metaphysical and political meaning of the excavations is not overlooked by Gay, who shrewdly remarks, "The exhumations ... that change and increase the great city's dimensions are the result of the excavations that in the past have shaped the national soul so as to dig up the tradition in which the imperial idea had lain dormant, an idea that means consciousness of bygone great deeds and revelation of a great destiny" (28). But not only do these excavations in Rome imply the beginning of a new empire. As a result of the spiritual unification of the country and the territorial unity achieved under Fascist rule (92–3, 134), Italy now also can aspire to the "resurrection of the imperial idea" and "cherish fantasies of greatness and well-being" (134), thus indirectly pointing to the present lack of imperial grandeur in Spain as well as the way to attain it. Gay's spatial approach to Italian Fascism manifests itself through the author's extensive observations of emblematic cities and towns (e.g., Genoa, 18; Naples, 33–4; Pompeii, 52–9; Herculaneum, 61–7; Milan, 84–9; Venice, 117–23; Verona, 131–6; Bologna, 136–40; Florence, 140–50) and through his underscoring the transcendental meaning and effect of the Fascist material spatial practices (253–5), particularly the construction of a transportation network "already present in Imperial Rome" (255).

In part 5, Vicente Gay expands his interpretation of Rome. He praises the Roman countryside "reorganized and fertile" (411) and narrates his visit to the Mostra della Rivoluzione Fascista (417–21), the Via Apia (424–5), the Catacombs (427–32), and the Vatican (433–44). The personal feeling of the Roman grandeur and the admired contemplation of the city from the Appian Way "have made me realize that the Romans had in their horizons yet another motive for the formation of their imperial ideal. The petty horizons and the still landscapes will be good for the ascetics and cenobites, but not for a people who associates its ideas and its life to world domination" (424–5). The sixth part of the book, "Madre Roma," offers the reader a metaphysical reading of Rome, which the author has reached through an analysis of the Fascist material spatial practices. Gay considers Rome to be the symbol and reality of the "great historical work of the formation of peoples; the focus of a great centuries-old culture that prepared what ... turned out to be Europe" (453). Rome was the "Lady of the Ancient World and the Mother of the Nations that filled out the real Europe" (453). Furthermore, in Rome there are "deep ideas" that aspire to rule as they did in the past (484–5). Fascism's roots "stem from the Roman tradition's trunk" (494). Spain owes to Rome its religion, law, and language. Spanish citizens are therefore Romans of sorts (497).

An epicentre of a totalitarian production of space as well as the capital of Spanish fascism, Rome provided the myth of Castile with a narrative of origins. Out of Rome's imperial and cultural grandeur – to which

Spain was thought to have contributed – emerges the heir of the Roman Empire: Castile. Without the consideration of Castile as the repository of Spain's essence or as the cradle of the first modern empire in history, the myth of Rome that was developed by fascists would lack its condition of possibility. This search for mythic origins required a stimulus. Such an impulse, manifested mostly but not only among fascists, led to the past as much as to the present.[54] In fascist discourse, "Rome" entails "national order" and "empire." Thus the adoption of Rome as the capital of Spanish fascism involved an imperial project. Castile might reign again as the engine and centre of an empire, but this time Rome would be its capital, the place providing both the grammar and the technology needed for an imperial production of space.

The Grammar of Empire

Of all the keywords of Spanish fascist discourse, *imperio* (empire) is without a doubt one of the most pervasive. From the early 1920s onwards, it appears once and again in political manifestos, speeches, articles, essays, poems, and novels written by fascists. To be sure, the omnipresence of *imperio* in fascist discourse was the actualization of a fundamental family resemblance of fascism – its imperialistic drive – also present, I should like to add, in liberalism and Western democracies from the nineteenth century to the present.[55] Kallis's assertion (*Fascist Ideology* 28) that, by means of specific fascist values (e.g., activism, elitism, violence), the fascist territorial expansion pursued long-term nationalist ambitions formulated earlier by parliamentary democracies is right on the mark, insofar as we keep in mind both the resilience of imperialism and the presence of fascist elements in contemporary democratic societies. This said, the discourse on empire in Spanish fascism has characteristics of its own whose underlying grammar needs to be analysed.

Although the fascist discourse on empire has merited considerable historiographic and critical attention, the current view of this phenomenon does not take in all its dimensions.[56] The intertwining of two factors has hindered a better understanding of the discourse on empire in Spanish fascism. The first of them resides in the contrast between, on the one hand, the territorial expansion of Nazi Germany and Fascist Italy and, on the other, Spain's military, economic, and political impotence to put into action Falange's declared imperialism in the aftermath of the civil war. This most characteristic demand of the fascist habitus – the military conquest of and political control over foreign territories –

would be forestalled two years after the fascist victory in the Spanish Civil War.[57] A complex set of circumstances hampered the wishes of Franco and the Falangists, publicly expressed well into 1942, to join the Axis so as to have a share in the new European order shaped by the Germans during the war. Hitler's tactical refusal of Franco's shopping list of territorial demands (i.e., the cession to Spain of most of France's territorial holdings in northwest Africa in exchange for Spain's entry in the war on the side of the Axis) at the summit of Hendaye on 23 October 1940 frustrated for good, as it turned out, the fulfillment of what the Falangists famously called *voluntad de imperio* or will-to-empire. The verification of this fact has led to the second factor that I mentioned earlier. For some scholars, as the result of the impossibility of having an empire, Spain's imperial pretensions – put forth in the early 1940s in essays such as José María de Areilza and Fernando María Castiella's *Reivindicaciones de España* (1941), Tomás García Figueras's *Reivindicaciones de España en el Norte de África* (1942), José María Cordero Torres's *La misión africana de España* (1941), *Tratado elemental del derecho colonial español* (1941) and *Aspectos de la misión universal de España* (1942), and Juan Beneyto Pérez's *España y el problema de Europa: Contribución a la historia de la idea del Imperio* (1942) – subsequently amounted to little more than wishful thinking. In this sense, *imperio* was an "empire-fiction" (Southworth 199–207) that did not correspond to imperial practices. Indeed, this lack of referentiality, the *décalage* between the concept of *imperio* and the impossibility of realizing an imperial project could induce us to think that the word *imperio* was, at best, a confusing keyword of Falangist discourse. Since the word was applied to a non-existing object, it would seem appropriate to conclude that it was not employed meaningfully. Thus the discourse on empire could be seen as an instance of nonsense. However, these conclusions are insufficient to capture the multilayered semantic and pragmatic nature of empire in Spanish fascism. The first step that we have to take in order to expand our understanding of empire in Spanish fascism will consist of looking carefully at the *different* meanings and uses of the word *empire*.

This is not a problem limited to the scholarship on Spanish fascism. Indeed, scholars who specialize in imperialism and empire do not usually take into account the different meanings and uses of the word *empire*, in all likelihood because its meaning is considered to be self-evident. According to the academic *doxa*, *empire* is the supreme and extensive political, administrative, economic, and military control exerted by a political society on the internal and external policy of other political societies.[58]

The scholarship on fascist imperialism is predicated, too, on this concept of empire.[59] There is, of course, nothing wrong with this assumption. Nonetheless, when discussing issues related to imperialism, critics and historians alike should be wary of accepting a definition of *empire* without subjecting it to further analytic scrutiny. Overlooking other meanings somehow reduces the scope of a phenomenon whose complexities might be better grasped if approached from different conceptual angles *simultaneously*. This is precisely one of the presuppositions underpinning this section: the discourse of empire in Spanish fascism needs to be studied in relation to the polysemy of the word *empire*.

In English, *empire* means, among other things, "supreme and extensive political dominion; especially that exercised by an 'emperor'" and "paramount influence, absolute sway, supreme command or control" (defs. I.1 and I.2). Similar definitions can be found in Spanish (*imperio*, defs. 1 and 3: "action of prevailing (to order)" and "political organization of state under an emperor") and French (*empire*, defs. 1 and 2: "authority, absolute domination" and "sovereign authority of a chief of state holding the status of an emperor"). Hence individuals (e.g., an emperor, but also a dictator in the modern sense) and groups can exercise "empire" over other people, irrespective of the society to which they belong. To put it differently, "empire" is not necessarily a function of foreign politics; it can be performed also within the borders of a politically organized territory. This is crucial for understanding FE-JONS insistence that the will-to-empire (*voluntad de imperio*) is a component of the individual's fascist habitus and an integral part of the state's policymaking. Such will-to-empire referred, to a great extent, to the fascist will to rule over fellow Spaniards through an authoritarian polity. Not to be overlooked is precisely the fact that in Spanish the verb *imperar* means "to order, to dominate" (def. 2). To FE-JONS, the projected fascist Spain had to *imperar* abroad *and* at home.

In the following pages, I will look at the fascist discourse on empire through the lens of a methodology inspired by the philosophy of Ludwig Wittgenstein. For this purpose, I have chosen a variety of articles, essays, and maps on empire or related to it from the 1930s and 1940s.[60] An examination of the concepts *imperio, imperial, imperar* and *voluntad de imperio*, as well as their underlying grammar – the grammar of empire – may dissolve, I believe, certain still-circulating clichés on the topic under discussion. Here grammar is understood in the sense proposed by Ludwig Wittgenstein, namely as the particular ways in which words, propositions, sentences, expressions, states, and processes are used. Grammatical rules are the criteria that determine which of them are used meaningfully and which are not. Essence, says Wittgenstein, is expressed by grammar (§ 371), which means that "grammar tells what kind of object anything is. (Theology as grammar)" (§ 373). Furthermore, grammar "does not tell us how language must be construed in order to fulfill its purpose, in order to have such-and-such effect on human beings. It only describes and in no way explains the use of signs" (§ 496). To establish the grammatical rules of words and expressions is thus an explanation of their meaning. Since grammar describes the way words are used, it follows that the analysis of the grammar of *imperio* in Spanish fascism – a language game indeed, to employ Wittgenstein's celebrated concept – will put on display *all* the uses of this word while laying out its interconnectedness with expressions such as *voluntad de imperio*.[61]

The word *imperio* as used in fascist discourse can be divided into two broad categories: what I call *exo-empire* and *endo-empire*. While the former category refers to empire as an enterprise related to foreign policy, the latter points to the imperial control exerted by a state on its own territory and citizens as well as the net of cultural, political, and economic exchanges. The category of exo-empire groups at least the following meanings/uses of the word *empire*:

1. Empire as territorial expansion (e.g., military conquest and political administration of foreign territories).
2. Empire as "living space" (a key constituent, let us remember, of the ideology and political practice of National Socialism).
3. Empire as the cultural and political hegemony over other countries, two manifestations of what Doyle terms as "informal" empire, that is, empire exerted – so to speak – remotely, without the occupation of the dominated territory (e.g., control of the Americas through the technologies of cultural control underpinning the discourse of *Hispanidad* and the academic discipline of Hispanism).

As regards endo-empire, one can determine the following:

1. Empire as a fascist production of the national territory.
2. Empire as the symbolic and physical imposition of the concept of "national unity," predicated on the view of the nation as an integral and organic imagined community.
3. Empire as the realization, through a particular production of space, of Spain's "essence."

4. Empire as the necessary first step towards the realization of exo-imperialism.
5. Empire as the strict control of the individual through technologies of the self set up and implemented by the state through its institutions.

In order to grasp the grammar of empire in Spanish fascism, it is crucial, first of all, to determine and to understand these two categories as discrete unities. Second, we need to take into account the combinations of all the possible uses of *exo-empire* and *endo-empire* vis-à-vis the ideal narrative that articulates them. In the five years following the end of the civil war, the Franco regime undertook two interconnected imperial projects. The most immediate consisted of the colonial, absolute control over Spain and its own citizens, considered as colonized subjects through a violent and paternalistic lens. The Nationalists thus considered their enemies as foreigners. As repeatedly remarked by historians, Franco's high command conducted the war with the tactics and strategies learnt in the Spanish protectorate of Morocco; thus the civil war was – to borrow Virilio's expression – an "endocolonial war" (Virilio and Lotringer, *Pure War* 93–6). The new regime adopted the tactics and strategies of colonial power, treating its citizens with firm, patronizing authority, as children in need of close surveillance – in short, as colonized subjects.[62] Though an end in itself, this project also was conceived of as a step towards the conquest and imperial control of foreign countries. Since that goal would never be achieved, Spain's dictatorial regime had to resign itself to *imperar* within its own frontiers. FE-JONS will-to-empire would be realized only as the imperial dominion exercised over Spain. In April 1939, Spain became an empire of itself.

Let us begin by examining the fascist projected exo-empire as expressed in written discourse. As the result to a great extent of Falange's hegemony within the regime, there was in Spain a strong drive towards territorial expansion in the early 1940s. These were years punctuated by the Germans' victorious blitzkriegs in Poland and Western Europe. In the seemingly unstoppable push forward of the Germans, the Falangists and Franco himself saw an opportunity to carry out a goal repeatedly expressed, if not always in clear terms, by Falange. A classic book in this respect, Areilza and Castiella's *Reivindicaciones de España* (1941) spells out what the authors consider as Spain's territorial ambitions: the devolution to Spain of Gibraltar and the Gulf of Guinea's territories seized by the United Kingdom and France, the incorporation into Spain's sovereignty of western Algeria, as well as of regions from Africa's hinterland so as to achieve, around Morocco, "a continuity of Spanish land between the Mediterranean and the Atlantic Ocean," and finally, the expansion of the Spanish protectorate of Morocco to the rest of the country, including the international city of Tangier (93).

Along the same lines, Cordero Torres, a prominent theorist of empire, wrote several books on the "pending" imperialistic mission of Spain and a tedious treatise on Spanish colonial law whose introduction starts out with the author proudly professing to be a convinced colonialist "who does not regret feeling the 'fetishism for the square kilometers'" (*Tratado* 7). Without colonies, contends Cordero Torres, Spain will not recover an acceptable status in world politics (7). A similar stance is taken in *Aspectos de la misión universal de España*, in which the author maintains that Spain has a pending "universal mission." In order to attain it, the government must set up a precise course of action in foreign affairs, as well as display an energetic, decisive attitude towards its colonial enterprise (*Aspectos* 9). All Spaniards, according to Cordero Torres, have the duty to participate in the country's colonial endeavours for the sake of the fatherland (14). In chapter 2, Cordero Torres indicates the characteristics of that universal mission, lists the territories that allegedly belong to Spain, and states some basic goals of Spain's territorial expansion: the bestowing to the world, as a gift of sorts, of Spain's "eternal values"; cooperation with Portugal and Latin America; and the cultural, economic, and political integration into the Peninsula of all those territories that constitute Spain's "living space" (15–16), which lies in Northwest Africa, from western Algeria to the south of Cabo Blanco, including the Oran region, Ain-Sefra, and Mauritania, as well as the territories contiguous to Equatorial Guinea (known as Spanish Guinea until that country's independence from Spain), especially those located between the Campo, Sanga, and Congo rivers (17). Moreover, Gibraltar, Andorra, Roussillon, Lower Navarre, Soule, and Labourd "are pieces of Spanish territory" (18). The last section of chapter 2 sketches several effects that "Spain's universal mission" will likely have on Spain's national politics (24–5). Symptomatically, the item listed at the end is the most relevant, for it shows the interplay between exo-empire and endo-empire. For Cordero Torres, carrying out the "universal mission" will mean "the strengthening of the unity of all the peoples of Spain, of its social classes" (25). Thus exo-imperialism becomes a function of the endo-imperial control of the national territory.

Cordero Torres elaborates upon the two key concepts underpinning his theory of exo-imperialism – the "living space" and geopolitics – in his

1941 *La misión africana de España* and in an article published the following year in *Escorial,* titled "Trayectoria y perspectivas de nuestra expansión territorial." Echoing a topos of National Socialism, he categorically
affirms in *La misión africana de España* that the Spanish people need colonies because their own land restricts their necessities and prospects for
improvement (8).[63] While Spain had an empire, their standard of living
was such that hunger was practically unknown in the country (8). Now
lacking an empire, argues the author, Spain must conquer other territories in order to obtain the basic products for its survival (26). The
imperative necessity to acquire territory to provide the Spanish people
with their basic needs intertwines with a reading of geopolitics. In this
respect, Cordero Torres maintains, "The fundamental truth of geopolitics, namely the natural inequality between states ... automatically leads
us to this other axiomatic truth: what rates and differentiates the states
lies in their foreign politics, and in the effects ensuing from it" (16–17).
Geopolitics and domestic affairs go, therefore, hand in hand: "Spain has
to profess and to practise an ideal common to all its peoples and social
strata, capable of joining all their efforts in the achievement of an objective ... the inner worries ... dangerously tend to bring Spaniards face-
to-face within the Fatherland" (27). Only a return to the great ideals of
"acting abroad" (i.e., a war) can unite all Spaniards (32). In his article
"Trayectoria y perspectivas de nuestra expansión territorial," Cordero
Torres concludes: "Spain has a noble mission to accomplish in the world:
to provide its concept of life and its eternal values to international relations; the exercise of its civilizing mission within its living space; the
policing of Gibraltar for the benefit of all nations; the promotion of its
civilization in the Hispanic world ... But in order to carry out this mission, its [Spain's] right to rescue its soil must be acknowledged ... as well
its right to expand into African territory" (274).[64]

In the 1930s the use of *empire* as cultural exo-empire was far more common than the uses analysed earlier. Mostly focused on Latin America, FE-
JONS' program was adamant in this respect: "We have a will-to-Empire.
We state that the historical plenitude of Spain is the Empire. We demand
for Spain a pre-eminent place in Europe.... Concerning the countries
of Latin America, we tend towards the unification of culture, of the economic interests, and of power. Spain puts forward its condition of being
the spiritual axis of the Hispanic world" ("Los 27 puntos" 4). The most
extensive and influential work advocating such an enterprise is Ramiro
de Maeztu's *Defensa de la Hispanidad* (1934).[65] A spatial concept that, in
principle, refers to Spain's legacy in Latin America as well as a set of val-

ues and a world view allegedly shared by Spaniards and Latin Americans, the *Hispanidad* is a technology of colonial control predicated on Spain's cultural hegemony vis-à-vis the Americas whose main purpose consists of the regeneration of Spain, Latin America, and the world through the dissemination and assimilation of "Hispanic values." Maeztu's nostalgia for the Golden Age, his defence of the counter-reform, his view of Spain as the repository of the spiritual values of Western civilization, his wholesale repudiation of the Enlightenment, liberalism, and Marxism – in sum, the uncompromising rejection of all European history since the eighteenth century – should not conceal the tacit modernity of an imperial enterprise based less on military might than on uncontested cultural hegemony. Maeztu's characterization of the Spaniards as the "chosen people" whose mission resides in the redemption of the world might sound odd if we focus on the wording of the idea rather than on the structure of modern cultural imperial enterprises. I am saying this because what Maeztu proposes is far from far-fetched or unfeasible. On the contrary, he expresses a phenomenon characteristic of the reorientation of Western colonialism in the twentieth century, particularly since 1947. The military and administrative colonial control exerted by the United Kingdom and France on countries all over the world was replaced, after the decolonization following the Second World War, by a cultural hegemony. In like manner, the world dominance of the United States has been achieved by a combination of military and economic might, as well as by the dissemination of American culture to all corners of the world, thereby consolidating its worldwide hegemony.

For Maeztu, the concept of man has three possible meanings: the liberal, the Marxist, and "the ecumenical attitude of the Hispanic peoples" (75). Such an attitude or position presumes that all men can be good. They need only to believe in goodness and realize it; such was the "Spanish idea" in the sixteenth century (75). Maeztu argues that "the historic mission of the Hispanic peoples consists of teaching to all men in the world that they can save themselves should they wish so, and that their elevation depends on their faith and will" (75). In a section whose title ("La misión interrumpida") links the present with the imperial past, Maeztu summarizes the path to follow: for the Spaniards the only possible way is the "old Catholic monarchy, instituted for the service of God and fellow men" (300). In his opinion, the peoples of Latin America are involved in a struggle to death against Bolshevism on the one hand, and against the "foreign economic imperialism" on the other. In order to prevail, they must embrace again "the common principles of the *Hispani-*

dad" (300–1). Maeztu's description of the political and economic articulation of these principles is a peculiar mixture of a theological concept of political power, fascism, and imperialism. To espouse the *Hispanidad* means living under the control of authorities "aware of having received their power from God ... and of the fact that this power has to be used to organize society in a corporatist fashion in such a way that the laws and the economy subordinate themselves to the same spiritual principle ... so that all the organs and corporations of the state resume the Catholic task of traditional Spain" (300–1). The means to carry out this project is intellectual, hence the relevance given to the performativity of language. Having asked the poets for help, Maeztu affirms that "the magical words are yet to be uttered." These "magical words" will articulate concepts already known: "service, hierarchy, and brotherhood" (305; see also 306).

The Franco regime undertook that imperial task. Under the cover of a "cultural mission," it created several institutions (most notably the Asociación Cultural Hispano-Americana, the Consejo de Hispanidad, the Instituto de Cultura Hispánica, and finally the Instituto de Cooperación Iberoamericana) whose main goals consisted of propagating the ideology of the regime through the discourse of the *Hispanidad* (Catholicism, anti-communism, empire, unity, race), counteracting the increasing influence exerted by the United States over the Americas, creating a movement of "Hispanic assertiveness," establishing a self-fashioned leadership in the "community of the Hispanic states," rehabilitating Spain's prestige, legitimizing a dictatorial regime, and presenting an image of the country more palatable to the international community. The primacy of political over cultural goals was clearly stated in a report written by the Dirección General de Relaciones Culturales on 2 February 1959. Its goal, says the report, is not the promotion of education or scientific research; rather, foreign policy should consist of the use and spreading of the spiritual and cultural values of a nation in order to have an influence on other countries (qtd. in Delgado Gómez Escalonilla 460–1).[66]

Ramiro Ledesma Ramos was among the first fascist theorists to employ the word *imperio* in an endo-imperial sense. Published in *La Conquista del Estado* on 2 May 1931, the article "El momento español" evinces Ledesma's fear that the country might disintegrate should the government comply with Catalonia's demand for political autonomy, and encourages readers to oppose what in the author's view would be a catastrophe (*Escritos* 151–4). For Ledesma, the real unity of the country can be attained only through empire. Due to its nature, Spain is and has to be "a candidate to Empire. The nationalist sentences are here imperial sentences

... Now, against the federalist projects, the nature of empire contained in the *Hispanidad* must be accentuated. *Let that grandiose concept of empire be the breath of air that presides over the articulation of the autonomous regions*" (*Escritos* 154; my emphasis). Ledesma Ramos elaborates upon his endo-imperialist stand in two subsequent pieces. In an open letter to Major Ramón Franco Bahamonde published on 9 May 1931, he contends that Spain's resurgence depends on the ability to find new collective projects, optimistically concluding that a "very strong craving for empire" is already materializing in Spain (*Escritos* 163–6) – hence the importance of everything concerning Catalonia, which he believes to be a sort of test for "our ability for empire." Echoing the Nazi's *Dolchstoßlegende*, the enemies of what he calls "imperial route" "are not as much the foreigners as the treacherous inner extras. The first battles have to be fought thus at home" (*Escritos* 165). In addition to being a function of the imposition of an authoritarian state, "empire" involves the political unity of the Iberian Peninsula as well. In line with other fascists, Ledesma argues that "the whole Peninsula must be subjected to an order ... Spain and Portugal are one and the same people ... Opposite to this degraded, withered, and old Europe, the Spanish empire ought to mean the great offensive: a new culture, a new economic order, a new vital hierarchy" (*Escritos* 165). An article of 30 May 1931, "España, sangre de imperio," summarizes Ledesma's concept of empire. In this piece he reiterates the notion that Spain needs to capture a national counterweight to hinder the confinement of the regional energies within the limited spheres of their lives. In this context, "the empire would be the common idea to assign a compromise of unity to the Hispanic peoples" (*Escritos* 191).[67]

Onésimo Redondo shared many of these ideas and concerns. In his unsigned editorial "Lo que somos y lo que queremos" (*Libertad* [13 June 1932]), he propounded four principles designed to unite all Spaniards "in the development of a great Fatherland." The first and the fourth principles have to do with the reconfiguration of the grammar of the national territory as well as with the relationship between a unified country and empire. Principle 1 deals with the "assertion of Spain as a united and imperial nation," whereas principle 4 works out the "systematic and forced reconstruction of the national land" (1). "Puntos de partida," the manifesto written by the future leadership of Falange published in *El Fascio* (16 March 1933), systematizes these ideas. Divided into six parts, this seminal text establishes two basic objectives of the future new state: unity and empire. On the one hand, "before 'territoriality' the new state will not allow artful fragmentations, political autonomies that diminish its absolute sovereignty." On the other, Spain must embrace the "Roman idea" again and thus re-establish its world hegemony. The two principles of the new state will fight communism ("the Orient") and individualism ("the West"). One year later, Falange Española would explain the meaning of (endo-)imperialism in the context of its resolve to take over the state. In "Estado e historia," published in *F.E.* on 25 January 1934, an anonymous author admits that both the nation and the empire are two necessary myths for the transformation of the country. In the author's opinion, without a will to rule (*de imperar*) Spain's integral, organic unity will not be possible. "Either the fatherland is conceived of in an upward function towards its unity … or it is conceived of as a degrading function of the autonomous regions" (1). That "upward function" (here implying "direction") cannot exist without a will-to-empire. "By losing its will-to-Empire, Spain has lost its unity and its freedom before the world" (1). For this reason, the national order cannot be static but rather it must be dynamic, led towards a "supreme driving force that justifies the unitary, totalitarian, and authoritarian function" (1). Like the Sorelian myth of the general strike, the fascist myth of empire is both a means to rally people to achieve a goal and the substance of such an objective (2). Spain needs a myth, the myth of empire, in order to rule over itself as well as over other countries and thus become a unified territory and an authoritarian state.

An interesting and idiosyncratic if somewhat obscure version of the endo-empire was propounded by Ángel María Pascual in his 1938 article "Tratado segundo de la Razón del Imperio." Pascual conceives of the empire as the mystical unity of the country, which, once attained, expands to the rest of the world. Applying the threefold path of Christian mysticism (the purgative, illuminative, and unitive stages corresponding to body, mind, and spirit), Pascual establishes three "missions" of imperial action. The first resides in conquering, setting up borders, and merging all particular (national, regional, local) histories. The second consists of governing all the peoples "so as to transform them into a universal, ordered, and intimate city" (46). Finally, in the third mission or unitive stage, the provinces receive "forms of unity" and all foreigners cease to be subjected people in order to become citizens (46–7). Pascual's metaphoric figuration thus may be translated: an endo-empire is the first step to the imperial perfection, that is, to exo-empire.

The intertwining of exo-empire and endo-empire pervades José Solas García's *La Nación en la Filosofía de la Revolución Española* (1940). For Solas García, the empire is an eternal good for humanity, the noblest thing on earth, the path leading men to God (133–4). Consequently, only the authentic dominating idea that gives rise to a real good for humankind will be called "imperial" (139). To exert imperial control on individuals means nothing other than the dissemination of the glory of God and the Church. Therefore, the idea of empire relates to religion and the national tradition. According to Solas García, Spain contains in itself, as a sort of gift bestowed by God, "the best Empire in the world," that is, the empire that provides eternal content to what he terms as "national mystique." In the past, the Spanish people performed their "providential mission" in a perfect manner (142). As in other fascist works, Solas García associates empire with a spiritual task that consists of spreading the word of God to countries other than Spain. But this is only part of the story told by Solas García. The author also devotes attention to the endo-empire, whose main characteristics are (1) the supreme hierarchy of the nation, (2) the state of national culture, (3) the archetypical idea of the nation, considered as the most perfect mode of a people's existence, and (4) the "austere architecture of a people" (148). A nation will find itself in a "state of empire" only insofar as it remains organically united (98). "The Empire is born," affirms Solas García, "when a people integrates completely within a political community, and it develops when this people, a master of its destiny, rises a civilization … until it establishes as men's benefit the glory of God and his Church" (150). Further, he points out, "Imperial is the state of a people living united and in control of its destiny." Accordingly, the "imperial moment" is defined as the highest degree of civilization achieved by a people in a particular historical period (151; see also 153).

Empire as cultural conquest may be used – as we saw earlier – in an exo-imperial sense, but it is also a possible meaning of *endo-empire*. The meaning of *empire* as the cultural conquest of the imperial country, that is, as cultural endo-imperialism, can be seen, for example, in José Luis Santaló Rodríguez de Viguri's *Introducción a la política del Imperio Nuevo* (1938).[68] After reviewing several fascist texts, the author concludes that to the Falange's leading ideologues "empire" is, above all, the "conscience of the unity of destiny in the universal through the hierarchical organization of the national territory [*de las patrias*]" (195). But for him, *imperio* contains a more specific meaning. In his discussion about the grounds for a nation's sovereignty, he argues that because it requires a hierarchy of power, the sovereignty is not based on "unities of culture," namely the specific culture of each social and regional group making up the nation. Instead, national sovereignty lies in empire, conceived of not as a brutal force or crude materialism, but rather as something essentially delicate and spiritual (196). In this book written during the civil war, Santaló Rodríguez de Viguri maintains that, since it is a spiritual task, the new empire has to be the "exactness, to the highest possible degree, of things cultural" (196). This requires respecting the tradition that at all times has to preside over and guide the new leaders of Spain. At its most essential, empire is culture (197). Spain has been invaded, Santaló Rodríguez de Viguri continues, by barbarians from the Orient (the Bolsheviks) who have tried to extinguish forever the light shed by Spanish culture (247–8). As it did in 718 and 1492, the country is fighting the invaders. Then as now, Spain does not defend things material; instead, it fights for something that transcends the duration of human life and the territorial extension of the nation: "It defends the Western culture" (248). As a result, "Spain ... emerges radiant, splendid ... out of this test.... here is the Empire announcing itself ... the New Empire of Spain ... the Empire of the Eternal Values, the Empire of Culture" (248).

To rule (*imperar*) over citizens' consciousness and behaviour is a precondition for taking over the state and controlling the country. This use of the word *imperio* can be found, among other instances, in the article "Unidad de destino," published anonymously in *Arriba* on 21 March 1935. Its author stresses that his purpose is far from repeating the deplorable, pretentious, and empty rhetoric about imperial Spain. The FE-JONS concept of empire "goes to the roots and to the foundations. It is neither attire nor verbiage, but rather cold, luminous, difficult architecture." Revealingly, these "roots" and "foundations" of empire have little to do with a drive to conquer new lands. Instead, they function as means to influence other Spaniards. Empire, according to the author, is a concept of "forming ... the consciousness, the way of being, the style of a new kind of Spaniards." To subjugate people's thinking, emotions, and actions with the ultimate goal of implanting in them a fascist habitus: that is the meaning and object of empire. FE-JONS used writing and public speeches to have an effect on other Spaniards. To write or to talk about empire entailed "ordering" a way of thinking, ruling through writing. Speech became a means of "having empire" over the recipients of fascist texts. By giving that definition of *imperio*, the author of "Unidad de destino" made explicit the perlocutionary effect intended in his article. The affective force of the word *imperio* is self-consciously spelled out. Hence we may conclude that uttering *imperio* amounts here to acting out its meaning.

One of the clearest and most complete contributions to the Falange theory of endo-empire can be found in Antonio Tovar's pamphlet *El Imperio de España* (1936). Tovar does not conceal the perlocutionary effect intended by his book. In his own avowal, he has undertaken the task of writing a synopsis of the history of the Spanish Empire with the sole aim of shaping readers' consciousness: "Falange wants to awaken in everyone ... the awareness of an imperial past. Because an Empire is built by both the consciousness and the will, we bring to the Spanish people ... this imperial vibration of the knowledge of the Spanish past, of the incorporation of the past into the national conscience, so that the people know what they want" (8–9). Empire, Tovar avers, is an "awareness of duties" (8). Thus, from the outset the concept is closely linked to the inculcation of a fascist habitus. To write about empire – which is a way to inculcate the reader with the "glorious" history of the former Spanish empire – entails disciplining the mind; it means to "exert empire" (*imperar*) over the ideology and habitus of the reader, with the ultimate goal of stamping on him a fascist habitus based upon the individual's subjugation and obedience to the authority, understood here in military terms (the *mando* or "command"). As Tovar maintains further on, with respect to Spain proper (*para dentro de España*), "The awareness of the duties to the Empire will suffice to maintain the idea of the unity of destiny. We cannot believe that before the greatness of a common undertaking there can be rancours refusing to take it upon their shoulders [*sic*]. Let us hope that those who feel resentful will know how to expand their hearts to the imperial winds ... Then, languages, customs, histories will find their exact freedom, under the sign – yokes and arrow – of the Empire" (14). An empire, affirms Tovar, is preserved and created only by the energetic will of a people that subjects itself to the "unity of command" (7). Empire involves personal self-sacrifice because it is, above all, "renunciation of comfort in order to achieve the eternal work" (8). In sum, faith, discipline, self-sacrifice, and historical consciousness are the four elements required for and demanded by the empire.

In his succinct history of the Spanish Empire, Tovar explicitly identifies empire with national unity. His section on the Visigoths says that much: the Visigoths anointed themselves with the imperial idea of "Spain's Unity" (35). This synonymy of empire, Spain, and national unity is expressed more clearly in the section devoted to the Cid, in which *Spain* and *empire* are interchangeable: the meaning of the Middle Ages in Spain is given by "this dream of Castilian-Leonese Empire [*sic*], the Cid, who dominates the Arabs and conquers Valencia, the idea that Spain – Empire – opposes Europe's universal Empire" (44). As national unity, *empire* also means individual subjugation, obedience, discipline. In Tovar's reading, from the anarchic Spain of the fifteenth century there suddenly arose the unity, discipline, and empire, adding that "the yoke and the arrows from the marriage of Ferdinand and Isabella do not symbolize a union solely. Castile and Aragon felt that the marriage was something more than a personal and dynastic union, that what was coming was nothing other than the Unity and the Empire. Discipline, tension, gravity.... Pride of service and discipline" (49–50). Further on, the author even refers to the "national Spanish Empire" in the eleventh century (53), an unmistakable view of empire as endo-empire. That "national empire" reached its full maturity during the reign of Ferdinand and Isabella (55). From Charles V onwards, it would overlap with an exo-empire; thanks to him, "Spain receives the dignity not of a national, peninsular Empire, but rather of the only Empire in Europe and the world" (53). Charles V understood that Spain "was able to embody a conjunction of the two Empires – his and Spain's" (53).

The grammar of empire in Spanish fascism consisted of the rules articulating the unstable, asymmetrical relationship between a dreamed exo-empire and the only empire that an impoverished country, devastated by the war, and with very limited military might, could actually enjoy: an empire of itself. On some occasions, the arguments deployed to use the word in one way or the other were illustrated with maps. This is the case of Tovar's *El Imperio de España*, a book that includes a map of Spain's empire in the sixteenth century (figure 3.5).

The comparison with an ideological map of Spain inserted in Rafael García Serrano's 1936 article "A Roma por todo y volver a reír" (figure 3.6) is revealing. Tovar's map depicts the Spanish and Portuguese Empires in the sixteenth and the seventeenth century. Here, Spain's imperial power lies buried in the past, and in the caption the reader is given no reason whatsoever to hope for a new empire. In contrast, the caption centres on another kind of empire: "Today, the Spanish Empire, disunited and almost with no say in the world, still has as a link two imperial languages upon which to rebuild its soul." Notice the expression "Today, the Spanish Empire, disunited." Here Tovar is not referring to an overseas empire (in 1936, "today," there was no Spanish Empire), but to Spain itself, irrespective of any territorial possessions abroad. For the author, what is at stake resides in the present-day lack of political and social unity of the country, which he calls the "Spanish Empire." At the same time, Tovar's mention of the Spanish and Portuguese languages as the two "imperial languages" that can rebuild the "soul" of the "Span-

Figure 3.5 "The Spanish Empire: Spain and Portugal in the World." Antonio Tovar, *El Imperio de España*, 1936

ish Empire" points to one way of unifying the country, namely through the imposition of Spanish (Portuguese would count as a possible official language, provided that Spain and Portugal united) as the only official language of Spain. As is known, this project was carried out after the war by the prohibition of the other three languages spoken in Spain. In the context of the map and the caption, one could say that the politics of language belongs to an imperial politics – a politics designed to unify a disunited Spanish Empire (i.e., Spain). While the map depicts a former exo-empire, the commentary below centres on the reconstruction of an endo-empire. The implicit cartographic acknowledgment of exo-imperial impotence and the endo-imperial project is even more evident in the ideological map of Spain in Rafael García Serrano's article. Of all

Figure 3.6 "Map in circle and Spain at the centre." Rafael García Serrano, "A Roma por todo y volver a reír," 1936

the phrases and sentences in the map, the only one making sense is "La unión hace la fuerza" (Unity is strength) placed just below the Falangist yoke. Both the image and the statement underscore the desired unity of the country under the yoke of one single party. Falange's arrows point to the conquest of territories in all directions (Rome, France, Germany, Africa, the United States, and Latin America). None reached their destination, and only the yoke would be successfully applied for almost forty years. Crucially, unlike Tovar's, this map represents Spain only. García Serrano might have given the same information on a map representing the world. Instead, he focuses solely on Spain, as if he were aware that the tension between reality and desire could be resolved only by leaving aside exo-imperial endeavours and by focusing on an endo-imperial enterprise. Insofar as the rest of the world lies outside of its visual field, the fascist gaze is first and foremost an endo-imperialistic one.

The analytic examination of the grammar of empire helps to understand points of overlap and divergence with similar grammars of empire in other countries, as well as to evaluate their significance in a wider international context. The Nazi endo-empire lasted twelve years (January 1933 to May 1945), and its exo-empire, if we consider the Anschluss as the beginning of Nazi Germany's exo-imperialism, scarcely seven (March 1938 to May 1945). Mussolini's dictatorship covered a period of eighteen years (January 1925 to July 1943), while Fascist Italy's empire over Eritrea, Somalia, Libya – territories all of them annexed by Italy before Mussolini's rise to power – and Ethiopia came to an end when the Allied armies captured these colonies in 1943. In contrast, Franco's dictatorship lasted much longer (April 1939 to November 1975) – a period during which Spain held its control over the protectorate of Morocco for seventeen years (April 1939 to April 1956), Equatorial Guinea for twenty-nine (April 1939 to October 1968), Ifni for thirty (April 1939 to January 1969), and Western Sahara for thirty-six (April 1939 to November 1975). What is remarkable in this comparison is, of course, Franco's ability to control his country for a much longer period than were the Nazis and the Italian Fascists in their respective countries. As stated earlier, scholars have noted the contradictions between the Falangist rhetoric of empire, considered as vacuous, and the non-realization of that will to conquer other territories. But a key to understanding such rhetoric and will-to-empire lies not in the desired exo-imperial control over other countries, but rather in the dictatorship's endo-imperialism, in its *imperio* over Spain itself. This consideration is important, for it demonstrates that a country limited to imperially rule over itself should not necessarily be seen as a failed empire. Three decades and a half of uninterrupted dictatorship – or to put it in spatial terms, of endo-empire – attest to the resilience of what began as a course of action forced upon the Falangists and Franco by extraneous events and ended as the imperial control of Spain by its state and hegemonic formations.

Chapter Four

The City

Hegemony and the City

More than any other social habitat, the modern city is the locus where antagonisms and hegemonic formations find a broad, complex, non-linguistic field of action. In the cities, the dynamism of life, the coexistence and overlapping of habitus, the provisional nature of the spatial grammar, and the instability of the subject's political alliances visualize, as it were, the defining unfixity and openness of the social. As outcomes and determinants of human action, urban centres make up and articulate social relations in a manner one may call *meta-urban*, for the city puts itself on display. Although hidden powers, anonymous dramas, latent violence, and mysterious figures lurk in its interstices and forbidden areas, the urban constitutes a multilayered theatre of sorts open for inspection. "Only in a city," has remarked Lewis Mumford, "can a full cast of characters for the human drama be assembled: hence only in the city is there sufficient diversity and competition to enliven the plot and bring the performers up to the highest pitch of skilled, intensely conscious participation" (116). Without the drama of urban life, Mumford points out, "half the essential activities of the city would vanish and more than half of its meanings and values would be diminished, if not nullified" (116). From the urban ritual and dramatic action arises what Mumford denominates "significant conversation" (116). Through dialogue, the city becomes a space of differences, of accepted oppositions. "The city is a place," concludes Mumford, "that depresses corporeal and promotes mental war" (117). Because of the city's somewhat exhibitionistic disposition, the study of the modern city allows for a deep understanding of hegemonic practices that exceed, without excluding it, any abstract analysis of the social, as David Harvey has shown in practice in his Marxian studies of class structure, capital accumulation, money, the inner contradictions of capitalism, and social change in capitalist societies (e.g., *The Urban Experience*, *Spaces of Hope*).

Under certain circumstances, cities promote not only "mental wars" but also unforgiving physical struggles, becoming deadly battlefields where agents of hegemonic practices fight each other. As Raymond Williams reminds us in his classic book on the country and the city, the modern city has been the setting where all revolutions have taken place since 1789 (*Country* 247), a somewhat logical consequence of the hegemony of the city and urban relations in modern society. "How could one aim for power," notes Lefebvre in an eloquent rhetorical question, "without reaching for the places where power resides, without planning to occupy that space and to create a new political morphology?" (*Production* 386). Consider for instance, in the time frame of this monograph, the street violence in St Petersburg and Moscow on the eve of the Russian Revolution, in Bologna, Torino, Milan, or Rome in 1920–2, in Munich, Berlin, and other German cities since the fall of 1918 until the Nazis' seizure of power, and in Barcelona and Madrid approximately since 1909 until the end of the Spanish Civil War. Indeed, interwar Europe experienced a militarization of political activity. In addition to the mental wars carried out in the usual forums of civil society (the parliament and senate, the media, political rallies, party propaganda, and the like), political agents roaming the streets clad in military-style uniforms began a different kind of war: the systematic practice of physical violence. New vectors crisscrossed many European cities, thereby modifying their urban grammar. As in wars fought by armies, spatial considerations were of prime importance in the planning and conduct of revolutionary action. The violent clashes between hegemonic formations, the proliferation and exacerbation of antagonisms, as well as the crisis of social identities manifested themselves in the dialectics between material spatial practices (e.g., streets rewritten by mass demonstrations, general strikes, pub brawls, street shootings, punitive expeditions, and so forth), representations of space (e.g., conceptualizations of space, spatial codes, and specialized knowledge representing conflicting political positions), and spaces of representation (e.g., politically determined inventions of new meanings and possibilities for spatial practices).

This phenomenon is an instance of what I call the *geography of hegemonic practices*, that is, the specific configuration of experienced, conceptualized, and lived space that articulates a social field shattered by antagonistic relationships and contingent events and circumstances susceptible to be appropriated by opposing political programs. Preoccupied as ever with the pivotal function of space in social and political relationships, Antonio Gramsci sketched out in his exploration of the tactics and strategy of revolutionary action an early model for the geographic study of hegemonic practices. Revealingly, he based his analysis upon an identification that will be of the utmost importance in this chapter, namely the one he sees between warfare and the political struggles of his time (229–39).[1] Although in Gramsci's shrewd topographical analysis there is no specific mention of urban centres, his logic, his political experience, and the images employed in his line of argumentation allow the reader to infer that cities are the main battlefields of political struggle. Gramsci likens the political struggle to the colonial and even older wars of conquest (229). There are at least, as he relates (229–30), three types of (political) wars: the war of movement (e.g., strikes), the war of position (e.g., boycotts), and underground warfare (e.g., the secret preparation of weapons and combat troops). Gramsci's use of military language emphasizes the point that he is trying to make. Thus he advises against falling into "easy ambushes" set up by the ruling classes (232). Weakened states are compared to "flagging armies," and the political agents who take advantage of the situation to "commandos" entering "the field" with the task of using illegal means (232). Political forces clash in the two strata of the social: the economic structure and the superstructure. For Gramsci, superstructures are "like the trench-systems of modern warfare" (235) while, at the level of the structure, in times of great economic crisis, politics follows a pattern analogous to a war of attrition. He concludes, "A crisis cannot give the attacking forces the ability to organize with lighting speed.... Similarly, the defenders are not demoralized, nor do they abandon their positions, not even among the ruins ... things do not remain exactly as they were; but it is certain that one will not find the element of speed ... of the definitive forward march" (235). Likewise, when the established power trembles as a result of social upheavals, the state is "an outer ditch behind which there stood a powerful system of fortresses and earthworks" (238). In another text in which he compares political struggle with warfare, Gramsci tacitly establishes a connection between tactical and strategic changes in the conduct of warfare during the First World War and the political struggles of his time (238–9). His conclusion frames some central themes of this chapter: in politics, the war of manouevre subsists only insofar as it is a question of winning provisional positions, but "when ... these positions have lost their value and only decisive positions are at stake, then one passes over to siege warfare ... In politics, the siege is a reciprocal one, despite all appearances, and the mere fact that the ruler has to muster all his resources demonstrates how seriously he takes the adversary" (239).

In the 1920s and 1930s, fascism became a key player within the geography of hegemonic practices, characterized in those years by the interconnectedness between hegemony, the urban, and warfare. Like their German and Italian travelling companions, the Spanish fascists considered political activity within the framework outlined by Gramsci. A well-known and widely discussed family resemblance of fascism, violence and its apologia can be detected already in the fascist writings of the 1920s: Sánchez Mazas's "La campaña de África" (1921) is a notorious case in point. But the systematic theoretical reflection on violence came about with the first fascist political organizations. Just a few months after founding the Juntas Castellanas de Actuación Hispánica, Onésimo Redondo published a somewhat programmatic "Justificación de la violencia" (*Libertad* [21 December 1931]). Blaming the Marxists for the introduction of violence in Spain – defamation, threats, "aggressive" strikes, "terrorist crimes" – as the primary method for conducting politics, Redondo considers violence a legitimate mechanism to defend oneself against the "socio-communist coercion against someone else's freedom." Violence can be fought only, according to Redondo, by violent action. Therefore, right-wing organizations can and must accept "the pressing need to prepare a possible physical action by the militants in order to contribute and protect the propaganda's spiritual activities." There is simply no other way than "one's own action," no other attitude than the "insuperable virility," and no other option than violence. Primo de Rivera used analogous arguments in his first mention of this matter. Notwithstanding his early tactical opposition to conduct reprisals in response to the violent attacks against FE-JONS militants and sympathizers, he ultimately had no qualms in justifying the use of violence as a last resort to achieve power. In a letter dated 2 April 1933, this otherwise charming aristocrat explained to his cousin Julián Pemartín that all political systems, including "bland" liberalism, had been imposed through violence (*Obras* 49–51). The use of violence, proclaims the fascist leader-to-be, is reprehensible only insofar as it is used against justice. One year later, the anonymous author of "Reflexiones sobre la violencia" (*F.E.* [19 April 1934]) repeated the same argument, while adding a sinister nuance: in violence resides, for the author, "the most honourable way that men have to offend each other."

In a more assertive way Ledesma Ramos and the fascist group La Con-

quista del Estado propounded direct action as the best means to achieve
fascist political goals. The group's manifesto of 14 March 1931, a veri-
table call to arms against "bourgeois social-democracy" and communism,
defends violence as the appropriate mechanism to create a new state.
The last point of the seventeen-point program summarizes the manifesto's apologia of violence: "Only revolutionary action until obtaining
in Spain the new state's triumph [*sic*]. Methods of direct action against
the old state and the old regime's old social and political groups" [*sic*]
(Ledesma Ramos, *Escritos* 48). As La Conquista del Estado would put it in
yet another manifesto, in violence lies the group's first mission (Ledesma
Ramos, *Escritos* 233–6). Believing Spain's unity to be in mortal danger, its
members openly and proudly acknowledged having adopted violence
as the basic method for political action, and justified the assassination
of political enemies (235). "War ... is today's first duty," and in order to
enroll Spaniards in their project, the "cult of force" must be launched in
Spain (235). Such ideas and attitude were repeated by Ledesma Ramos
ad nauseam. In his book *¿Fascismo en España?* he states that fascism seeks
a new meaning of authority, discipline, and violence (55). As he puts it
in "¡Españoles jóvenes! ¡En pie de guerra!" (21 March 1931), the destiny
and interests of the country can be safeguarded only by "citizens' militias" and politicians "with a sense of the military, a sense of responsibility
and fight" (Ledesma Ramos, *Escritos* 61).[2] His most comprehensive theoretical exposition of his theses on violence can be found in "La Revolución y la violencia" (23 May 1931; in *Escritos* 179–82), where violence is
taken as a legitimate and energizing force in the revolutionary struggle
against parliamentary democracy and a debilitating pacifism.

Direct action was predicated on spatial considerations. To begin with,
Spanish fascists were perfectly aware that, in order to attain absolute hegemony, the masses – this most modern technology for the production
of space – had to be domesticated, manipulated, and used against the
status quo.[3] Control of the masses entailed control of the street and,
ultimately, the appropriation of social space. As Joseph Goebbels observed, "Whoever can conquer the street can also conquer the masses,
and whoever conquers the masses, conquers the state" (*Kampf um Berlin*
[1934]). Let us not forget that the masses imply movement and carry in
themselves the possibility to reshape spatial relationships and the normativity of space. In her classic study on the origins of totalitarianism, Hannah Arendt has shown that totalitarian regimes rest on the support of
the masses (*Origins* 306). "Totalitarian movements," Arendt notes, "are
possible wherever there are masses who for one reason or another have

acquired the appetite for political organization" (311; see 305–6).[4] In accordance with this family resemblance of fascism, Bedoya admits in his 26 February 1934 piece "Renovación violenta" that "it will be necessary to agitate ... and to move the people so that they respond to the task of forging a new Spain ... and give a hand for this task. The masses' commitment will be essential in order to develop enough force to end the great undertaking." For Ledesma Ramos, in today's politics nothing can be done without the "masses' very active collaboration" ("Movimiento español JONS," *El Fascio* [16 March 1933]); whoever refuses or puts aside the masses as something annoying or negative "is outside ... of the reality we are now living in." This is a tactic that Ledesma defended time and again. According to him, "There is no great, free, and strong Fatherland" without the support of the masses; likewise the "national Spanish revolution can't do without them" (*Discurso* 241).

Another basic spatial consideration was the fear of a possible dissolution of the country's territorial integrity and essence. "Their purpose is the dissolution of the Fatherland," wrote Ledesma Ramos on 13 June 1931, and for this very reason it is imperative to persuade the people "to protest with weapons" (*Escritos* 213). Spaniards must join in to destroy through direct action what he identifies as the "germs dissolving" the country (*Escritos* 261). Of all the articles connecting the call to arms to the perception of Spain as a territory endangered by separatists, Marxists, and others who are "anti-Spanish," Manuel Olivera Tarancón's "¿Es lícita la violencia?" stands out (*Libertad* [30 July 1934]). He lays out the problem unequivocally: "Only in the case of a civil war caused to destroy the Fatherland and subvert the civilization is violence admissible, and for us glorious ... it is licit to use violence ... to defend ... the freedom and dignity represented by a civilized nation in the process of losing its legitimate free will" at the hands of barbarism. Conceiving of violence as a kind of "just war," Olivera Tarancón's wording of his answer to the rhetorical question posed in the title of his article would become a topos of Spanish fascism: "Against the international and barbarian Marxism, against the anti-Spanish separatism, and against Freemasonry any kind of violence is legitimate and holy: *Hail the youth that gets rid of the easy and cowardly comforts [of life] and joins the ranks of the national militias for Spain's freedom and greatness!*"

For all their idealization of the countryside and vilification of the city, to the Spanish fascists the city was the main theatre of war – for war it was. Even the folkish faction of fascism assumed the centrality of cities in this regard. On 10 August 1931, an article by Onésimo Redondo published in *Libertad* acknowledged the role of the city in the practice of revolutionary politics. Today's problem, claims the author, resides in the incorporation of the proletarian class within the control of the state – in other words, "The demand ... for power by the workers of all nations presented and kept in the street" ("El peligro"). Logically, the struggle against this domination will have to take place in those same streets. Two months later *Libertad* published "El monopolio de la violencia" (26 October 1931), in which Onésimo Redondo establishes two types of violence: the physical one, carried out in the streets and addressed against people and symbols, and the intellectual one. Whoever has the command of the streets will control the state; hence it is imperative to go out into the streets. In an anonymous article published in *Libertad*, "Sin título" (8 January 1934), the author underscores the decisive function of the streets in the struggle for hegemony. Instead of trusting a parliament controlled by the Freemasonry, "Wouldn't it be better to go on the offensive and go out on the street ... with the stick in the hand, the dagger in the belt, and the pistol ready?" Only a properly armed "national" youth can frighten away the "Marxist nightmare." "Let us begin today to go after the Marxists ... Let us take up the street, which is ours, the Spaniards'." Finally, the clandestine journal edited by FE-JONS while Primo de Rivera and other fascist leaders were in jail, *No importa: Boletín de los días de persecución*, notes that fascism was born "in the street." Fascism, so the author claims, germinates in anarchy and in democracy. The national revolution "is taking place in the street, with the chest offered to the bullets [*sic*]. Falling facing the sun" ("¿Un fascismo de Azaña y Prieto?" [20 May 1936]).[5] Most of those pieces must be read against the background of the violent clashes between FE-JONS rank-and-file and members of leftist political parties. Indeed, *jonsistas* and Falangists had participated throughout the 1930s in violent incidents on university campuses, undertook punitive expeditions, and assassinated political enemies.[6]

The links between the city, the production of space, violence, and the struggle for uncontested hegemony in the 1930s therefore constitute a capital phenomenon deserving detailed topographical inspection. While it is true that fascist violence has been explored by historians and literary critics alike, the main scholarly foci have been for the most part the performance of physical violence and/or the cultural artefacts propounding the practice of direct action.[7] In contrast, the constitutive spatiality of these violent practices and the performance of symbolic violence have been somewhat neglected. Instead of exploring the location of fascism within the geography of hegemonic practices, historical and literary scholarship have preferred to concentrate their attention on history – a methodological procedure that has obscured another crucial factor of the struggle for hegemony: the discursivity of the social.[8] By transforming the city into a battlefield of contending hegemonic formations, fascism brought into the open the textuality of both the social and the urban.[9] The struggle for hegemony in the 1930s may be viewed therefore as a battle undertaken at the material and symbolic levels for both the non-linguistic and the verbal control of a space considered by many as a "text" – the city. That struggle took place within what may be described as a semiotic system of relations and shared values, within a grammar with its corresponding rules of formation and articulation actualized, through the daily actions – "speech acts," as put by de Certeau (97–9) and Lefebvre (*Urban* 50–2) – of its inhabitants. Languages and cities make up human communities. The condition for their intelligibility lies in their actualization, and any actualization depends on the competence, knowledge, historical horizon, and hermeneutic skills of individuals. The textuality of the urban thus relates the city to any text. Conversely, reading a text is a form of reading a city. In Lehan's words, "The ways of reading the city offer clues to the ways of reading the text, [with] urban and literary theory complementing each other" (9).

The next sections explore the location of fascism within the geography of hegemonic practices through the study of the *fascist urban writing* on Madrid as materialized in spaces of representation, representations of space, and, to a lesser extent, material spatial practices in the context of the violent struggle for hegemony in Spain during the 1930s. Preference has been given to the spatial analysis of written products, particularly of novels.[10] Discursive practices with political goals themselves, fascist novels condense better than any other cultural form the violent struggle for hegemony that took place in cities. In general terms, fascist urban novels refract, in their own rhetorical organization, the urban grammar of the cities that they describe, represent political antagonisms, provide a textual map of the geography of hegemonic practices, and function as passionate utterances that attempt to make readers accept a fascist production and articulation of space. Their language and images, more often than not unusually violent, symbolically mimic the fascist violence performed in Spain's streets in 1931–9. In this sense, urban writing is also war writing. In order to uncover the urbaneness and perlocution of fascist urban writing, I have paid special attention to the novels' urban texture, mainly because it refracts material spatial practices while suggesting ways for producing urban space. The fact that, with one exception, all the novels studied in this chapter were published after the war seems to confirm the hypothesis according to which the novels' perlocution was intended to condition the readers' perception and experience of space. If it is true, as Wirth-Nesher (3) contends, that the urban reality is the place of the tensions and contradictions of the novels on cities and also of the historical moment in which they are inscribed, then the critic's gaze should focus on the narrative articulation of such an urban landscape as well as on its own urban rhetorical configuration.

Spatial Antagonisms and the Rhetoric of Walking

Madrid de corte a checa, a novel by the first-hour Falangist, writer, and diplomat Agustín de Foxá, will be the point of departure of our exploration of the fascist struggle for hegemony within the context of the geography of hegemonic practices in Spain between 1931 and 1939.[11] Published in 1938, this otherwise splendid novel describes urban space in terms of spatial techniques, represents the struggle for hegemony since the fall of Alphonse XIII until the first two years of the civil war, and imagines possibilities for fascist material spatial practices completely opposed to the "Reds'."[12] The tacit purpose of Foxá's reading of urban space lies in the symbolic imposition of a fascist concept of space onto the reader. Although *Madrid de corte a checa* can be classified on the one hand as a Bildungsroman focused on the political ideology and sentimental life of the main character (a young aristocrat and Falangist named José Félix), and on the other as a historical novel, both personal story and national history are told through the representation of space. The title's word order ought to be read precisely in this way: the representation of "Madrid" organizes and gives meaning to the process of urban decline and national disintegration initiated in the last days of Alphonse XIII's reign (the "court"), speeded up by the Republican politicians and the masses, and completed during the war, a period in which Madrid became a sinister "cheka."[13] To put it differently, the configuration and value of places and spatial relationships determines the signification of personal and historical events. In *Madrid de corte a checa*, antagonism is *spatial antagonism*, while the struggle for hegemony translates into the struggle for *spatial hegemony*. Notwithstanding the third-part division of the novel, which implies chronology ("Flor de lis," "Himno de Riego," "La Hoz y el Martillo"), *Madrid de corte a checa* has many features of what Joseph Frank has labelled as *spatial form*, thus mimicking at the discursive level its spatialization of antagonism and hegemony. To a degree, Foxá's novel could be read as a cartography of the hegemonic practices in the Second Republic.

A fundamental, all-encompassing literary device used to display spatial antagonism is what we could call the *principle of dramatization*. Most chapters of *Madrid de corte a checa* embed dialogues whose underlying structure is no other than the antagonism narrated by Foxá since the very first scene of the novel. Lively conversations – on politics, theosophy, literature, the government – taking place in the Ateneo (948–52), the Café Varela (973–8), the Café Pombo (1046–8), and the Royal Palace (954), as well as in aristocratic (1001–3) and bourgeois (1004–6) houses, permeate the novel, thereby representing a city engulfed in a massive ongoing dialogue. However, these are dialogues impregnated by violence. In *Madrid de corte a checa*, the dialogue is a tool used to activate antagonism. The principle of dramatization deflects the readers' attention from temporality to the spatiality constitutive of any scene while conferring to the novel an urban density and articulating the intersubjective climate of violence that traverses the space described in the novel. The "verbal confrontation" characteristic of urban life does not lead to the creation of a space of accepted oppositions, but rather to a civil war and ultimately to the impossibility of any – to put it again in Mumford's words – "significant conversation."[14] In Foxá's magnum opus, the violence exuding from many of its dialogues thus points not only to the partial destruction of the city during wartime, but also, and perhaps more importantly, to the erasure of the conditions of possibility for *any* conversation. The type of physical violence narrated in the novel, often difficult to reduce to language or to clear-cut political slogans, points in that direction. Foxá uncovers an urban world ruled by an aggressiveness shared by many of the city's inhabitants. Street fights between Catholic students and members of the leftist student union Federación Universitaria Española, Civil Guard charges against students entrenched in the university, the assassination of Falangists by socialists and vice versa, the infamous *paseos* (a word used in a figurative sense to refer to the "walks" on which the executors killed their victims), and the state's alleged "organized" crime directed against right-wing individuals and supporters of Falange are some instances of violent behaviour that go beyond ideology. Instead, such aggressiveness could be described as a *structure of feeling*, a term coined by Raymond Williams (*Marxism* 128–35) that refers to those structures that cannot be labelled by the usual concepts of *world view* or *ideology* and extends to meanings and values as they are actively lived and felt by a whole community.

Consistent with the principle of dramatization, or, to put it differently, with the constant circulation of ideas, the novel prioritizes the movements of the characters over the description of static positions. To say it with de Certeau's terminology (119–22): the *tour* (i.e., the set of discursive operations needed to proceed from one place to the other) predominates at the expense of the *map* (i.e., the description of a place in terms of the distribution of all its elements as well as their static relation with other places). Thus the reader's attention falls on the spatial antagonism and conflicting appropriations of urban space. As depicted by the novel, a complex net of vectors discursively articulated whereby a rhetoric of walking and the opposition that it generates transforms Madrid's grammar, meaning, and pragmatics. Walking thus plays a crucial role in Foxá's novel.

To walk, let us remember, is at once a formative activity and one of the most basic technologies for the production of space. As Edmund Husserl has noted, through the act of walking the body constitutes itself as well as a coherent world nucleus (238–50). When I walk, I give a spatio-temporal unity to the near sphere of the familial and the far-off sphere of the non-familial, of the unknown. At the same time, my body's act of walking configures and gives life to the places where it goes by or rests in. Naturally, this intentional act described by Husserl connotes acquired dispositions and personal objectives. For this reason, walking on the one hand can be linked to certain ways of conceiving of and practising literature (e.g., Wordsworth, Baudelaire), philosophy (e.g., Rousseau, Kierkegaard), or politics (e.g., the people who participated in the Commune of Paris). On the other, such movement may be considered as a speech act endowed, according to de Certeau (97–9), with a triple enunciative function. First of all, it is a process of appropriation of a topographic system; second, it is the acting out of a place; and third, it implies relations between differentiated positions. In the context of the urban, each walk through the city is, more often than not, a simple yet idiosyncratic actualization of the rules and norms governing individual behaviour and urban transit. As put forth by de Certeau, all spatial practices square with the manipulation of the elements of a prefixed order. The representations of space provided by architects and urban planners contain implicitly the "correct" readings of a city, similar to the "correct" use of language according to the prescriptions of the grammarians and linguists. But in moments of great social tension, the normativity of the city is susceptible to being questioned and even subverted.[15] As happens with speech, in a city there is always the possibility of deviations from the "literal meanings" defined by the urban system. In *Madrid de corte a checa*, walking is a function of the political; it spatializes political action. To walk amounts to an act of reshaping the city in terms of the political slogans of leftist political parties and unions. The rhetoric of walking consists, therefore, in the political appropriation of urban space. To Foxá and other fascists, the real drama lies in the modification of the city map through the revolutionary tours – which henceforth I will call *itineraries* – undertaken by the masses.

As portrayed by Foxá, an ensemble of hegemonic practices has indeed activated a revolutionary rhetoric of walking, perceived by the implied author as an unwelcome, shocking transgression of the urban normativity. According to the implied author, the new rhetoric of walking deconstructs the external aspect of Madrid, alters the relations among places, and worsens antagonisms; it is a structuring of spatial activities that destabilizes meaning. The author conveys his critique of the Republic precisely by means of that spatial technique. The examples are legion. Shortly after the proclamation of the Second Republic, as a result of the quick succession of spatial changes the pro-monarchical households feel excluded from "their" city; they are no longer in the hegemonic centre. Thus beaten down by the fall of the monarchy, José Félix's parents give instructions to close off all their balconies (1021), thereby "blinding" themselves to the decisive changes in the country's polity. From the standpoint of José Félix's family, the monarchy's collapse is closely related to something at first sensed only by the novel's right-wing characters but soon confirmed: the birth of a new, to them inauthentic, Madrid. After a brief stay in this most aristocratic summer resort of Biarritz, José Félix's family returns home, only to find that Madrid has turned into something else: "José Félix understood that the city was evolving; it was becoming tawdrier and noisier. There were more bars, more cabs, more ballrooms. From the shop windows the crowns and emblems of the 'Royal House's purveyors' had been scrapped out. The theatres no longer bore the names 'Infanta Isabel,' 'Reina Victoria'" (1039).

The changes in the urban toponymy are obvious consequences of a polity that attempts to erase the past, thereby providing the city with significations consistent with the new hegemonic practices. In general terms, the rewriting of the urban space opens up places and spaces once banned to some sectors of the social (e.g., the working class), allowing for a closer identification between space and citizen. Thus the command over urban writing, which refracts at the symbolic and spatial levels the pro-Republican hegemonic formations' conquest of power, has conse-

quences for the characters' vectorialities. In a city, the renaming of places and streets provides new emblems, unveils fresh meanings, reorders
the patterns of traffic, opens up unexpected directions, and can liberate
places from past constrictions or close them off. José Félix and his family
face a city whose renaming of its streets tells them a story of loss – the loss
of their social class's hegemony in the city. In its stead, a new law of the
place applies to the city. Detached from their old identitarian function,
places like the aristocratic Casa de Campo, now accessible to any citizen,
deepen José Félix's alienation (1030–1). And yet this is just one of many
figures of the new rhetoric of walking. Describing the Puerta del Sol,
the narrator sharply criticizes the break-up with the city's old normativity: "People swarmed around the Puerta del Sol. The whole city's atmosphere had changed. One could see new faces, new people. The workers
dared already to go downtown, and they stayed on the Bar Flor's side-
walk. The 14th of April had taught them a path they would never forget.
The middle class also stepped with more confidence ... the cabs honked
with more boldness ... the well-to-do people were withdrawing" (1024).

A plebeian, degraded downtown it is. After reading letters and newspapers sent out from Madrid, José Félix, vacationing as usual in swanky
Biarritz, muses, "In that delicate world [Biarritz] ... how ... barbarian
the dusty Madrid of the Republic seemed to him, with its plebeian smell
of strips of fried dough [*churros*]" (1034). Back in town, he notices with
disgust what to his classist, elitist eyes amounts to the city's complete
proletarization. José Félix encounters "a terrible Madrid of hatred ...
The railroad workers, the porters, the taxi drivers had a defiant coun-
tenance ... From the balcony at the calle de la Magdalena he saw the
first proletarian parades" (1172). Coming downtown from the suburbs
(1172),[16] the participants in mass demonstrations vented their anger, hatred, and vengefulness, they "were threatening," so the narrator relates,
"with fists," bellowed, intoned revolutionary songs, made up a grotesque,
repulsive crowd of "ugly, hunchbacked women ... anemic and dirty children, gypsies, lame people, blacks from the cabarets, undernourished
students, workers with a stupid gaze, nightmen"; in sum, "All the filth
of losers, the sick, the ugly, the inferior and terrible world, stirred up
by those sinister banners" (1173). In this passage, Foxá echoes the fear
of the masses already experienced in the nineteenth century by some
social sectors and represented in literary works (e.g., Victor Hugo's *Les
Misérables* [1862], Gustave Flaubert's *L'Éducation sentimentale* [1869], José
María de Pereda's *Pedro Sánchez* [1883], Benito Pérez Galdós's *La de Brin-
gas* [1884], Émile Zola's *Germinal* [1885]). In the context of twentieth-

century revolutionary politics, F. Guillén Salaya's *El diálogo de las pistolas* (1931) is the first Spanish novel devoted entirely to the masses and their participation in urban life and politics,[17] while fascist novels like Alfaro's *Leoncio Pancorbo* (86–92, 125–8, 131–3), and to a lesser extent Francisco Camba's *Madridgrado* (40–1), Manuel Iribarren's *La ciudad* (195–206), and Felipe Ximénez de Sandoval's *Camisa azul* (27, 57–9) show, as in *Madrid de corte a checa*, a mixture of anxiety about and fascination with the masses who threateningly roam Madrid during the Republic and civil war. In Raymond Williams's apt summary of this issue on a wider, European scale, "The evident fear of crowds, with the persistence of an imagery of the inhuman and the monstrous, connects with and continues that response to the mob which had been evident for so many centuries and which the vast development of the city so acutely sharpened. As late as the early twentieth century, one main response to the city ... identified the crowding of cities as a source of social danger: from the loss of customary feelings to the building up of a massive, irrational, explosive force" (*Country* 216–17).[18]

The masses' accession to Spanish politics was a decisive change in the history of the country.[19] The vectorialities of the masses had been facilitated by the evolution of the city since the mid 1920s. Juliá (*Madrid* 45–50) reminds us of the existence in Madrid in the 1930s of a "popular city" apparent in the concentration within a small space of a great variety of business activities. For Juliá, the existence of this "popular city" facilitated the access of the masses to the Puerta del Sol to participate in all kinds of events, political or otherwise. The student from San Bernardo, argues Juliá, goes down easily to the Puerta del Sol, "the clerk who fills the cafes goes out immediately to Sol, and the worker and artisan from the adjacent poor neighbourhoods go to Sol with no problem whatsoever" (46). What happens is that Madrid at the beginning of the 1930s is also the new Madrid of urban expansion, the outlying districts, the adjoining villages. The characteristics of this new city, according to Juliá, are *grosso modo* the same as those of the cities at the beginning of industrialization, with the peculiarity that Madrid lacked an industrial infrastructure. The overlapping of the two cities, unsupported by an industry that would have imposed an abstract discipline to the new population, explains the kind of conflict that was unleashed in Madrid beginning in the summer of 1933 (Juliá, *Madrid* 59). The Republic would be the political framework in which the antagonisms caused by the chaotic growth of the urban periphery affected the centre of the city, thereby modifying the relations between social classes.[20]

Foxá does not elucidate the social processes that had created the conditions of possibility for the masses' new prominence; instead, he narrates the new vectorialities crisscrossing the city as well as their effects. In its lack of a historical account and political explanation resides precisely the novel's ideological positioning in this respect. By omitting such historical background, the novel hinders real understanding, the reader's possible coming to terms with complex facts. The kind of spatial perspective taken by the author buries history and time, thereby facilitating the novel's condemnation of the masses' appropriation of urban space and political power. For the implied author, their presence in the city meant the arrival of the altogether other, of an element deemed external to the urban community. Perceived as a destabilizing element for the social and the individual, the proletarian crowd is the urban equivalent to the uncanny in the sense given by Freud to the word in his classic essay *Das Unheimliche* (1919). In Freud's definition, "The uncanny is that class of the frightening that leads back to what is known of old and long familiar" (17: 220). It arises as the reactivation of something long forgotten or repressed in earlier psychic stages of our lives (e.g., childhood). In *Madrid de corte a checa*, José Félix's intimate, familiar, home-like (*heimlich*) Madrid metamorphoses into an eerie, uncomfortable, strange, "un-homely" (*unheimlich*) space as soon as there comes back to conscious life what once had been repressed and pushed out to the urban periphery, thus remaining "secret," "hidden," and therefore potentially "dangerous" – the poor. That notwithstanding, the novel's attitude towards the masses is somewhat ambiguous. On the one hand we have the *unheimliche* dimension of the crowd. On the other, the problem sometimes seems to lie rather in the ideological direction governing its urban itineraries, as evinced in a comment made by Ramiro Ledesma to Ernesto Giménez Caballero apropos of a demonstration that both are watching: "Ernesto, some day these masses will be ours" (Foxá, *Madrid* 1015). The masses have certainly violated the limits, but in the wrong way. The pending task for the fascists resides in redirecting the masses' vectorialities.[21]

A series of embedded stories about the city in the past, overlapping with the descriptions of Madrid during the Republic, comprise another spatial technique used to stress the city's decadence and its "sovietization" during the war. The nostalgic description of an amiable, traditional, almost community-like Madrid in Ferdinand Tönnies's definition of the concept *community* (*Gemeinschaft*) stands in stark contrast with its present-day inauthentic nature. Against this backdrop one ought to interpret the episode in which the nuns, taken out of their convents in or-

der to vote, realize to their dismay that the Madrid of their adolescence
has little in common with the city that they now contemplate speech-
lessly (1107). Don Cayetano's evocation of the Galdosean Madrid of his
youth allows for a similar reading (1162–3). Right after the outbreak of
the war, this sense of loss increases as a result of the transformation of
the city into a rotten, chaotic, "Soviet-made" space where workers roam,
driven by murderous instincts (see 1212, 1319–20).[22] After 18 July 1936,
Madrid completes the carving out of its own essence. "With the same
buildings and the same people," notes the narrator, "that was already
a new city.... In spite of the geography, that wasn't Spain any longer"
(1212). Confronted with these changes, Aunt Úrsula utters an exclamation apropos of her evocation of her childhood that constitutes one of
the novel's leitmotifs: "How far-off was all that!" (1254). José Félix shares
that feeling of loss in his remembrance of the city of time past while trying to escape from Madrid: "They crossed San Carlos. And he evoked the
happy terrace roofs of his young days ... How far-off was all that!" (1321).
Foxá's device consists in superimposing a diachronic map of Madrid with
a map of contemporary Madrid so as call into question the Republican
hegemony. The stories of a former idyllic Madrid make up a palimpsest
erased by the Republic. In view of the novel's urban design, of the significant number of embedded stories, songs, and poems, of the open
intertextual dialogue with other authors (most particularly Ramón del
Valle-Inclán), and finally, of the poetic character of many descriptions of
Madrid, we may conclude that Foxá at once conceives of the urban as a
literary palimpsest and the novel as a verbal city. While Madrid is rewritten by actions, memory, and literature, the novel duplicates the urban.
Such homology underscores, paradoxically, the tension between Madrid
and *Madrid de corte a checa* at the textual level.

Parts 2 and 3 of the novel portray Madrid as a huge theatre where
people act out phony roles, hence becoming simulacra of themselves. By
means of this decisive spatial technique, the narrator conveys the notion
that in the Republic everything and everybody is artificial, inauthentic.
Theatre and fashion dominate human behaviour. The coteries swarm
with snobbish intellectuals (1047, 1076); to praise Moscow is considered
an elegant thing to do (1079); and in the parliament the most important
matters are dealt with frivolously (1058): its sessions are nothing more
than theatrical performances (1058) and in its cafeteria the MPs con-
verse amicably, regardless of their party affiliations (1037); "They treated
each other," affirms the narrator with irony, "with the affection proper
to actors after a performance" (1058). In a meeting of revolutionaries,

people eat jam and toast in a festive fashion (1010–11; see also 1012, 1165, 1071, 1079). The conservative classes are not excluded from the narrative voice's fascist criticism either (1029, 1088–9). In this theatrical universe in which everybody simulates and strives to fulfil his most selfish interests, the narrator vents his anger against politicians who, far from defending their ideas with honesty, merely pretend to acquire a social and/or political prominence and thus satisfy their vanity. The unmerciful portrayals of Manuel Azaña (minister of war [1931], prime minister [1931–3, 1936], and president [1936–9] of the Second Republic) (951, 1011, 1061, 1071) and Niceto Alcalá Zamora (president [1931–3] of the Second Republic) (1010, 1165) present both politicians as conceited individuals. In his denunciation of the selfishness of left-wing politicians and revolutionaries alike, Foxá follows a literary tradition that depicts supposedly altruistic revolutionaries as no more than overambitious people who manipulate the masses for personal reasons (e.g., Fyodor Dostoievski's *Demons* [1869–72]; Émile Zola's *Germinal* [1885]; Joseph Conrad's *The Secret Agent* [1907] and *Under Western Eyes* [1911]).

At the end of the novel, the reader gets a hint of what the fascist production of space is all about. In the last chapter José Félix, now a soldier in Franco's army, has arrived at Carabanchel and observes the city. This scene is narrated by combining the spatial techniques of the map and the itinerary. The former describes the city's neuralgic sites (the Telefónica building, the Royal Palace, the Ministries of the State and of Foreign Affairs) while the latter presents a desolate urban landscape: José Félix "scoured Madrid's paving, the tramway's tracks ... and the trolleybus's cables, fallen, without electric current ... The houses had been pillaged by the militiamen ... One could see apartments, once happy, with beds without mattresses" (1337). Life thus has yielded to death. In spite of its physical proximity, Madrid is still a far-away city, a place stubbornly resisting the Nationalists' siege. José Félix's location and actions make this painfully evident, while they connote both a fascist conception and production of space. In this episode, the novel's main character, entrenched alongside a group of comrades, aims his rifle at Madrid: "He saw the city," writes the narrator, "covered by a light of danger. It would still be a long time before he could go there" (1337). With his field glasses he looks at "the most remote city in the world" (1338). *Madrid de corte a checa* has narrated in detail the process whereby José Félix and other citizens have been excluded from the city. José Félix has become a complete outsider in his own city, for he is physically elsewhere and Madrid has turned into an alien city, thus expelling him from its network of spatial relationships. His gaze upon Madrid through the field glasses and the rifle's front sight refracts the novel's mapping out of the urban on the one hand, and its perlocution – namely, the purpose to impose onto the reader a fascist absolute space – on the other. The association of field glasses with literary mapping underscores a crucial aspect of the novel. The homology between literary rhetoric and the rhetoric of walking established in *Madrid de corte a checa* enhances the novel's urbaneness. *Madrid de corte a checa* presents itself as a verbal urban space homologous to the urban space that it describes. And this is precisely what the novel *does*: it opposes the fascist rhetoric of walking set up at the level of the discourse to the Republican production of space narrated at the level of the story. In the novel, the fascist production of space lies not only in that confrontational stance, but also in the imposition of an ideologically determined discourse on individual behaviour.

Now, the gaze through the rifle's front sight reinforces a crucial element of the fascist production of space. It is, needless to say, a violent gaze. In Foxá's novel, the words uttered by the hero and the narrator about the urban are accompanied and strengthened by a weapon, by the thread of deadly force, by a menacing military gaze projected over the city. If we take into account *Madrid de corte a checa*'s ideological discourse, this final scene functions as an emblem of the novel's spatial techniques. José Félix's military gaze reproduces Foxá's violent literary mapping of the urban. *Madrid de corte a checa*'s performance of symbolic violence aims at the control of movement and ultimately at the elimination of the "other." For Foxá, the decadence of the country is such that Spain's regeneration can come only through its destruction. And the construction that fascism aspired to, as its literature shows, must be accomplished through aggressive words and violent action. Hence the subjugation of a city and the attainment of hegemony imply necessarily the conquest of a language, as witnessed in the novel's last scene: the hero and the rebel troops prepare themselves for that multiple conquest.[23]

The City at War

The rebels' failure to take Barcelona and Madrid – by far the two major metropolitan centres in economic, political, and cultural terms – as well as their conquest in the first weeks of the war of backward, conservative, agrarian towns such as Burgos, Salamanca, Ávila, Soria, Vitoria, and Pamplona belongs to "the urban logic that marked the war" (Ucelay-Da Cal, "Spanish Civil War" 39). In Ucelay-Da Cal's shrewd interpretation, since its inception the war was waged for the control of the cities, "and the defense or fall of urban centers decided campaigns and, ultimately, the conflict itself" (39). Hence the Spanish Civil War could be considered "a war of cities."[24] But the urban logic of the war had yet another dimension. Immediately after its outbreak, the antagonism among the hegemonic formations that had defined urban practices in 1931–6 acquired a new urban expression: the war split cities like Madrid and Barcelona into warring small "cities." In the first place, we have the "loyal city," initially appropriated by hegemonic formations (basically communism and anarchism) that for several months eluded all the government's attempts to rein them in. Far from being a unified space, the loyal city had divisions of its own that, more often than not, derived into open confrontation (the ruthless elimination of the POUM's leadership by Stalinist agents in Barcelona in May 1937 is a widely known case in point). There was also the "passive city," inhabited by people without political affinities, and the "secret city," comprising an ensemble of places and spaces that gathered together and sheltered fascists, members of anti-Republican parties and organizations, and all sorts of people hostile to the Republic.[25] As of 17 July 1936, spatial antagonism would be settled between heterogeneous visibilities and ghostly presences. The war of cities was, too, a *war within cities* fought by spies, hit men, informers, traitors, and saboteurs.

Fascist spaces of representation depicted the "cities" within the city, certainly not a surprising fact, since they fully participated, consciously or not, in the struggle for hegemony. Some, like *Madrid de corte a checa*, Adelardo Fernández Arias's (pseud. "El Duende de la Colegiata") "reportage" *Madrid bajo "El Terror," 1936–1937 (Impresiones de un evadido, que estuvo a punto de ser fusilado)* (1937), or Concha Espina's novel *Retaguardia: Imágenes de vivos y muertos* (1937) had done so as part of the war effort, but their republication shortly after the war placed them alongside the works published as of April 1939 on the same topic. All these spaces of representation belong to the production of space undertaken by the new rulers, if in a peculiar way. Their function did not consist in the propagation of the principles, goals, or realizations of the Francoist production of space, but rather in its justification. By representing the wartime urban divide within the binomial good/evil structure so characteristic of authoritarian fictions, these works set about to impress on the reader the pernicious, deadly effects of one production of space (the Republican) along with the need to restructure the urban and the national space upon the norms and rules established by the new state. Instances of these kinds of spaces of representation that appeared during the postwar era are Samuel Ros's autobiographical nouvelle *Meses de esperanza y lentejas (la Embajada de Chile en Madrid)* (1939), Alfredo Marquerie's *Cuatro pisos y la portería* (1940), Enrique Huidobro Pardo's Catholic ruminations *Escarmentemos... Meditaciones de un refugiado con un epílogo de asalto al Consulado* (1940), and the most important of them all: Tomás Borrás's notorious novel *Checas de Madrid* (1939–40).[26] To this work we will now turn our attention. An examination of the structure, ideological direction, and perlocution of this novel uncovers fundamental elements of the fascist urban writing and reveals the fascist mapping of a crucial locus in the geography of hegemonic practices in 1936–9: the city at war with itself.

Checas de Madrid is the finest and one of the most successful actualizations of the fascist urban writing centred on the war within cities.[27] Interesting for many reasons, Borrás's expressionist novel draws a map of two opposed spatial practices in the streets and places of Madrid. Construed as a battleground between different conceptions of space and structurally divided into five parts, the story of *Checas de Madrid* is organized around three main plots: (1) the arrest and imprisonment of the young Falangist Federico Contreras along with doña Fuenciscla's search for her missing son, (2) the activities of the chekas, and (3) the secret missions of the Falangist double agent Sagrario Milán. In general terms, the narrator centres his attention on the arrests, tortures, murders, lootings, and house confiscations carried out by the Republicans; his story, to put it in Nora's precise words, is a "hallucinated vision of a capital of terror, tortured and insane" (3: 377). Those horrific acts and itineraries of violence have as a point of reference a place that emblematizes, for Tomás Borrás, the Republic – the chekas.[28]

While in *Madrid de corte a checa* the Republican authorities and the masses alter urban space, in *Checas de Madrid* the *milicianos* (members of the main political parties' and trade unions' militias) transgress the law of the places by assigning them a function different from the one for which they had been originally conceived. The Republican actualization of places therefore becomes at odds with the grammar of these sites. A train station has, for instance, two opposed functions, being as it is both a point of departure and a detention centre; an old people's home has become a cheka where the detainees are sadistically tortured and eventually murdered; an unnamed palace houses don Roque and Sabino's sinister cheka, known as "Comité de Investigación Popular"; the elegant Palace of Argüelles houses the "Comité de Abastos CNT"; a kindergarten is now a prison of the Servicio de Investigación Militar or

SIM (Military Intelligence Agency), nicknamed as the "Lubianca de San Lorenzo" ("San Lorenzo's Lubyanka," an obvious allusion to the KGB's headquarters and prison in Moscow); and finally Saint Martin's Church has been transformed into a lively brothel.

Repression, torture, assassination, debauchery, and greed modify the urban beyond recognition, reassigning new laws to the places and thereby creating a grotesque urban landscape whose places lack stable norms of coexistence. In describing the train station, the narrator asserts, "The train station, a common metaphor of precision and order, was in a state of chaos and noise, like in a fair" (36). Private places share with public spaces that grotesque quality. Thus, about don Roque and Sabino's cheka, the narrator writes, "Between the morose exquisitenesses, the militiamen, pigs in intention and mud, shrilled" (273). As Huidobro Pardo put it in *Escarmentemos*, for the "Reds" "there is no other art than murder and assassination ... they worship all things ugly" (223). Such an improbable combination of classic beauty with immoral behaviour and physical vulgarity generates a *contradictio in adjecto* (Borras, *Checas* 273–4).[29] This is evident, too, in a theatre converted into a cheka led by one of its former prompters, a person with a deep resentment towards actors (223–4). At one point the prompter climbs onto the stage and unexpectedly begins to perform in front of both the detainees and guards. During this performance, the detainees must keep silent, thus repeating in a reversed context the silence required from the spectators during any theatrical performance, the violation of which may be met with disapproval by other spectators. At the end of his bizarre impromptu performance, the prompter forces the appalled detainees to applaud. In a multifaceted reversal of roles, the prompter has taken over the acting, and the public is now a group of detainees awaiting the worst.[30] *Checas de Madrid* denounces forcefully the formation of spaces that transgress the original law of the place. The Republican politicians, militiamen, and sympathizers radically modify the stable, traditional meaning of the places. However, the transformation of the place goes beyond the grotesque, for in almost all the Republican places described in *Checas de Madrid* acts of sadistic torture, medical experiments on human beings, and arbitrary assassination are routinely carried out. The spatial disorder, the aesthetics of the grotesque, and the evil that underpins the Republican hegemonic practices entail symbolic and semantic chaos. This close connection between abject places and immoral behaviour openly indicates the double nature of the constitutive evil of the Republicans and points out the aesthetic and ethical consequences of the Republican rewriting of the law of place.[31]

Like *Madrid de corte a checa*, Borrás's novel is an instance of spatial form. Thanks to its discursive fragmentation, *Checas de Madrid* refracts, at the formal level, the urban discontinuities and spatial disorder, as well as the seemingly random itineraries that, by eradicating all type of boundaries between neighbourhoods, leave Madrid in a state of absolute decomposition. In addition to private interiors, entire neighbourhoods and streets have lost their ordinary aspect. Readers are told about barricades and wire fences in Argüelles (164–5), destroyed banisters, houses swallowed up by explosions, streets with no pavement, broken doors, windows, and balconies (345), a city literally split in two (412) that has been "slowly dissolving" (345). An "aesthetics of the ruin" underpins *Checas de Madrid*'s cartography of the urban.[32] It is a ruin brought about less by the war than by the militias, de facto rulers of the city, always on the move, seeking to settle old scores, to fulfil their murderous instincts, or more prosaically, to satisfy their greed. "Free mobility" seems to be in the final analysis the implied author's bête noire. A wide range of itineraries crisscrosses the city map. First, those motivated by the militiamen's death drive; in this group the persecutions, street patrols, arrests, and *paseos* predominate. Then there are those originated on economic grounds, constituted basically by the itineraries of house confiscations and the evacuations of the well-off in exchange for handsome sums of money. In direct contrast to them are the itineraries coming from the "secret city," a defensive, resented zone whose residents long for a denotative, classist, authoritarian syntax, semantics, and pragmatics of space. Borrás determines two basic itineraries coming from the "secret city." The first is the itinerary of the victim, which groups the itineraries of the hiding, the search for missing people, and the flight from the militias. Alongside this defensive set of itineraries one can find a second group, the itineraries of resentment, actualized in two different vectorialities: the march of Franco's army towards and subsequent siege of Madrid, and the itineraries of the spy, without a doubt the most important to the novel's storyline and ideological direction.[33]

A natural product of the "secret city" in wartime and perhaps the purest expression of anti-Republican *ressentiment*, in a Madrid split into two warring sides the spy functions as a bridge that links and opposes insularities, at once destroying autonomies and opening up spaces.[34] Within the logic of the urban, the bridge, to put it in de Certeau's words, "offers the possibility of a bewildering exteriority, it allows or causes the reemergence beyond the frontiers of the alien element that was controlled in the interior, and gives objectivity ... to the alterity which was hidden inside the limits, so that in recrossing the bridge and coming back within the enclosure the traveler henceforth finds there the exteriority that he had first sought by going outside and then fled by returning" (128–9). That this role is played in Borrás's novel by Sagrario Milán, a well-mannered, pious, prudish young woman who belongs to the ranks of the haute bourgeoisie, is far from accidental. If we consider their marginality in public life, women in the 1930s (and in previous times, for that matter) could be described, to borrow the term from Ralph Ellison's masterpiece, as "invisible." Naturally, the fifth column took full advantage of this invisibility, as proven by the decisive importance of Falangist women in information gathering, subversion, and sabotage missions.[35] But aside from reflecting a historical fact, Borrás invests his character with a very particular spatial signification, for Sagrario is a double agent working for the Falange Clandestina *and* the Republican intelligence agencies. Not only is she the perfect image of an urban space split up into different "cities"; the psychic consequences of her duplicitous secret activities also make her a living metaphor of the war within the city. Like other characters in the novel who have adopted false identities in order to survive, Borrás's female hero, whom the narrator calls, tellingly, "dual Sagrario" (420), has to act out the habitus of militiawomen, radically different from her own. Sagrario's duplicity estranges her from her own social milieu as well as from herself. Wherever she goes, she is seen as an unpleasant presence, as a potential threat. In the street, people look at her with profound distrust, even hatred, because they take her for an SIM agent (e.g., 347). The same happens in the bourgeois houses upon which she calls to investigate families suspected of supporting the rebellion, especially on a particular occasion in which she deliberately blows her own cover in the house of a Falangist family. She unveils her identity, says who has sent her and why, gives them the Falangist watchword, and makes the Roman salute; but to Sagrario's desperation, no one believes her (270–2). The urban is thus a foreign, inhospitable, even dangerous territory: the double agent's home is at once everywhere and nowhere, his or her location resides in a no-man's-land where accidental death will inevitably be an anonymous event.

To the spatial estrangement corresponds a psychological split. Having to behave and talk like a militiawoman – a type deeply despised by fascists and anti-Republicans in general[36] – is extremely painful because it contravenes Sagrario's education, ideology, and habitus. The first time she utters "comrade," the word sounds to her "as if she were listening to herself … a repulsive swearword [*sic*]. 'I am serving them and I am serving my people.' This double game ... made her soul totter" (266–7). Sagrario does not take long to feel disgust for herself (e.g., 352, 402–3) as well as remorse (348). To behave and to dress with the vulgarity expected from any militiawoman (e.g., ugly clothes, bad manners, provocative gestures, swearing) is as toxic to her mental health as her participation in espionage-related activities whose effect may be the assassination of anti-Republican people – her people – is harmful to her conscience. As a way of being, duplicity destabilizes Sagrario's identity; it alters her sense of place, her self-perception, her psyche. While her activities as a double agent make her an embodiment of the split of the urban, their psychological effect allows us to conclude that the psyche of the novel's main character refracts the war within the city. This double spatial function plays an important role in the ideological direction of the novel as well as its perlocution. Sagrario's duplicity and identity crisis are meant to be a lesson; they point out to the reader the peremptory hygienic necessity to maintain a stable, one-dimensional identity. For the implied author, any dialogue with the enemy – as Sagrario's story demonstrates – has pernicious effects. To establish bridges makes sense only insofar as they lead to the destruction of the "other." While free mobility is tacitly opposed by absolute space, psychic contradictions, the subject's unfixity, and ambivalence towards hegemonic formations need to be replaced by unidimensionality. In other words, the absolute subjection of the individual to a one-dimensional identity as well as to (absolute) political power is a correlate of the fascist defence of absolute space. By expanding his mapping of the urban to the mental space of his characters, Borrás is consistent with a primary fascist goal: the moulding of the subject, the imposition of a fascist habitus upon the individual. The fascist production of space involves the reshaping of this most secret of places – the human psyche.

Almost invariably, fascist literature written on the war portrays the "Reds" as abject, murderous, vulgar, depraved, profit-seeking, Mongoloid-like *Untermenschen*, as evil figures lacking political convictions whose sole purpose is the extermination of Spain. This topos, which appears again and again in fascist narrative,[37] would be elaborated in metaphysical terms by José María de Pemán in his *Poema de la Bestia y el Ángel* (1939). Borrás made this topos the main thread of his novel and reduced it *ad absurdum*. In *Checas de Madrid*, the "Reds" are sadists: "The red Beast feels indescribable joys causing pain. The revolution's preparatory technique has had only two phases: first, to extirpate the moral defences ... to put out the spiritual education; and second, as soon as the being gives

in to basic instincts, to arouse them in order to resurrect what's left of
the Beast" (396–7).

By mapping the militias' itineraries, places, and spaces, Borrás draws
a topography of evil. The narrator describes in great detail the many
sadistic tortures performed by the Republicans and the medical experiments on detainees, evocative to the contemporary reader of similar experiments routinely performed by Nazi doctors on Auschwitz inmates.
Madrid is no more than a vast prison with a chamber of torture where
corpses, wounds, body fluids, and rot are common currency.[38] Borrás
represents a space of abjection where the distinction between subject
and object has been lost, a space that breaks down meaning. The novel
makes us stare at the abject (in Julia Kristeva's sense of the word); we
are forced to face an object that, once a subject, has now been cast out
from the world. Situated outside the symbolic order, the abject means
the eruption of the Real (in Jacques Lacan's terminology). Take, for instance, the corpse, which Kristeva uses to exemplify her theory of the abject. The corpse condenses the dissolution of the border between subject
and object, it upsets whoever confronts it. "Refuse and corpses," argues
Kristeva, "*show me* what I permanently thrust aside in order to live" (3).
Body fluids, defilement, excrement "are what life withstands," and every
time one contemplates them is at the border of his condition as a living
being (3). "The corpse," according to Kristeva, "is the utmost of abjection. It is death infecting life. Abject. It is something rejected from which
one does not part, from which one does not protect oneself as from an
object. An imaginary uncanniness and real threat, it beckons to us and
engulfs us" (4).

Taking into account the meaning and significance of the abject, one
may conclude that *Checas de Madrid* is an attempt to create in readers a
feeling of horror. As a consequence of the Republic's advent, Madrid
turned from a space of life into the habitat of the abject. Therefore, everything related to the Republic must be eliminated. On first inspection
this seems to be a fundamental component of the ideological direction
of the novel. Now, Borrás's literary treatment of the abject is ambiguous,
and for this reason the previous conclusion needs to be qualified. In
the first place, the novel's expressionism as well as its symbolic violence
reproduces, at the level of discourse, the violence carried out by the militias. As with the work of Jean Genet, Louis-Ferdinand Céline, and Curzio
Malaparte, reading *Checas de Madrid* is far from a comforting activity. It
cannot leave the reader indifferent, not only on account of its contents,
but also, and basically, because of the way the stories are told. *Checas de*

Madrid puts its reader in a situation analogous to the one faced by the victims described in the novel. The narrator lays on the readers a symbolic, sometimes unbearable violence, which parallels the physical violence committed against some characters in the novel. Moreover, Borrás shows an unabashed fascination for the murders he describes, so much so that in many instances he clearly enjoys his description of abjection.[39] The discourse of the novel participates mutatis mutandis in the violence and evil of the militias. To put it differently: Borrás indulges in the sadistic narration of the repulsive, bestial scenes to which he devotes many pages. This apparent contradiction belongs, though, to a wider context. Speaking of its dual relation with the abject, Kristeva notes that contemporary literature "seems to be written out of the untenable aspects of perverse or superego positions while maintaining a distance as regards the abject.… The writer, fascinated by the abject, imagines its logic, projects himself into it, introjects it, and as a consequence perverts language – style and content" (16). But "on the other hand, as the sense of abjection is both the abject's judge and accomplice, this is also true of the literature that confronts it. One might thus say that with such literature there takes place a crossing over of the dichotomous categories of Pure and Impure, Prohibition and Sin, Morality and Immorality" (16). That crossing over and impurity notwithstanding, literature, like art, purifies the abject, it performs catharsis of sorts (17); for this reason, "the artistic experience, which is rooted in the abject it utters and by the same token purifies, appears as the essential component of religiosity" (17–18).

Gareth Thomas might be right when he argues that the lack of measure in novels like *Checas de Madrid* is pernicious in their purpose to instruct the reader; in this sense, it could be said that the moralizing discourse of the novel fails because the work leaves the reader "insensitive to the atrocities" (Thomas 28). Indeed, the violence inherent in Borrás's novelistic discourse seems to cancel out the Manichaean ideological message of the novel. But Thomas's conclusion misses an essential factor of the novel's perlocution. I am referring to its cathartic function, which liberates the reader from the abject. *Checas de Madrid* purifies a space of abjection. For Borrás, free mobility and individual freedom are consubstantial to the abject. In the novel's axiology, to purify the abject amounts to putting things back into their "proper" place, it means bringing back order, borders, rules, identity, thus reinstating the threatened morality and law. Therefore, *Checas de Madrid* attacks a hegemonic formation through a critique of its revolutionary production of space and its abjection. From the novelist's standpoint, the military uprising of 17 July 1936 was a rebellion against all that. *Checas de Madrid* maps out the spatial practices that the military endeavoured to eliminate and the abject space that it sought to purify. Like other fascist works published during the war or immediately afterward, Borrás's novel creates a distorted image of the Republicans that justifies the military rebellion, its subsequent repression (a "cleansing" of "undesirable" people), and a new production of space. *Checas de Madrid* thus may be seen as part of a complex constellation of tactics and strategies of the new state.

Spatial Form and the Rhetoric of Mapping

As previously pointed out, both *Madrid de corte a checa* and *Checas de Madrid* are instances of spatial form. In each novel, the novelistic discourse breaks up the chronological order of events and fragments the story. Simultaneity predominates over sequentiality. The juxtaposition of storylines with their own temporality and the fact that they are usually if not always told discontinuously create a fictive world whose fragmentation refracts the city's polymorphism as well as the simultaneity of urban experience. Neither novel allows for a purely sequential interpretation. Instead, both need to be apprehended as unities built up by narrative patterns. This is also true of other instances of fascist urban writing, such as Iribarren's *La ciudad*, Camba's *Madridgrado*, Ledesma Ramos's early Bildungsroman *El sello de la muerte* (1924), and, to a certain extent, Torrente Ballester's *Javier Mariño*. Closely related to the spatial history so common among some fascists, spatial form permeates such a significant number of urban novels that it could be said to constitute what Roman Jakobson has termed the *dominant*. If we were to consider on the one hand fascism's attempt to bury historical time under absolute space, and, on the other, the connection between spatial form and works underpinned by a reactionary or fascist ideology (e.g., Wyndham Lewis, Ezra Pound, Filippo Tomasso Marinetti, Céline, Giménez Caballero), it follows that spatial form in fascist urban writing is a discursive technology whereby novels spatialize time in order to symbolically control the dynamism of human activities. Given fascism's preference for absolute space, spatial form could be seen as a discursive technology of the fascist production of space.

Among the different components of that technology there is one of particular importance vis-à-vis the fascist preference for absolute space and the intended perlocution of the urban writing. I am referring to a device already pointed out in this chapter albeit not in detail: the rhetoric of mapping. As seen before, mapping coexists with other elements of spatial form, such as the rhetoric of walking. However, sometimes mapping turns out to be the main technique, if not the only one, in fascist urban writing. When this happens, the novels refract the totalitarian drive inherent in the fascist politics of space. Hence the importance of such works: they reduce to the absurd a technique present in other fascist urban novels. In their merging of spatial form and absolute space, these novels reveal with great clarity the fundamental coordinates of fascism's location within the geography of hegemonic practices. Our attention will focus now on a milestone of Spanish fascist literature: *Plaza del Castillo* (1951), by Rafael García Serrano, an unrepentant Falangist who authored works that have defined Spanish literary fascism, such as *Eugenio o proclamación de la Primavera* (1938), one of the most important depictions of the fascist hero; *La fiel infantería* (1943), an outstanding representative of fascist war writing, analysed further in this chapter; and *Diccionario para un macuto* (1964), an interesting, somewhat nostalgic collection of . fascist expressions and songs produced during the civil war.[40]

Not unlike *Madrid de corte a checa*, García Serrano's novel at first sight seems to prioritize time over space. Its story takes place in Pamplona during the *sanfermines* of 1936 from Monday, 6 July, to Sunday, 19 July, and each chapter bears as a title the date of the events that it tells. Whereas Foxá's novel narrates the story of the country's "decadence," *Plaza del Castillo* concentrates on the days immediately leading to the outbreak of the war. As the novel makes obvious throughout, the *sanfermines*' defining bloodiness stops on 14 July (the last day of the festivity), only to reassume three days later when the colonial army posted in Morocco rebelled against the Republic. The author makes a disturbing link between a traditional festivity and a fratricidal military confrontation. Nevertheless, a more careful inspection reveals this chronological arrangement of events to be in fact articulated by a concentric structure in which chapter 8 plays a crucial role in the symbolic dimension and fascist political discourse of the novel, stated explicitly in several passages (e.g., 42, 181–2, 225–8). The chapter is set in the structural centre of this fourteen-chapter novel as well as within the storyline, for it covers the day of the last *encierro* (13 July); hence it functions as a hinge of sorts between the festivity and the war: in the end of the festivity is the beginning of the war. The narrator furnishes in this chapter a short but substantive history of Pamplona's Plaza del Castillo, its significance for the people, its symbolism, its political function, its metaphysic nature. Chapter 8 constitutes, therefore, the structural, symbolic, and ideological "main square" of *Plaza del*

Castillo in which everything converges. In view of this, the title of the novel underscores the priority of space over time, hints at the structural and symbolical importance of Pamplona's main square, and stresses one crucial element of the absolute space proposed by fascism as the nation's organizing principle – stasis. While streets, avenues, and boulevards facilitate movement, squares foster stability and closure. In the last analysis, "Plaza del Castillo" and *Plaza del Castillo* are emblems of absolute space. The novel, whose structural, thematic, and symbolic centre lies in chapter 8, mimics Pamplona's urban layout. *Plaza del Castillo is* Pamplona, and chapter 8, or the novel's "main square," constitutes the "main square" of that discursive Pamplona. García Serrano's novel hence may be considered as a city built by language and organized around a main square that, according to the author, symbolizes Navarre and the rest of Spain.

The events leading to the novel's "main square" function as the prologue to the restoration of the Plaza del Castillo to its original meaning. An ominous atmosphere of violence and abjection permeates the first seven chapters of *Plaza del Castillo*. For the narrator, Spain is a "latrine" that must be cleaned up; specifically, the task to be performed consists of "cleaning up the heads of the Spaniards, the grime of the Spaniards, the filth of towns and cities ... the ugly instincts ... [as well as] creating a big national garbage dump, and thus begin to live in a place that doesn't smell of urine where there are ... no mental dungs" (43; see also 86). Interestingly, for the implied author abjection is a valid means to fight the Republic. Apropos of the Republican dismissive consideration of bullfighting as "barbaric," the narrator approvingly notes that "the street prayed its own way, it prepared the festivity, and in addition it didn't give a shit about the Republic, a gesture otherwise as elegant as it is just" (35). Alongside this anonymous resistance there is the Falangist and Carlist conspiracy against the Republic and the above-mentioned connection between the *sanfermines* and the imminent war. The examples are many. Thus, reacting to a friend's announcement that the rebellion has been put off to a date later than 15 July, a character voices his disappointment by saying, "It would have been much better to dovetail the two fiestas" (155); in yet another example, the narrator relates the *encierro* of 12 July with military language (130) and compares reveille with the sound of the church bells (131). Unsurprisingly, in *Plaza del Castillo* the *sanfermines* are perceived as a festivity whose Christian sediment unites the people while erasing social antagonisms. Falangists, Carlists, socialists, communists, republicans, and monarchists participate in the *sanfermines* as a single people, as brothers and sisters happily sharing the same traditions.

During the *corrida*, unity replaces antagonism: "All of them participated with all their hearts, in the fiesta, all of them offered themselves jubilantly to danger" (133). Antagonisms re-emerge, however, as soon as the *corrida* on Pamplona's streets is over (136).

The novel's "main square" consists of a series of overlapping palimpsests, an "urban palm" (165) that contains the past, present, and future of the city, and of several social, political, and metaphysical functions and significations hierarchically articulated. It is worth remarking that the first thing the reader is told about the square is its military function: it is the "parade ground" of an "entire people" (163). In essence a military locus at the service of a "people's community," the main square has gone through many changes since the Middle Ages, the most negative one a result of the modern rationalization of Pamplona's urban layout. As in other fascist urban narratives, spatial antagonism (traditional/modern Plaza del Castillo) cannot be dissociated from ideological hostility (folkish traditionalism/modern rationalism). In modern times, says the narrator, "Pamplona needed to widen itself to the countryside and break the crust of the city walls and look out at the green landscapes"; however, the real problem lies elsewhere: "Then someone thought of breaking through the Plaza del Castillo," and as a consequence, "the square's tight and perfect unity broke up on one side, and Menéndez had the impression that a new life, good or bad, different in any case, that no one could predict would come in through it, and that avenue ending in the square or starting there might very well be a sign of the city's good fortune, or also a clear sign of ill luck" (165). Notice here that for the narrator a material spatial practice brought about by modernity may not necessarily lead to its purported negative logical consequence; in fact, it could derive into its opposite, that is, the restoration of the main square's essence. But this will not come about by itself, as a natural outcome of the modern grammar articulating the city and its main square. Rather, the key for that to happen resides, if we take into consideration the entire novel and the *intentio textis*, in *doing something about it* – war.

Decisively, the Plaza del Castillo condenses Spain, a synonymity that projects Pamplona's spatial antagonism to the rest of the country. The Plaza del Castillo/Spain comprises a folkish habitus based on Spanish nationalism and Catholicism, as argued in a passage that links habitus and production of space with hegemony: "Nobody knows ... that the first thing to do is to reinstate in our people the national and Christian soul, and the rest will be added unto it ... Spain is ... the Plaza del Castillo: there is an enormous breach between the old and the modern ... The problem consists of linking up the two things, of building a solid arch leading ... to the future. Primary school, bread, justice, and a common enterprise" (207). An earlier novel of García Serrano's, *La fiel infantería* (1943), already had spelled out how to solve that problem: "The square wanted the war because it summed up the city. And the city was a placard of Spain. What a violent midday in my old square!" (38).

The Plaza del Castillo is thus both a physical place and a metaphysical ground, a unifying force for the inhabitants and fellow Spaniards, a bearer of a tradition based on Christianity, an embodiment of culture and humanism (165). Only war can restore an essence eroded by modernity. Indeed, the square recovers its centrality, signification, and social function thanks to the military rebellion; it becomes itself as soon as the cleaning up of the Republican "filth" begins, an event told in the last two chapters. From the Plaza del Castillo to the countryside and back, and hence to Madrid: these are the two axes of the Nationalists' itineraries. *Plaza del Castillo* focuses only on the former itinerary, thereby underscoring key concepts, such as *centre, absolute space, stasis,* as well as the spatial form upon which the novel is built.

To recover stasis and absolute space, movement in relative space-time must be brought into play. The movement is both centrifugal and centripetal, a circularity that reinforces the perception of Navarre as an absolute land (i.e., a region unified by the same culture and traditions) comprehending a "people's community." First, Falangist agents are ordered to go to villages of Navarre. To them, the names of those villages, so familiar, now sound new, recent, as "if they were being used for the first time" (227), a somewhat logical perception: to reinstate places as they were in the past entails looking at them anew. In order to achieve it, the spatial centre must be changed. Following thus a folkish tradition, García Serrano situates the root of the solution in the countryside. Further in the text we read that, after the call to arms, "the whole land of Navarre was sending to Pamplona" (227) volunteers to fight the Republic – a sentence whose syntax stresses the region's agency. Navarre is basically the main agent of folkish revolutionary action. Right after giving the order to his fellow comrades, Joaquín recalls a folkish passage from a book saying that Spain will not be back in history until "impassioned men go all over the fields and the villages to inflame the atmosphere with this expression: 'Hey, you the provinces, on your feet!'" (227). And this is precisely what they are doing, as Joaquín himself considers (227–8). Soon "the voluntary procession [*romería*], both subversive and military ... coming up from the very land, would flood the city and fill with clean water the Plaza del Castillo" (235). After this call to arms many volunteers arrive in Pamplona and gather in its main square. A revolution to carry out a new production of space begins in the centre of a city, itself the centre of Navarre. Remarkably, the production of space is performed by an entire region, as if this region contained in itself the spatial grammar that had to be applied to the rest of Spain (233). Navarre rises up in arms to reshape Spain according to its own values, which are identical to those of the nation, if we consider the synonymy between that region and the nation. In a passage that perfectly exemplifies the novel's geographic approach to history and social reality, the narrator says, "The entire country of Spain was within those men and landscapes ... As if this were a harmonious synthesis of Spain, taking hold of the Pyrenees on one side and on the other calmly spreading out through the Ebro's lowlands ... From the mountains' blond and primitive race to the Ribera, Navarre has everything, it is a geographical and spiritual compendium of Spain, summary and cipher of the beautiful Fatherland" (234).

As if relieved, the narrator points out that with the arrival of the volunteers the Plaza del Castillo has recovered its military meaning and function; it is again a "plaza de armas" or a parade ground, a meeting place with "immutable roots" (239). A purifying task, a "national *sanfermin*," a "military pilgrimage" is being undertaken at the Plaza del Castillo: "It was necessary ... to be born again, to be different ... to sweep the manure ... to open the windows and breathe that impetuous and purifying air" (240). This means that from now on military discipline will shape all spatial relationships and vectorialities on the one hand, and individual lifestyles and ways of thinking on the other. The Plaza del Castillo imposes a discipline, erases individuality, and stamps a military habitus on the men gathered there. The geometry of the square, applied to the novel through the practice of a spatial form, projects itself into the discipline imposed on people. In the Plaza del Castillo, says the narrator, "They were called to fall in. The battalions' restless geometry fits soon to an absolute rigidity" (246).

Since *Plaza del Castillo* is a discursive extension of the Plaza del Castillo in Pamplona, it may be said that the novel carries an illocutionary force. Just as other fascist works we have seen, García Serrano's novel *orders an order* to the readers; it commands them to accept and fit in a static space. *Plaza del Castillo* could be considered as an authoritarian illocutionary act, as a military novel of sorts performing the verb *to command*, thereby imposing absolute space at the thematic, structural, symbolic, and pragmatic levels. From the implied author's standpoint, literary mapping re-

turns everything to its original place. In the context of the role played
by literary discourse within the geography of hegemonic practices, *Plaza
del Castillo* brings to the fore essential characteristics of the fascist urban
writing's performativity. "To act against" hegemonic formations and "to
fight for" spatial hegemony were actions performed not only in Spain's
streets. Words could do the job just as well.

Into the Battlefield

Total wars make particular demands on literary critics, for their all-encompassing nature (e.g., the involvement of the entire population of
the countries at war, the instability of the usual limits between civilians
and the military, the targeting of civilians by enemy armies, absolute
enmity) may blur the usual borders between literary subgenres. This is
most true of war writing and urban novels about cities in wartime: separating one from the other is often a doomed undertaking. In a way, the
urban novels studied in this chapter more closely resemble such classics of war literature as Ernest Hemingway's *A Farewell to Arms* (1929)
and Siegfried Sassoon's *Memoirs of an Infantry Officer* (1930) than they
do such milestones of urban writing as Andrey Bely's *St Petersburg* (1913–
14), John Dos Passos's *Manhattan Transfer* (1921), Italo Svevo's *La cosci-
enza di Zeno* (1923), or Alfred Döblin's *Berlin Alexanderplatz* (1929). Not
infrequently, urban writing and war writing overlap to such an extent
that to elucidate their ascription to one category or the other is as difficult as it is futile. I am thinking of André Malraux's *L'Espoir* (1937),
George Orwell's *Homage to Catalonia* (1938), and Arthur Koestler's *Spanish Testament* (1937), works in which the accounts of fighting coexist with
the textual prominence of the urban. Furthermore, the perlocution of
urban writing produced during the war and war writing itself is similar if
not identical. As a constitutive part of the war effort, their intended perlocutionary effect resides in "winning over" the reader for the cause that
they defend. For all these reasons, it is advisable to study urban writing
and war writing in tandem. In order to better capture the significance
of fascist urban writing, it is important to understand the workings and
function of war writing. Within the above-mentioned urban logic of the
civil war, the urban and the battlefield tend to overlap, and so do the
literary works dealing with one or the other. The actualizations of fascist
war writing are as many as they are diverse. Other than the abundant poetry produced during the war, some of it collected in anthologies such
as *Poemas de la Falange eterna* (1939) and Jorge Villén's *Antología poética*

del Alzamiento, 1936–1939 (1939), in the literary field stand out Cecilio Benítez de Castro's *Se ha ocupado el Kilómetro seis (Contestación a Remarque)* (1939), Felipe Ximénez de Sandoval's *Camisa azul (Retrato de un falangista)* (1939), Edgar Neville's *Frente de Madrid* (1941), Rafael García Serrano's *La fiel infantería* (1943), and Pedro García Suárez's *Legión 1936* (1945).[41] It is true that most of these novels, understandably enough, were published after the war. But despite this fact, these works did collaborate with the military in regard to the consolidation of the rebels' victory. By way of example, I will centre on one of the best fascist war novels ever written – *La fiel infantería.*

García Serrano's *La fiel infantería* is a true classic of Spanish fascist literature. Little has been written on the novel, but this lack of scholarly work has more to do with the secondary status of literary fascism in specialized criticism than with any other consideration.[42] *La fiel infantería* is one of the better-known, if not always read, fascist war fictions. Its themes, figures, and values (e.g., the fascist hero, folkish ideals, exaltation of soldierly life and disdain for the civilian world, politics of space), its bellicose language, and its joyful depiction of physical violence, among other fascist family resemblances, have contributed to the novel's preeminence within the fascist literary canon. Awarded the 1943 Premio Nacional de Literatura "José Antonio Primo de Rivera," García Serrano's second novel tells the story of three young Falangists – Miguel, Matías, and Ramón – who fought in the civil war, first as members of Falange's militias and later as commissioned officers. Far from accidental, this metamorphosis reflects Franco's strategically intelligent subordination of the militias to the armed forces (Preston, *Spanish Civil War* 210–11), and more importantly, it underpins an ideological direction of the novel – pointed out by its very title – whose main proposition could be expressed as follows: the fascist habitus reaches its plenitude under the army's discipline. The novel's *dispositio* is based upon that proposition. Of the three parts composing *La fiel infantería,* the first two are narrated in the first person by a Falangist – Miguel in part 1 and Matías in part 2 – whereas the anonymous extradiegetic voice narrates the third, devoted to the military training at the Military Academy at Ávila of the two Falangists whose autobiographical narratives end, rather significantly, shortly after being called up by the army. The disciplining of personal behaviour and the utter elimination of individual freedom initiated in the Military Academy is thus reflected by the narrative erasure of the characters' own voices, absorbed by the extradiegetic narrator whose anonymity mirrors the army's impersonal control of its troops.

La fiel infantería may be considered as the militarization of the fascist habitus, ideology, and discourse. Likewise, the constellation of places and spaces on the one hand, and the relationship between the city and the countryside on the other, are controlled by a military gaze. Cities (i.e., Madrid, Pamplona, two unnamed cities) and the countryside relate to each other antagonistically; in addition to the usual folkish arguments, the urban is the object of the narrators' disdain or mockery for its association with civilian life, while the country is related to things military and for this reason exalted as the locus of true manhood and authentic life. Instead of presenting that *longue-durée* structure in an antinomic fashion, the novelist has opted for a dialectic method; each dialectical moment corresponds to one of the novel's three parts: folkish Castile as a model space (thesis), the urban and civilian life (antithesis), and the militarization of the folkish ideals to be imposed upon the urban (synthesis alluded at the end of the novel).

Largely centred on the march of fascist volunteers from Pamplona to the Guadarrama front, in the first part of *La fiel infantería* the implied author condemns, if briefly, Madrid's proletarization and easy life. In his position during a moment of rest, Mario reflects on tramways full of stinky, sweaty people (24), the pointless literary gatherings and the literary coteries' naiveté vis-à-vis the increasing social and political tension (26), and his worries about the potential effect of the sharp political disagreements among his friends (25). Vaguely realizing the outcome of antagonisms, Mario feels overwhelmed by confusion and melancholy (26). After Mario's remembrance of his life in the city, Madrid is never mentioned again in *La fiel infantería*, as if by this absence the author wished to symbolically eradicate, to expel to the margins of representation the much-hated Republican Madrid. In counterpoint, the narrator continues his narrative with an exaltation of Castile. In their position near a Castilian hamlet, the Falangists find much more than a place to rest: "It simply smelled of country. Of Castile.... Now he [Mario] guarded Castile's land with a rifle in his hands ... Mario felt how the landscape dazzled him" (28–9). In that land viewed through folkish lenses, not only do the fascists fertilize Spain "by the firing of guns" (19), but they also have themselves become a state "on the offensive, with its troops and unwritten codes" that imposes its law by "clean shots" (18), thereby identifying the new state in progress with the fascist habitus and military action – an issue to which I will return later.

Precisely in the overlapping of the violence joyfully conducted by the fascists and the military striation of space and places resides the produc-

tion of space represented in and performed by *La fiel infantería*. Part 1
shows that overlapping as it materialized in the first months of the war,
and presents fascist violence as performed in the weeks before 17 July.
At the front, Miguel remembers the fascist punitive expeditions undertaken against leftists in Pamplona (30–1), the gathering of volunteers at
the Plaza del Castillo (45–6), their progress by bus to Madrid through
Logroño, Soria, Aranda, and Somosierra until they were forced to halt
at a point eighty kilometres from the capital (86), whose conquest he
and his comrades-in-arms conceived of as a rape to be performed (87).
Encountering no opposition to their advance, the narrator notes, with
characteristic fascist bravado, that they travelled through Spain cheerfully "as armed tourists" (54), a statement that points to a production of
space identified more with leisure than soldierly manners and military
discipline. The order to join the Military Academy at Ávila announced
at the end of part 1 establishes a sharp contrast with the "touristic" trip
from Pamplona to the Madrid front. At the Military Academy, Miguel
will be taught how to produce space in a military way. Perhaps anticipating the army's design to discipline Falange, before his departure to the
Military Academy Miguel defensively claims that "we would be – forever –
the best thing of the war. We and those landscapes. Hereafter … only we
and our landscapes would know exactly why the war was fought" (110).
These thoughts would be qualified at the Academy.

Part 2 of the novel shifts the focus from the battlefield to an unnamed
walled city in "national" territory. Matías, its intradiegetic narrator, tells
the story of a leave spent in his hometown in November 1936. Now a
new man born out of his combat experience, he feels the apparently
unbridgeable gap between soldierly life and the Falangist revolutionary
spirit on the one hand and the bourgeois lifestyle of the cities, "well ordered, earnest, without scandals" on the other (125). Repeating a topos
of modern war fiction set up by Barbusse in *Le Feu* (323–30), García
Serrano depicts the social consequences of the radical metamorphoses
that occur in people who have seen combat. Since the civilians' indifference and incomprehension might awaken in the soldier feelings of
frustration, resentment, hatred, and superiority, the battlefield is a potential threat to the urban and civilian society at large. The roaming of
the *Freikorps* in the streets of Germany and the anti-democratic stance
of many German First World War veterans who, feeling betrayed by the
political caste, ended up joining the ranks of fascism, constitute two instances (masterfully portrayed by Joseph Roth in *Das Spinnennetz* [1923])
of such a potentially dangerous effect of the front on the home front. "I

am different from what I used to be," acknowledges Matías (119). Except for his comrades-in-arms, "there is no one worthy enough for me to drop my backpack ... so as to give him a hug" (120). Melancholia, disappointment, and a sense of emptiness and disgust overwhelm him at home (120–1, 127), at a coffee house (121–4, 125), in the streets (124, 125, 127–8), at a brothel (125–6). "This is the civilization," ruminates Matías, "a series of pleasures" whose comforts sap his finest primitive instincts (122). The mere fact of sitting in a coffee house amounts to an unwilling defence of "the whole Western world that crushes me with caresses" (122). Just a few months earlier, Matías thought they had kicked "the old world's butt"; their goal resided in "fertilizing the Fatherland with the uprising's [*Alzamiento*'s] violent powder so that a different world could be born" (122). The daily activities and routines of the city, still untouched by Falange's revolutionary spirit, deeply depress the narrator and main character. This situation is felt more painfully at the brothel, whose suffocating "provocative atmosphere" is located in the antipodes of the battlefield: "On the field the rain will sound. There are going to be prayers, changing of the guard ... anguish. Comrades will die" (126). In the episode devoted to the march from Pamplona to Madrid in part 1, the narrator had already criticized the stultifying effect of living in cities. Leaving that Navarrese city to take Madrid meant quitting an urban habitus. In Pamplona, affirms the narrator, stayed what they had been until the uprising: "good sports from San Luis Gonzaga, *sanfermín*'s boozers, rich young students ... cheerful little hypocrites ... Finally, now we were something profoundly grave: soldiers" (45).

The fascist habitus thus does not belong to the city. They are, according to the narrator of the first part, "men of voice and rifle" (77). 19 July (the date of the rebellion in Pamplona) gauged the stuff that people were made of: some joined the rebellion, but others preferred to stay home: "Unquestionably, that day Spain was at stake, and while we marched towards the clash covered with roses, they threw roses to us from the sky of their indifference or cowardice" (77–8). The bourgeois, properly dressed with English-style elegance, will see the fatherland passing in front of them "in shirtsleeves, hoarse and brave" (78). Hence Falange embodies the new military-style Spain. Similar scornful statements against the comforts and refinements of the cities, against Western civilization, and against the "cowardly" civilian population in relation to the Falangists' readiness for violent action pervade part 3 as well (216–17, 269–71, 294).

The third part provides the answer to the Falangist disorderly way of marching and fighting the enemy and to the alienation felt by Matías in the city, away from the battlefield: the army. In the army, whose intrinsically violent habitus as well as its disciplining of individual behaviour have so much in common with fascist ideology, lies, so to speak, "absolute fascism." Not coincidentally, the extradiegetic narrator devotes a great deal of textual attention to the military training of the three main characters at the Military Academy of "El Santo Tomás de Ávila," located in the outskirts of that Castilian town (149–213).[43] Of all the places described in the novel, the Military Academy is the most important in regard to La fiel infantería's intentio textis. In that heterotopia of crisis – to use Foucault's terminology (Dits 2: 1575–6) – the Falangists are no longer simple members of FE-JONS; they are now cadets, individuals placed in a liminal situation about to undergo a rite of passage. Therein the three Falangist friends refine their fascism, internalize the military technologies to produce space, and decisively realize the fundamental connection between those technologies and Spain's essence. This internalization of the military ethos and army regulations leads to a new perception and use of space rooted in the fascist politics of space, as well as in the structure of what Theweleit calls (military) "machinery," which "transforms functions such as 'thinking,' 'feeling,' and 'seeing' ... into movement and movements of the body" (2: 153). In one of the first marches outside the Academy, the narrator establishes the connection between the army's habitus and the military production of space: "Here, not making mistakes was of the essence. To begin with, the right foot wasn't the same as beginning with the left one ... While in formation one cannot speak ... It is unclear if one is allowed to think" (159–60). Furthermore, he correlates the marching in tight formation with the Falangist cadets' discovery of a new Spain. Little by little during the march, thanks to the army, Miguel, Matías, and Ramón become aware of "Spain's new dawn" (159). Through such discipline, the military academy has given them "the knowledge of an unprecedented dawn" (160). The military production of space encompasses the whole national territory.[44] Crossing the land surrounding Ávila in yet another march, the three Falangists experience a new and intimate connection with Spain, represented as a metaphysical wedding: they feel themselves "tied to the land they were stepping on, rooted until becoming trees or rocks or bushes, and they felt how the deep cold was coming up through their legs to mix with their bones and blood, to transfuse them with the bones and blood of thousands of generations settled in the age-old land ... They knew all too well that what they were doing in Santo Tomás de Ávila wasn't a mere short course ... They knew that they were celebrating … mythical weddings with their Fatherland, and that all that blood was a nuptial one" (161–2).

Since in the countryside dwells the fatherland, the peasant is the perfect Spaniard; according to Ramón and by extension the implied author, "the peasants understood the land" because "those who work the land know a lot about the Fatherland" (235). For this reason, Ramón, now an infantry officer, focuses specially on the workers, "uprooted from the most-holy unity" (235), whom he indoctrinates so as to instil in them folkish ideals (235–7).

Equally important is the fascist and military production of the city. While marching through the streets of Ávila, the three Falangists realize that they were fighting in defence of an urban life based upon agrarian values and traditional lifestyles; in other words, their ultimate goal was the imposition of a folkish model of city over modern urban centres. To striate Ávila by military means (e.g., military occupation of the city, tight marching through downtown, and so forth) is almost identical to a military production of Spain: "It did matter to walk along the Calle de los Reyes Católicos … Ramón, Miguel, Matías, the entire 2nd Company were singing with energy.… It was a taste of heaven … the wonderful last stanza: 'Spain, we will make you One, Great, and Free / even though we are going to die.' … The sections writhed geometrically" (177). This episode plays as an emblem of the ongoing military striation of the country, while it foretells the military striation of the main Spanish cities by means of victory parades that were performed shortly after their conquest by Franco's army. The victory over the urban must be a complete one, as Ramón thinks further in the novel: "To achieve full victory: he reflected on how his entering the liberated cities would be like. He wanted to see the hoist of triumph, not on the flagpoles, but instead in the crowd's eyes" (260). At the level of the story, *La fiel infantería* narrates the aim to take and control towns and cities by military means. It is also, as we saw earlier, a militarization of fascist discourse. But in its pragmatic dimension, García Serrano's novel consists of an aggressive, unforgiving passionate utterance whose perlocution resides in impressing onto the reader the idea that only military action and the countryside can regenerate both the city and the nation.

Longing for the City

Despite sharing with *La fiel infantería* the exaltation of military values, the more than sympathetic portrayal of the military production of space, the recurrence of macabre images, the morbid description of combat scenes, and the concept of the urban, Felipe Ximénez de Sandoval's *Camisa azul (Retrato de un Falangista)* (1939) approaches the fascist struggle for hegemony and offers coordinates of fascism's location within the geography of hegemonic practices from a substantially different standpoint.[45] A career diplomat, for a time the national delegate of Falange's Servicio Exterior,[46] the Cabinet chief of the Minister of Foreign Affairs Ramón Serrano Suñer until the minister's dismissal in September 1942, Primo de Rivera's fellow student, friend, and unconditional admirer, and the author of an important avant-garde novel titled *Tres mujeres más Equis* (1930) as well as a successful biography of Primo de Rivera, *José Antonio: Biografía apasionada* (1941), Ximénez de Sandoval has bequeathed to Spanish literature the most comprehensive fascist Bildungsroman. As a consequence of its generic form, *Camisa azul* articulates and discursively actualizes the fascist/military production of space through individual experience. Certainly, the *Bildung*, thinking, and deeds of the main character (a charismatic, somewhat preachy twenty-two-year-old student of philosophy and history whose name – Víctor Alcázar – sums up both his own heroism and a darling of the Francoist mythology of space) are meant to symbolize the fascist habitus, as the title itself points out. Víctor is thus a type rather than an individual. All the same, by narrating through a fixed internal focalization, the novelist allows for an understanding of the fascist struggle for hegemony vis-à-vis the urban from a personal point of view. And this differentiates *Camisa azul* from all the novels previously studied.

Ximénez de Sandoval's novel tells the story of Víctor Alcázar's alienation from the urban and of the main character's subsequent longing for the city and struggle to win it back. In the first part, the narrator centres his attention on Víctor Alcázar and fellow Falangists' political activities in Madrid in the days preceding the rebellion, their participation in the failed defence of the barracks known as Cuartel de la Montaña, and finally Víctor's arrest, imprisonment, trial, and sentence to death. Part 2 – whose action takes place at the Guadarrama front, Ávila, Toledo and its Alcázar, and the static front of the Ciudad Universitaria – narrates Víctor's escape from his executioners, the Nationalists' combats to take Toledo and Madrid, and the protagonist's death on a combat mission in the Ciudad Universitaria. *Camisa azul*'s failed circular structure (downtown Madrid–Castilian towns–Madrid's Ciudad Universitaria) reflects what could be regarded as the main story of the novel, that is, the story of a spatial loss and the military attempt to recover and rewrite what has been taken away: Madrid. As happens with other actualizations of fascist urban writing, in *Camisa azul* antagonism translates as spatial antagonism.

Following an already-studied pattern common to other fascist urban novels, *Camisa azul* depicts Madrid as a "foreign" city shackled by the "Reds," especially since the victory of the Popular Front in the general elections of February 1936. The examples of this resented vision abound. There are references to the streets' new ominous look (11–12), to the strikes and riots that have emptied Madrid of its "essence" (27), to the new meaning and function of public and semi-public places (81–2, 112–14), and to the people (*pueblo*) giving support to the Republic, which under the narrator's elitist eyes does not consist of a group of working men and women, but rather of a "jumble of layabouts, thugs, criminals against decorum and honesty, prostitutes, pimps, and other fauna from the brothel or the prison: the whole sub-humanity that sells and rents itself for riots, for elections, and for all the other democratic regimes' masquerades" (55; see 111 for analogous pejorative comments).[47] All in all, Ximénez de Sandoval's portrayal of Madrid is very similar to that of Foxá, Borrás, and Camba – to mention just a few – excepting the conclusions Víctor draws from the Cuartel de la Montaña fiasco.

Víctor interprets the Republican storming into the Cuartel de la Montaña as a turning point for the urban and the Republic. Alongside the "well-to-do's Madrid," on 20 July died "the intellectuals' state, artificially created behind the back of the nation by a coterie of clerks and journalists … pettifoggers and coffee-house geniuses" (78–9). Walking through Madrid, Víctor feels like he is stepping on "rubble" and "ruins" (79). The city resembles a "sinking ocean liner" (79), in itself not a bad sign indeed, because this is taken as the precondition for the Republic's final demise and the ensuing fascist appropriation and re-articulation of Madrid. As Víctor mutters while fleeing from the Cuartel de la Montaña, "Madrid is dead. Long live Madrid!" (79). A new society is thus born "amongst blazes and the thunder of the cannons" (113), a society that will be either "red" or "blue" (113). Reflecting on the refashioning of the law of the place in the Círculo de Bellas Artes (112–13) – a place built for the exclusive enjoyment of the dominant classes now turned into a cheka – Víctor Alcázar realizes that the war is being fought for the hegemony over space. Earlier, he had pointed out Falange's constitutive spatiality as well as the party's program for the organization and administration of the social. First of all, according to Víctor, Falange is, like all architectural wonders, "a marvel of equilibrium and harmony. José Antonio created it as Bramante and Michelangelo [built] St Peter's dome in Rome; as those architects ... that built the Parthenon or the Pyramids. They provided the plans, the geometry of space and time" (72). Second, for Falange, Spain was and has to be again an absolute space. Paraphrasing Primo de Rivera, Víctor affirms that from the stars one sees "Spain, *total and great, as a bull on a large map*. The rivers, as blue ribbons; the roads, as plaster strikes; the mountains, as wrinkles. The whole of the earth's flesh, *without incision nor wound. From the Pyrenees to Gibraltar, just one brown and hot massif*' (17; my emphasis). Spain is by no means the people who besieged the Cuartel de la Montaña, but the countryside, the ruined castles and the sumptuous churches, the folklore, the "imperial language," the inland and the coastline, the foggy North and the sunny South, Don Quixote, Teresa of Ávila, Columbus and the conquistadors, the Escorial's austerity (57–9). The concluding sentence, a summary of this long list of national traits, unambiguously underscores the fascist conception of Spain as an absolute, static space, as well as its military nature: "It is twenty centuries of grace, of stone, of banners' music, of the West's imperial history" (59). Not unnaturally, violence is the chosen technology to clean up this space from "hired henchmen from an icy and yellowish Moscow, with Oriental hatred and Mongoloid barbarism" (59). The "coating over Spain's clean flesh," says Víctor, must be pulled away by violent means (45), even if fascists are the victims. Writing on the three exit wounds in Enrique's dead body, the narrator claims that the bullets opened up three trails of blood fertilizing a country "with a new geography and climate" (30–1). Hence violent action actualizes both a key component of Spain's essence – the military – and the fascist habitus. Part 2 amply demonstrates this proposition.

An important factor in *Camisa azul*'s production of space resides in its narration of the rebel's take of Toledo and its besieged Alcázar, as well as the interpretation it provides on what is left of them (290–303).[48] This is the high point in the novel's treatment of space. As somehow foretold by his last name, Víctor Alcázar is part of the troops sent by Franco's high command to take Toledo and relieve the military resisting in the Alcázar. Before the final assault, he looks at the city through his field glasses. By means of his character's violent gaze (similar to José Félix's at the end of *Madrid de corte a checa*), Ximénez de Sandoval conveys to his readers the historical and metaphysical significance of the city and the Alcázar held for the Nationalists. In former times, these "broken walls" and "rubble" were the most heroic castle in Europe, a "Caesar's mansion" (291). The Alcázar is "the most graphic example of a race" (291) as well as Spain's heart (292). Comparing the Alcázar with Numantia, Sangunto, and

Zaragoza, the radio and heliograph messages issued by the rebel military withstanding the siege are described as the "resurrection" of the words of General José de Palafox (commander of the heroic resistance of the people of Zaragoza during the siege by French troops in 1808–9), along with the "gestures" of Guzmán el Bueno (sobriquet of Alonso Pérez de Guzmán, an aristocrat and military man who in 1294 led the defence of Tarifa on behalf of Sancho IV against the troops of the king's uncle, don Juan), with the Cid (292).

Such exaltation of the ruins and heroism permeates a vast number of coeval texts (e.g., memoirs, essays, poems, articles, war journals), and the Alcázar would soon become a convenient common place in fascist and Francoist discourse.[49] In "Ruinas gloriosas," P. Félix Gabola gave a complete summary of the meaning and function of the Alcázar's ruins (*Arriba* [11 August 1939]). The Alcázar, an "immense ruin," is "Spain's moral peak, born out of its pain," a sanctuary of militant heroism, a holy place. "Today," Gabola writes, "the Alcázar in ruins is the sublime witness of a resurrected Spain … that asserts its will to be." Upon such ruins rises the moral greatness of a country just born. The Alcázar's ruins therefore signify the triumph of the spirit over matter, as well as the resurrection of Spain's imperial spirit. For Agustín de Foxá, Toledo has never been so complete: in its ruins lie men's faith, hatred, passion, and soul ("Arquitectura hermosa de las ruinas," *Vértice* [April 1937]). Thus the ruins would be a reminder of the destruction brought about by the Republic, a symbol of fascist heroism and Christian faith, and the spatial expression of the new state.[50] The Alcázar was called to be, along with the Valle de los Caídos, a capital myth of the Franco regime. In accordance with the contents of that myth, Víctor's wondering about the possible destruction of Toledo by "Asiatic barbarians" is only logical: "Romantic Toledo, what will be left within you? What will the long-nailed thieves … who have raped with their blasphemies your mystical corners, have left of your wonders? Upon which torn-to-pieces crucifixes will those mangy and stinky militiamen … have wallowed?" (293). Once taken, the Toledo area "belongs again to Spain" (295), "the Alcázar, which had always been the Fatherland, now belongs entirely to the Fatherland" (296).

Indeed. But the myth of the Alcázar in *Camisa azul* cannot be dissociated from Víctor's *Bildung*. In the final push to take the citadel, Víctor fights in a Legion unit. By merging Falangism and the legionary ethos, the novel makes explicit the close connection between the legionary and the Falangist habitus. Ximénez de Sandoval had already pointed out the similarities and differences between that military unit and Falange in part

2, chapters 8 to 10, centred on the conversations taking place in the military hospital at Ávila between several legionnaires and Víctor. Gradually, the young Falangist realizes not only that Falange and the Legion have a lot in common (e.g., cult of death and the fallen, war as an activity that regenerates the individual and the nation, ritualism, vitalism, centrality of the hero figure, rhetoric of glorious violence and death in combat), but also, and decisively, that the Legion enjoys an advantageous position over Falange: as a military unit, the Legion has the might to achieve hegemony. Falange's call to and practice of direct action simply does not compare to the Legion's military power, already tested in Morocco in the 1920s. Hence a legionnaire embodies, more effectively than a Falangist, the (fascist) Übermensch. *Camisa azul* inscribes Falange within the Legion's habitus and ethos. Persuaded by the legionnaires, Víctor agrees to join their unit provisionally, a momentous occasion in his life: "The little philosopher, an admirer of the Nietzschean Übermensch, is on its way to the legionary glory [*gloria legionaria*] so as to blend it with his Falangist glory" (278). Víctor's fascist philosophy of violence becomes, therefore, a way of life. In addition, in his own avowal, he is a legionnaire "because the Legion is Spain" (348). As if to emphasize the synonymy between Falange and the Legion, at the end of the novel there is a reversal of roles. Upon finding out about his girlfriend's murder and Primo de Rivera's death sentence, the novel's main character becomes a nihilist who believes his life to be no more than a "balloon inflated by José Antonio's [Primo de Rivera] spirit" (395–6); now his only wish is to die in combat. Alexis, the legionnaire, replies as a Falangist would. First, so he notes, Falange is a gospel, a work of art, a mystical and philosophical treatise that will survive its prophet. The party's twenty-seven-point program "will make the world Falangist" (395). Second, Primo de Rivera's death makes him a useful myth and provides him with an "evangelic mission" (396). That the merging of Falange and the Legion in the figure of Víctor occurs in the operations undertaken to break the siege of the Alcázar is certainly no coincidence. Ximénez de Sandoval associates the fusion of Falange and the Legion with the myth of the Alcázar and thereby stamps onto such fusion a mythical aura. As implied in *Camisa azul*, Spanish fascism reaches its absolute state, its perfection, when Falange and the Legion join ranks in the takeover of the Alcázar. Ultimately, that episode brings out Falange's submission to military control, indicates the military means to achieve and maintain hegemony, and finally, stresses the kind of space that fascism intends to produce: absolute space, embodied here in the myth of the Alcázar.

Camisa azul comes full circle in the last chapters, whose action takes place in the Ciudad Universitaria. Stopped by the Republican troops and the International Brigades defending Madrid, Franco's army cannot embark on its production of the urban. Víctor's return to his longed-for city is thus a failed one: his movement towards the conquest of Madrid has been halted. As happens in other fascist novels (e.g., Foxá's *Madrid de corte a checa;* García Suárez's *Legión 1936;* Neville's *Frente de Madrid*), Madrid is seen from a distance, it is both near and immensely distant, it is a stubbornly denied presence, the story of a loss, the vivid image of repulsiveness that must be destroyed (319–29). Posted as corporal of the Legion to the Ciudad Universitaria, Víctor states peremptorily, "We all know that Madrid has a red layer of coating and pus, that it is not Madrid proper, and that it is necessary to destroy it" (317). For Víctor, the rewriting of Madrid will involve motifs, themes, and intertexts from Spain's Golden Age: "When [José Antonio Primo de Rivera] returns, by his order new angels ... for St Anthony, new upright spears for Breda's sky ... and new serges for Zurbarán's or Ribera's anchorites will be painted. José Antonio [Primo de Rivera], recreator of Spain's lyrical and epic spirit, will inspire paintbrushes, quills, and burins in order to make golden the century that the Marxists and the Freemasons from the *Ateneo* have tried to make out of bronze" (317–18). The resemblance between this image of Madrid and Toledo is further underlined by a fellow Falangist who claims to share Víctor's "feeling for Madrid": "Out of Castile's brownish earth, or Andalusia's green coasts ... will arise squads of painters. And the models for the new calling ... will be Falangist!" (354–5).

Víctor's death in a suicidal mission is the sign of a momentary impotence, but most important, it is also a mystical event, for his body fertilizes the soil, it lays out a basis for a new spatial grammar and for a state whose capital will be not a modern city, not a place freely acted out by its inhabitants where the dynamism of life, the unfixity of the subject, and the significant conversations so prominent during the Second Republic define spatial relationships and dialogue with political power. Rather, fascist Madrid shall be a Toledo of sorts, an atemporal, pre-modern locus, a place whose stasis will reflect a hierarchical structure of the social as much as the nature and self-perception of the state. Such a fascist image of Madrid-as-Toledo is in accordance with the fascist concept of empire and the state's practice of endo-imperialism. Víctor says as much in his explanation of the Falangists' will-to-empire and Falange's concept of empire, which here translates, markedly, as endo-empire. "We want the empire," says Víctor, "although built by free men having an imperial will

… We conceive of the Empire as the most gigantic democracy: the will of all Spaniards raising their arms to affirm that they want Spain one, great, and free. Without candidacies and polling stations. Without parties and coalitions. Spain one and only" (46). Two instruments will be used to implement this (endo-)empire: work and discipline, "which is not tyranny, but the awareness of duty and hierarchy" (46), adding, as if to accentuate Falange's endo-imperialism, "And one thought only: Spain. And one mission only: Spain. And one worry only: Spain. And one joy only: Spain" (46). Not only does Víctor Alcázar long for a fascist city, a city whose grammar is somewhat imbedded in the main character's last name. He also longs for an endo-empire whose capital will mirror Toledo. And this is *Camisa azul*'s ultimate contribution to the fascist production of space.

Representing Fascist Urban Space

Javier Navarro, the main character of Edgar Neville's war *nouvelle Frente de Madrid* (1941), fantasizes about a fascist Madrid as he lies mortally wounded in no-man's-land on the outskirts of Madrid. Moments before dying, Javier pictures his hometown covered with Falange's and the red-and-yellow national flags: "Legions of young men wearing blue shirts will parade on the streets; they will keep the same step, the same direction, the same interest" (81). Javier's dreamed city is a militarized absolute space controlled by the Falangists where the subject melds into masses that, by means of their military marching through Madrid, rewrite the city's grammar after a fascist ideology. In this fascist Madrid, everybody would go in the same direction and share identical purposes. The autonomy of the individual would be a thing of the past. History would prove this fantasy to be much more than wishful thinking.

The interconnected aims to produce a new grammar of the place and new spatial relationships were ever-present in the Nationalists' designs for Spain. Noticeably during the war, on 25 March 1938 the rulers-to-be of the country created the Servicio Nacional de Regiones Devastadas y Reparaciones, the first of a series of institutions whose purpose was the reconstruction of a country devastated by the war, as well as the modelling of places, spatial relationships, and customs after the new regime's ideology. In this respect, the Instituto Nacional de la Vivienda, the Instituto Nacional de Colonización, the Dirección General de Arquitectura, and the Dirección General de Regiones Devastadas – agencies created in 1939 by the Franco regime – would play a crucial role in rebuilding the country. A significant number of representations of space underpinned the work of the architects and urban planners working under political guidelines in the war's aftermath. That is the case of the "Ideas Generales sobre el Plan Nacional de Ordenación y Reconstrucción" (1939), written by the Servicios Técnicos de FET y de las JONS; J. Paz Maroto's *El futuro de Madrid: Plan General de Ordenación, Reconstrucción y Extensión de Madrid* (1939); Pedro Muguruza Otaño's *Sistematización técnica en un Plan Nacional de Resurgimiento* (1940); and the *Memoria comprensiva del primer Ayuntamiento después de la liberación de Madrid* (1945), prepared by the city hall of Madrid.[51] Architects and urban planners worked hand in hand. Held in Madrid in June 1939, the National Assembly of Architects was an event in itself indicative not only of the professional awareness of the need to find technical solutions to the architectural and urban problems posed by the ruinous state of the country, but also of the keen understanding that architectural forms and urban planning designs ought to express and impress onto the citizens the new hegemony.[52] The preface to the law that on 23 September 1939 established the creation of the Dirección General de Arquitectura states it in unequivocal terms: "The destruction [caused by the war] … the need to order the country's material life after the new principles, the representational importance that the works of Architecture have as expressions of the state's strength and mission … lead to assemble and order all the different professional expressions of Architecture in an office for the service of the public interest. Thus by getting involved in the official agencies, the professionals will be the representatives of a syndicalist-national architectonic criterion previously established by the supreme agencies that will have to be created with that purpose" (qtd. in Cirici 120).

Despite their resentment against the city for its resistance to Franco's army, the Nationalists envisioned Madrid as the capital of a new empire. For this purpose, the government created in April 1939 the Junta de Reconstrucción de Madrid. Its advisory body, the Comisión Técnica de Reconstrucción, was assigned the task to produce a general plan for the reconstruction and organization of Madrid and its environs. An Oficina Técnica of the Comisión would in effect undertake the job. Headed by the architect and urban planner Pedro Bidagor, the Oficina Técnica finished its task in December 1941. The Plan General de Ordenación de Madrid was published in 1942 and approved by the Cortes (Franco's non-democratic parliament) in 1944, but did not come into effect until after an enabling act of 1946.[53] Indebted in part to the rationalist plan designed by Secundino Zuazo and Hermann Jansen in 1929, the Plan Bidagor articulated a fascist vision of the city, conceived of as an "organic" unity defined by a principle of hierarchy and considered as a reflection of the state; as the Plan itself states, the urban layout must represent the "ideas of hierarchy, service, and brotherhood upon which the regime is based" (in Sambricio, *El Plan Bidagor*). The Plan contains important elements that, while not fascist in themselves, define nonetheless a fascist project if they are taken together vis-à-vis the historical moment and the Plan's political dimension:

1 Its understanding of town planning as a fundamental strategy of political power that aims at affecting urban development and the individual acting-out of the urban grammar.
2 Its *overarching, total* approach to urban planning.
3 Its rewriting of Madrid by taking as the main point of reference its status as the capital of Spain and centre of power; in this context, Madrid was thought to have three functions:
   a efficient organization of the political and economic direction of the country;
   b exaltation of Spain's traditional values; and
   c symbolic representation of Spain's force and mission; accordingly, the Plan suggested to build buildings representing the "New Spain's" three fundamental principles (religion, fatherland, and FET-JONS) and to name the projected three main entrances to the city as "Vía de la Victoria," "Vía de Europa," and Vía del Imperio."
4 The hierarchical organization of the historic part of the city by dividing the old neighbourhoods into districts.
5 The idea of creating three green belts surrounding the city that separate the residential areas from the working class.
6 The radial organization of the road system connecting Madrid to the periphery.

In the end, the Plan Bidagor did not really materialize, largely because, just as throughout the country from the late 1950s on, capital, and not the fascists, would be the key factor in determining urban development and growth in Madrid. By comparison, architecture would be far more successful than urban planning in disseminating and stamping a fascist ideology on social space.

These institutions and representations of space were supplemented by newspaper articles, newsreels, literary works, and essays that circulated, justified, and prescribed the concept of space underpinning the plans to rebuild the country. Their capacity to reach a wide readership allowed these cultural products to play a significant role in the ongoing multidisciplinary production of space. While the above-studied novels focused on Madrid and spatial antagonism during the Second Republic and the war, coeval essays and articles presented a quite different image of Madrid: the Madrid of the victors. Giménez Caballero's *Madrid nuestro* and Puente's *Madrid recobrado* are two cases in point.

In 1944, Giménez Caballero published a collection of articles whose terse title constitutes an unambiguous declaration of principles: *Madrid nuestro*. Certainly not a pleasant, comforting read for the people of Madrid who suffered the war, most particularly those battered Republicans doing their best to carry on, Giménez Caballero's book may be considered as the discursive equivalent of the activities of an occupation army and administration. As the author himself flatly acknowledges in an introduction misleadingly titled "Amor a Madrid," his is a "*combat book*" (14). Of combat indeed, but also, as the title of the first part spells out, of conquest ("conquistaciones" in Giménez Caballero's idiosyncratic phrasing) of a city that, according to the author in the first section ("Exaltaciones de Madrid," originally written in 1937), had betrayed him as well as its imperial past and political function. Gone are the times when Madrid, during the war no more than an abominable, treacherous Babylonic city of masses in flip-flops (22, 35, 36), was the centre of a military empire, of a new Rome whose destiny consisted of "Spain, one! Madrid, one! Madrid free and great! Spain great, free, and ecumenical!" (34). Fallen into an unstoppable decline since the eighteenth century, Madrid turned away from its unifying and centralizing mission (64), or, as the author says, further from its (Falangist) mission of "destiny," "unity," and "empire" (65–6). The armed rebellion against Madrid's new urban grammar (described in some detail on 26–9) will spring out only, as the author states, from the fatherland's soil, from the countryside, from the unpolluted depths of the land (41). Accordingly, in this piece written in 1937 Giménez Caballero rallies the people from the countryside to rise up in arms and march towards Madrid (41). Once taken, Madrid will be under "the fasces and the yoke" (43), that is, under Falange's direct and strict control.

Giménez Caballero's use of the country/city structure, a constant in fascist urban writing as we have seen, serves to justify the book's basic goal: the discursive production of urban space. Properly speaking, such production begins with the second essay collected in the book, "Alocución a Madrid liberado," originally a speech broadcast by Unión Radio shortly after the city's surrender. In a threatening, resentful, vengeful,

and authoritarian tone, Giménez Caballero lays out from the beginning
the military character of both the messenger and his message. As he
points out at the beginning of the speech, the person addressing the
people of Madrid is not Giménez Caballero the writer, but a "Franco
soldier" about to tell the city "all the truths" (47). Through this text,
the author of *Genio de España* participates in the conquest and occupation of Madrid in three different but complementary dimensions: the
non-linguistic world (as the soldier of an army), the intellectual field (as
an intellectual *engagé* with the regime), and the metaphysical grounding
of the subject (as a native of Madrid talking about that city). The last
dimension is the most interesting of the three for many reasons, among
them for its political undertones. Giménez Caballero considers himself
no longer a "son" of Madrid. As a matter of fact, he has become its father:
"I was your son. But not anymore. Because as of now you have come to
be my son: ours. Now we are your parents. Now it is us to whom you owe
your life. And to whom now you will owe your destiny" (49). These are
strong words indeed, for they indicate an authoritarian father taking full
charge of the son's future. In a stark admonition to the people of Madrid
– one has only to imagine its intimidating effect upon the listeners – Giménez Caballero points out the real nature of the space generated by
the new regime as well as the three father figures governing it: "Madrid,
gone are the times in which sons and wives lived their lives freely! Among
us life belongs to the paternity of the home, and the home is the state,
the supreme father. And the state belongs to a flesh-and-blood father: a
Caudillo.… From now on Madrid will depend on God, the Fatherland,
and the Caudillo" (49).

   In order to prevent a return to the past, the new rulers will impose on
the city a military spatial structure controlled by the ever-present authoritarian gaze of the dictator. Discussing the possible places that Franco
might choose as his official residence, Giménez Caballero notes that Toledo could be one of them, "so that every day he may keep a watch on
you [Madrid] and look after you with field glasses" (57). The military
nature of the new space is explained further by comparing it to the former spatial organization of the city: "May your naiveté at last turn into
loyalty and discipline; your feast-day, bullfight, and football tumult at last
turn into manly, stentorian, and military joyfulness" (59). As he notes in
another essay of the book, the Caudillo's gaze, projected from his "command post" (85), will be the ultimate *logos* regulating places and spatial
relationships. By establishing his command post in El Pardo after "taking
Madrid," the Caudillo showed that in fact he possessed "great prudence"

(85–6), for "as long as it doesn't re-nationalize, as long as it doesn't become loyal to the Escorial's and Toledo's genius, Madrid deserves only to be kept under surveillance by field glasses from a command post in the outskirts" (86). Because of the resentment towards and suspicion of the city (64), both the military control of the urban and the Caudillo's military gaze will remain in place for awhile. Evoking the entrance of the rebel troops into the city and the victory parade, in 1941 Gimenez Caballero writes that two years after taking Madrid "as soldiers," they still keep watch on Madrid "with a rifle": "Our Caudillo – in his Palace of El Pardo – in the outskirts, as if in a command post, watches you with field glasses" (69).

Madrid nuestro can be read as a supplement of Madrid recobrado: Crónicas de antes y después del veintiocho de marzo (1939), a collection of newspaper articles by José-Vicente Puente. Madrid "ours" and Madrid "regained" complement each other. While the former connotes exclusive ownership, the latter refers to the operations carried out to "regain" Madrid, the dispossession felt during the war by the "rightful owners" of the city, and the city's new image. Madrid has been "regained," it is "ours" again. Nonetheless, the past participle recobrado does not fully convey the reality described by Puente. Although Madrid had been conquered by the Nationalists and was therefore part of Franco's Spain, it was the place where thousands of men and women who supported the Republic were still living. For some, among them Giménez Caballero and Puente himself, the city had not been completely "regained." Immediately after the entrance of Franco's troops in Madrid, the new authorities established mechanisms for "cleaning up" the city – an ongoing process in the rest of the country – of "enemies" or potentially dangerous individuals.[54] Madrid recobrado is predicated upon the author's suspicion of the people of Madrid's real feelings vis-à-vis the victors of the war. While the administration proceeded at full speed with its repressive measures in the city, symbolic artefacts like Madrid nuestro and Madrid recobrado set about to inculcate in the reader a fascist meaning of Madrid. Puente himself stated this goal with unmistakable fascist language in the prologue to his book: "To Madrid we will give back its precisè and exact outline, we will move away from it everything noxious, and we will work with the same ardour as that of the martial days so as to remove the false bushes that cast a paltry shadow over its nobility. We are all involved in this undertaking … Here, our intolerance will shine with its purest line" (7–8).

This idea would be further elaborated in a passage devoted to the hegemony of the "hicks" (paletos) during the war and to the imperative need to give back to the city its long-established elitist flavour (94). Puentes's opinion of the working class was shared by more than a few Nationalists. In his view, people who in the countryside would find a more humane quality of life should not linger around splendid buildings; the excessive number of workers living in the city has been Madrid's undoing (94). Unsurprisingly, with the tacit objective to create a negative image of the Republic and thereby justify the production of space projected by the victors, a great deal of attention is given to the city during the war, in particular to the changes affecting the streets of the city (45, 87–90) and the modifications in the decoration and function of bourgeois domestic interiors (55–8). As an alternative to the Republican city stands a militarized urban space. We will see more of that in the next section, but suffice it here to mention Puente's sympathetic description of the militarization of the university: "The university has a new face. It looks like an encampment devoted to studying ... It seems that after the silence of weapons the talents are going to engage in battle" (155–6). In part because of its rhetorical simplicity, *Madrid recobrado* makes evident the fascist articulatory practice whereby material spatial practices, representations of space, and spaces of representation – such as those of Foxá, Borrás, Ximénez de Sandoval, and García Serrano – reshaped places, spatial relationships, social allegiances, habitus, and individual identities. One could argue that these texts complemented the tasks conducted by the armed forces, which applied a pattern borrowed from the tactics and strategies of colonial control.

The Performance of Victory

Complying with an order issued on 6 May 1939 by the Chamber of Commerce, Madrid's shopkeepers decorated their windows with pictures of the Caudillo and Primo de Rivera, with the Movement's and the two-coloured national flags, and with slogans (e.g., "Franco, Franco, Franco," "Gloria al Caudillo," "España Una, Grande y Libre," "¡Arriba España!") that condensed both the semantics and pragmatics of the upcoming victory parade. The shops had been taken over by the Nationalists, their windows literally and figuratively reflecting the rebels' victory; as an article published on 13 May in *Arriba* remarked, "Madrid's windows are today a cry of victory, a precise chord within Victory's and Peace's general symphony" ("De cara" 5). The entire city was a work in progress.[55] Madrid's urban landscape had experienced significant changes since the victorious entrance of Franco's troops and the FET-JONS militias in the city on 28 March 1939.[56] Not unnaturally, one of the first measures taken by the new rulers consisted in changing the city's toponymy. Under the belief that Madrid had to be cleaned of "all the symbols and names left on its public thoroughfares by a corrupted regime," on 24 April the city hall proposed to the Comisión Municipal Permanente to restore to all thoroughfares the names that they held before the Second Republic, to create for this purpose an ad hoc committee, and designate some streets and avenues with new names. Important instances of this renaming of public spaces are the following (comp. Ortíz Mateos 29–30):

Present name	Proposed name
Paseo de la Castellana	Avenida del Generalísimo
Calle Gran Vía	Avenida de José Antonio
Plaza de las Cortes	Plaza de Calvo Sotelo
Calle del Príncipe de Vergara	Avenida del General Mola
Calle de Abascal	Calle del General Sanjurjo

At the paradigmatic axis, the significance of these proposed changes is quite clear. While the main avenue was to be renamed after Franco's honorific military rank, the modern boulevard par excellence would be designated by the name of the co-founder and first leader of the party. Thus the transit along the north–south axis of the city would be symbolically controlled by the ultimate military authority, and half of the east–west axis (Alcalá–Gran Vía), the "cosmopolitan Madrid" in Baker's apt characterization, where in the late 1920s and early 1930s many entertainment and leisure activities had been concentrated, by a disciplinary, watchful, prudish fascist political power. On the other hand, the Plaza de las Cortes, located next to the parliament, was to be named after a harsh, anti-democratic critic of the Republic and leader of the opposition in the period following the victory of the Popular Front in February 1936. At the syntagmatic axis, that list establishes in decreasing order a hierarchy of importance: (1) the Caudillo, (2) the executed Jefe Nacional of FE-JONS, (3) the leader of the opposition whose assassination on 13 July 1936 outraged the political right and the armed forces, (4) the head of the military conspiracy against the Republic who had died in an aviation accident on 3 June 1937, and (5) the general initially chosen by the rebels to be the head of the new state, killed on 20 July 1936 when his plane crashed. On that list everyone but Franco was already dead.

On the streets of Madrid, foulards and worker overalls – the garments that during the war had expressed the hegemony of a politics of egalitarianism – disappeared altogether as a result of the rebels' military victory over what the fascist and conservative intelligentsia derogatorily called "el populacho" (the plebs). From the balconies of the numerous apartments confiscated by Falange now hung the party's red-and-black flag, and the FET-JONS yoke and arrow was everywhere to be seen. On 1 April 1939, Falange squads occupied factories, schools, and convents, and the next day saw the beginning of the confiscations of emblematic buildings such as the Capitol and the Palacio de Bailén. Incessant impromptu Falangist parades, their participants marching in tight formation and making the fascist salute, punctuated the streets of Madrid, emphasizing at the material level the multifaceted fascist/militaristic urban *écriture* and its simultaneous erasure of the Republican urban space. Madrid had an "indigestion of super-Falangism" (Bravo Morata 13: 48–9), so much so that Manuel Valdés, the chief of Falange in Madrid, prohibited the use of the Falangist uniform in dance halls, coffee houses, and pubs. Just as overwhelming was the presence of the army. Since the end of the war, the streets of the capital had been flooded by thousands of cheery soldiers and cocky officers, living emblems of the strict, intimidating military control of the city – and of Spain, for that matter – as well as the hegemony of the armed forces within the new state. Official reports attest to the presence in Madrid right after the war of about 25% of the armed forces' 30,000 officers (Bravo Morata 13: 48–9), an impressive proportion indeed. In sum, barely one month has elapsed since the end of the war, reports an exultant anonymous journalist, and Madrid already looks like a "civilized city" ("Madrid," *Arriba* [28 April 1939]).

An executive order, signed on 16 May by Minister of the Interior (*Ministro de la Gobernación*) Ramón Serrano Suñer, announced that a victory parade would take place in Madrid on 19 May.[57] In a sense the last of the victory parades organized by the Nationalists during the war in recently conquered cities (e.g., the victory parade in Barcelona on 21 February 1938), this one was also meant to be the culmination of a series of victory parades carried out in other Spanish cities since 3 May, the central stage of collective celebration, and crucially, the performance of victory, as hinted by the first disposition of the executive order: 19 May, the date of the victory parade, would be designated "Día de la Victoria" (Victory Day). In this executive order, it was established that on 18 May all Spanish provinces would hold parades, festivals, and religious celebrations, and on the next day both the proclamation read by Franco on 19 July 1936 upon taking the command of the colonial army and the last dispatch issued on 1 April 1939 by the Generalísimo's headquarters (penned by Franco himself) were to be read in the "main squares of all of Spain's cities, towns, and villages."[58]

In addition to the illocutionary force of the decree (it officially *declared* and *established* what it said), the overlapping of the designation of 19 May as "Victory Day" (actual victory had been achieved, let us remember, almost fifty days earlier) with the announcement of the public reading of these two texts by Franco was far from accidental. On the contrary, it had a perlocutionary force, for its purpose consisted of impressing upon all Spaniards the essential features of the new state. In effect, the event itself – the reading of the texts on "Victory Day" – was to a great extent conceived of as a perlocutionary speech act. First of all, by being ventriloquists of Franco, the officials in charge of reading both texts became mere carriers of absolute power, unquestioning members of the administration whose function was no other than uttering the words of their master, sole bearer of truth. Second, the two texts read by the officials framed the countrywide ceremonies within a war narrative narrated by Franco; moreover, since a public reading was imposed on the entire nation in all cities, towns, and villages, such a war narrative discursively refracted the military conquest and control of the country. Third, a victory parade on "Victory Day" conveyed the message, as the voice-over of the newsreel on the parade produced by the Departamento Nacional de Cinematografía put it, that the parade was in fact "the war's last military event" (*El Gran Desfile*). Hence the parading army also was conceived of and featured as the army *taking Madrid* immediately after the city's surrender *and ending the war* as it was marching through the city *on 19 May*.

To emphasize this overlapping of temporalities and events, the General Staff and motorized units of the Army of the Centre, directly involved in the Battle of Madrid, would head the parade. Possibly following instructions of the Delegación de Prensa y Propaganda, the *ABC* journalist reporting on the parade interspersed his comments about each unit passing in front of the podium presided over by Franco with a brief narrative of its war deeds ("El día de la victoria" [20 May 1939]), thereby making the parade a war narrative. Consequently, the victory parade was designed as the ultimate war narrative of the civil war and the spatial practice that, by simultaneously representing the war and performing final victory, connected the two texts of Franco read by officials across the country. The Caudillo's opening and closing of the parade, an obvious refraction of the order and connotations of the two texts (one written at beginning of the war, the other effectively *ending* it) underscored

Franco's self-fashioned role as Omniscient Narrator, Main Character, and Great Hermeneut.

No means were spared to create the right mood among the people of Madrid. The streets would be plastered with propaganda posters while coffee shops, movie houses, and theatres were allowed to decorate their facades with billboards, pictures of Franco, and the official flags. Before 19 May, countless portraits of the Caudillo, twenty thousand metres of percaline, and 100,000 flags would be sold by the Army's Stockpiling Service. Pennants hung from the top stories to the street in buildings on the Gran Vía and the Calle de Alcalá, from Sol to the Plaza de la Independencia. Squads of workers built arches and platforms around the clock. Madrid, so reports *Arriba* on 18 May, was ready to receive the Caudillo: "The whole city was full of imperial coats of arms, of portraits of the Caudillo and José Antonio [Primo de Rivera], of lights, of garlands, and of the Movement's emblems" ("Madrid" 1). Franco's entrance in Madrid on 18 May could be considered as the prologue to the parade. The Caudillo conspicuously stayed on in loyal, folkish Burgos after his army entered Madrid in triumph on 28 March, symbolically expressing, on the one hand, the incommensurable distance between the leader and his people intrinsic to fascism's *Führerprinzip,* and on the other, Franco's displeasure towards Madrid for its stubborn two-and-a-half-year resistance to his besieging troops. In the first paragraph of his executive order, Serrano Suñer described the event with words whose purpose consisted of stamping on everyone the symbolic meaning of Franco's entrance in the capital: "The war reaches its symbolic end and Victory its highest crowning with the Caudillo's official entrance in Madrid" (*Arriba* [17 May 1939]).

The victory parade, a mixture of fascist ritual and military victory parade *sensu stricto,* was an impressive, carefully orchestrated ceremony. Already by six o'clock in the morning a crowd of thousands – 500,000 according to *ABC* ("El día de la victoria" 9) – swarmed in the area, comprising the Paseo de la Castellana, Paseo del Prado, and Calle de Alcalá. Wearing a somewhat unflattering yet politically well-chosen uniform (a Requeté red beret and a Falangist blue shirt under his army uniform), Franco opened the ceremony in a characteristic fascist fashion. Aloof, making the fascist salute to an enthralled crowd, the dictator arrived in an open car escorted by his Moorish guard by 8:45 a.m. at his podium.[59] "Our Caudillo looked like an inaccessible demigod," wrote an ecstatic Josefina de la Maza (qtd. in Sueiro and Díaz Nosty 1: 11). After the formal welcome by the awaiting generals, ministers, and members of the political elite, right arms fully extended and wearing a military uniform, the vice-president of the government and minister of foreign affairs, Count of Jordana, read the decree that granted to the Generalísimo the Gran Cruz Laureada de San Fernando – the highest distinction in the Spanish Army. After a brief, rather ungainly speech, General Varela conferred the medal on Franco. The parade began right after this symbolically loaded ceremony. Between 9:00 a.m. and 2:00 p.m. on a rainy Friday, 120,000 troops divided into thirty-one groups (including Falangists, Requetés, legionnaires, Regulars, Moroccan mercenaries, Portuguese volunteers, and members of the Condor Legion and the Italian Corps of Voluntary Troops) marched along the Paseo de la Castellana (renamed as Avenida del Generalísimo), Paseo de Recoletos, and Paseo del Prado, from the Glorieta de Castelar to the Plaza de Cánovas (see figure 4.1).

The total figure of units and materiel is staggering: 115 infantry units, twenty-seven cavalry squadrons, three thousand cars and trucks, two hundred artillery batteries, twenty anti-aircraft batteries, twenty-five anti-tank batteries, five hundred motorcycles, 150 tanks, and 450 aircrafts. These figures are all the more impressive if considered in relative terms vis-à-vis the total number of troops composing Franco's armed forces in May 1939 (735,000 men) and the population of Madrid (about one million people by the end of the war). The resulting percentages are as astonishing as revelatory: about 15% of the armed forces paraded in Madrid on 19 May, with the ratio of troops to population consisting roughly of one soldier per twelve inhabitants – an intimidating proportion indeed, especially within the context of a "victory parade" performed on "Victory Day."

A parade may be considered as a collective process that manipulates space through movement, creates its own specific space according to norms and rules, and stamps new values on places and space (Marin 40). As Louis Marin points out, its syntax can be studied in terms of (1) the places and spaces crossed or passed by the cortège, and (2) the internal organization and articulation of the parade. Both are equally important to a proper understanding of the pragmatics of this kind of event – the former, because parades are ritualistic processes of spatialization that aim to reproduce and, in some cases, produce a network of places; the latter, for the reason that the order of the parade is a mechanism by which its organizers seek to transmit civic, religious, political, or social "messages" (Marin 45).

As regards the network of places and spaces related one way or the other to the victory parade, I should like to comment on the parade's

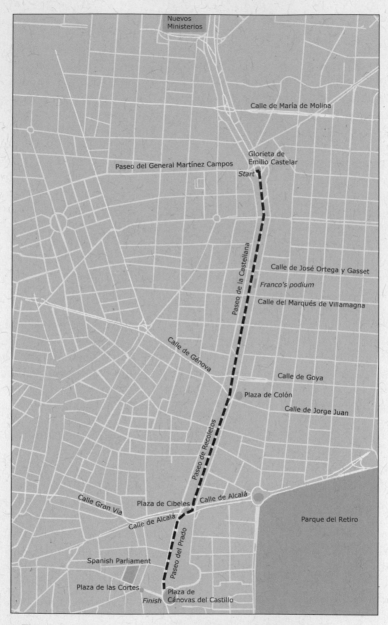

Figure 4.1 Itinerary of the Victory Parade (Madrid, 19 May 1939).
Image created by the author

direction. The parade started out at the Glorieta de Emilio Castelar (intersection of Castellana/Calle de Francisco Giner, a street named today as Paseo del General Martínez Campos) – not far from Nuevos Ministerios – and ended at the Plaza de Cánovas, where all units dispersed; from there, each unit returned to its corresponding cantonment by following a pre-established route.[60] Logistic considerations aside (the Paseo de la Castellana was, and still is, a logical choice for a military parade), the points of departure and arrival as well as the direction of the parade had a political purport. In the first place, the cortège commenced very near to a space representative of a yet-to-be-established political power (in fact, many units gathered at the Nuevos Ministerios before the parade). Begun in 1933, construction of the Nuevos Ministerios was halted by the war, and only after the war would the project be brought to completion (1942). In the context of the victory parade, both the unfinished character of the complex and its political function made the Nuevos Ministerios a useful marker of a political power still to be centralized in Madrid.[61] Emerging as it were from the new hegemony and legitimized by its origin in power, the parading army of 120,000 men marched downtown in a straight line on the most important boulevard crossing the city north–south (the stretch Paseo de la Castellana–Paseo de Recoletos–Paseo del Prado forms a north–south axis that splits the city in two).[62] Thus the cortège, bearer of the new hegemony, brought that hegemony to the centre of the city, specifically to two places (i.e., Plaza de Cibeles and Plaza de Cánovas) with special significance for spatial relationships, social meaning, and political power. On the Plaza de Cibeles, which links the north–south axis and the most important east–west axis, that of Alcalá–Gran Vía, there is a pivotal centre of Spain's economy (i.e., the Banco de España building) as well as the main post office (i.e., the imposing Palacio de Comunicaciones building). The Plaza de Cánovas, the finishing point of the cortège, is located just five minutes walking distance from the parliament, that is, the constitutional body representing the Spanish people. Hence one could say that the direction of the parade somehow re-enacted the war: the military force sprang out as it were from a not-yet-completely-established absolute hegemony, then moved towards, or, perhaps more precisely, *against* the core of the Second Republic. The end of the parade thus was equivalent to the end of the war, to the final victory of fascism, the military, and the anti-democratic organizations over parliamentary democracy.

In a sense, the military cortège played as a counter-image of the mass demonstrations and general strikes that had taken place during the Republic. As mentioned before, these demonstrations flowed basically from the working-class districts on the outskirts to the centre of Madrid, particularly to the area of the Puerta del Sol. Despite the political slogans of these mass demonstrations, disorderly movements and unruly behaviour were the order of the day, features otherwise rather common to that kind of event. The victory parade "corrected" the "anomalies" of the mass demonstrations. Working-class garments were replaced by army uniforms, the voicing of political slogans by martial silence, the concentric direction of the masses by the lineal one followed by the military cortège, the popular origin of the mass movements by a movement originated in absolute power, the chaotic, non-normative marching of the masses by the mechanical, disciplined, normative march of the soldiers, the obedience to political slogans and party guidelines protesting the government by the unquestioning obedience to military regulations and political power.[63] This multiple substitution – in effect a replacement of one type of urban spatial practice by its opposite – did not go unnoticed at the time. Agustín de Foxá, whose novel *Madrid de corte a checa* displays, as already seen, an acute sensitivity to the meaning of the mass demonstrations, pointed out the contrast between the two spatial practices in an article published in *ABC* on 20 May, in which he suggests that his readers remember the "trusting Republic's humble parades, when a bunch of failed pettifoggers and top-hated members of the Ateneo took up the place of the heroes." Comparing the march of the army over the Castellana to a sword in its sheath – a phallic image underscoring the violence underpinning the military production of space – Foxá writes that, instead of the "red disorder," it has shone the dazzling line of the parade ("Pasa el Ejército" 7). "Seeing them," adds Foxá, "one understands that the army – opposite to the 'red' militiamen's disorderly rejoicing – is a system of order [*sistema de orden*]." In "La llegada esperada," appearing in *El correo español–El pueblo vasco* on 7 May 1939 (collected in *Madrid recobrado* 75–8), José-Vicente Puente made analogous observations on the entrance of the army in Madrid after the surrender of the city: "Over the asphalt trod [in the recent past] by the murderous militiawomen's dirty espadrilles and the international gangs' far-off boots, Spanish men solemnly, imperiously parade" (77). In short: the army erased the people's urban writing while imposing its own.

The internal order and the articulation of the parade deserve critical attention as well. In this respect, I should like to pinpoint three striking elements of that order: (1) the role played by the air force in the parade's syntax and pragmatics, (2) the distribution of the Italian and German troops in the cortège, and (3) the Caudillo's framing function.

At eleven o'clock, the air force made its appearance in the skies of Madrid. Squadrons of bombers, fighters, and reconnaissance aircraft flew over the Paseo de la Castellana. The buzz of the approaching aircraft, their deafening noise once flying over the city, and the decreasing din of their motors as the squadrons flew away must have been heard with shudders and fright by people who only a few months earlier had suffered aerial bombings. For that reason, we could say that, compared to the troops and materiel parading on the Castellana, Franco's air force had a stronger capacity to awaken memories of war among the people of Madrid than did the army, and therefore executed better than any other unit two of the parade's main functions: to intimidate and to subjugate. In addition, the air force produced writing, a fact of the utmost importance. The first squadrons drew a *V* and an *F* ("Viva Franco" [Long live Franco]), and a later squadron composed the surname *Franco* with the skilful formation of its aircraft. By so doing, the air force constituted both a threat and a potent urban *écriture*. Instead of dropping bombs, this time the aircraft dropped words. They wrote over the city, stamped Franco's signature on the skies, and dragged it along the Avenida del Generalísimo, thereby mirroring in the air what had already been written on the ground: General Francisco Franco, *Franco* in the sky, the *Generalísimo* on the avenue, was the absolute master, the owner of Spain's land and sky, the victory parade's narrator and protagonist, the man whose shadow was projected from the sky through the fuselage of his airplanes. Far from being "one of the most bizarre expressions of the cult to the Caudillo" (Platón 14), the aerial writing conveyed a very powerful message. While the direction of the parade told a narrative of origins, the story of the war, and the replacement of a democratic polity embodied in the parliament by an authoritarian one based on overwhelming military might, the order of the airplanes unambiguously stressed the identity of the narrator of those multiple stories and of the master of national space. That this was done through the aircraft formations and not only, as it has been suggested (e.g., Preston, *Politics* 35), in smoke coming from their motors, indicates a willingness to remain, to continue, to impose military might as opposed to a fleeting, evanescent, somewhat "soft" presence connoted by smoke. Finally, the air force's writing constituted a meta-language, for it commented on the ground parade, it provided the non-verbal event with words.[64]

Another remarkable aspect of the parade's internal syntax and pragmatics is the order in which the Italians and the Germans paraded in relation to the other units: the Italian CTV was the second unit to march, while the Condor Legion was the last important unit from the last. These facts, along with Franco's framing function (he opened the parade and ended it when he left his podium as soon as the Carlist and Falangist hymns as well as the national anthem were over) make up the following circular structure:

[Franco]
Spanish unit (Army of the Centre)
Foreign troops (Italian)
Twenty-three ground units and 450 aircraft
Foreign troops (German)
…
Spanish unit (72nd Division motorized section)
[Franco]

Apart from imposing its logic on the streets and skies of Madrid, this structure also tells the story of the foreign armies' involvement in the war and their ideological relationship with the new regime. Admittedly, the symmetry is not perfect because five motorized units (made up of the Quartermaster corps and sanitary units) paraded after the Condor Legion, but these were minor units, and only the last one to parade carried military weight: the 72nd Division. Placing them second and (almost) second from the last underscored the importance of the Italian and German involvement and constituted an homage of sorts. But important as they were, the CTV and the Condor Legion had been conspicuously placed between Spanish units and framed by the Caudillo. In the parade's order, the relative closeness between Franco and the Italian and German troops indicated at once an ideological proximity and a calculated political distance.

In all parades, action and spectacle intertwine in such a way that dissociating one from the other would misread their pragmatics, ritualistic structure, and social function (Marin 50–1). Spectators standing on the street, sitting on balconies, or glued to the windows of their homes are also actors who participate in the performance; some of them (e.g., writers, journalists, artists, memorialists) will re-enact the parade through spaces of representation. To some extent, the spectators' role in the production of the parade is isomorphic to the one played by the presiding authorities, whose involvement is at once active and passive. The thousands of cheering men and women from working-class districts like Vallecas, Ventas, Estrecho, and Villaverde made the parade a felicitous illocutionary speech act. Thanks to their somewhat surprising presence – some of them had fought during the war against the very soldiers whom they were now enthusiastically applauding – all the conventional procedures and pragmatic conditions that allow something to be done through saying were there.

For the parade to be completely successful, the politically motivated vectorialities of the working class during the Republic (i.e., mass demonstrations and strikes flowing downtown from the outskirts in a concentric movement) and their meaning (i.e., opposition to power) had to be redirected, absorbed by the logic of the victors' production of space. From this perspective, 19 May constituted the decisive starting point for the spatial domestication of the working class and of all those who opposed the new regime. In short, the Nationalists' "victory" parade on "Victory Day" *performed victory*. The parade consisted at once of a ritualistic commemoration, a rite of passage for the inhabitants of Madrid and the Spanish population at large, the performance of victory, a re-enactment of antagonisms (the "war isn't over," the Caudillo and others kept repeating),[65] the spatial deployment, display, and imposition of hegemony, and finally, the writerly constitution of a *communitas*, to use somewhat freely Victor Turner's celebrated concept (94–165). As politically conceived, ritualistically articulated, and discursively manipulated by speeches, essays, poems, and the like, the victory parade attempted to place its participants and spectators within a liminal locus framed, on one end, by the disintegration of the former regime and, on the other, by the formation of the new state. By means of a victory parade designed in part as a rite of passage, Spaniards were released as it were from the Republican organization of the social into a *communitas* in order to be *trained for* and later *incorporated into* a different articulation of social, political, and cultural relationships. In this sense, the rite of passage may be viewed as a rite of institution, that is, as a rite that sanctions and consecrates an order.[66] If we take as a rite of passage the parade and all the activities carried out in the rest of the country to celebrate "Victory Day," it follows that all Spaniards were forced to play the role of neophytes in liminality, of *tabulae rasae* that need to be shown, to quote from Turner, "that in themselves they are clay or dust, mere matter, whose form is impressed upon them by society" (103). Hence the parade may be viewed, on the one hand, as the production of *communitas* through the representation and performance of victory, and, on the other, as a rite that instituted an exclusion (consecrating the separation between those who "joined in" from those who opposed the new order) while discouraging the members of the new community from transgressing that order.[67]

An ensemble of written and oral products as well as visual material (e.g., newsreels, documentaries, photographs) related or devoted to the victory parade established the codes for its "proper" interpretation and extended to the rest of the country its illocutionary force and perlocution. Fernando Fernández de Córdoba's broadcasting of the event on Radio Nacional played in this respect a noteworthy role. Not only did Fernández de Córdoba bring to every corner of Spain what only the people of Madrid could see, nor did he provide only factual information about the parade. More decisively, his characteristic pathos, his exalted comments, the tone set up from the very beginning of the retransmission by his emphatic reading of Rubén Darío's poem "Marcha triunfal" made the broadcast a perlocutionary act clearly addressed to the listeners' feelings rather than to their intellect. The same could be said of the documentary produced by the Departamento Nacional de Cinematografía, the ample photographic coverage of the parade, and the many articles appeared in the following weeks. Radio speeches by the Caudillo, Rafael Sánchez Mazas, Ernesto Giménez Caballero, José María Alfaro, and many other writers and politicians apropos of the victory parade had the same purpose of extending both in time and space the parade's significance and performativity.[68] These texts should not be considered as mere supplements of the event, but rather as an integral part of it. Consequently, one ought to see the victory parade as a constellation of spatial practices, linguistic products, and iconographic material that, when combined, produced physical, conceptual, and lived space.

A set of spatial practices, representations of space, and spaces of representation, the victory parade points out and performs key elements of the fascist production of space. It is, too, the most complete expression of fascist urban writing. Within the geography of hegemonic practices, Spanish fascism had settled in on a new location. The fascist direct action carried out in Spain's streets during the 1930s had finally achieved – if by a convoluted route not always determined by FE-JONS – its objective: the complete destruction of the enemy, the conquest of power, absolute hegemony, and the fascist/military rule over those same streets. The days of FE-JONS direct action in Spain's streets were over. From armed Falangists to parading soldiers, from the paramilitary struggle in space to the military control of space, the victory parade staged a narrative of origins, but more importantly, it presented hegemony as spatial hegemony. This was neither a coincidence nor an association exclusive to fascism. On a theoretical level, we could conclude that antagonism and hegemony are played out in space regardless of the ideological direction of the hegemonic formations. For this reason, their study should not be dissociated from the topographical analysis of spatial relationships, as I hope to have shown in this exploration of fascist urban writing vis-à-vis fascism's location within the geography of hegemonic practices.

Chapter Five

Russia: Spectres and Paratopos

Returning a Courtesy Call

Of all the myths created by Spanish fascists to narrate Spain's military involvement in the Second World War, there is one of particular interest, considering our previous discussion on the technologies of tropological striation and the fascist habitus. I am referring to the spatial myth according to which the División Española de Voluntarios was sent to the Soviet Union to return the "courtesy call" paid by the Russians to Spain in 1936–9.[1] The Russians had gone to Spain – so the myth goes – to help the "Reds" impose a communist regime in Spain, committing countless crimes in the process; now it was time to take revenge on them. As José Luis Arrese, the then secretary-general of FET-JONS, put it in the directive he dispatched on 26 June 1941 to the regional leaders of the party, ordering them to open recruitment offices, "Russia sought to destroy Spain, and to a great extend destroyed it; [Russia] wanted to appropriate it in order to shatter the Western world, and the ransom that Spain had to pay exceeds one million dead … We have to make up for our fallen … We have to avenge Spain" (qtd. in Moreno Juliá 82; Ramón Serrano Suñer would speak in a similar vein in his radio address of 27 October 1941). Spain, the first country to defeat communism in the battlefield, was offering itself to fight it again, this time, in the words of a veteran, "in its own den" (Eizaguirre 14). Franco's troops had expelled the "Reds" from Spain; now they would cooperate with the Germans to eradicate for good the bacillus of communism and thus save the world from it. Some of the banners carried by the people showing their support to the German invasion of the Soviet Union condense this myth eloquently: "Let's return Russia the visit it paid us in 1936."[2]

Fostered *pro domo sua* by the Falangists and bombastically articulated by the media, the pro-German enthusiasm that paraded through Spain's streets immediately after Germany's surprise attack on the Soviet Union on 22 June 1941 reached its paroxysm in the impromptu speech given by Minister of Foreign Affairs Ramón Serrano Suñer to the crowd that had gathered in front of the Secretaría General del Movimiento on 24 June. Elated by the situation, impeccably dressed that day in a white Falange summer uniform, Serrano Suñer blamed Russia for the civil war and the present state of affairs ("Russia is guilty! Guilty of our civil war! Guilty of the death of José Antonio [Primo de Rivera], our founder, and of the death of so many comrades and so many soldiers fallen in that war because of the aggression of Russian communism!"), demanding no less than the extermination of Russia (qtd. in Moreno Juliá 75). The subsequent organization of an expeditionary corps of volunteers to be sent to the Soviet Union, in fact already considered by Serrano Suñer, Dionisio Ridruejo, and Manuel Mora Figueroa on the eve of the German onslaught, was proposed by the minister of foreign affairs to Franco on 22 June, discussed the next day in a Cabinet meeting, and formally announced on 27 June.[3] In addition to this unit, the regime would create an air force squadron (the Escuadrilla Expedicionaria de Voluntarios Españoles de Aviación, known as Escuadrilla Azul, or the Blue Squadron). Thousands of young men – some of them minors who could not fight in the civil war and wanted now to emulate their victorious fathers – rushed to the recruitment offices to enlist in the Spanish Division of Volunteers.[4] A leading force in the genesis of this expeditionary corps, FET-JONS would have fourteen of its leaders enrolled in it, among them figures of such political relevance and public prominence as Agustín Aznar (national delegate of Health Care), Pedro Gamero del Castillo (member of the National Committee of FET-JONS), Manuel Mora Figueroa (chief of the Militias General Staff), and Dionisio Ridruejo (member of the Junta Política). The fascist habitus, forged, as we saw in chapter 2, during the Rif War, would once again find in battle as well as in its cultural representations an ideal field of action.

Long would be the march, and long would last the courtesy call. The staggered troop convoys from Spain to the Bavarian military training camp of Grafenwöhr;[5] the excruciating fifty-three-day trip from the camp to the front (see figure 5.1); the boundless brutality of a war of extermination; the frequent suicidal missions executed with limited materiel under extreme weather conditions in the Volkhov River and Leningrad fronts; and the hardships endured by approximately four

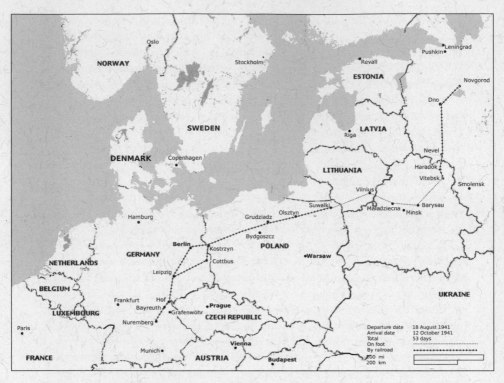

Figure 5.1 The Blue Division: From Grafenwöhr to the front. Image created by the author

hundred POWs in the transit and concentration camps of the Soviet Gulag would be milestones of a journey that began on 13 July 1941 with the departure by train of the first troops to Grafenwöhr. For some, that journey would end thirteen years later, when the *Semiramis*, at 5:35 p.m. on 2 April 1954, safely docked at the port of Barcelona carrying the 248 haggard, battered, morally ruined ex-POWs repatriated, after diplomatic negotiations, from the Soviet Union.[6] The authorities presided over by Franco's ad hoc representative and minister of the army, General Agustín Muñoz Grandes,[7] along with the thousands who for hours had been anxiously awaiting the arrival of the remnants of the Blue Division, the Blue Legion,[8] and the surviving diehards who decided to fight on under Wehrmacht or Waffen-SS units until the very end of the Third Reich,[9] could hardly conceal, with their display of pathos, the huge human cost of a military expedition cynically manipulated by the Spanish government in a remarkable exercise in political tightrope walking.[10] During the two-and-a-half years of the campaign, the division of 46,000 men suffered 25,000 casualties – 56% of its fighting force. The most reliable sources (e.g., Moreno Juliá 311–12, 322) list 4,954 dead and missing in action, 8,700 wounded, 2,137 cases of amputation or *mutilados*, 1,600 victims of frostbite, 7,800 seriously ill, and around 400 prisoners of war. It was a deadly courtesy call indeed.[11]

As Moreno Juliá (94) and Payne (*Franco* 148) have noted already, the Blue Division is perhaps the military unit with the highest number of learned soldiers and officers in the history of the Spanish army. The strongly ideological call to arms drew university students and professors, doctors, lawyers, mayors, and civil governors who joined the division, more often than not, out of idealism (e.g., anti-Marxism and/or disenchantment with Franco's regime for its partial implementation of the Falangist program), or the wish to fulfil an adventurous spirit, the need to clean a "red" past, the hope to desert to the Russians, or the pressure some felt to join in this call to arms.[12] Following a pattern established in the First World War (studied, among others, by Paul Fussell in a seminal book), this fact resulted in a large number of cultural representations produced by *divisionarios* (as the members of the Blue Division are known in Spain), especially during the 1950s. In their 1989 annotated bibliography, Caballero Jurado and Ibáñez Hernández list 132 books of poetry, memoirs, novels, and short stories, two movie scripts, and four films.[13] Moreover, as Payne reminds us, "the total amount of publications about this unit is greater than that concerning any other division of any of the belligerent countries [in the Second World War]" (*Franco* 146).

Whereas the history of the Blue Division, as well as Spain's intricate foreign policy during the Second World War, has merited scholarly attention,[14] what I will call the *Blue Division culture* has been neglected by literary critics; even the scholars who have explored Spanish literary fascism have surprisingly left out the Blue Division's cultural legacy.[15] However, the Blue Division is much more than a simple military unit endowed with a political function; it is also what Pierre Nora has termed a *lieu de mémoire*, that is, a set of documents and monuments making up the narrative of Spanish fascism as well as the multilayered substratum of the narratives whereby Spaniards remember, reconstruct, and reinterpret, still without a global consensus, their traumatic civil war. Therefore, it ought to be integrated into the scholarly discourse on fascism. Exploring the Blue Division culture uncovers, I believe, hidden layers of the topography of fascism in Spain. The double bind of spatiality and fascist habitus, both condensed in the myth of the courtesy call, will be the focus of this chapter. As the result in part of the division's ideological uniformity, the veterans' works share significant family resemblances, among them the linear chronology, the cartographic gaze, the poetics and experience of liminality, an explicit political discourse, an ideological and personal *ressentiment*, the fascist habitus, the consideration of war as a decisive formative event, and spectrality. In the pages that follow, I will expand four propositions through the analysis of these family resemblances in some of the most important works of the Blue Division culture. The first proposition claims that the tropological striation of space is carried out from the experience of a *paratopos*, a concept defined further in this chapter. The second proposition considers a number of works as "spectral" and their protagonists and/or authors as "spectres"; as I hope to show, writing constitutes, in these cases, the *house of the spectre*. This proposition is particularly important to understand the third: in this chapter I argue that, after the Second World War, Spanish fascism became, to a large extent, a haunting spectral presence. In this sense, the Blue Division culture would be both the bad conscience of the political establishment and the public display of such spectrality. Finally – and this is the fourth proposition – the Blue Division culture, in its encounter with the paratopos, can be considered as a topography of fascist resentment.

Territorial Alterity and Absolute War

The Blue Division and the Blue Legion fought in a territory – comprising the Novgorod area, the suburbs of Leningrad, and in the latter's case, Nikolajeska, Jamburg, Kostovo, and Luga – the topography and climate of which have little in common with Spain's (see figures 5.2 and 5.3). The "landscapes" were, we read in Carlos María Ydígoras's 1957 novel *Algunos no hemos muerto*, "identical and inhospitable ... A wasteland tormented by the snow, by the thaw, and ... by the heat" (126–7). In his dull, but informative, war memoir *La División Azul en línea* (1967), General of Staff José Díaz de Villegas depicts the Russian territory where the division had been deployed as "*geographic monotony*" and speaks of the "*anguish of immensity*" (45). Here men are not "kings," but rather "slaves" of the milieu. The horizon "recalls the sea's"; the steppe stretches to the infinite, and when the forest crops up, it seems to have no limits either (45). The same monotony applies to the soil: "The earthy ground, cov-

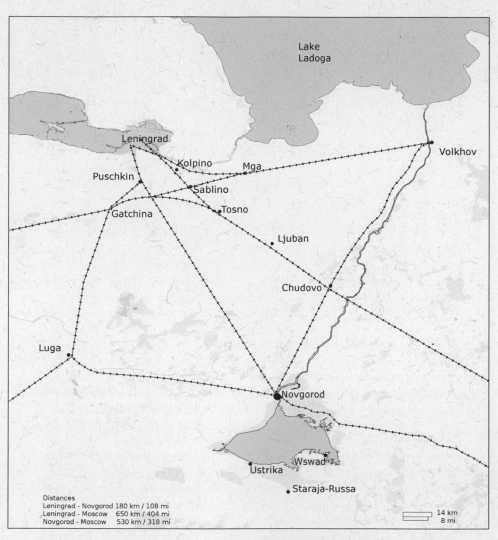

Figure 5.2 The two fronts of the Blue Division: The Volkhov River and
Leningrad. Image created by the author

ered by snow six months every year, another three by mud, hardened
only in the summer, is completely clayey" (45).

We owe to Dionisio Ridruejo, whose acute capacity to perceive, feel,
and enjoy landscapes has been acknowledged by the writer himself, one

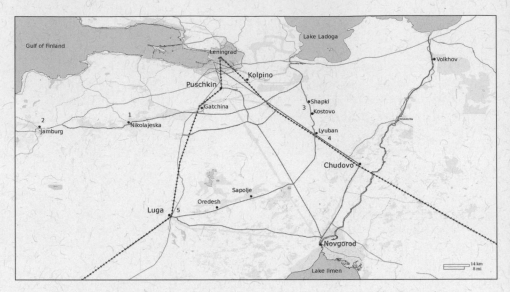

Figure 5.3 The five fronts of the Blue Legion. Image created by the author

of the finer and more insightful depictions of the strangeness felt by the
soldiers in the country to which they were paying their "courtesy call."
Posthumously published by his widow in 1978, Ridruejo's war diary is
also an extensive, wonderfully written series of sketches of Russia's towns,
landscapes, peoples, and customs, as well as an account of the author's
shifting impressions of his surroundings. Upon entering into Russia, the
flatness and wide horizons of the steppe remind him of his native Castile.
But soon Ridruejo perceives an uncanny side of the Russian countryside.
Already in the entry of 1 October 1941, Ridruejo observes, "At night a
dazzling moon merges, which spills over the earth. Thus the plain looks
flatter and more desolate, and the confines ... suggest an abyss: an abyss
certainly infinite" (*Los cuadernos* 121). Walking there could only mean
"going enveloped in terror" (121). Indeed, it is the landscape of the dying: with snow or by moonlight, "I think of ... heading towards the horizon, walking alone, as if such a thing were the act of dying; as if the
act of dying were ... a walking of that kind, outside the world" (121).
To the resemblance between this landscape and Castile noted in previous entries he adds a new, ominous spiritual layer; instead of eternity, it
suggests the nothingness (121). "A new, strange world": such is the land
he is acquainting himself with, as he succinctly puts it in his entry of 5

October 1941 (125). Prior to this observation, the writer had scribbled in his diary that a mujik's house in a hamlet near the Volkhov River was for a while "our home," and yet, "what a sensation of feeling lost and very far away from everything, from our own world!" (144). In addition, several of the poems he wrote during his sojourn in Russia (collected in *Poesía en armas (Cuadernos de la campaña de Rusia)* [1944]) evince similar feelings of estrangement. His "first and estranged vision of the Russian land" is conveyed in the triptych "Soledad (Tierra de Rusia)" (*Cuadernos* 89–94). The Russian landscape is a "relic of nothingness in sea of lead" (line 42). "To walk, to walk, to walk. Am I living?" (line 29), or, as the poetic voice says further, "Along the finished steppe / The spirit drifts hazy / Until it sinks in the nothingness of the present. / Only my pulse is alive, alone, alone" (lines 47–50).[16] Ridruejo would always regard Russia's land with admiration, so much so that at the end of his war service he professed his fondness for the country, its people, the exceptional beauty of its landscape: "I felt that I was drinking Russia in my heart. All the love that I have accumulated for this land, for this great and sad people ... has suddenly merged in myself to such a degree that I almost cried" (*Los cuadernos* 285–6).[17]

A strange land indeed. But even stranger to the rank and file (less so, understandably, to the professional military personnel), and far more deadly was the kind of war waged on the Eastern front, deeply conditioned by the Russian climate, and above all, by the National Socialists' theory of *Lebensraum* as well as their ideological position with regard to the Slavs, the Jews, Bolshevism, and the Soviet Union.[18] The Nazis conceived the war as a "crusade" against "Judeobolshevism."[19] The German officers and troops who fought against the Soviet Union were, to quote Arno Mayer, "not only military combatants but *political warriors* as well" (210; my emphasis) whose purpose was the complete annihilation of the Soviet Union. What led the war to its exceptionally murderous power was the priority given to racial (anti-Semitism) and political (anti-communism) principles.

From June 1941 to early May 1945, the war of annihilation fought between Nazi Germany and the Soviet Union was, in effect, an instance of what Carl von Clausewitz famously termed as *absolute war*. By *absolute war*, let us remember, Clausewitz means war as an independent and unconditioned reality, or, to put it differently, war waged according to its intrinsic rules and irrespective of external factors. Defined as "an act of force to compel our enemy to do our will" (75), war is composed of "primordial violence, hatred, and enmity" (89). Since all belligerents must necessarily

hold this view, it follows that "military operations could not be suspended ... until one or the other side was finally defeated" (579). In its absolute form, war lacks a "nonconducting medium" (579); the only result
that counts is the complete fulfillment of the intrinsic elements of war
in the absolute: the annihilation of the enemy's forces. For Clausewitz,
absolute war became another way of waging war after the French Revolution. Bonaparte, according to him, brought war, "swiftly and ruthlessly,"
to a state of "absolute perfection" (580); he waged war "without respite
until the enemy succumbed" (580). Clausewitz maintains that during
the revolutionary wars, and especially in the Napoleonic campaigns,
warfare "attained the unlimited energy we consider to be its elementary
law" (217). The subversion of the limit permeates Clausewitz's analysis
of absolute war as practised during the Napoleonic campaigns. There
seemed to be no end to the resources mobilized to conduct war, and "all
limits disappeared in the vigor and enthusiasm shown by governments
and their subjects ... [war had been] untrammeled by any conventional
restraints, had broken loose in all its elemental fury" (592–3). Absolute
war is the realm of the "pure element of enmity" (605), or, to borrow a
useful concept coined by Carl Schmitt, of *absolute enmity* (*Theory* 85–95).
Like Kant's *unjust enemy* (*Metaphysik der Sitten* §60), absolute enmity is
predicated on the absolute injustice of the enemy's cause. The enemy is
not – as Hegel would put it – "negated otherness," but rather a criminal,
a wholly unfettered evil. While it is undeniable that past wars had been
waged in the name of absolute, transcendental categories (e.g., "true religion"), the sheer vastness of the resources employed, the fact that wars
from then on would be fought in the name of the nation, and not the
Crown, as well as the universal claims of the enlightened ideals underlying the French Revolution, gave an entirely new dimension to war and
increased the brutality of absolute enmity exponentially. And this is precisely, as Bellamy explains in an important book, what happened in the
war between Nazi Germany and the Soviet Union in 1941–5. Several of
the veterans from the Blue Division noted this fact. "This war," Antonio
José Hernández Navarro writes in *Ida y vuelta* (1946), "shows no mercy.
A matter of life and death is the sign of the struggles of these times; and
if tomorrow I met during an assault, face to face, the Russian with whom
today I sincerely shook hands, I would kill him without a trembling of
my will" (230; see also 104). Remembering in 1967 – to give one more
example – the destruction witnessed in Vitebsk, Fernando Vadillo concludes: "In effect, the spectacle was horrible ... that was a total war ...
all over the horizon a scorched and wretched land outstretched. Ware-

houses and arms depots, kolkhozes and electrical power stations, forests and sown fields, granaries, stables, and telegraph poles. The world was burning towards the east, and the smoke from the fires darkened the sun" (*Orillas* 1: 227).

The Paratopos

The Russia of 1941 was hardly a good choice for a visit. Following an identical temporal sequence (i.e., a round trip from Spain to the Soviet Union), a significant number of works written by *divisionarios* can be read, in the framework of the spatial terms discussed earlier in the chapter, as a journey from home to a barren, hostile place; after spending a period of time butchering at the front, the soldier returns home. While it would be inaccurate to generalize it to every veteran's work, there is in the Blue Division culture a powerful existential feeling that ultimately subverts the conventional, more common meaning of a trip from home to a foreign land and back again. Some of the men who had enlisted out of an idealistic impulse felt used and betrayed – during and most particularly after the campaign – by the government and the party, ignored by the media, and misunderstood by their fellow countrymen.[20] Back in Spain, the *divisionarios* found themselves in a somewhat unexpectedly alien locus. Returning home was, in reality, going to a new place. This type of locus I will call *paratopos*. Let me pause for a moment and clarify this concept, as it is important to understand an essential component of the Blue Division culture.

By *paratopos*, I am referring to those anthropological habitats whose affective association with their former inhabitant(s) has been suspended altogether.[21] Under certain circumstances, a place in which the former inhabitant had invested his affectivity excludes him. The personal relation between place and individual has been so radically discontinued that the place alienates the former inhabitant. A place becomes a paratopos as soon as the smooth and seemingly natural links between habitat, former inhabitant, and the latter's habits is lost, something lived by the former inhabitant, more often than not, as an alienating experience. Places cannot be dissociated from the traces left by human beings. *Inhabitare* (to dwell) entails the inscription of one's *habitus* (habits) onto a *habitat* (place). As Maurice Merleau-Ponty has phrased it, places are not defined "as objective positions in relation to our body's objective location, rather, they inscribe around us a varying range of our aims and gestures" (178–9). Our habits, Merleau-Ponty explains, express our ability to widen our being in the world and consist of knowledge irreducible to thinking (179). "The habit," the French philosopher further clarifies, "resides neither in the mind nor in the objective body, but in the body as mediator of the world" (180). In the case of the paratopos, the problem does not lie only in the impossibility of experiencing the old centre of gravity as if it still were an extension of the self, but also in the fact that such place projects a blurred image of past habits within the rules of an extraneous grammar. On the one hand, the visibility of these sedimented habits generates a process in which the individual perceives his past experience as uncannily alien; on the other, the intimate familiarity of the subject with his former place hampers his possible attempts to adjust. In a paratopos, one has lost an anchor in the world; the former inhabitant seems to be "out of touch." Paratopoi are places that for some people have lost their capacity to function as habitats. In short, *a paratopos is an alienating habitat to its former inhabitant(s)*. It lies alongside of, near, in comparison to, and contrary to a locus lived by other people simply as a place: hence the prefix *para*. Not a mere mental construction, a paratopos is an outcome of the production of space. It should be noted that the broken links between habitat, inhabitant, and habit require an adjustment that may bring into being spatial practices and spaces of representation that have the potential to alter the alienating grammar. The paratopos transforms the previous inhabitant into a stranger, but a stranger with the capacity to alter it, even to make it again his dwelling, an action that ultimately clears away the paratopical component of the place.[22] The estrangement also has the capacity to confer new meanings to paratopical spaces. Therefore, paratopoi set out important problems of adjustment which may lead to creative ways of producing space.

In modern times the number of paratopical experiences has increased exponentially. "Homelessness" has been widely experienced in our time to the point that it is one of the defining traits of modernity, a phenomenon closely related to the mobility so characteristic of the modern age. To a degree, the modern being-in-the-world may be understood as a being-out-of-place. We live in a world of nomads, refugees, migrants, displaced and homeless people.[23] "The house is past," wrote Adorno shortly after the Second World War. "The bombings of European cities, as well as the labor and concentration camps, simply continue what the immanent development of technology had decided on houses long ago. These are now good only to be thrown away like old food cans" (*Minima* 57). Sometimes the individual's possessions lose their familiar physiognomy; they do not seem to be "in their place" any longer. The place has wholly lost its connection with self-identity, becoming instead what could be called a *centre of alienation*. To other people, these *centres of alienation* look just like regular places, structurally homogeneous to their own. But to émigrés or veterans, these places have turned into paratopoi. *Coming* home, for the political exile, for the expatriate, for the veteran, for displaced persons thus may involve *going to* a place that has been taken over by other, alien meanings. In this sense, a paratopos is a type of place widely experienced in modernity.[24]

Houses, neighbourhoods, hometowns, countries, even institutions and the entire world are potential paratopoi. Imagine a well-known experience. A person, after many years of living abroad, decides to visit the family country house where he spent his entire childhood and adolescence. From afar, the house looks as it did in the past: its structure, its surroundings, its ecology have not changed. Smells, sounds, the breeze from the north, so familiar to him, take him back to times past. He walks down the road, opens the gate, knocks on the door. A complete stranger opens it. Upon hearing the purpose of this man's call, he invites him in. Once inside, the visitor suddenly realizes his mistake: the few pieces of furniture left by his family have been removed to the basement, there is a new staircase, the quaint drawing room is now a rather conventional living room, and his childhood bedroom a tastelessly decorated guest room. These and other changes belong to a new grammar, the rules of which have been established by the present dwellers. The place has hidden his personal history, thereby breaking the affective connection between the things and his being. The house is not the visitor's habitat any longer; his longing will never be fulfilled, his past has been cut off from him. The individual feels alienated, expelled from something fundamental, excluded from the place as well – and more decisively – from what it represented and is there no more. The house, his former – to quote from Gaston Bachelard's *La Poétique de l'espace* – "well-being" is now a paratopos that sets him off-limits. Imagine now four other situations. After – say – twenty uninterrupted years abroad, a family returns to their hometown. To their surprise, the hometown has changed substantially. They discover new streets, new buildings, new lifestyles; the old urban grammar has been altered in unexpected ways. The inhabitants seem also to behave a bit differently. The town, the "habitat," expresses new "habits" that hinder the former inhabitants from adjusting to their hometown. Analogous experiences have occurred among convicts upon being released from prison, survivors of death camps, and veterans.

The out-of-placeness felt by the veterans in their own country after having served abroad has been studied extensively.[25] Moreover, the corpus of cultural artefacts produced in the twentieth century depicting the out-of-placeness of the veteran is vast.[26] A number of works written by *divisionarios*, especially by the most ideologically committed of them, belong to such a corpus. Some Blue Division veterans felt an ideological alienation akin to the sense of estrangement experienced by the *camisas viejas* ("old shirts," as the members of Falange Española before the civil war were known) vis-à-vis the Franco regime. It is also important to note here that organizations have the capacity to function as places and paratopoi. That was the case of Falange Española, a political party denaturalized after Franco's Decree of Unification in 1937 and by the massive increase of its membership right after the civil war. Both events dramatically diluted the fascist ideology of the party as conceived of by its founding fathers. To the bitterly disappointed and frustrated "true" Falangists, the party had ceased to give expression to their political thinking. By transforming a fascist party into an umbrella political organization in which fascists and Carlists had to cohabit, Franco placed the *camisas viejas* into a paratopical space.[27] Not a few *divisionarios* tore up their membership cards for this reason. From an ideological standpoint, their Spain, the Spain they had fought for in the Soviet Union on behalf of fascist ideals, had metamorphosed itself into *something else*. In this transformation, the correlation between fascism and the "new" Spain had been lost. Spain did not "host" fascist ideals, it was not the "house" they had hoped to build. As regards the veterans' fascist identity, the country – and let us add, FET-JONS – had become a paratopos. In 1945, and more so in the 1950s, the Spanish government had shifted its course from openly embracing fascism, especially its language and symbols, to a rapprochement with the winning side of the war, a piece of acrobatics that required an abandonment, at least in public discourse, of fascism, thus beginning a long process of – in Payne's useful neologism – "defascistation" (*Fascism* 363–479).[28] After nearly a decade of international isolation, Spain signed its first bilateral agreement with the United States (1953), and joined the United Nations (1955) and the World Bank (1958). Consequently, the Blue Division became a political embarrassment. During the war, Franco's government had been pressed by the United Kingdom and the United States to withdraw the Blue Division from the front. Its eventual dissolution in October 1943 and the almost furtive creation of the otherwise ephemeral Blue Legion (October 1943–February 1944) were derived from the opportunistic double orientation of the regime in a decisive turning point in world history. Before long, the soldiers and officers of the Blue Division who made it home realized that there they were not regarded as heroes but rather as adventurers. Russia had been a strange land to which they had simply "paid a courtesy call." But now Spain was no less alien to them. Interestingly, while for the veterans "home" had ceased to have its usual meaning, for the Francoist regime the returning *divisionarios* constituted a sort of *Unheimliche* (uncanny). As a result, the fascist *divisionarios* haunted Franco's regime as much as they were haunted by the individuals and institutions who had ideologically occupied "their" place, thereby changing it into a paratopos.

A "lost generation," according to Tomás Salvador (*División* 6), the Falangists who had joined the Blue Division did indeed feel uneasy back in the Spain of Franco.[29] Eugenio, a character from Rodrigo Royo's 1956 novel *El sol y la nieve*, expresses the disappointment no doubt felt by other *divisionarios*: he went to Russia out of disgust with the political situation, because after three years of a fratricidal war "we are going back to our old ways, and [now] the old enemies come and snatch the flag from us or put us aside, as if we had gone to kill and be killed on their behalf in order to bail them out, to defend their grime and pettiness as well as their social and political lethargy," adding that he is the product of a political nausea (37–8). In a similar fashion, a character from José María Sánchez Diana's fictionalized memoirs remembers with a bit of melancholy the hopes of the volunteers: "We all thought that, after returning to Spain, a new 'political spring,' without capitalists, or aristocrats, or Christian democracy, would begin, that we would enjoy social equality and real justice ... Our idea was that upon their return to Spain the fighting youth would impose their political goals, the land reform, and the destruction of capitalism" (*Cabeza* 158). Sánchez Diana himself, in the prologue to his book, attacks the opportunists and social climbers who joined FET-JONS and those who secretly worked to destroy "Falange's revolutionary youth, sending it far away, the further the better" (16); after the war emerged "the generation of opportunists, technocrats, capitalists," all of them afraid of the "revolutionaries," of "that enthusiastic youth who could have carried out a great Revolution and save Spain from so much pettiness and corruption" (16–17). While they were away in Russia, "the state of the right . . . the neo-capitalist state of bureaucrats and submissive unionists was developed" (17).

In the prologue to the 1954 edition of *Ida y vuelta*, Antonio José Hernández Navarro vented his resentment without sparing harsh words against those who – so he believed – had betrayed the *divisionarios*. At a dinner party held in honour of the POWs just repatriated from the Soviet Union, the guests talked about the old times, about the present, about their prospects "as if they were still soldiers ... And we have sung the old and beloved songs of the campaign, and made a tacit profession of hope turning our backs on the civilian failure of many heroes who in the battlefield were demigods, and in the peace of the urban jungle have been wounded treacherously by those who have the rare ability to enjoy the victories won by others" (59–60). Coping with the new situation would not be easy, as Salvador's novel *Camaradas 74* (1975) clearly demonstrates. Its characters' deep sense of personal failure and social maladjustment is yet another instance of the *divisionarios'* awareness of living in a paratopos. A character of the novel named Luis points out to a former comrade-in-arms that as soon as a war is over, heroes are not needed any longer: "It is the time of the administrators ... All this is fine, in theory, in a bled nation that must be rebuilt.... But ten, thirty years go by, and everything stays the same. The same because the silencing of the public opinion doesn't let them notice the widening distance between theory and practice" (64–5). Pedro agrees with Luis completely, and further in the novel he gives free rein to his self-pity: his life as an "honest industrialist" is meaningless while his mediocre professional life is complemented by the no less pointless participation in the veterans associations whose members gather year after year for the burial of a comrade, resentfully adding: "And to feel that one loses the Fatherland by falling asleep ... And you go to the store, to the brotherhood [of veterans], to the bank, and ten, twenty, thirty, even forty years elapse, and they let you grumble a little bit, and you let them grumble a little bit, and you put on the [blue] shirt for the parades ... but you end up not knowing what, or whom, or how to honour ... little by little you realize that wars are waged so that those who win them may have power ... and this is what makes one sad: that at some point the retirement comes ... And everything will die, apart from the memories, from the right to complain" (270–2).

The last sentence is crucial: the key to overcome such a pitiful situation lies in memory. Some *divisionarios* would find in the practice of writing a place of their own where they would put things back into "their place." Thus writing is much more than the space where absolute war and paratopoi are symbolically expressed and articulated; it also has to be considered as a new "home" for the veterans. The repeated metatextual references to the act of writing and of remembering underscore indirectly the existential function of literature.[30] Memoirs, poetry, novels, and short stories functioned therefore as loci in which *ressentiment*, historical testimony, self-vindication, and self-creation intertwined.

The House of the Spectre

Tomás Salvador – a veteran of the Blue Division, prolific novelist, and literary critic of note during the 1950s and 1960s who had joined the Spanish police in 1944 – published in 1954 the first novel ever written on the entire history of both the Blue Division and the Blue Legion, from their creation to their dissolution: *División 250* (Spanish translation of the official denomination of the Blue Division within the Wehrmacht: 250. Infanterie-Division).[31] Published by the prestigious Ediciones Destino and well received by the public, meriting three editions in six months, Salvador's novel evinces mastery of narrative form as well as a nuanced treatment of human suffering that make it one of the better works of its kind. Its structure, divided into a prologue, four parts, and an epilogue, follows a circular pattern: the prologue ("Doce años después") and the epilogue ("Soneto final, soneto de amor con estrambote") frame the lineal story within the temporal horizon of the author – the epilogue is dated "22 March 1954" – thereby stressing the existential and ideological gap between the war and a purportedly mediocre, demoralizing present. Similarly to other works of the Blue Division culture, *División 250* draws a stark line separating the present of the discourse from the war experience told in the story. Accordingly, the novelist locates his work in what we could call a *parachronos*, namely a point in time in which a person feels "out of place." *División 250* alternates an extradiegetic voice and a handful of embedded narrators, and each section composing the four parts focalizes on at least one soldier. The clever intertwining of focalizers immerses the reader into a shared, collective universe with no leading voice: properly speaking, the only protagonist of *División 250* is, as announced by the title, the Blue Division itself. By narrating the history of the division from multiple angles, Salvador destabilizes the frontiers separating voices, gazes, and spaces. The overlapping of historical horizons and narrative perspectives springs up, as we shall see in the next section, from a poetics of the limit.

Written in part to set the record straight with those who have given a distorted, prejudiced image of the Blue Division (6–7), *División 250* is built upon an apparently bizarre theory of the *espantajo* (scarecrow) that intersects the above-mentioned ideological, historical, and existential gaps. To emphasize the importance of this theory, the prologue of the

novel starts with an account of what the author understands by *espantajo*.
A good comprehension of the *espantajo* will clarify several key issues not
only of the novel, but also of Spanish fascism itself. Let us begin by stating that the *espantajo* is a spectral figure linked to war whose haunting
presence compels the author – so he claims – to write:

> Ten years have elapsed, and I had forgotten many things.... But I have re-
> membered the 'scarecrow.'... The scarecrow ... is the sum of all the emo-
> tions that lead men to the sacrifice ... It is everything ... it will always be
> there, between the furrows turned into tombs, shouting like a nutcase.... It
> doesn't frighten, it isn't amusing, it doesn't even praise: it only accompanies
> us ... This is basically what has forced me to write. Because all notwithstand-
> ing, it has been good enough for me to open up a gap for the remembrance
> in order to immediately find myself in front of the face of the dead. I have
> seen the scarecrow's shadow ... Because of this, I have understood that I will
> never be able to disown the past. (6)

The title of the prologue's first section, "Invocación. Tiempo," clearly
points to the origin of Salvador's writing: the purpose to conjure up the
spectre.[32] From this perspective, the writing of *División 250* could be considered as a hauntology, a concept proposed and explained by Jacques
Derrida in *Specters of Marx*. *División 250* is not concerned with recovering the fullness of being but rather with the dislocation that corrupts
identity, with the undecidability between flesh and spirit. To follow the
trace left by the spectre and conjure it up so as to recover the repressed
in history (generated, according to Derrida, by the "mode of production
of the phantom" [*Specters* 120]), to be aware that the outcome of such
a task, a mourning of sorts, will always be provisional, to show that the
décalage is the condition of possibility of justice and emancipation: these
are some of the main if tacit presuppositions and objectives of Salvador's
novel.

The fascist ideology articulating both *División 250* and its spectrality demonstrates the dangers of associating the emancipatory power of
hauntology with justice understood within the parameters of progressive
political thinking.[33] Derrida calls for an exorcism "not in order to chase
away the ghosts, but this time to grant them the right ... as *revenants* who
would no longer be *revenants*, but as other *arrivants* to whom a hospitable
memory or promise must offer a welcome :... out of concern for *justice*"
(220). But the return of the repressed may acquire different directions,
some of which – beyond the mourning necessary to overcome "a his-

torical trauma that has been erased from conscious memory but which makes its presence felt though its ghostly traces" (Labanyi, introduction 6) – might lead to unexpected paths.[34] A fascist novel on fascist spectres, *División 250* is a case in point. In this novel, the connection between the spectre and deadly violence is symptomatic indeed. Like so many, if not all, veterans, Salvador and several of his characters seem to live surrounded by spectres – the spectres of the fallen and killed, the spectres, as it were, of death itself. A spectre, Derrida reminds us, has a paradoxical phenomenality that distinguishes it from the spirit: on the one hand, we have "the furtive and ungraspable visibility of the invisible or an invisibility of a visible X," while on the other, "the tangible intangibility of a proper body without flesh, but still the body of some*one* as some*one other*" (*Specters* 6). Thus the definition of the spectre is twofold: it is the phenomenal body of the spirit (169) as well as "the impatient and nostalgic waiting for a redemption" (170). The latter point has a social import, as Gordon demonstrates in *Ghostly Matters*. A ghost, she argues, is not the invisible. Rather, it has "a real presence and demands its due, your attention. Haunting and the appearance of specters or ghosts are one way … we are notified that what's been concealed is very much alive and present, interfering precisely with those always incomplete forms of containment and repression ceaselessly directly toward us" (xvi); the spectre is, in other words, a "social figure" (8, 25). Spectres and the living coexist in an unstable liminal space without exteriority: as Derrida rightly asserts, to possess a spectre means necessarily to be possessed by it (*Specters* 165). For this reason, it could be argued that the location of the spectre is at the crossroads of remembrance and writing. By encapsulating this logic of the spectre in *División 250*, or, to put it differently, by centring on invisibilities and exclusions, Salvador's novel could be considered as a ghost story. To set the record straight implies, in this case, the conjuring up of spectres. "Perceiving the lost subjects of history," Gordon claims, "makes all the difference to any project trying to find the address of the present … To write a history of the present requires stretching toward the horizon of what cannot be seen with ordinary clarity yet" (195).

In the section titled "Retirada" (146–60), the invoking function of writing is explicitly stated in a metafictional passage focused on a character named Dionisio who is modelled after the Falangist poet Dionisio Ridruejo. On guard duty at a position covering the retreat of the surviving defenders of Posad, Dionisio, overtaken by deep melancholy, begins to think about his fallen comrades: "The dead … They would never be abandoned. He knew that in the last days it had not been possible to bury them, and that the dead remained in a shelter, awaiting" (146; see also 150). What they are awaiting is the conjuration of writing, for war writing consists of "giving form" to the anxiety suffered by Dionisio and to the dead. Literary form provides new life to the fallen; it is a recognition of the spectre. The word offers the spectre a "hospitable memory" (Derrida, *Specters* 220). Writing, aside from being contaminated by the undecidability of the spectre, turns itself into *the house of the spectre*. Were Dionisio to survive the war, he would represent his dead comrades' anxiety. "The bodies would rise ... They would reveal their faces sunken in the snow, their mouths full of earth, their shattered limbs ... He could see them! Amongst the ruins, amongst the trees ... burning the roots, tormenting the memory" (151). Haunted by the spectres of his comrades, envisioning the project to conjure them up (Dioniso, on guard duty, will be the "guard" protecting the spectre from being repressed to the margins of history), this alter ego of Ridruejo sees the sudden apparition of a scarecrow wearing a uniform who, getting up off the snow, "skeletal, without blood and without sex" (151), exclaims, "Dead, dead all! On your feet!... You, the endless, the damned, the forgotten ...! Soldiers of mine, you belong to me ...! You ... are castles in my land ... Dead! I will be with you. I will recount the mad things you did" (152). This episode on haunting may be considered as a metafictional comment on the major role played in the novel by the conjuring up of the spectre. Dioniso understands that the dead "are never left alone" because the spectre, "the soldier's real glory," has the mission to always accompany the dead soldiers and shout next to their graves "the tremendous importance of their sacrifice"; the *espantajo* "would keep for them the last gesture, the best emotion" (152).[35] Crucially, this character understands that the surviving soldier's pain will diminish through poetry. By writing, he will come to terms with his traumatic experience. As Horkheimer and Adorno put it, "Only the conscious horror of destruction creates the correct relationship with the dead: unity with them because we, like them, are the victims of the same condition and the same disappointed hope" (215). Dionisio's final ruminations refract the inextricable relationship between writing and the act of conjuring the spectre in *División 250*: "As days, and months, and years go by, the pain would decrease, floating on the lake of memories. The verses that he would write some day would be like an offering ... to the unassuming comrades" (152). The thematization of the act of writing in other passages of the novel (14, 113–14, 202–6, 293, 365–9) underscores the invoking function of *División 250*'s writing and its relationship with war and fascist ideology.

Not unnaturally, conjuring up in Spain a spectre born and seen in Russia brings to the native country a haunting, threatening presence. Eleuterio Paniagua points to this itinerary of the spectre in an episode of his novel *Los hombres se matan así*. Paniagua's narrator devotes a chapter to the "Position of the Ghost," thus baptized because the soldiers believed the position to be haunted (201–15). In this position, "one could breathe the terror when the ghost showed up, and the soldiers, unafraid of men, walked and talked as if they were afraid of something else. A fear of the ghost" (208). It was a deadly ghost, for it enjoyed killing soldiers when the Russians were not attacking and it always followed them wherever they went. Crucially, "they even say that they saw it en route to Spain" (209). Discourse would be the path taken by the spectre. Haunting first the veterans, it would come through their speech, written or spoken. In certain cases, conjuring up the spectre liberates the possessed from its negative power. Take, for instance, Sánchez Diana's *Cabeza de puente*. In its prologue, the author affirms that his novel does not pretend to be a lesson; instead, he has written it to get rid of this "nightmare": "There are nights in which the reflex acts from insomnia, the lights from the snow, the flares crossing rivers and swamps come out, in which I can hear shouting unique things, in which the word *Spain* has then a meaning. And one can't live like this" (17). The spectre thus comes home through literature. For the veteran, returning home is an act followed by his determination to write. Frustration, resentment, and paratopical experience find an outlet in writing, the house of the spectre, built in part to haunt the reader and the political establishment. That is precisely the last itinerary of the spectre: the itinerary traced by the pen. The narrator of *División 250* underscores this when he narrates the repatriation of the Blue Division (330–5), connecting space, remembrance, memory, and writing: "All that silent land, full of funnels and puddles, of torn open trees, and of ruins, belonged to the strange region where the war set up. But in the trenches full of mud, at the crossroads, in the shelters, and in the machine-gun nests set up another strange theory of the wounded, broken, anxious humanity ... Floating over the minefields remained ... the strange memory, unrequited, forgotten, but everybody knew that it could emerge at any moment" (330).

The Visit

In the Blue Division culture, writing is a locus in which the borders between life and death are blurred. The true place lies, for the veteran, in writing, and once immersed in it he locates himself in an interstitial, liminal place. As seen in chapter 2, liminality is as much a transition between states in the context of ritual initiations as a place of habitation or "position" (Pérez Firmat xiv), the latter being a structure made up of the relationship between a centre and a periphery. Furthermore, the unstable liminality defining the relationship between the living and the spectres counters the alienating effect of the paratopical space found by veterans upon their anticlimactic, almost clandestine arrival into Spain. While this instability reproduces the above-mentioned dissolution of the limit caused by absolute war, the liminal locus constitutes, too, a discursive space from where the writer applies a cartographic gaze over the territory occupied by the Blue Division, thus proceeding to a tropological striation.

División 250 puts into a practice a poetics of the limit closely linked to the recursive thematic presence of the border. By *border*, one should not understand a static topographical site between two fixed loci, but rather "an interstitial zone of displacement and de-territorialization that shapes the identity of the hybridized subject" (Gupta and Ferguson 18). As Anderson and O'Dowd have noted, borders "are at once gateways and barriers to the 'outside world,' protective and imprisoning, areas of opportunity and/or insecurity, zones of contact and/or conflict, of co-operation and/or competition, of ambivalent identities and/or aggressive assertion of difference" (595–6). Migrants, exiles, smugglers, and soldiers configure and reconfigure an ambiguous entity of hybridization enclosing and giving meaning to a territory. By the same token, a place has anthropological content through the imposition of limits. Territories are humanly produced entities. The inherent ambiguity of the border is an important technology of tropological striation present in the Blue Division culture. Salvador's novel as well as other narratives by *divisionarios* show a penetrating consciousness of the performative power of borders.

Examples abound. Crossing the border between Spain and France is an important topos of the Blue Division culture. The young volunteers passed over that threshold with much emotion, for at the border they began to realize the real purport of their decision to fight in the war. The narrator/protagonist of *Cabeza de puente* repeats a commonplace in his re-enactment of that event: "The moment to take the decisive step was approaching: the crossing of the border [between Spain and France].... It was an epic moment that still makes me shudder.... We had left behind the flags of the Spanish towns, the music and the colour of our sky, the white streets and Spain's accent. It was four o'clock in the afternoon of the nineteenth of July of '41" (Sánchez Diana, *Cabeza* 31).[36] Likewise, to Ydígoras the act of crossing into Russian territory represented the penetration into a world articulated by an uncanny grammar. In their first halt in the Soviet Union, the protagonist of the novel and his comrades witness, completely horrified, a scene functioning as a metaphor of a new, violent spatial relationship between territory and subject. Stopping next to a group of hanged bodies, the narrator feels forlorn "in the world's most inhospitable corner," adding that "looking towards the group of hanged persons who, by way of old Muscovy's welcome, swung half a hundred metres further from where we were, I muttered, as if frightened by the acknowledgment of my great adventure: 'I am in Russia'" (Ydígoras 73; the same scene in Hernández Navarro's *Ida y vuelta* 135). In Salvador's *División 250*, crossing the border with Russia does not imply, however, the perception of any change; quite the opposite: "And one fine day they learnt that they were already in Russia. No visible border showed it.... The comrades were surprised. They expected to find something different, strange, sombre perhaps. And that land was just like all the rest. With the same sky, the same destroyed towns, the same people" (*División* 74). It goes without saying that the border does not shape the meaning of its contents *by itself*; this requires the encounter of the border and a transcendental subject, a fact that explains the different feelings and interpretations of the *border* and *crossing the border* in the Blue Division culture. Through one focalizer, Salvador sketches a theory of the border as a basis for the previously quoted experiences; apropos of the German border, "Ortega, the intellectual, was the first to realize it.... Something had changed. It couldn't be anything other than an exchange of countries; Germany on the horizon and a new music in the air.... Ortega was a thinker ... he knew that borders are the consequences of many centuries [of] fighting, intrigues, and blood. A border couldn't go unnoticed because it symbolized the change from one world to another ... Only when he saw ... some children wearing the characteristic uniform of the *Hitlerjugend* would he be convinced" (*División* 25).

Literally at the centre of this crossing of boundaries lies the military training camp of Grafenwöhr, a liminal space, since it marks an interstitial process of ritual initiation already studied in chapters 2 and 4. Here the volunteers receive training that will cast them out of the civilian society and put them in a world where the act of hurting other human beings is not only *in order*, but *ordered*. No longer an exteriority, from now on the border will be located within the individual himself – a mere volunteer before entering into Grafenwöhr, a trained Spanish soldier wearing a German uniform upon leaving it. The multiple unstable liminality stamped on the Spaniards (volunteer/soldier, Spanish/German soldier, badge with the Spanish flag and the noun *España* sown on the upper right shoulder of his army jacket / German uniform) was interestingly extended to the Blue Division itself (corps of Falangist volunteers / commanded by professional officers, official name División Voluntaria de Españoles / Falangist nickname "División Azul"), a military unit that operated with autonomy from the Wehrmacht under its own chain of command while being assigned first to Army Group Centre and shortly afterwards reassigned to Army Group North. Sánchez Diana states it unequivocally: "We learnt [in Grafenwöhr] something very important ... that before we perceived only on a sentimental level. The observance of the ordinances and the consideration of the military turned into a religion [*sic*] stamp on men a distinctive character" (*Cabeza* 55–6). The volunteer unavoidably acquires a military habitus. When he left Grafenwöhr for the front, the autodiegetic narrator of *Algunos no hemos muerto* writes, "I bade farewell to a life begun only two months before ... a life in which thousands of men prepared themselves for a monstrous and legal assassination" (Ydígoras 50). In a similar fashion, during his military training Paulino reflects, "It would be too difficult an effort to explain what he was feeling, or, possibly, too futile to be specific about how he was emptying his inner self in order to clear the way for a new man. A man who was learning a new trade: the trade to kill" (Salvador, *División 250* 44). In what constitutes perhaps the most telling example of the liminal experience lived by the Spanish volunteers, Ydígoras's narrator bitterly remembers his training in Grafenwöhr: "A new life was starting out in which the thousand customs, habits, and reactions that an ordered existence had formed in us would become blurred until they disappear. Men would become numbers, tamed by discipline. During the military training period, we would learn how to do away with guerrillas, to throw grenades ... We had to always obey orders ... Only this way would we become good soldiers ... dummies without initiative ... The war wanted fighting men, a little insensitive, a little stultified. And for this to happen, it would be necessary to get rid of many things, of all lyricisms" (47–8).

The threshold, the ultimate border, the epicentre as it were of all borders resides in the ceremony of the Hitler Oath, in which the volunteers pledged "absolute obedience to the Chief of the German Army Adolf Hitler in the struggle against Bolshevism." This is the decisive liminality, for *to pledge* is a binding performative that, in the case of the army, questions self-identity, thus erasing the soldier's individuality. Meditating on the meaning and consequences of the speech act *to take an oath*, Donato – one of *División 250*'s many characters – realizes what will be expected from them henceforth: upon hearing the words of General Muñoz Grandes in the ceremony ("What a Spaniard swears, he fulfils"), Donato "felt that he had suddenly grown ten years older. Oath …, fealty …, duty.… And like all the others, in order to fulfil his committed word he had to give himself over to a fight to the finish. Perhaps the oath was a new helmet" (Salvador, *División* 41). And he adds, in yet another insightful reflection on the oath, that he was not even twenty years old, that he had never taken an oath, and that "the first thing that he was committing to was his own death. He knew, through his father, about that Spanish ceremony … in which the flag is kissed … But that oath seemed different to him. It wasn't the fatherland anymore, a physical entity bounded by the borders and rocked in the customs and in the language. It was the intuition of the idea … And he was afraid. Afraid of the possibility that calamities might soften his bones, disillusion him, purloin from him the mystical content of his ideals" (41). This must have been a common thought among the volunteers. Sánchez Diana's main character, for instance, remembers in similar terms his oath to Hitler to fight communism: "Do you pledge obedience to the German Führer in the struggle against communism? YES, I DO. It was a real, unanimous howl … For the first time, I felt the enormous feeling of the universal history burdening us.… There was something in us that wasn't anymore what it was before. We had the spirit of war stuck in our blood" (*Cabeza* 51).

Performing the oath was the necessary precondition for the violent production of space as well as the fascist's insertion within the military structure. The tensions between the army and FET-JONS from the genesis of the division to its dissolution, manifested within the division itself in the frequent disagreements between the volunteers and their officers, should not conceal the military component of the fascist habitus shared by many officers and volunteers alike. In the Blue Division, the Falange's fascist habitus was integrated within the military field, a location that allowed the fascist volunteer to legally put into practice the violence inherent in his habitus – a habitus, as we shall now see, directed towards the fulfillment of the Falangists' will-to-empire. At the level of the story, *División 250* narrates in detail the itineraries followed by the soldiers: the trip from Spain to Grafenwöhr (13–32) and the march from Grafenwöhr to the Volkhov River front (54–86), the military operations (e.g., Posad, 119–33; Otenki, 133–8; the "Posición Intermedia" or Intermediate Position, 165), the epic suicidal mission at Lake Ilmen (171–92), the soldiers' days on leave in rearguard positions or cities like Riga (86–363), the reassignment of the Blue Division to the Leningrad front (238–41), the bloody Battle of Krasny Bor (10–13 February 1943) (274–91), and the return home of the Blue Division (330–5) and the Blue Legion (352–63). A dense net of vectorialities crisscrosses *División 250* – certainly not a surprising fact in itself, given the obvious basic modus operandi of any army, but of interest if we look attentively at the distinctive characteristics and meaning of those vectorialities vis-à-vis the fascist production of space studied in this book. Above all, it is significant because the changing emotions that tinge the itineraries in Salvador's novel (enthusiasm, hopefulness, fear, pain, disappointment, resentment) tell a story that intertwines with ideological drive, existential transformation through the war experience, a sense of political failure and/or personal frustration, and the return to a country soon to be perceived as a paratopos. Thus the temporal construction of the novel is somewhat secondary to the crucial overlapping of spaces with the emotionally and politically loaded vectorialities connecting places.

In *División 250* and other Blue Division narratives, the production of space works on at least two different levels. First, it consists of the military reorganization of the space occupied by the Spanish expeditionary corps, thereby imposing new meanings to it. Second, it may be interpreted as the individual's attempt to give meaning to his existence as well as transform (that is, *produce*) a depressing political space considered to be in the wrong hands or inadequately managed. Dionisio Ridruejo put it very clearly in his war diary. In an entry of 18 July 1941, he spells out what he and other *divisionarios* expected the Blue Division to be "now and upon returning": "a force of a new political fermentation" (*Los cuadernos* 19). The vast majority of volunteers feel, according to Ridruejo, "a kind of messianic conscience" that has to do with the fact that "almost all of us are disillusioned Falangists, in disagreement with how things go in the reactionary Spain that has been set up" (19); indeed, one has the impression that this "revolutionary interest in regard to Spain" is stronger than the Blue Division's objective: to fight against the Soviet Union (19). In an entry of his war diary dated 18 September 1941, Ridruejo summarizes a conversation that he had with a prominent Falangist and comrade-in-arms, Enrique Sotomayor (110–12). They came to the Soviet Union not only to fight communism: "We aspired to earn a right, a privileged position within a less unjust organization: to remedy our duties and force

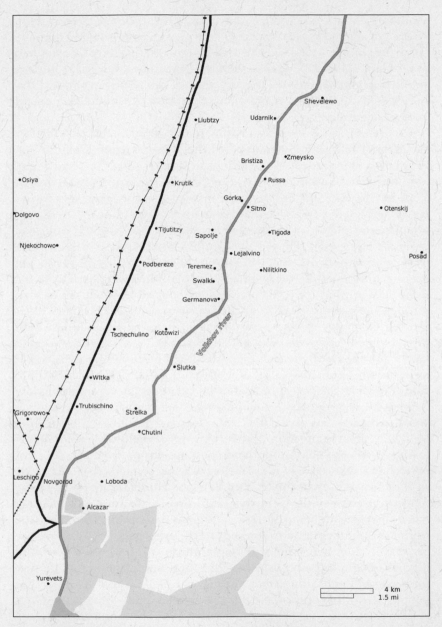

Figure 5.4 The Volkhov River front. Image created by the author

Spain to live in the behaviour proper to a universal people. In this sense
we are the agents of a total Spanish interventionism, or failing that, the
redeemers of Spain's impotence to intervene with its own character and
on her own" (111–12). Thus *going to Russia* amounted to *going to places
located in or related to Spain*. The structure of *División 250* produces this
crisscross of physical places and itineraries vis-à-vis their being a function
of Spanish politics.

At the level of the novel's story, the march towards Russia is seen by
some characters as a "liberation" of the Russians from communism.
"They were not invaders," Duez affirms in *División 250*, "they were libera-
tors" (72). Duez's thought was no doubt shared by many. General of Staff
Díaz de Villegas (7–8), for instance, insisted that the "blue volunteers"
had gone to Russia to fight communism and not the country. The somewhat condescending sympathy towards the Russian people manifested
in several passages of *División 250* (e.g., 195–6, 222) can be detected easily in other narratives.[37] Such an attitude was reflected in the very act of
walking, different from the Germans' way of dealing with the conquered
space. Take, for instance, the *divisionarios*' behaviour in Vitebsk, as seen
through the astonished gaze of the Germans, who often found "their
Spanish comrades in pairs, even alone in neighborhoods where only
heavily armed groups dared to go. The Spaniards carried only machetes
and ... pistols. Their audacity, their treating the Russians as their equals
... surprised them, too" (Salvador, *División* 81–2). The Blue Division
culture depicts the Spaniard soldier befriending the local population,
treating his prisoners fairly, unafraid of going into supposedly dangerous areas, always ready to breach the German prohibition to interact
with the civilian population. Vadillo's history of the Blue Division offers
many instances of this appropriation of space, which of course does not
preclude the existence of racist feelings among some *divisionarios*, as we
shall see further. In a similar vein, Ydígoras emphatically refers to the
differences between the German and the Spaniard way of appropriating
space. In the conquered territory, Ydígoras's narrator claims that the
Germans "plundered and despised the Russian people. To them, the
invaded ... were men who could be humiliated and whose wives could
be robbed with impunity ... Never did those stupid policemen in uniform realize that ... they were dealing with a good and hard-working
people" (245). In contrast, the Spanish soldiers "made fun of the *staros-
tové* [town mayors] for being the German administrators' favourite collaborators ... sometimes we helped to work their fields, and it was not
hard to find us involved in a fight, as an equal, with a prisoner" (245).

In a rather telling scene in *División 250*, the narrator expresses the deep resentment of the members of a Spanish platoon from the Blue Legion ordered to evacuate and raze to the ground Kruti Rutski, a village that was suspected of collaborating with the partisans (341–6). The suffering and sheer fear of the inhabitants, the nervousness of the Spanish soldiers, and their bad conscience are described in detail. "The truth is," concludes a soldier, "that they are afraid of us ... We haven't been able to liberate them.... Tomorrow, we, the Spaniards, will torch those houses" (344). A leitmotif of the scene condenses the shame of the Spanish soldiers: "This is not for us." They are soldiers, exclaims one of them; they haven't come to Russia to do this. Nevertheless, not only do they do it, but they also feel a slight pleasure in it, while never losing sight of the inhumanity of their mission: "He and the rest of them, men who would give their own lives for defending their homes, burned down others', and even took some pleasure doing this, forgetting what they were doing" (345–6).

Salvador's descriptions of places focus on their destruction, on the new grammar brought about by war. Grodno (60–1), Vitebsk (80–1), the annihilated villages where combats to the last man take place (e.g., Posad, 119–33; Otenki, 133–8), Novgorod, Leningrad's suburbs: at all these sites, the Spanish soldiers inhabit a landscape of death. Of all the descriptions, three deserve close critical inspection: those of Novgorod (193–6), Riga (206–11), and Leningrad (249–52). The narrator sees Novgorod, one of the oldest Russian cities, as an emblem of the destruction of Russia (193). Novgorod is an "anchor" of a land, stiff like a corpse under a grey sky gravitating over ruins and human beings (193); the beauty of the "mother of the Russian cities, the most Russian of all the cities, the most beautiful," had not been respected (193). War, this most potent technology for producing space, has altered its grammar to such an extent that the narrator describes the city as having been the direct object of the enemy's attack: "Everything is dead. The death of men attacking the stones, the monument ... the bridge. The war was everywhere: on the square, on the crossroads, in the cemetery, on the eternal ruins" (193). The military murders the space it produces: "The immense pile of ruins," writes the narrator, "had some points of reference that soon entered into the soul of the Spaniards.... Almost everything ... was rubble" (194). Significantly, Casto, the focalizer of this passage, feels empathy for its inhabitants when he reflects on the unburied: "One needed more imagination than usual in order to capture at once the tremendous emptying of their lives, their state of abandonment, their conformism. Because those dead represented the instant, the drama of Novgorod, of Russia itself. Old men, women, children" (195–6). This Spanish soldier "loved the unburied dead's life [sic] as well as the city, also unburied" (196), stopping short of considering Novgorod as his own hometown (196). Novgorod would resuscitate some day, "the earthy walls of the Kremlin ... still standing ... Its Slavic soul ... was withstanding the inclemency as the mujiks had always endured the everlasting tyrannies" (193).[38] The esteem for the Russian territory and its inhabitants, a topos in the Blue Division culture, permeates *División 250*. In the chapter titled "Relevo" (222–5), one character of the novel echoes Casto's belief in Novgorod's renaissance after the war, although now this assurance goes beyond one single city, for it embraces the whole country. Men die, but the land survives, reproduces itself. This permanence of space is pointed out by Lieutenant Grau, who upon his arrival in Russia shares with an embedded narrator his surprise about the landscape. Going to Russia "full of gloomy images," he finds the opposite: "little houses ... unmowed lawn in every corner, pure air ... Russia is a whole world" (222). Men cast a pall over nations, but they pass away, and along with them their ideas. In contrast, the prairies, the lakes, the rivers will remain (222). Like in the scene analysed previously, Grau professes his love for Russia: "I love Russia. In these plains I see the European land that resembles Spain the most. I deeply regret the fact that its men are our enemies" (222).

The description of Leningrad involves different strategies of symbolic appropriation, in part due to the fact that, unlike Novgorod, this city would never be taken by the enemy.[39] The cartographic gaze applied in the novel brings to mind the description of the still-unconquered Madrid in fascist novels analysed in chapter 4. At the same time, the point of view relates intertextually with Tolstoy's narration of the Battle of Borodino through the short-sightedness of Pierre Bezukhov in *War and Peace* (1865–9) and with Zola's recounting of combat in the Battle of Sedan through a bespectacled school teacher in *La Débâcle* (1892). In *División 250*, the cognitive limitations of the focalizer, a soldier named Barahona, lie in his lack of knowledge. Unlike Tolstoy's and Zola's novels, Salvador's presents its cartographic gaze of the city and the war with a mixture of desire, longing, political discourse, and threat. In Ydígoras's summary, the Spaniards looked at Leningrad with "assassins' or poets' eyes" (375). Such is the case with Barahona's cartographic gaze, a violent tropological striation focused on two overlapping spaces: the civilian space and the militarized territory. From the last story of the

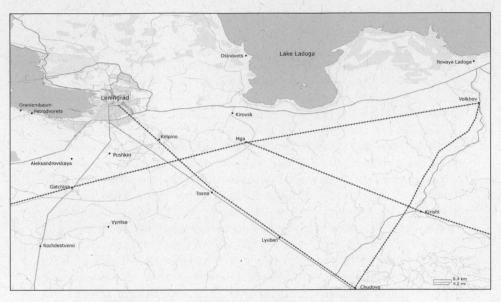

Figure 5.5 The Leningrad front. Image created by the author

Summer Palace in Pushkin (a building commissioned by Catherine the Great), Barahona

> made out the parks, the ponds … One couldn't see much. The pressing need
> to conceal the positions from the enemy's observation … made them look
> strangely changed. That long avenue … yes, up to Nowaja, where the 11th
> was breaking its neck … And over there, on the left, the road up to Pulkowo
> pointed out the line of trenches. Yes, all consisted in getting used to a bird's-
> eye view. Looking to the right one could see Slutz, among gardens, forests,
> and roads where the 269th Regiment and the 1st Group of Artillery had their
> command posts. There was even a cemetery … Further down, in Propos-
> kaya's stately residences, was the Headquarters. (Salvador, *División* 250)

Threatening but cognitively limited, in Barahona's gaze the visual and
military encirclement of space, vague geopolitical considerations, and
Falangist anti-communism intertwine. "Barahona," writes the narrator,
"would have liked to shout from the palace, 'You, the ones from St Petersburg, look … We are right here, but don't inhabit the palace. It is de-

stroyed, and we don't inhabit it" (251). Echoing a conviction shared by
the Nazis, Italian Fascists, and Falangists, they went to Russia on behalf
of Europe. "We are Europe," apostrophes Barahona to the unsuspecting
inhabitants of Leningrad, and would like to open up again, for their
own benefit, "the window to the west shut by your tyrants" (251). Aware
as he is that this is being done through an invasion, "the truth is that the
great transmutations in history occur by force only. By the force that you
lacked to knock down your oppressors'" (251).[40] In "El día de San José"
(305–11), the relationships between violent cartographic gaze, epistemological uncertainty, short-sightedness, and not-yet-conquered enemy territory are further emphasized. Marugán, an artillery observer, looks out
from the roof of a house. "There was always something to inspect ... The
thousand details of war, interpreted day by day" (306). But Marugán's
vision is far from optimal for the job he has been assigned: he wears
glasses, "his nightmare." "A soldier with glasses, and that this soldier was
an observer on an advanced position were things hard to believe ... And
yet there he was, protecting his lenses when the light's refraction was too
intense, painstakingly cleaning them when they misted up" (306).

Riga, a rearguard city where the Blue Division had its most important
hospital, a place seemingly untouched by the war, whose westernized inhabitants carried on with their lives, made the soldiers feel at home.[41]
It was perhaps for this reason that in Riga some *divisionarios* realized
the futility of war and developed a far-reaching resentment. Salvador devotes an entire chapter to this matter. The focalizer, a deserter named
Juan, "keeps fresh in his memory the incredible hardships of the previous months in Sitno, in Nitkilino, in Tagoda. And a deep resentment re-
gurgitated in his palate. Whose fault was it? Whoever it was, to hell with
him" (207). He is literally fed up (207). Ydígoras's autodiegetic narrator
is clearer in this regard: feeling forlorn on a bridge over the Duina River,
Lalo concludes that he now belongs to a strange world: "the world of
the old and the disappointed.... The life that he had voluntarily chosen
... erasing years and lustra, had taught me everything vertiginously, had
made me bitter, contemptuous.... When my parents ask me the terrible
question 'And now, what do you plan to do with your life?,' I wouldn't
know how to answer, because the nostalgia for the war ... would be my
ultimate world" (172).

The military production of space is conceived by one of Salvador's
characters as interlocked with a new type of modern epic. Duez, a high-
school history teacher, reflects on the route they follow on their way to
Russia; he knows that they are penetrating Russian territory along the

route of the great invasions. "They had left behind Poland the martyr; the Lithuanian border ... and now they were following the Grande Armée's route, to Moscow via Smolensk. Half of Europe's history ran along those roads" (72–3). But of course, teaching history is one thing, and living it is entirely different; thus he finds that the "modern epic" possesses bitterness and dirt: "Jews forced to remain in their ghettos; whole towns destroyed, farms where only women or the elderly were left. In Molodezh, he had run into three men hanging from a gallows ... The Germans had executed them" (72–3). Writing on the campaign cannot obviate the destructiveness of the military production of space. Even in the most committed fascist's work, the tropological striation of space would show the *décalage* between the ideal (e.g., the conviction of fighting for a good cause) and its destructive power. Through symbolic expression, writing reproduced the destructive military production of space. In this light, the Blue Division culture centres on the remembrance of ruins. Its writing builds on destruction, a destruction populated by ghosts living between the lines, between the words and silences of the *divisionarios*' literary works. Amid the devastation and ruins described in *División 250* and other narratives spring up spectres haunting both authors and readers. The Blue Division culture constitutes a compelling multifaceted testimony of this devastation brought upon Russia. On the other hand, Russia in ruins refracts the ruins of the Falangist ideals. Russia would be both the climax and the end of many Falangist dreams. The "courtesy call" or visit turned out to be a costly one in more than one sense. Calling upon the Russians placed the volunteers within a phantasmagoria of sorts. In the end there would be a beginning: the beginning of the spectre.

The Being-for-War

Whereas *División 250* centres on the history of both the Blue Division and the Blue Legion through overlapping perspectives and war experiences, *Algunos no hemos muerto* (1957), by the *divisionario* and novelist Carlos María Ydígoras, focuses on the life of a sixteen-year-old Falangist volunteer named Lalo.[42] Narrated by the main character, this novel tells the story of an unusual apprenticeship, unusual because the apprentice's self-discovery coincides not with plenitude but with emptiness – the complete estrangement of the self. The self-consciousness of this apprenticeship in nothingness is perhaps one of the most striking characteristics of *Algunos no hemos muerto*. The title itself, a pathetic if self-assertive statement, condenses the constitutive spectrality of the main

character's ontological structure and of the novel's discourse. Notwithstanding the scarcity of explicit references to spectres, the reader cannot fail to notice the insidious, fateful appearance of a spectre born out
of and nurtured by war. Indeed, not all the *divisionarios* lost their lives
in the battlefields of Russia: "some of us have not died." But a sort of
death took over those who did come back. Haunted by memories of war,
the veteran lives within a world no one but another veteran can truly
understand.[43] This commonplace of war writing and personal experience receives in *Algunos no hemos muerto* a special texture furnished by its
main character's fascist ideology and habitus. To a greater extent than
the POWs' memoirs – as we shall see in the last section of this chapter
– *Algunos no hemos muerto*'s voice presents, from the inside as it were, a
most frightful experience, that is the comprehension of having crossed
a line one should never have passed: the line separating the living from
the dead. By participating in a war of extermination, Lalo becomes a
dead-in-life, an undead being, a ghost. Dubious survivor of the abyss, battered, morally ruined gazer upon nothingness, Lalo slowly but steadily
metamorphoses into a being-for-war suited only for killing and, interestingly, for writing about it. The spectre, a being-for-war, is at once a killer
and a writer. However, this transformation does not lead to a rejection of
fascism.[44] On the contrary, Wilfred Owen's "pity of war," present as it certainly is in *Algunos no hemos muerto*, uneasily overlaps with a fascist ideology and habitus reinforced during war. This cohabitation of fascism and
war in the context of the mentioned metamorphosis crucially unveils the
constitutive negativity of fascism.

Unsurprisingly, the being-for-war emerges not in the recruiting office,
nor even during the cheery journey by train with the rest of the volunteers to Germany, but in Grafenwöhr. There, amidst "pines and swans"
(50), German and Spanish military instructors inculcate in Lalo and his
fellow volunteers this most typical component of fascism: the military
habitus. The narrator's criticisms of the meaning and consequences of
this constituent of the fascist habitus ought to be interpreted less as a
repudiation of fascism than as the ambiguous feelings arising from the
comprehension of and further reflection on the real scale of the self-
alienation and murderousness involved in the fascist habitus. Thus in
the otherwise idyllic town and landscape of Grafenwöhr, where, if the
divisionarios are to be believed, recruits on leave dated young women,
took pleasant walks in the countryside, and enjoyed long sessions of
heavy drinking in local pubs, a wholly new life began, a life in which
men would be transformed into tamed and disciplined automata (47–8).

What differentiates this particular learning process from analogous ones already studied in this book is Lalo's stark and startled consciousness of the emptying of the self entailed by the military habitus as well as the physicality of a life without transcendence. In other words, one of the distinctive characteristics of *Algunos no hemos muerto*'s main character resides in the vivid self-consciousness of going through a liminal process that ultimately leads to his alienation, to a being-for-war, to a spectrality located within fascism.

Killing and hurting are two activities the bloodiness of which raw recruits tend to repress, willingly or otherwise. The mental disorders most commonly associated with fighting point to the tension between, on the one hand, personal expectations and societal myths, ready-made images and prejudices, and on the other, an autonomous world ruled by a rationality of its own. This explains the sense of unreality experienced by the soldier in his baptism of fire, graphically described by Clausewitz (113–14) in his seminal treatise on war. Lalo's remorse after his first combat (123–5), though not particularly special in generic terms, is remarkable, considering our previous discussion on spectrality vis-à-vis fascism. After the attack, a horrifying phantasmagoria – in which the dead men who were killed by his platoon cry out and accuse – haunts him (123). The enemies thus come back as revenants. In *Algunos no hemos muerto*, Lalo's war experience is framed and haunted by this phantasmagoria. At the end of the novel, a soldier from his unit suddenly asks for silence so as to better hear the dead ("Listen up...! The dead!" [415]). Despite being told that the dead cannot talk, he insists again and again, "They are calling me! They shout at me!" In a reversal of the structure of the conjuration, the spectres conjure up the private by intoning the Spanish version of the German song "Ich hatt' einen Kamerad" (I had a comrade), also known as "Der gute Kamerad" (The good comrade): "I had a comrade, the best amongst all ..." (416).[45] Upon repeatedly hearing the enchanting voices of the spectres of the fascists (or should we say, perhaps more adequately, "fascist spectres"?), this private wants to join them: "I am taking off," he shouts to his comrades. "I leave you here ... Good-bye, good-bye! Good luck! Good luck, magnificent and useless dead! They shout at me! They shout at me!" (416). Lalo understands him better than the rest of his platoon, for he is aware that all of them are haunted by the dead comrades "that we left in enemy territory" (416). The spectres of Russians and Spanish fascists make up a maddening symphony conducted as much by imagination as by bad conscience. The latter is a formidable obstacle to carrying out the ghastly business of killing – so says the nar-

rator – and makes Lalo regret the day he joined the Blue Division (123).
But at the same time, as an officer tells him after his baptism of fire, "It is
only after the first combat that we react like this. Afterwards, you will get
used to it, you will fight and kill with no remorse," and "one day you will
kill a fellow man with joy" (125). The haunting spectres of the Russians
killed in battle will cohabit with the spectralization of the consciousness
itself, which is split, as a result of Lalo's baptism of fire, into the self prior
to combat and a new one that feels alive only amidst destruction and
death. Solely in war can the being-for-war be a *being* and feel *at home*.

Lalo thus has been impregnated by war. He feels "happy," for instance,
in the peasants' house where his platoon lodges amid weapons, helmets,
and ammunition boxes; camaraderie, a steaming kettle, a *paso-doble*, and
warmth help create a cozy atmosphere: "That was a home at the front"
(185). In contrast, in the rearguard city of Riga, Lalo's feeling of forlorn-
ness makes him realize not only the absurdity of a world to which he
now feels trapped. More importantly, he comes to the conclusion that he
has now become a being-for-war (172). Restless in the military hospital
of Riga where he has just checked in to recover from war injuries, he
insists on going back to the front (175–8) after having heard from an
officer what really has happened to him: war transforms men into surly,
silent, permanently maladjusted beings; all wars have left "a balance of
millions of men who would be good only for waiting for the moment to
hold a rifle again" (176).[46] Shortly after this conversation, Lalo indeed
runs away from the hospital back to the front. Amidst its wasteland, he
feels at home. Dead cities, destroyed railway stations, columns of civilians
and prisoners of war, villages, paths and forests set up in flames: that was
"my world, the heavy and cold world of war. I had come back to it, and,
strangely, I felt happy" (179). Riga had been "an unsubstantial dream"
not to be repeated, and he concludes that he is already a "man defini-
tively won by war" (179).

As is well known, war represents a decisive experience for those who
live it out. "War," states the narrator, "had made us, normal people ...
into strange, resignedly wild beings who kill and let themselves be killed
with indifference, with boredom perhaps" (313–14). These alterations,
however, do not appear to preclude the possibility of enjoying it. In fact,
war has also, as the narrator himself acknowledges, a "wild good side"
(388). The way by which he explains it associates the being-for-war with
two basic components of the fascist habitus that we have seen throughout this book: violence as a form of life and the cult of death. "In the
midst of the fighting," writes the narrator, "[the soldiers] feel the beauty

of combat and sing and are happy. It is the strongest emotion that youth can experience! We are overcome with that joy when … we see the enemy in rout…. Yes, no one who hasn't been in a war can say that he had been once a young person" (388). Defiantly marching towards a "beautiful" death, so claims the narrator, makes them feel as "gods" and, more significantly to our analysis of the spectre, as "resuscitated." Going forward like "visionaries," they actively seek and indulge in danger. They may die, "but our joy lies in the fact that we have gotten rid of the fear that one attributes to married men, to cowards, to content people" (388). Consequently, Lalo prefers to stay on in Russia with the newly created Blue Legion than to go back to Spain (389–91).

Not coincidentally, cemeteries play an important role in *Algunos no hemos muerto*. These heterotopias make their appearance at the very beginning of the novel. Posad, a village and Spanish position – where the Spaniards, against all odds, resisted waves of merciless and deadly Russian attacks before finally retreating – "resembled," according to Lalo, "a cemetery rather than a town" (16).[47] After two years of fighting, the narrator perceives Russia as a huge Spanish cemetery – a perception that fuels Lalo's resentment for the futility of such huge human sacrifice (374–5). What the different places described in the novel share is their quality of being "cemeteries": "Between towns and towns, landscapes and landscapes, [there were] tombs, many tombs" (71).[48] The *divisionarios*' fixation with cemeteries derives in part from their resentment and the fascist cult of death, and ought to be correlated with the presence of the spectre in Russia and Spain. The cemetery is the heterotopia where the flesh decomposes, but also a reminder of the presence of the absent. Russia, a bloody battlefield and consequently a huge cemetery, becomes the space of the being-for-war. At the same time that Spain – through the shifts in its foreign policy and the changes in society in the soldiers' absence – is slowly acquiring the structure of a paratopos. Russia – the land of the enemy, the communist country to which the Spaniards were paying a "courtesy call" – is becoming the space where the spectres of both the fallen and the survivors feel at home. In this ironic inversion of spatial alliances, the volunteers' *Bildung* has been completed. Few fascist works have portrayed with such detail and in such a compelling way the *Bildung* and paradoxes of the being-for-war, the structural element of the fascist habitus as well as its cultural representations. Spectrality has such a powerful presence in Ydígoras's *Algunos no hemos muerto* that, as we shall see, it even goes so far as to contaminate the discourse of this novel.

To the implied author of *Algunos no hemos muerto*, the paratopos lingers amidst the veterans' fate as soon as they return to their former civilian lives. Three veterans of the civil war share with Lalo the alienation they had suffered once the civil war was over in 1939. Their remarks supplement the theory of the paratopos proposed earlier. As can be deduced from the veterans' words, places become paratopoi as a result of the veterans' longing for their soldierly life of violence and camaraderie. A being-for-war cannot feel at home in civilian spaces. On 28 March 1939, while triumphantly marching through the streets of Madrid, Sergeant Matías experienced "a strange fear of the peace ... I began to think about the monotony of an existence ... grey and cold" (225). A dreadful perspective, bleaker than the possibility of death in the battlefield, haunts the veteran, who imagines with dismay the Sundays in which the people, "tired like flocks," walked aimlessly on the streets: "This frightened me more than the war!" (225). Thousands of people acclaimed, kissed, shook hands with the returning soldiers, true, "but so what?" (226). Although during the war they had wanted peace, now the veterans fondly remembered situations and events of the war (226). Nonetheless, such yearning for the abyss is not the only problem facing the veterans. The attitude towards them that civilians display is equally hurting. As soon as final victory had been achieved, recalls Ambrosio, nobody remembered them: *"No one was interested in us any longer"* (226). Civilians looked at them with pity, but also with distrust, for they considered the veterans slightly unsavory and emotionally unstable (226). When walking on the streets of Barcelona, everything that Ambrosio saw caused in him a "ridiculous giggle": "I looked at them ... and wanted to imagine them with the face full of mud and coagulated blood ... but it was impossible" (227). So great was the difference between them and the soldiers that he finds it hard to believe that all belong to the same race (227). Antón corroborates Ambrosio's grim assessment with a summary of his civilian life: "I thought I would die from laughing the day I put on a civilian's suit." He looked like a scarecrow (227). At night, he slept in a bed with sheets and for as many hours as he wished, but "can you imagine," he asks his comrades, "what eight hours without cannon shots, shouts, mud and lice are like?" (227). To this sequence of perception and experience, Ricardo provides a logical conclusion: "In most cases, war transforms people, it turns them a little insensitive, maladjusted. Many manage to recover, but some continue being apathetic and are forever disappointed. They are men who believe only in war ... *'I am a man of war,'* we all muttered" (227–8).

In Luis Romero's collection of short stories, *Tudá (Allá)* (1957), the
being-for-war's alienation is presented in a similar fashion. Having become a being-for-war during the civil war, a character of the short story
"El golpe de mano" (77–114) joins the Blue Division so as to return
to his real home – war: "He could not completely return to civilian
life. Something strange … was inhibiting him from his surroundings.
Among others, this was one of the causes that led him immediately to
the Blue Division's recruiting office … He and his parents … realized
that their relationship was not as before. And as with his parents it happened with the rest of the family and even with the city itself" (106–7).
He could not go back to his life as a student either, which had as little
interest as "the slow, static, ordered [civilian] life." Realizing that his life
had experienced a radical change, he concludes that he could not be
happy in that environment after three years of war (107). The difficulty
or failure to adapt to civilian life that is experienced by the fascist being-
for-war carries the potential for violence as well as resentment, as shown
in a dialogue in Hernández Navarro's *Ida y vuelta*. "You'll see," Agustín
warns a comrade. "What is terrible is adjusting to these customs that one
despises … It will be a few months … of fighting against yourself" (368).
Before crossing a street, a traffic policeman will tell him whether to proceed or to stop, and then "you will recall … the times that, during an
assault,… bullets had halted you, and you will feel a strong desire to skip
the prohibition" (269). The same will happen at the university, where
"you will have to endure an insignificant gentleman's yells or sermons
… You will feel then a terrible and primitive wish to kill" (269). The
relation between the being-for-war and the paratopos parallels the tension between the fascist ideology defended in key passages of *Algunos no
hemos muerto* (e.g., 33, 56–7, 67–9, 386–91, 416) and the regime's Realpo-
litik – a regime that had only partially implemented the "revolutionary"
Falangist social and political program. Lalo and other characters show
a bitter disappointment with the Franco regime. The civil war was good
for nothing: landowners, bankers, the well-to-do will continue enriching
themselves at the expense of the working class. The political life is thus
a paratopos as well. Both "home" (civilian life) and "fatherland" (the
projected fascist new state) become paratopoi of spectres longing for
violence. The divide between civilian and military life on the one hand,
and the contrast between political ideas and their failure on the other
seem almost insurmountable. Lacking a field for action, the being-for-
war might redirect his death drive towards civilian life, thus becoming a
threatening presence.

Algunos no hemos muerto projects that divide into the narrative discourse by splitting up the autodiegetic narrator's voice, for Ydígoras has embedded in his novel fragments in italics in which the narrator reflects on episodes or elaborates with sharp criticism on political, religious, and existential issues. In the passages in roman font, there is a powerful erotic of violence in which Ydígoras indulges in vivid, morbid, expressionistic, repulsive descriptions of intense fighting, dying soldiers, rotten corpses, rape. The server of a machine gun, for instance, has been hit so hard that "in his head, scarcely attached to the torso by a dirty muddle of arteries and muscles, the explosions seemed to represent multiple forms of laughter, of amazement, and of terror" (13); a fallen soldier was no more than "rag, a monstrous head" (21); the defenders of the Intermediate Position had been "nailed down on the snow ... Some corpses were naked, and revealed genitalia turned into horrible confusions ... other [corpses] had the genitalia cut off and stuck in the mouth" (196–7). No gruesome detail is spared in the descriptions of the dead or dying soldiers (e.g., 15, 21, 323–9). The narrator seems to enjoy narrating hand-to-hand combat in particular. One example will suffice. After successfully repelling a Russian attack, the Spaniards gleefully go after the disbanded Soviet soldiers running for their lives: "Ours were shouts of triumph, and shouting like this made me feel wrapped in a pleasant unconsciousness ... I could hear moans, I stepped on men, on people injured or dead, who cared! I felt strong, invincible ... Now I belonged to a virile, wild world in which men kill each other 'with pleasure.' And I found it appealing, marvellous" (118; see also 33–4, 237, 242). Logically and in accordance with other fascist narratives already studied, war in *Algunos no hemos muerto* is considered a beautiful spectacle. On one occasion, Lalo perceives a combat as if he were a spectator in a movie theatre (154), adding, "I never thought that the war could offer so many strange instants; that unique and marvellous emotion produced by facing a game ... Groups of men ... retired from the battlefield ... from the game" (155). Once again, fascist writing carries out a symbolic violence that stems from the violence constitutive of the fascist habitus.

This erotic of violence intertwines nonetheless with passages in italics of an entirely different nature. As it happens in *División 250* and other works written by *divisionarios*, spectral presences haunt the narrator of *Algunos no hemos muerto*. Most important, in Ydígoras's novel even the writing itself becomes a spectre of sorts. Taking into account the existential resentment, the political criticism, the being-for-war, and the paratopos, the alternation of fragments in italics with text in roman characters transform the novel itself into *spectral writing*. There, in the interstices between the two types of characters, the spectre finds its discursive locus. Consider, for instance, the first italicized fragment, written apropos of Lalo's feeling of loneliness and horror at a first-aid station. Reflecting on the wounded soldiers, hungry children, and terrified mothers he sees there leads Lalo to a spiritual crisis, to his questioning of God's justice (22–3). Further in the novel there is another instance of this crisis: having lost his faith in the Battle of Posad, in Riga's cathedral he demands from God a justification of all that is going on at the front (163). The reasons for going to war, as well as its effects and ultimate absurdity are also questioned by the narrator in several other italicized passages. He reflects that the soldiers, cannon fodder, *"keep dying, why? Those whom they face, aren't they civilized as well? ... The ones who survive hang the rifle, return to their homes ... And when, as years go by, they reflect on their past fighting, and see that everything went back to normal, ask themselves: why did we fight?"* (291). In yet another example of this critical attitude, after deconstructing the reasons put forward to justify the war, the narrator asks rhetorically if the war was the fault of *"those freakish 'office-men' who in each speech utter the word Peace one thousand times ... or the amorphous and stultified masses ... [who] in the boulevards and train stations gesticulate and sweat and yell their support to the soldiers who are going to die"* (292; see also 326). Notwithstanding this criticism of war, expressed with so much pathos, war is, in the end, worth the while to be experienced. Lalo, a being-for-war, believes that *"it is magnificent to be involved in a conflict and to know the ultimate limits of rage, goodness, apathy, love, comradeship"* (292–3). Behind this undecidability, underlying the impossibility of conciliating the critique and defence of war resides the logic of spectrality.

The splitting up of the narrative form manifests itself in the very origin and space of writing: an old notebook originally owned by a *malenki* or Russian boy. Near Lake Ilmen, Ydígoras exchanged a small can of food for the boy's old, worn-out notebook (11). "There," says the author in his 2002 prologue to the novel, "I began to scribble the names of towns and rivers, combats ... and feelings. The little *malenki*'s notebook was the origin of this book" (11). Food in exchange for a place for writing, nurture for the body in exchange for a locus for the spirit: thus the survival of the *malenki*'s body becomes the precondition for the re-creation of the haunting past. Compare the meaning of the Russian boy's notebook with two other notebooks used to keep a record of emotions and actions: Sánchez Diana's and Ridruejo's. While the former chose a German grammar, the latter used a more conventional blank notebook. In Sánchez

Diana's work, the writing is over a German text. Still in Spain, the author bought a German grammar book that would later become a notebook of sorts where he scribbled his personal impressions and wrote down all the data that would turn that grammar book into a war diary. "I was more obsessed with preserving the pencils than in keeping my rifle clean; I wanted to write my little history, and I believe that I have achieved it" (*Cabeza* 22); it is as if the author somehow corrected, nuanced, crossed out the German point of view, the German "rules" determining the war as well as what can be said about it. To Ridruejo, the blank notebook signifies the possibility of being himself again, purified from his deep involvement with a regime he had helped to build and from which he felt increasingly estranged. Going to Russia could be a new beginning, but also a possibility for encountering unexpected, beautiful landscapes. In this case, the borders of the white page refract both the limits of a new being and the horizons of the space to contemplate. Ydígoras dialogues with neither the Germans nor with the Spanish political establishment, but rather ironically with the Russians, for whom he feels a strong empathy. But the inverse alterity in Ydígoras's novel has yet another layer of meaning. The Russian boy gives to the Spanish invader what will be the place of writing and therefore the remembrance of a failed war of conquest. This exchange is the condition of possibility of Ydígoras's narrative. Without this symbiotic relationship between the Russian and a member of the occupying forces, there would be no writing at all.

In the "Russian" notebook, in the "Russian" space of the white page, the narrator writes the chronicle of the occupation of the Russian territory. The correspondence between the military technology of striation and the technology of tropological striation could hardly be more evident. The place of writing, a Russian boy's notebook, involves a double conquest: the written word of the invader "occupies" a "foreign" white page – the colour itself refracting the snowy steppe – while it produces space through a technology of tropological striation analogous to the one analysed in chapter 2. However, whereas the tropological striation of Morocco went hand in hand with a successful military victory over the rebellious harkas, in Russia the outcome, by contrast, would be disappointing. At the most basic level, we have the narration of the main battles in which Lalo participates: Posad (13–32), the Intermediate Position (193–202), the crossing of Lake Ilmen to liberate a besieged German position (214–42), the *Bolsa* or pocket (243–56), and Krasny Bor (335–59). The narrator's cartographic gaze – this most characteristic technology of tropological striation – looks at the landscape drawn by desire and by an increasingly maddening sense of failure. At the same time, in Ydígoras's novel the tropological striation of space cohabits with the criticism of war. Thus, writing contains a critical purpose.

This performativity of writing is twofold. On the one hand, it conquers the "other" by means of a technology of tropological striation; on the other, it intends to persuade the reader of the accuracy of the accusations, pointed out metatextually at the end of the novel in a passage devoted to the Blue Legion's departure from the front. During the withdrawal of this unit, the exhausted Spanish soldiers do not hide their rage or frustration. After the announcement that the march is over, Private Fernández, aware that Lalo keeps a record of everything in a notebook, entreats him – already a sergeant – to write about what they have seen and gone through: "Write!, Sergeant, write!" (403). The pathos of the exclamation points to the need to leave a testimony of what has happened. It must not be forgotten, and it must be denounced too. The haunting performed by writing has therefore a pragmatic dimension, for writing is addressed to affect, to haunt the feelings and political thinking of the reader and of the political establishment. And yet, writing denounces so as to reaffirm a fascist ideology based precisely on a violent habitus, as can be seen in the dedication of the novel: "To you, the magnificent Absent Ones, as an offering of apologies ... To you, the First Ones, I dedicate this book. I owed you the remembrance ... And may I now be in peace with myself. Facing Life" (9). The dedication's Falangist language and style, as well as its last sentence, an obvious allusion to the title of the Falange hymn, place violence and the fallen within the world of the living. At the same time, by conjuring up the spectres of the fallen, Ydígoras comes to terms with his war experience. He gives the spectres their due. His spectral writing is therefore an act of justice.

Unforgiving

Antonio José Hernández Navarro's *Ida y vuelta* (1946) – the only major work of fiction written by this Falangist lawyer and *procurador en Cortes* (member of Franco's non-democratic parliament), officer of the Spanish Army, and prolific journalist – wholly embraces war as a form of life and, equally important, as *écriture*.[49] War represents much more than a type of violence by which the fascist intends to shape a new political and societal structure. *Ida y vuelta*'s narrative voices and implied author express the close relationship between the structure of war and fascist writing.[50] This novel, provocatively published shortly after the Allied victory over Nazi Germany and Japan, merited a second edition in 1955 by no less than Editora Nacional, and a third in 1971 by the equally highly regarded publishing house Espasa-Calpe in its popular paperback series Colección Austral.

Overlapping the vitalism of the fascist soldier and the resentment of the veteran, *Ida y vuelta* illustrates both the ambitions and the limits of Spanish fascism. In the Soviet Union the victors of the Spanish Civil War faced the contradictions and paradoxes inherent to their will-to-empire. In the extremely cold winter of 1941–2 (temperatures sometimes reaching -50° C), they were to realize that marching as victors on the streets of Moscow would not be as easy a task as some had fantasized. The apparently straightforward title of the novel contains several layers of meaning. Not only does it reflect the round trip of Agustín, a twenty-two-year-old poet and Falangist college student, the main character and occasional intradiegetic narrator who follows a not unusual itinerary among the *divisionarios* who survived the war (Spain, Grafenwöhr, the Volkhov front, sojourn in Riga, back to the front, the Leningrad front, back to Spain). In addition, the title underscores two contradictory notions: on the one hand, the Falangist's will-to-empire, and on the other, the unpleasant recognition that such an imperialist project was little more than wishful thinking. The fascist exo-imperial dreams died on the Russian steppe. The *vuelta* (return trip, military withdrawal) therefore can be interpreted as the forced renunciation of a fundamental component of the fascist habitus – its will-to-empire over other countries. If only for this reason, Hernández Navarro takes the fascist war writing one step further, a step that places fascist writing on the defensive. Chronicling a wild, murderous enthusiasm unexpectedly turned into a bitter, resented withdrawal, *Ida y vuelta* points to the definitive direction of Falange's will-to-empire. In dropping for good its exo-imperial dreams, Spanish fascism would limit its will-to-empire to Spain itself. After Franco's death in 1975, transformed, modified so as to make it more palatable to the population, the fascist habitus would insert itself within the political and social texture of Spain as it had happened to a certain degree – let us repeat – in Western democratic regimes after the Second World War. Hence "ida y vuelta" has been the path followed by fascism in Europe. *Vuelta*, I should like to stress, does not mean that fascism went elsewhere and is now coming back; rather, fascism is "back" because somehow it has always been "around."

A convinced fascist with no regrets whatsoever, Hernández Navarro produced an otherwise interesting novel whose characters share an unforgiving fascist habitus. While the will-to-empire inevitably permeates the narratives and memoirs of many Blue Division veterans, *Ida y vuelta* makes it proudly explicit. In a conversation in the training camp of Grafenwöhr, Félix says, "The same has happened to me every time that I've gone there [El Escorial]. In order to believe that I was in a cemetery, I have had to visit the tombs of the princes and the *infantes*. I always stopped in front of don Juan de Austria's. In front of it, I invoked the princes' name with a mental 'Present!' I would have liked to be his soldier because he would have been a Falangist captain and I would have been in Lepanto" (77).To this Falangist topos, Agustín adds a nuance apropos of the not infrequent quarrels between German submarine crews and *divisionarios* on leave or convalescent from war injuries in Riga when he proposes to an officer that he not stop a brawl because this too is "to build Empire" (349). In fact, says Agustín, "To fight is a very Spanish virtue; to fight head on ... we have fought all over the world and loved all over the world as well ... We have always built Empire through three capitalized gerunds: Loving, Fighting, and Dying. A not very productive Empire ... but nonetheless more noble that all the Empires in history; an all-generous Empire" (349). This is imperialism at its most basic, a will-to-empire over the "other" as a sort of training ground for higher enterprises. A fascist bravado, a defence of what Primo de Rivera notoriously called the "dialectics of fists and pistols," Agustín's suggestion points to the primitive manifestation of fascist violence, the pub brawl, while relating it to its latent goal: the will-to-power, here in its imperialistic form.

This said, Hernández Navarro's novel focuses not so much on the "grand design" of fascist violence. Rather, *Ida y vuelta* depicts some of its grounding forces, three in particular: the death drive, the cult of the absolute, and the cult of death. As one of the characters puts it, enrolling in the Blue Division was a question of having or lacking honour: "About Falange it won't ever be possible to say that it is not on the first row when the award is death. It is no doubt a tragic fate, but a Falangist one; so Falangist that without it we would stop being ourselves and would be orphaned of spirit, like the bourgeoises" (66). War is a "call," but one that simultaneously bears two meanings: an order and a "vocation." Accordingly, *Ida y vuelta*'s characters enjoy violence, especially Agustín, who upon learning the positive result of his X-ray exclaims, "I would really like to shout that ... I will be able to run and jump again; that I will be able to keep being violent and to make war" (227). Enjoying violence and war belongs to the Falangists' penchant for the absolute in its meta-

physical, existential, and political dimensions. As Félix says, so much do
they like the absolute that without the risk of dying they would not like
war: "There is no solution for us: we are born to be like this" (181). This
death drive cannot be separated, of course, from the fascist cult of death,
already studied in this book, the climax of which is reached in an auto-
referential passage (171–3). To the murderous impulse caused by the
death of comrades at the hands of "a bunch of dirty soldiers filled with
lice, matter with no spirit at all" (171) follows a "poetic mystique, the
Falangist mystique in the comrade's death" (171). Expressed in characteristic Falangist language, Agustín imagines a scene with blasphemous
undertones: "Comrade Javier… had fulfilled his last and best service;
his death had lit up a new bright star [*lucero*] in the Eternal Guard's
constellation, and in his spirit he would enjoy José Antonio's [Primo de
Rivera] presence. The captain would have been saluted upon arrival,
and later, he would have hugged him…. Afterwards he would assign him
a place in the fell-in, impassive *centurias* of dead Falangists. Javier would
go through the ranks recognizing old comrades towards his place in his
squad, where he would stand at attention forever and ever until the resurrection of the flesh" (171–2).

But to Agustín, this is not enough. A sort of resurrection of the flesh
can be accomplished by literary means, through poetry, thereby transforming the fallen captain into a spectre. After learning about Javier's
death, Agustín – so he says – felt pain, rage, despair, but at some point he
reached serenity. His coming to terms with his friend's death is achieved
through the conjuring of the spectre: "My imagination has made me see
Javier's death with our mystique and poetry. I have seen … Javier's arrival
at the bright stars; his salute to the captains; his going to his post and his
remaining in it amongst the comrades who preceded him. I wanted to
imagine the same scenes again, and my memory has turned into poetry"
(172). The poem, embedded in the novel (173), reproduces Agustín's
"vision" of his friend's ascension to the "bright stars."

In accordance with its will-to-empire, *Ida y vuelta* proceeds self-consciously to a tropological striation of space. In a telling passage, the
narrator establishes the link between the blank page and the occupied
Russian space: "Wirytza's days and nights passed by. It was like turning
the page of an imaginary book. In one page, Wirytza; its landscape of
pines and wooden guesthouses; the street market … In the next, the
position of his company before St Petersburg … the deep trenches, the
shacks full of lice … two hundred metres of minefields" (340). Writing,
the landscape, and the militarization (that is, the striation) of space

merge into one single entity, thus reproducing symbolically the military occupation. To a degree, writing is the technology that Hernández Navarro employs to conquer the Russian space. The link between writing and space is grounded in an unforgiving gaze.

Of the novel's five chapters, the third – the structural core of the novel – is significantly titled "Rusia en la mira de los fusiles." This fascist cartographic gaze finds its ultimate expression in a remarkable scene. At the Leningrad front, the protagonist compensates for the boredom caused by lack of action with an aggressive cartography of his surroundings, the grammar of which has naturally been altered by war. Agustín found himself in "a semi-civilized environment ... It took him no little effort to adjust to his new life ... Paulowska, in a forest that once had been a garden, with the Palace of the Tsars ... with the villas of the aristocracy.... Pieces of furniture, books, and walls turned upside down" (340). The narrator, focalizing his vision through Agustín, describes Gatschina ("full of monuments, gardens, palaces, churches, factories, and barracks") and the palace of Catherine the Great (340–1). Agustín's gaze over Leningrad through his binoculars refracts the military threat lingering over the city, but it also implies the failure of the undertaking, for the distance between gaze and object underscores the Russians' resistance to the besieging troops. There are other instances of mapping through a cartographic gaze: Grodno (113–15, 118), Vitebsk (151–2), Riga (339–55), and Hoof (363–5).

To this mapping must be added the narration of the itineraries followed by the characters of the novel. The violent production of space through military marching refracts the production of space carried out by Agustín and the narrator via an aggressive cartographic gaze. There are several instances of this violent production of space. In *Ida y vuelta*, marching is considered as a speech act of spatial conquest. To march and to conquer are almost synonymous. In a passage devoted to Grodno, the narrator writes that the Spanish soldiers crossed the bridge over the Neman River in a soldierly fashion: "The nails of their boots beat time harshly" (115). Identical military production of space is carried out when the soldiers cross the Russian border; in their crossing of the border, the soldiers striate space: with a slight shiver, they "mark Russia's lintel with the nails of their boots" (135). In Riga, two *divisionarios* laugh and mark their steps with force: "The empty streets returned the echo of the soldiers' laughter and of their hard stepping; a hard stepping as if Riga were theirs" (353). In Hernández Navarro's *Ida y vuelta*, the production of space is thus a joyful act of military violence.

Unlike the novels of Salvador and Ydígoras, *Ida y vuelta* espouses a racist attitude towards the Russians, characteristic of certain trends in Falange's folkish faction. The lives of the Russians are not seen as – to use a concept recently developed by Judith Butler in *Frames of War* – "grievable." On the contrary: in a scornful, chilling description of a concentration camp for Russian prisoners in the vicinity of Seyni (103–4), the narrator remarks that it was reminiscent of a gigantic fold enclosing a brownish, dirty flock. Almost all the prisoners looked like the walking dead, monstrous and dirty dead "who threw themselves to the ground like beasts to fight … over peels of fruit or a bone. There were few of them who hadn't lost their humanhood" (104). Shuddering with horror and disgust, Private Ángel concludes, in an interesting association of racism and absolute war: "Beasts!… It would be a merciless war" (104). In another passage there is a scene that displays an identical attitude. Aboard a train en route to the front, Agustín and his comrades see, on a nearby track, a train loaded with crammed, starving Russian prisoners without proper clothes for the cold weather. Commenting on the Russians' reaction to the tobacco and food thrown to them by the Spaniards, the narrator states that, upon receiving "any of those things they fought themselves as beasts. Agustín felt pity … not because they were hungry, cold, or destitute, but because they did not know how to suffer their setbacks" (153); Agustín considers that he would rather let himself die of hunger "before losing like that his human condition" (153). The murderous substratum of this racism is acknowledged in a passage that summarizes Agustín's merciless fascist habitus: "[Agustín] felt a physical need to kill … but not to kill humanely, but rather to ravage enemy lives … He despaired, thinking that a bunch of dirty, lice-ridden soldiers, all matter with no spirit at all, could have cut off … the valiant and intelligent life of his dead comrades" (171). Interestingly, in Nazi fashion, *Ida y vuelta* correlates racism towards the Russian people, anti-Semitism, and a drive to rape the "other" – the Jew. Walking in Grodno, Agustín and his comrades come across a beautiful Jewish woman. "Her face," thinks Agustín, "was beautiful, and her lips … smiled with a mixture of triumph and scorn…. Everything in her was arrogance … Like the others, Agustín admired her. He desired her perhaps even more than the others because possessing her would entail a victory of sorts" (117; see 114–16, 117–18 for further anti-Semitic references).

As we have repeatedly seen, war is waged not only by military means, but also through strategies of symbolic production. The military commanders as well as the politicians leading the war effort are well aware of this and act accordingly, trying as much as they can to control the network of cultural objects produced apropos of the ongoing or projected war. I have already analysed this phenomenon and there is no need to go over it again, but it is nonetheless important to take it into account so as to better understand Hernández Navarro's novel, for *Ida y vuelta* evinces an awareness of the interrelatedness of political power and war writing. Despite the author's claim that his is a book of a soldier and not of a writer (61), the truth is that literature plays a prominent role in *Ida y vuelta*. The intertwining of narrative voices (i.e., the extradiegetic narrator, Agustín's embedded journal, Matías's narration on the fate of his company during the taking of Tigoda, and Félix's recounting on the Battle of Posad through narrated speech) attest to the need felt by some characters to relate and make sense of their war experience. The literaturization of war through fascist writing focuses mostly on Agustín, a "lover of things messianic" (177) and a poet. Some of his poems are embedded in the novel: a ballad (173), a poem entitled "Nostalgia" (231), the first lines of a ballad (290), and an untitled poem (335–6); in addition, he states in his journal that he wrote a poem in Sapolje (228). Of these poems, the most interesting is the first ballad, written as homage to a fallen friend. Falange's fascination with death as well as its spectrality could hardly be more evident:

> Falangist Comrade …
> Falange's and Spain's
> Natural hierarchy.
> You headed towards the bright stars,
> Where the captain awaits
> His men's arrival …
> Centuries of silver and sun
> Formed a tight guard for you …
> You saluted the captain
> With your hand open and high
> And later he hugged you
> The friend and comrade. (173)

Another character, Félix, talks about his purpose in writing an epic ballad on Posad, a "ballad to live for centuries after we are gone" (248). He finds this task difficult: "I write the first verses, and as soon as I finish them, they seem insignificant to me … [the poem] sounds incomplete" (248). According to Agustín, this is an impossible undertaking, for the adequate language to express what happened is perhaps a ballad of "verses, stone, and music" (248). The problem lies therefore in finding adequate language to represent an extreme experience – a war of extermination. Félix and Agustín return to this issue in a dialogue in which both friends acknowledge the need to conjure up the spectres of the fallen: "When they retreat from Posad, or when Posad succumbs," says Félix, "the hundreds of Spaniards and Falangists dead ... heroes whom nobody will ever know, will be verse, stone, and music, as you have said; verse, stone, and music of our greatness throughout all the centuries that will pass by this devastated and hostile land, which will make up legends with Spanish names" (257). Agustín seems to share this view. On one occasion, he considers the moon's gleam as the symbol of the bloody Battle of Posad, and remembers the ballad that Félix will have to write: "verse, stone, and music, and still this will not be enough for our greatness in Posad" (264–5). Only the soldier has the authority to write about it (231).

At the end, the soldier, who must not forget what happened in the battlefield (233), becomes a writer. Back home, the protagonist of *Ida y vuelta* daydreams about the possibility of writing at some point the "novel of his remembrance" (371). It will be a novel of war, love, and death, but most importantly, a novel exalting the will-to-empire. Writing and power, therefore, go hand-in-hand: they need each other, they cannot be dissociated. Agustín's novel must relate both, for the will-to-empire exists in empirical reality as well as in discursive practices. The protagonist will write about "The exalted Loving, Fighting, and Dying of the men who build Empire" (371). For this reason, the main character must not die at the end: "Almost all the war novels he knows about end with the main character's death.... But no. Comrade Agustín is back. Comrade Agustín won't be the main character of a war novel, but rather one among many in the war" (371–2). At the end of the novel lies its own beginning: "Agustín sits down and begins to write a letter: 'Madrid, 7 June 1943. My dear: I have just decided to write a novel about my war in Russia. A novel on my division. It will be titled "Ida y vuelta." The topic is ...'" (372). Thus the novel begets itself, beginning as it ends. Such a circular construction stresses the decisive role played by representation within the structure of war and encloses war within writing. War is also discourse – in Hernández Navarro's case a fascist one. Such a relationship of identity raises important questions. Does this fascist novel represent a relationship between war and discourse essentially different from the purportedly non-fascist accounts of the same phenomena? Does Hernández Navarro not unveil the fascist nature of the non-linguistic and symbolic conduction of modern wars? Perhaps this is a lesson one learns by reading disturbing fascist works like *Ida y vuelta*: that fascism lurks in activities associated with ideologies and habitus not considered as fascist.

Ghostly Cities

The bombing and utter destruction of European cities during the Second World War, along with the displacement of millions and the Nazi extermination camps, is a potent *lieu de mémoire*. The replay, in contemporary mass media, of documentaries and films on the ravages brought about by war on urban centres, as well as the literary and artistic archive depicting horrifying, ghastly scenes have stamped lasting images on our minds. They have created the conditions of possibility to manipulate citizens (as Torgovnick has proven in *The War Complex*), and – among other effects – produced a new spatial order in Europe. Told as always by the victors, the net of stories of this most sinister production of space has until recently diminished, justified, or silenced the suffering of those Germans living in cities like Hamburg, Dresden, Hannover, or Cologne – to mention only a few – during the mass raids carried out by the Allies.[51] The Germans' guilt and sense of shame, as Sebald has sharply pointed out, has limited the number and determined the belatedness of the literary works on those dramatic events by German authors. Although this is not the place to narrate them, they must be kept in mind in any analysis of the fascist literary portrayal of the production of space through destruction during the Second World War.

Consider, for instance, Louis-Ferdinand Céline. Not a fascist like, say, Pierre Drieu la Rochelle, Robert Brasillach, or Lucien Rebatet, Céline nonetheless did more than enough to be considered as a writer with close affinities to fascism.[52] His rabid anti-Semitism, his vicious pamphlets against – albeit not only – Jews and Communists (*Mea culpa* [1936], *Bagatelles pour un massacre* [1937], *L'École des cadavres* [1938], *Les Beaux draps* [1941]), his friendly relationships with, for example, Karl Epting (director of the German Institute in Paris), the well-known artist Arno Breker, Gerhardt Heller (in charge of the censorship of books in Occupied France), and Hermann Bickler (chief of the Intelligence Bureau on Political Activities in the occupied territories of Western Europe who was under the direct orders of none other than Reinhard Heydrich, the "hangman" in Adolf Eichmann's telling word), his contacts with the German Ambassador Otto Abetz, and his attendance at the inaugural

session of the Institute of Studies on Jewish Affairs, to whose director
he wrote an openly anti-Semitic letter, show the extent of Céline's ideological and personal positioning during the war. Céline, who periodically received threatening letters and sinister miniature coffins in the
mail, left Paris to go into exile with his wife Lucette on 17 June 1944.
After a nine-month journey through a ghostly Germany, they finally
reached their destination: Copenhagen. This nightmarish journey gave
the French writer the chance to witness the effects of what was known as
the "area bombing" of German cities and towns. On the basis of his escape to Denmark, years later he would write a masterful trilogy of novels:
D'un château l'autre (1957), *Nord* (1960), and *Rigodon* (1969). Some of the
most memorable philo-fascist depictions of the destruction of Europe
can be found in the pages of these novels. By employing expressionistic
techniques, Céline maps out the horror and death inflicted on Berlin,
Augsburg, Ulm, Hannover, and Hamburg by the English and American
bombers. In that trilogy, Céline puts into practice a modernist conception of writing, consisting in the mimesis of the bombings and their destructive power through an expressionist, violent, and broken syntax, as
well as plotlessness. In other words, the representation of destruction is
carried out through the destruction of representation. This modernist
mimesis of destruction contains an aggressiveness addressed ultimately
against the reader.[53]

The Blue Division culture also has produced, naturally enough, abundant depictions of cities in ruins; we have already seen some of them.
In addition to the *divisionarios'* texts studied in this chapter, works like
Fernando Vadillo's describe in some detail the destruction brought on
Grodno, Minsk, Vitebsk, Novgorod, Leningrad, Berlin, not to mention
the towns and hamlets where units of the Blue Division lodged in and/
or fought the Red Army – cities and towns belonging to a geography of
ghostly space. In the Blue Division culture, there are two fascist works
that, despite lacking altogether Céline's expressionistic literary techniques, display nonetheless a Célinean type of destruction. I am referring
to *Encrucijada en la nieve: Un servicio de Inteligencia desde la División Azul*
(written in 1978; published in 1996) by Ramiro García de Ledesma, a
member of the Legion and double agent in the Soviet Union and France
during the Second World War; and to *Berlín, a vida o muerte* (Portuguese
version 1947; Spanish version 1975) by Miguel Ezquerra, who after the
dissolution of the Blue Legion fought on with the Germans and participated in the Battle of Berlin. Both books focus on cities emblematic of
the suffering inflicted on the civilian population – Leningrad and Berlin.

The type of involvement of each author (Waffen-SS officer fighting for his life against the Red Army in Ezquerra's case, a spy infiltrated in enemy territory in García de Ledesma's) conditioned their attitude towards space. While the Blue Division did not participate in urban combat nor occupy urban centres, both authors witnessed firsthand what happened in Leningrad and Berlin. With these two works, the Blue Division culture completes its symbolic production of space and its portrayal of absolute war. Hence their importance.

Encrucijada en la nieve is the memoir of a spy whose career begins at the Centro de Información Especial in the fall of 1940. His first mission consists of infiltrating the French Resistance to provide intelligence on its activities. After his training as a spy, he enrols first in the Legion and later in the Blue Division to "defect" to the Russians and show them he is a true Communist. From the Soviet Union he flies to the United Kingdom and is ferried from there to France to join the Maquis. The main character's fascist habitus is clear from the beginning. In the Legion training camp, he displays a deep emotion for military things as well as admiration for the legionary ethos (62, 65, 68). Chapters 12 and 13 are devoted to Leningrad (141–85). Interestingly, the main character, in spite of his anti-communism and fascist habitus, does not have animosity towards the Russians. Once cleared by the Soviet secret service, he walks through the desolate streets of the besieged Leningrad. In the Prospekt and Nevski boulevards, he sees with a sympathetic gaze the ravages of war: buildings reduced to rubble, dirt, corpses all over, starving men and women, the craters in the pavement caused by mortar bombs, grief, destitution, hundreds of people wandering like somnambulists (155). Further on, in his visit to the cemetery of Piskarevski, he is overtaken by compassion for the inhabitants of the city: "Thousands and thousands of tombs ... unburied corpses ... Workers digging nonstop ... Weeping, tears, grave gestures, vanquished pain, resignation ... The procession of corpses was impressive: they came from the hospitals, from the streets, from the nearby front. Soldiers, elderly people, women, children ... It was a dance of ghosts, because the living looked ... more dead than the dead themselves. And then the trucks loaded with victims – dead due to the bombings, to hunger, to illnesses ... It was death's darkest face" (168–9). The narrator admires the inhabitants of Leningrad, who, in spite of their suffering, try to carry on a normal life. In his visit to the School of Ballet, he concludes, "To some, the war was just an accident ... incapable of bringing to a halt the artistic activity [of Leningrad] ... The miracle of the theatre paralleled the miracle of the radio, the press, literature, and the cinema. There were moments in which it didn't look like a besieged city" (175; see also 176–7). He learns to "admire, revere, and love that grandiose and beautiful land" (212; see also 190), and he feels sorry for the destruction of the city, for the famine suffered by its inhabitants.

Miguel Ezquerra's war did not come to an end with the dissolution of the Blue Legion. It had started in 1936 and would not end until early May 1945 in Berlin, where he commanded a Waffen-SS unit, the "Unidad Ezquerra," during the Battle of Berlin.[54] Taken prisoner by the Russians (95), Ezquerra managed to escape and return safely to Spain. Within Ezquerra's fascist habitus, an ideological idealism and a restless vitalism intertwine. To him, violence was a vital need. His resentment after the dissolution of the Blue Legion was the expression of both a personal and an ideological frustration. Tellingly, his memoirs begin with a mixture of resentment, anti-communism, fascist idealism, and an irresistible penchant for a life of action: in Spain, he did not like what he saw – his country's political atmosphere asphyxiated him – but above everything, he longed for the war in Russia "defending the European civilization against the steppe's onslaught" (13; see also 64–5). Compared to the autodiegetic narrator of *Algunos no hemos muerto,* Ezquerra is an unrepentant, joyful being-for-war. To him there is nothing worse than stasis. In the French town of Cauterets, "away from the battlefields, he feels like a fish out of water. He wasn't cut out for that kind of life" (23). The same happens in Wiesbaden, where he has been sent by his superiors (48). But soon his captain proposes that he become a member of a commando unit (51). He goes to the training centre of commandos in Koblenz (52), where he meets members of the unit of Spaniards whom he will command (52). They participate in the Ardennes offensive, where the unit is decimated (54–5). Ezquerra and the surviving soldiers then go back to Berlin (59). There he is told by General Faupel to group in a special unit all the Spaniards fighting on different fronts (61). This unit, under Ezquerra's command, will be a Waffen-SS unit (113). When reflecting on the unit, Ezquerra interlaces violence, war, and idealism: "In my unit there were no rookies nor fainthearted … My soldiers weren't a mercenary troop, but rather men illuminated by an ideal and ready to defend the remaining redoubts of civilization, threatened by the red tide. It was formed by three companies of Spaniards, plus the Frenchmen of Doriot and some men from the Degrelle Division" (69). In chapters 4 to 6 (69–96), Ezquerra goes on to narrate a story unique in the history of Spain during the Second World War: the active participation of a handful of Spaniards in the defence of the capital of the Third Reich. With the addition of a few Latvians and French volunteers, the "Unidad Ezquerra" fiercely fought the Red Army, almost to the last man, in key areas of Berlin (the Moritz Platz, the Air Ministry, the Potsdamer Platz, the Stettiner Bahnhof). Ezquerra describes a completely destroyed city (69, 70, 72, 73, 81). As he and his men exit into the street from the Friedrichstrasse subway station, the platoon finds itself before a "sight both horrific and disconcerting. Berlin's ruins seemed to be ablaze, and the grenades exploded everywhere. The commands muffled by the groans of wounded soldiers" (87). While the Russian tanks roamed through the streets of Berlin, they fought "for each building, for each floor, for each square, for each street, for every inch" (78). Berlin was no more. After many turns in a long winding path, for a handful of fascist diehards the "courtesy call" to the Russians would end in a wasteland.[55]

Revenants

The repatriation in April 1954 of the surviving ex-POWs brought a renewed interest within Spain in the Blue Division. Curiously enough, the first book on the Gulag experience would be written based on the testimony of a *divisionario* who, defying the explicit prohibition issued by the Spanish government, joined the Germans to defend the Third Reich: Second Lieutenant Lorenzo Ocañas Serrano, taken prisoner by the Red Army after the Battle of Berlin. Entitled *Yo, muerto en Rusia: Memorias del alférez Ocañas*, this book by Moisés Puente was published in 1954 in Madrid by Ediciones del Movimiento. One year later Captain Palacios Cueto published his memoirs, *Embajador en el infierno*, which were hailed by critics and readers alike. In the first year alone after its publication, no fewer than 27,500 copies were sold. Awarded in 1955 with the Premio Nacional de Literatura and the Premio "Ejército" de Literatura, these memoirs attracted the attention of the film industry, and on 17 September 1956 a motion picture based on the novel, *Embajadores en el infierno*, directed by José María Forqué, was premiered in the Palacio de la Música in Madrid. The year 1955 also saw the publication of a memoir by *divisionario* Ramón P[érez] Eizaguirre, *En el abismo rojo: Memorias de un español, once años prisionero en la URSS*. Another important work on the Gulag experience, Major Oroquieta Arbiol's *De Leningrado a Odesa*, would appear in 1958.[56] Much has been written about the vicissitudes of the Spanish POWs,[57] many of whom (between two hundred and three hundred) had been taken prisoner in the Battle of Krasny Bor (10–13 February 1943), by far the deadliest battle fought by the Blue Division.[58]

One of the most remarkable family resemblances of these memoirs is the omnipresence of a cartographic gaze. The authors want to make sense of an extreme experience by mapping out the Gulag's grammar. This might sound obvious, considering the nature of any internment in a concentration camp. However, common as it is among survivors of concentration camps to describe the grammar of places designed to harm and/or exterminate human beings, Oroquieta Arbiol, Ocañas, Palacios Cueto, and Eizaguirre evince an acuteness for spatial issues that make their works stand out from similar memoirs. Furthermore, it should be noted that a few years before Aleksandr Solzhenitsyn depicted the struggles and hardships of camp life in *One Day in the Life of Ivan Denisovich* (1962) – a novel that had a huge impact both in the Soviet Union and abroad – these four *divisionarios* provided the Spanish reading public with a thorough, relatively precise picture of the Soviet Gulag from a fascist perspective.[59] The remarks of Ocañas, for instance, recall Giménez Caballero's idiosyncratic analysis of space; thus Ocañas states categorically that communism has attempted to merge the "Oriental hut" and the "skyscrapers from the West" (Puente, *Yo, muerto* 60). Similar observations punctuate all four memoirs. More interestingly, in these books the analysis of the Gulag focuses not only on the concentration camps themselves, but also on a crucial characteristic of the Soviet camp system: the constant mobility of prisoners. The memoirs of *divisionarios* portray a seemingly paradoxical "confined world on the move," what Palacios Cueto called an "infinite prison" (25) located nowhere and everywhere. "Internment" in the Gulag meant, as a matter of fact, "internment in speed." As described by the *divisionarios,* the Gulag may be seen as a concentration camp system that based its torturing of the prisoner on a never-resolved dialectics between stasis on the one hand, and unexpected and unexplained movement on the other. Since, as Virilio has rightly pointed out ("Kosovo"), the possession of territory has to do with laws and contracts as much as with movement, the Gulag depicted by the *divisionarios* demonstrates, in a dramatic and extreme way, the connections between power, territory, and movement.

A clear indication of their understanding of the inherently spatial dimension of the torture inflicted on the inmates, some memoirs include a map of the Soviet Union, from its western borders to the Urals, with the names and locations of the concentration and labour camps where the *divisionarios* had been confined, as well as the inmates' itineraries from

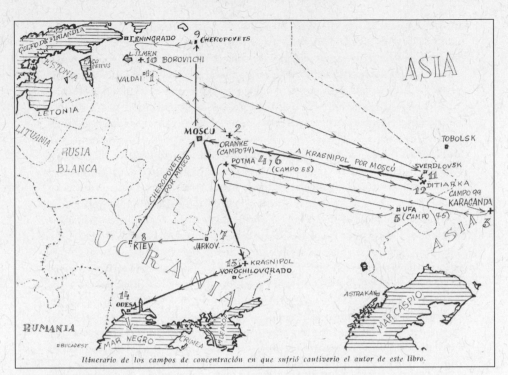

Itinerario de los campos de concentración en que sufrió cautiverio el autor de este libro.

Figure 5.6 In the Gulag: Transfers from camp to camp of Blue Division
volunteer Eusebio Calavia Bellosillo. Eusebio Calavia Bellosillo and Francisco
Álvarez Cosmen, *Enterrados en Rusia*, 1956

camp to camp. In the span of almost thirteen years, Ocañas spent his
internment in twelve different camps, Oroquieta Arbiol in fifteen, and
Palacios Cueto in thirteen. A reading of the map (figure 5.6) inserted in
Eusebio Calavia Bellosillo's memoirs, *Enterrados en Rusia* (1956), shows
the seemingly arbitrary nature of these itineraries, for the *divisionarios*
were sent sometimes for no apparent reason to camps where they had
already been. The memoirs are saturated with the narratives of itineraries; some examples are the transport to Susdal, camp number 160 (Oroquieta Arbiol and García Sánchez 189–95); the excruciating seven-day
transport to the Svarlov region, on the Asiatic side of the Urals (Palacios
Cueto and Luca de Tena 257); the transfer to Borovichi (Palacios Cueto
and Luca de Tena 201–2) and to camp number 27 in Moscow (Pala-

cios Cueto and Luca de Tena 59–61); the trip to the first concentration camps (Puente, *Yo, muerto* 32–46); sudden changes of destination (Palacios Cueto and Luca de Tena 71); and the transport to the Borovoski camp, near Cherepovetz (Puente, *Yo, muerto* 55). As Palacios Cueto concludes, "If one had to reduce to a graphic formula our stay in Russia, I would hesitate between the vignette representing barbed wire, or that of a truck or train packed with prisoners crossing the frozen immensity in all directions at any time" (Palacios Cueto and Luca de Tena 36). Further in the book, he insists on the incessant mobility of the inmates, what Eizaguirre called "the transportation of death" (79–85): "Since they captured us at the Kolpino front, the cities or camps of Leningrad, Cheropoviets, Moscow, Suzdal, Oranque, Potma, Jarcoff, Ohrms, Leningrad again, and Borovichi had been the milestones ... of an endless journey" (Palacios Cueto and Luca de Tena 258). Or, to put it with Puente, "to set off, to set off and never to arrive: that seemed to be the horrible fate of the prisoner in Russia" (*Yo, muerto* 156). Puente himself explained the reasons behind this constant mobility of – in his own words – the "concentrationary army": "This movement obeys the principle that the prisoner cannot remain longer than one year in the same place in order to ensure that he doesn't trust people and doesn't get to know the terrain and escape" (*Yo, muerto* 140–1). Furthermore, this mobility was often determined by economic considerations (141). To emphasize those considerations, in several memoirs there are also descriptions of the cities crossed by the prisoners en route to concentration camps, especially of Moscow (Palacios Cueto and Luca de Tena 62, 72; Puente, *Yo, muerto* 102–3) and Leningrad (Oroquieta Arbiol and García Sánchez 82). The memoirs include many detailed portrayals of concentration and labour camps, prisons, punishment cells, kolkhozy, and mines, as well as their functioning and the living conditions in the camps.

The most analytical of the four *divisionarios* is Ocañas, who provides a thorough view of the Gulag system, a real and "strange" world (Puente, *Yo, muerto* 48), a "true concentrationary universe where men, throughout the years, are transformed into wordless robots, into a working machine, while suffering a complete moral and physical mutilation" (48). The Gulag constitutes, he says, a microcosm of the Soviet Union based on slave work, along with police control and repression. For this reason, the camps are also a microcosm of the state (71; see also 166–7). Inevitably, this technology of imprisonment and torture dehumanizes the prisoner, as the memoirs make evident (e.g., Puente, *Yo, muerto* 168–9, 191–2). Surviving in the Gulag depended mostly, like in any concentration camp, on physical strength, the numbness of the sensibility, and the ability to avoid an intellectual reflection on the camp (Eizaguirre 126; see also 113, 117). As Ocañas himself points out, "Generally, only the crafty and the morally strong survive" (Puente, *Yo, muerto* 57). In addition, Puente includes a short history of the Gulag from its creation by the Cheka in 1923 (although the Gulag proper was founded in 1930 under the control of the secret police) to the 1950s, as well as a detailed description of its division in systems, sections, and camps (*Yo, muerto* 182–8). Nobody is free in the Soviet Union, not even those in power, for the system works by itself, "annihilating the very brains and arms that keep it moving" (198). The Soviet Union's ultimate goal consists, according to Puente, in transforming the world into an immense concentration camp (206). In the camps and the trains transporting them to other camps, the *divisionarios* encountered a multinational population, most of it made up of POWs from other countries, frequently mixed up with Soviet political and common prisoners. Among the many people they met stand out the deserters and the Republican Spaniards working in the Soviet Army and intelligence agencies seen through the prism of fascist anti-communism.[60] The POWs from the Blue Division and the Republican Spaniards re-enacted, in the concentrationary universe of the Soviet Gulag, the civil war.[61] It is a remarkable reversal of fortunes, not only because in this case the fascists are on the losing side, but also because they are completely at the mercy of their enemies, both physically and linguistically, since the only way the POWs can communicate with the Soviets is through the Spanish interpreters (see, for instance, Oroquieta Arbiol and García Sánchez 63–80), considered much worse than their Soviet "masters." The animalistic images and derogatory, insulting language used to describe the "Reds" in the narratives studied in chapter 4 reappear in these memoirs. Ocañas remembers how unbearable their life was in Chaika, especially the "interrogations performed by Spanish communists" (Puente, *Yo, muerto* 96). The language employed by Oroquieta Arbiol to describe the Republicans imprisoned by the Soviets is consistent with the profound hatred towards Republicans and deserters of the Division present in *De Leningrado a Odesa*, and it summarizes perfectly the fascist POWs' perception of the Republicans: "Amid the inmates there were plenty of individuals with low moral standards, illiterate ... resentful, and full of hatred. We avoided them ... Amongst them stood out a man more repulsive that one can imagine. It was an anarchist ... who boasted ... about the killings of the 'fascists' that he had carried out in what was the red zone during our War of Liberation"

(Oroquieta Arbiol and García Sánchez 206; see also Palacios Cueto and Luca de Tena 119).

As pointed out earlier, Republican airmen and merchant sailors stranded in the Soviet Union after the civil war were sent to concentration camps. Oroquieta Arbiol and Palacios Cueto talk about them with sympathy while feeling superior to them. The latter of the two *divisionarios* hints at a reconciliation as a result of the moral purification of the Republican pilots: "In the heart of Russia the two Spains had flattened their differences. Here they hugged each other forever ... They merged in a hug of blood and sacrifice, and, shoulder to shoulder, fought together, suffered trials, endured sentences. The civil war ended for us in the Russian concentration camps! If any of the pilots who came to Russia were sincerely a communist, what they had undergone cut off from them the last rosy seed of Marxism. They crossed the Jordan and came out clean" (Palacios Cueto and Luca de Tena 227).

Perceived as victims of the Soviet State, the Russian population are often depicted with condescending sympathy. As Eizaguirre writes of the Russian workers in a mine where he was sent to work, "As a prisoner, it was the first occasion that I had to talk with the simple Russian people and admire the limitless resignation and stoicism with which those female peasants performed ... tough tasks in the mine. In spite of thirty years of Soviet power, it hasn't been possible yet to uproot from the Russian peasants their streak of Christian charity. Contrary to what we expected, they received us gladly" (96). In similar terms, Palacios Cueto understands the abject subjection of the peasantry by the Soviet state (Palacios Cueto and Luca de Tena 94–6; see also Oroquieta Arbiol and García Sánchez 277), underscoring further in his memoirs the disproportion between the riches of the country and the sheer poverty of the population (175). In the Soviet Union, individuals are not considered as human beings, as "bearers of eternal values," but as numbers, as "heads of cattle" (Oroquieta Arbiol and García Sánchez 309). This perception of the Russian "other" is in full accord with the authors' anti-communism. In fact, the memoirs could be considered as passionate utterances destined to affect the readers' perception of the Soviet Union and communism. Eizaguirre makes clear the purpose of his book: "If anyone reading this work finds emotion in it, and perceives in its content yet another warning cry against a regime that aspires to destroy the fundamental principles of our society, the author will feel quite happy" (10). In a similar vein Oroquieta Arbiol writes that the stories included in his book "have to be ... a passionate declaration against communism ... with the ideological reasons that led us to the fight ... The essence of this book could be no other than that" (13).

The memoirs written by ex-POWs who survived the Gulag are the manifestation of the spectre through discourse. Take, for instance, Palacios Cueto and Luca de Tena's extremely successful *Embajador en el infierno*. Torcuato Luca de Tena, who penned these memoirs in the first person based on a series of interviews with Palacios Cueto, was one of the journalists who boarded the *Semiramis* in Istanbul to meet the ex-POWs and accompany them on their trip to Barcelona. In the prologue to the book, he describes the *Semiramis* as a ship "populated by ghosts" (Palacios Cueto and Luca de Tena 7), a "new boat of Charon, between the banks of death and life" (7–8). During the trip, he closely observed the ex-POWs' behaviour "in their new awakening to life" (7). As if to corroborate Luca de Tena's first impressions, one of the repatriated *divisionarios* explained to him, "It is as if one dead felt, suddenly, his sensibility renewed and began to perceive around him murmurs, reflections, faint clouds of light emerging from the silence and infinite shadows surrounding him. The resurrected would never know which of those belonged to the world of the shadows and which were already the result of his conscious activity" (7). Hence the ex-POWs were ghosts waking up to life, or, to be more precise, revenants, animated corpses returning from hell, as underscored by the title of the memoirs. For Luca de Tena, these revenants will be received in Spain as "the absent ones" (8), thereby associating them with the regime's "first ghost": Primo de Rivera, *el Ausente* (The Absent One). In effect, the main character of the book will be, as Luca de Tena announces to the reader, "the Absence and Death surrounding the [ex-POWS'] back" (9). Palacios Cueto / Luca de Tena revisit(s) this idea at the end of the book. Narrating the repatriation trip, Palacios Cueto perceives his comrades as "dead standing up" (281). Aboard the *Semiramis*, he feels himself awakening to life. The *divisionarios* are "resurrected" in that "back-to-front boat of Charon" (283–4). To the Spanish authorities and journalists who welcomed them in the harbour of Istanbul, "We looked as resurrected Lazarus. They said that they didn't understand us because we spoke very quietly, as if afraid of hearing our own voices, and ... because when we spoke we didn't move our lips" (287). In the *Semiramis*, "we were now travelling to the bank of ... life" (288; see also 294–5). Identical perceptions and feelings can be found in other memoirs. Oroquieta Arbiol remembers his arrival into Barcelona as "the signal of the resurrection to a new life" (18), and Moisés Puente refers to the ex-POWs as "dead souls" (*Yo, muerto* 12), "beings resurrected from their tombs of pain" (12), men with a "lost, faraway gaze" who "return to life" (14). Puente sees them literally as revenants: the ex-POWs are "returning dead" (14) who are coming back from the netherworld (15).

The presentation of the ex-POWs as revenants should be understood in relation to two different factors: (1) the conditions of their internment set up by the Soviets and the mark left on the prisoners by the Russian concentrationary universe, and (2) the paratopical nature that Spain would have for those *divisionarios* who believed that the regime had betrayed Falange's doctrine. As regards the former, we have to take into account the Soviets' treatment of the Spanish prisoners of war. In contrast with the conditions placed upon POWs from other countries, the Soviet authorities allowed no communication between the Spanish inmates and their families. Although news leaked out piecemeal about the fate of a limited number of *divisionarios* through ex-POWs from other countries who were repatriated in the wake of the Second World War, as time went by many families assumed the worst, and some even held funeral services to mourn their beloved ones. The moving cablegrams and radio messages exchanged between the *divisionarios* in the *Semiramis* and their relatives waiting in Barcelona attest to the logical emotions shared by families who learnt that sons, husbands, or brothers for long thought to be dead were in fact alive. But were they? Were they "alive" after having spent almost thirteen years in the Gulag?

In a chapter devoted to the Argentinian *desaparecidos* during the 1976–83 military dictatorship, Gordon remarks that those disappeared who had the luck to survive never returned alone, for the *desaparecido* "always bears the ghost of the state whose very power is the defining force of the field of disappearance" (127). The repressive state that has kidnapped and tortured these people generates an identity that "remains to haunt those marked by its hand and all the others to whom that hand is extended" (127). The act of making contact with the disappeared means, according to Gordon, "encountering the specter of what the state has tried to repress" (127). The disappeared thus carry the message "of the other door" (127). The *divisionarios* had been possessed by the structure that held them in captivity. As Friedrich Nietzsche wrote in *Jenseits von Gut und Böse* (1886), "He who fights with monsters should be careful lest he thereby become a monster. And if thou gaze long into an abyss, the abyss will also gaze into thee" (chapter 4, §146), insight beautifully elaborated by Jorge Semprún in *L'Écriture ou la vie* (1994) and present in countless works on or by survivors of Nazi concentration and extermination camps and on extreme situations such as wars. After surviving the abyss, the horror of the absolute unknown shines in the gaze of the former inmate. In *Yo, muerto en Rusia*, Moisés Puente observes that, in the first hours of the *divisionarios*' "return to life," he could notice in them a "lost and distant gaze, an extreme gravity on [the] face, a slowness in the answers," and adds, in a very important passage, that the long captivity "has stamped on them its trace, a trace that will have to be erased with great tact and understanding" (*Yo, muerto* 12). Ocañas, according to Puente, seems even to have Russian traits (210). Like other inmates of concentration camps, Ocañas has become a haunted being, but a haunted being who, through writing, will haunt those who come in contact with him.

In some instances, the logic of the spectre imprinted by the Soviet repressive power onto the inmate is heightened by a symptomatic literary technique: properly speaking, the revenant did not write his memoirs. Although he signed them, they were penned by another person based on the information provided by the *divisionario* while assuming the latter's identity. The memoirs were written in the first person *as if* the revenant had himself authored the book. Luca de Tena, for instance, takes up the role of a ventriloquist by lending his voice to Captain Palacios Cueto, an "undead" of sorts. Other memoirs follow the same logic. Moisés Puente narrates in the first person the memoirs of Second Lieutenant Lorenzo Ocañas (*Yo, muerto en Rusia: Memorias del alférez Ocañas de la División Azul*), as do César García Sánchez with Major Oroquieta Arbiol's from the latter's "copious notes" (*De Leningrado a Odesa*) and Francisco Álvarez Cosmen with Eusebio Calavia Belosillo's (*Enterrados en Rusia*). In a game of spectres mirroring each other, the spectre's speech would be represented – rather fittingly – by a *ghost*writer. By channelling the communication between the earthly world and the netherworld, the ghostwriters of the memoirs furnished the spectres with voice and shape. Therefore, the ghostwriter, the author-turned-into-a-ghost, provided flesh to the ghost-turned-into-an-author. In a literal sense, those memoirs have been *ghostwritten*. Writing, itself the house of the spectre, is thus a ghost itself – a ghost set up to haunt the reader.

The spectres coming back from the Gulag found themselves in the situation characteristic of the veteran returning home. Their homeland had changed without them. But in this particular case, the paratopical nature that the native country might have had for some veterans was enhanced by expectations stemming from the Falangist ideology of some *divisionarios*, an issue already addressed in this chapter. Through their presence in public discourse and, more decisively, through their literary products, they reflected the bad conscience of the political establishment and ex-

pressed the resentment felt by the *camisas viejas* toward the Franco regime. In a historical juncture marked, as we saw, by the rapprochement of
Franco's regime to Western democracies and international institutions,
the spectres of the Blue Division became a somewhat embarrassing presence. In general terms, Spanish fascism became after the Second World
War a spectral presence. In its encounter with the paratopos, the writing
produced by the Blue Division veterans may be viewed as a topography
of resentment, as the mapping of failed dreams and dead ends. The journey that began in the Rif seemed to have ended on the Russian steppe.
Thereafter, the history of fascism in Spain would be a ghost story of sorts,
an unfinished tale about spectres haunting the living.

To be sure, spectres populate and stroll through the history, spaces, and
places of Spanish fascism. The cult of death and the fallen so characteristic of fascism, explored throughout this book, reached its climax with the
enshrining of José Antonio Primo de Rivera, the so-called Absent One.
Executed by a firing squad on 20 November 1936, the improbable Jefe
Nacional of FE-JONS became after his death a politically useful spectral
presence in Franco's Spain. A decree by Franco of 16 November 1938
declaring the date of Primo de Rivera's death as National Mourning Day
initiated the massive cult of the Falangist leader, "without precedent in
the history of modern western European politics" (Payne, *Fascism* 233).
The transfer of Primo de Rivera's remains from his tomb in Alicante to
San Lorenzo de El Escorial, carried out with elaborate ritual from 10 to
20 November 1939, constituted the ultimate expression of the fascist cult
of the dead.[62] Primo de Rivera was turned into a national hero, into a
symbol – in the Caudillo's own words – "of sacrifice to the youth of our
time" (qtd. in Payne, *Fascism* 233), into a spectre. He did not die, Franco
affirmed in a speech broadcast on 20 November 1938, the day he was
executed: "The matter decomposed, but the spirit lived on" ("Discurso
de S.E."). As Torrente Ballester put it in the prologue to his *José Antonio
Primo de Rivera (Antología)*, the "myth is the 'operational way of being'
by which José Antonio lives on in the conscience of today's youth" (10).
The making of Primo de Rivera into a spectre, a being neither living nor
dead, brought spectrality to political and social life. But one cannot possess a spectre without being haunted by it. The visibility of the invisible,
the tangibility of the intangible, the omnipresence of the omni-Absent
throughout almost four decades would remain a characteristic paradox
at the core of a regime that succeeded only partially in erasing from public view its fascist substratum.

The burial of Franco on 23 November 1975 in a tomb right next to Primo de Rivera's in the basilica of the Valle de los Caídos belongs to the logic of spectrality.[63] After many years of trying to conceal the impertinent presence of the absence, Franco finally assumed his ideological affinities – emphasized by the physical proximity of the two tombs, placed in a vertical line with the giant 150-metre-tall cross standing atop the Risco de la Nava mountain – with Primo de Rivera and hence with fascism. Lying next to a spectre, Franco himself would become one. The fact that both men died on the same day and month underscores, if only by a happy coincidence, a merging that took place in death. Bodily proximity and ideological closeness in a fascist memorial turned the connection between the two spectres into what we could call the *ur-spectre* of Spanish fascism. This ur-spectre constitutes a spectre of spectres, a paradoxical origin without original moment as well as the effect of a process projected not so much into the past or the no-time of death as towards the future of the living. A presence whose inscription had been partially crossed out by a regime that did its best to hide its fascist substratum, the ur-spectre rose to the surface, unabashed, in an exhibitionistic and calculated ritualistic way, at the very end of the dictatorship, as if the main purpose of the dictator's burial were to haunt the very space controlled by the Franco regime for thirty-six years. Franco's burial can be interpreted, therefore, as the ultimate expression of the fascist politics of space, for the ur-spectre emerged from a monument built not only as a gigantic tribute to those who died for the "crusade," to the "martyrs" who – in the Caudillo's own words in the inauguration of the Valle de los Caídos in 1958 – "command" all Spaniards to teach their children the "permanent principles of our Movement" ("Inauguración"). This huge celebration of nothingness, this shrine inhabited by spectres commanding the living, this monument erected in "the centre of our Fatherland" (Franco, "Inauguración"), was also conceived of as the materialization of the dictatorship, as a tale of a "holy war" between good and evil, as a tool of social control, as an everlasting statement addressed to political enemies, as a place of pilgrimage, as an unfinished narrative (as Franco himself hinted in his inaugural speech) to be continued, under the regime's tutelage, by future generations. Emerging from a fascist place that, by its very nature, eludes any well-intentioned attempt to give it a non-fascist meaning, the ur-spectre has brought to the present the ideological core and political direction condensed by the Valle de los Caídos.

The ur-spectre of Spanish fascism and the Franco regime roams in space in many guises. In contemporary Spain, it exerts its haunting power through the signatures that it has etched on space. It talks through the names of streets and squares, through symbols and monuments; it rewrites space by public demonstrations and events; it keeps underground the corpses of its victims, thanks to the political agents who are possessed by it. The spectre of fascism thus still haunts Spain. Repressing it – as literary scholarship, for instance, has done by neglecting the thorough study of fascist Spanish literature for decades – only intensifies its power. Out of justice for both the spectres *and* the living, exorcism needs to be performed not solely on the disappeared, on the still-unaccounted-for victims of a murderous regime, but also on the spectres of the perpetrators. Only those who read and record the deeds and signatures of the spectre, argues Giorgio Agamben, "will perhaps be able one day to reopen that breach in which history – in which life – suddenly fulfills its promise" (*Nudities* 42). Hence we may conclude that there is a logic underlying these topographies of fascism: the logic of the conjuration.

Notes

Introduction

1 The official name of the law, which came into effect on 28 December 2007, is "LEY 52/2007, de 26 de diciembre, por la que se reconocen y amplían derechos y se establecen medidas en favor de quienes padecieron persecución o violencia durante la guerra civil y la dictadura" (see Spain, Law 52/2007).

2 On the residues of fascism and Francoism in contemporary Spain, see Merino and Song; Rodríguez Puértolas, *Historia* 1: 16–33, 2: 1021–1109. This fact, however, needs to be framed not only within the history of Spain, but also in relation to the presence of fascism in the structure of modern democracies across the world (Adorno, *Critical* 90, 98–9; Virilio, *Speed* 134–5) and in the flourishing of neo-fascist organizations and political parties in Europe (see, for instance, Gregor, *Search*; Laqueur 93–215).

3 José Antonio Primo de Rivera – son of Miguel Primo de Rivera, a general of the Spanish Army and the dictator who ruled Spain in 1923–30 – was called "José Antonio" by fellow Falangists and coeval politicians in the 1930s in order to differentiate him from his father. While many people have ever since referred to the co-founder of Falange Española by his first name only, throughout this book José Antonio Primo de Rivera will be referred to by his surnames. In order to avoid confusion, his father's name will always be preceded by the latter's Army rank.

4 For the full text of the ruling, see Garzón.

5 Eatwell, *Fascism*; Gentile, "Fascism" 229–51; Griffin, *Nature*; Mann; Mosse, *Fascist* 1–44; Paxton; Payne, *History* 3–19, 441–95; Sternhell, *Birth*.

6 Griffin, *Fascism*; Iordachi, *Comparative*; Laqueur; Linz 3–123; Mosse, *International*; Nolte; Paxton, *Anatomy*; Payne, *History*.

7 For Spain: Ellwood; Payne, *Fascism*; Rodríguez Jiménez, *Historia*. For Germany: Evans, *Coming, Third Reich in Power, Third Reich at War*; Friedländer; Kershaw, *Hitler*. For Italy: De Felice, *Mussolini*; Gentile, "Fascism," *Sacralization, Struggle*; Morgan; Sternhell, *Birth*; Tasca; Whittam. For France: Milza; Paxton, *Vichy France*; Soucy, *French Fascism: First Wave, Second Wave*. For the United Kingdom: Linehan; Thurlow.

8 The centrality of architecture and urban planning in fascism is commonplace among scholars devoted to the study of fascism. On architecture and urban planning in Spain during the early Franco regime, see Blanco 17–40; Cirici 44–6, 110–50; de Terán 141–5, 223–321; Díaz Nosty 23–6; Doménech Girbau; Flores López 347–60; Llorente Hernández, *Arte* 67–85, 275–302; Moneo; Sambricio, "El Plan" 115–36, "La arquitectura" 173–97, "De nuevo" 12–18, "La renovación" 234–9, "La vivienda"13–84, "Madrid" 289–328, "¡Que coman!" 199–243; Urrutia 353–85. For information on Nazi architecture, urban planning, and public works, see Giesler (one of Hitler's top architects); Petsch; Scobie; Speer (Hitler's most important architect whose memoirs are still a very valuable document); Spotts 312–85; Teut; R. Taylor. An introductory account to the same issues in Fascist Italy can be found in Ciucci (*Gli architetti*) and Cresti.

9 For Spain: Di Febo. For Germany: Thamer 172–90; Theweleit 1: 429–35, 2: 3–142. For Italy: Berezin; Falasca-Zamponi; Gentile, *Struggle* 77–87, 109–25.

10 On the "spatial turn" in the humanities and social studies, see Warf and Arias's representative multidisciplinary collection of essays.

11 For other adaptations of Lefebvre's model, see, for instance, Harvey, *Condition* 218–19, *Cosmopolitanism* 142–3; Soja, *Postmodern, Thirdspace* 68–9. See also Neil Smith's sophisticated Marxist approach to the production of space in contemporary society.

12 Compare Lefebvre's spatial triad with Ernst Cassirer's differentiation between three types of spatial experience (42–9): "organic space" (the environment where every organism lives, that is, the space of action), "perceptual space" (the space lived through all the different kinds of sense experience), and "symbolic" or "abstract space" (the abstract apprehension of space and spatial relationships through symbolic thought).

13 To emphasize the materiality of spatial practices, throughout the book I use Harvey's renaming of Lefebvre's concept: "material spatial practice" (Harvey, *Condition* 218).

14 On the concept of *habitus*, see Bourdieu, "Habitus," *Le Sens* 87–109.

15 For Spain: Carbajosa and Carbajosa 107–29; Rodríguez Puértolas, *Historia* 1: 49–52. For Germany: Klemperer; Steiner 95–109. For Italy: Falasca-Zamponi; Gentile, "Fascism," *Sacralization*; Spackman.

16 The concept of *symbolic violence* has been developed by Žižek (*Violence* 1–2, 58–73).

17 On this score, see, for instance, de Terán 141–5, 223–321.

18 See Díaz Nieva and Uribe Lacalle's thorough, partially annotated bibliography of the primary and secondary material concerning Spanish fascism.

19 Albert, *Vanguardistas, Vencer*; Carbajosa and Carbajosa; Gracia; Mainer, *Falange*; Naval; Peloille; Rodríguez Puértolas, *Historia*; Schmolling; Trapiello; Umbral; Wahnón.

20 For a theory of generic fascism, see, for instance, Eatwell, "Nature"; Griffin, *Nature*; Mann; Mosse, *Fascist*; Nolte; Paxton, *Anatomy*; Payne, *History*; Sternhell, *Birth, Neither Right*. Two representative anthologies of scholarly works defining generic fascism are Iordachi's *Comparative Fascist Studies* (51–161) and Kallis's *Fascism Reader* (64–100).

21 The concept of *family resemblance* has been proposed and developed by Ludwig Wittgenstein (see *Philosophical Investigations* §§65–71, 92, 108, 114).

1 A Politics of Space

1 This is the main thesis of Kohn's book on "radical space."

2 Foucault, *Dits* 2: 1090–1; Harvey, *Cosmopolitanism* 260–83; Ucelay-Da Cal, *Llegar*.

3 On the connections between politics, power, and space, see, for instance, Foucault, *Surveiller, Dits* 1: 1389–93, 2: 28–40, 190–207, 1089–1104; Kohn; Harvey, *Cosmopolitanism*; Lefebvre, *Production, State*; Smith.

4 Watch Peter Cohen's classic documentary *The Architecture of Doom* (1989), which explores Hitler's ideas on art – most particularly architecture – as well as their influence on policymaking. Not to be overlooked is the title of the documentary itself.

5 In Harvey, *Cosmopolitanism* 134–41, *Social Justice* 13–14, 168–9, 184–7.

6 On the fascist organizations as "movements," see Arendt, *Origins* 243–66, 305–15, 323–6, 341–88, 389–92; Klemperer 225–30.

7 See also Gentile, "Fascism" 245–6.

8 Much has been written on the son of General Miguel Primo de Rivera and co-founder of Falange Española. His biography has been the object of many books, articles, and notes, most of them from a pro-fascist point of view (see the items listed in Díaz Nieva and Uribe Lacalle 101–11). Two sympathetic critical studies of Primo de Rivera's thinking are Brocà Tela, *Los antecedentes* and *Falange*. Scholarly approaches on Primo de Rivera are Ellwood; Gibson; Payne, *Fascism* 69–71; Rodríguez Jiménez, *Historia*; Saz Campos, *España* 138–49.

9 *Neither Right nor Left* is precisely the title of Sternhell's important book on fascist ideology in France. For Sternhell, fascism was, as he writes in another of his works, "a variety of socialism which, while rejecting Marxism, remained revolutionary. This form of socialism was also, by definition, anti-liberal and anti-bourgeois, and its opposition to historical materialism made it the natural ally of radical nationalism" ("Fascism" 55).

10 The official movement received its name – Falange Española – in the organizational meeting of 2 November.

11 On the *khora*, see Derrida, *Name* 89–127.

12 Laín Entralgo summed up that view of Falange in his 1937 article "Meditación apasionada sobre el estilo de la Falange"; for Laín, those under the spell of fascism are like poets of an immense "collective poem" (165). The "literary" dimension of Falange has been a critical commonplace since the first newspaper accounts of Primo de Rivera's speech (see Payne, *Fascism* 92). Thereafter Spanish fascism would be frequently dismissed as a "poetic movement" concerned mainly with language and style.

13 On Ledesma Ramos, see the two standing – if not always reliable – biographies written by Borrás (*Ramiro Ledesma*) and Sánchez Diana (*Ramiro Ledesma*). See in particular the following critical studies: Gallego [Margalef], *Ramiro Ledesma*, "La realidad"; Payne, *Fascism* 54–61; Rodríguez Jiménez, *Historia* 66–72; Saz Campos, *España* 118–22. Some fascist approaches to Ledesma Ramos are Aguado's, Cuadrado Costa's, Macipe López's, Montero Díaz's (*Ramiro Ledesma*), Schneider and Cuadrado Costa's.

14 The programmatic "Puntos de partida" published in *El Fascio* on 16 March 1933 categorically stated, "Before the 'territoriality' the new state shall not allow artful divisions, political autonomies that diminish its absolute sovereignty" (3). See also Ledesma Ramos, *Discurso* 234–5, *Escritos* 122, *¿Fascismo?* 83–7; "Los 27 puntos" 3; Primo de Rivera, *Obras* 66; "Unidad de destino."

15 In addition to Primo de Rivera's definition, see the anonymous article "Unidad de destino," published in *Arriba* on 21 March 1935. The Falangist expression *unidad de destino en lo universal* ("unity of destiny in the universal") is in fact an idiosyncratic translation of *Schicksalsgemeinschaft* ("unity of fate"), a concept put forth by the Austro-Marxist thinker and statesman Otto Bauer in *Die Nationalitätenfrage und die Sozialdemokratie* (1907). As of the 1920s, *Schicksalsgemeinschaft* would be a keyword of the National Socialist discourse.

16 On politics as architecture, see also Primo de Rivera, *Obras* 398, 663.

17 See, for instance, Hitler, *Mein Kampf* 263–6 (on German cities, their lack of monuments, and the capital meaning and function of the monuments and monumental buildings for the constitution and the representation of the

"people's community") and most particularly Hitler's important speech at the Kulturtagung of the Reichsparteitag of September 1937, wherein the Führer spelled out the driving force, signification, and purposes of a vast building and urban-planning program set in motion that year throughout Germany and Austria (in Hitler, *Speeches* 1: 592–6). For an excellent introduction to that building program, see Spotts 332–85.

18 Justly considered by many as the most important fascist intellectual in Spain in the 1930s (Arconada; Rodríguez Puértolas, *Historia* 1: 119–20; Valls 11; Wahnón 17), Giménez Caballero has been, and still is, the most-written-about Spanish fascist writer. On his life, works, and fascist ideology, see Albert, *Vanguardistas* 47–58, 353–60; Carbajosa and Carbajosa 33–5, 51–6, 82–5, 138–9, 192–4, 221–3; Foard 93–214; Payne, *Fascism* 51–4; Rodríguez Jiménez, *Historia* 53–62, 134–41; Rodríguez Puértolas, *Historia* 1: 119–33, 364–71, 2: 861–71; Selva; Wahnón 17–69.

19 On Giménez Caballero's ideas on architecture, see Albert, "'El saetazo,'" *Vanguardistas* 356–8; Pérez de Tudela; Carlos Ramos 131–45; Selva 221; Wahnón 49, 56–69. Mermall's article on the rhetoric of architecture and of geometry in Falangist culture offers a good context for understanding Giménez Caballero's reflections on space and architecture.

20 *Genio de España* merited five editions in seven years (1st ed. 1932; 2nd ed. 1934; 3rd ed. 1938; 4th ed. 1939; 5th ed. 1939). On this work, see Foard 173–88; Hernando 175–208; Labanyi, "Women"; Saz Campos, *España* 110–18; Selva 204–19.

21 Giménez Caballero had already written what has been considered as the first piece expounding a fascist doctrine in Spain: "En torno al casticismo de Italia: Carta a un compañero de la joven España," published in *La Gaceta Literaria* on 15 February 1929.

22 On Giménez Caballero's view of art as revelation and the poet as a prophet, see Albert, *Vanguardistas* 354–6; Wahnón 29–33.

23 See Hernando 247–60 for a good analysis of what the author calls "architectonic schemata" in the works of Giménez Caballero produced in the 1920s.

24 See Kern's authoritative book about the new modes of understanding and of experiencing time and space between 1880 and the Great War.

25 See Mosse, *Fascist* 137–55.

26 "Fascism itself," Griffin argues, "can be seen as a political variant of modernism. This peculiar genus of revolutionary project for the transformation of society … could only emerge in the first decades of the twentieth century in a society permeated with modernist metanarratives of cultural renewal which shaped a legion of activities, initiatives, and movements 'on the ground'" (*Modernism* 6). While this assessment is, in general terms, correct,

it must be taken with a grain of salt. As Mosse has observed (*Fascist* 137–55), there was an essential tension between the artistic avant-gardes on the one hand, and fascism's nationalism and the political necessities of modern mass movements on the other.

27 On the relationship between Futurism and Italian Fascism, see Berghaus, *Futurism*; Gentile, *Struggle*. Hewitt (*Fascist Modernism*) has analysed the spatiality of Marinetti's work as well as the connection between said spatiality and Fascism, and Virilio has underscored the connection between Futurism and the Nazi death camps by asserting that "the slogan of the First Futurist Manifesto of 1909 – 'War is the world's only hygiene' – led directly … to the shower block of Auschwitz" (*Art* 16).

28 On Lewis's fascism, see Jameson, *Fables*. On Pound and fascism, see Hickman 89–131.

29 See Albert, *Vanguardistas*.

30 Taking as the point of departure Theweleit's known theses on the topic, Labanyi ("Women") explores the fascist fear of dissolution as expressed in *Genio de España*.

31 See Harley 51–107, 149–68 for a magisterial analysis of the connections between political power, ideology, and cartography.

32 On the semantic field of *alma* in fin-de-siècle Spain, see Mainer, *"Alma española."*

33 This cartographic technique employed by Giménez Caballero in *Genio de España* was not new to his work. He had already used it in *Julepe de menta* ([1929] 67–75) in a critical presentation of Spanish art since the sixteenth century. On the praise of the machine and modernity in Spanish literature in the first three decades of the twentieth century, see Cano Ballesta, *Literatura*.

34 See, for instance, Marinetti, "Manifesto dell'aeropoesia" (1931), Marinetti et al., "Manifesto della aeropittura" (1929), Alceo Toni, "Aeromusica: la musica e il volo" (1933). Outstanding works of aeropittura are Fedele Azari's *Prospettive di volo* (1926), Gerardo Dottori's *Trittico della velocità* (1927), and Enrico Prampolini's *Spiritualità cosmica* (1932).

35 On this score, see, for instance, Berghaus, "Futurism" 8–14.

36 For an overview of Italian Fascism and aviation, see Piper 95–103. It is far from coincidental that the first serious treatise on aerial warfare, *Il dominio dell' aria* (1921), was written by a supporter of Mussolini: the Italian general Giulio Douhet, who emphasized the importance of strategic bombing (i.e., against the civilian population). An authoritative survey of aviation since the 1910s through the Second World War can be found in Gibbs-Smith (167–243).

37 Likewise, in his "Manifesto tecnico della letteratura futurista" (1912), Marinetti had argued that the "speed of air travel had greatly increased our knowledge of the world" (*Critical Writings* 108). According to Marinetti, "Seeing things from a new perspective, no longer frontally or from behind, but straight down beneath me, and thus foreshortened, I was able to break the age-old fetters of logic and the leaden wire of comprehension" (112).

38 On the relationships between war, aviation, representation, and the act of seeing, see Virilio, *War and Cinema* 20, passim.

39 An early survey on aerial photography can be found in Winchester and Wills's 1928 book; for a comprehensive synthesis of the topic, see Piper 63–126.

40 For a sound introduction to cartography and war, see Livingstone 216–59.

41 For more information on *Arte y Estado*, see Albert, *Vanguardistas* 353–60; Cirici 56–75; Foard 202–7; Hernando 220–4; Rodríguez Puértolas, *Historia* 1: 131–3; Selva 219–25; Wahnón 17–69. Silva's panoramic and comparative account of fascist art in Europe frames within a wider context Giménez Caballero's aesthetics.

42 On the fascist art theory and literary criticism in early Francoism, see Llorente Hernández, *Arte* 33–65.

43 Some examples are González Ruiz, "Función social de la crítica" (1941); Pérez de Urbel, "El arte y el imperio" (1938); Sánchez Mazas, "Textos sobre una política de arte" (1942); Torrente Ballester, "Razón y ser de la dramática futura" (1937); and Vivanco, "El arte humano" (1940).

44 On Giménez Caballero and the *escorialismo*, see Wahnón 109–12, 222–3.

45 The spatial form of *Arte y Estado* articulates, too, a fundamental book on literature of that period, *Mirador literario: Parábola de la nueva literatura* (1931), by the fascist-to-be F. Guillén Salaya. See Albert, *Vanguardistas* 35–9, for an interesting exploration of the fascist elements of Guillén Salaya's important essay.

46 For more information on Giménez Caballero's concept of art as propaganda, see Albert, *Vanguardistas* 358–60; Cirici 58–60; Selva 221–3; Wahnón 39–42.

47 See, for instance, Giménez Caballero's essay "La arquitectura y Madrid," collected in *Madrid nuestro* ([1944] 161–81).

48 See Carlos Ramos 131–6.

49 See Diéguez Patao 58–63. On the different architectural movements hegemonic in Spain at the time (rationalism, expressionism, the classicist functionalism of the Generation of 1925), see Bohigas; Diéguez Patao; Carlos Ramos 87–8; San Antonio Gómez, *20 años* and *El Madrid del 27*; Urrutia 241–353.

50 On Le Corbusier and French fascism, see Antliff 111–53. On Le Corbusier
   and Italian Fascism within the context of the architect's visit to Italy, see Ciucci, "A Roma."

51 "What is a city? And, to begin with, what is a man? It is an unlimited potential of energy placed between two contradictory and hostile fatalities: the
   individual and the collective. The equilibrium point … is to be found between those two destinies" (qtd. in Giménez Caballero, *Arte* 68).

52 The expression "architecture, art of the state" was probably borrowed from
   an important article by Pier Maria Bardi titled precisely "Architettura, arte
   di Stato" (1931). See Ciucci, *Gli architetti* 108–28 for a good account of the
   debates in Fascist Italy about that concept of architecture.

53 Giménez Caballero's ideas on the unionization of the artists, guilds, broth-
   erhoods, and artisanship have been examined by Foard (206–7), Selva
   (224), and Wahnón (34–5).

54 Founded by Julián Tellaeche, Manuel Aizpurúa, and other Basque artists,
   the "Gu" attempted to apply to art the fascist theory of corporatism and
   promoted all kinds of activities with the purpose to disseminate the new-
   est trends in art and architecture. After its resounding inauguration in the
   summer of 1934 (attended by no less than Pablo Picasso and José Antonio
   Primo de Rivera), it became an important and very dynamic cultural centre
   with close ties to Falange visited, among other artists, writers, and intellectuals of note, by Max Aub, Pío Baroja, and Federico García Lorca. On the
   "Gu" and fascism, see Martínez Gorriarán and Agirre Arriaga 224–9.

55 In the wake of the civil war, the Franco regime unionized the artists. It
   founded the Sección de Bellas Artes (attached first to the Sindicato de
   Actividades Diversas and moved later to the Sindicato de Profesiones Libe-
   rales), and made the old Unión de Dibujantes Españoles dependent of the
   Central Nacional Sindicalista (see Llorente Hernández, *Arte* 57).

56 For more information on Giménez Caballero's interpretation of El Escorial,
   see Albert, *Vanguardistas* 356–8; Cirici 73; Pérez de Tudela 1001–13; Carlos
   Ramos 140–5; Wahnón 56–62.

57 José Ortega y Gasset expounded his interpretation of El Escorial in *Meditaciones del Escorial* (1915; in *El Espectador* 6: 167–87).

58 Shortly after the fascists' victory in 1939, Sánchez Mazas related El Escorial
   to the new totalitarian state and its imperialist drive ("Textos" 17).

59 The normative meaning of El Escorial would be further emphasized in
   the aftermath of the civil war. In certain cases, El Escorial was conceived
   of as an illocutionary speech act: its classicist order *ordered* (in the sense of
   "ordering" and "commanding") norms of behaviour. Thus, Sánchez Mazas
   asserted, "El Escorial dictates to us the best lesson for the Falanges of today

and the future. It summarizes our entire conscience, it orders our will and corrects, implacable, the least error in our style. It teaches us the authentic meaning of our relationship with Spain and ... the skies" ("Textos" 20–1).

2 Morocco: The Forging of a Habitus

1 For a global approach to the connection between fascism and colonialism, see Arendt, *Origins* 123–302. Although this interconnectedness has been studied by the scholarship devoted to the relations between Spain and Morocco during the first half of the twentieth century (Balfour; Madariaga, *Los moros*), it is surprisingly absent from the main histories of Spanish fascism, which place the origins of fascism in the confluence of a constellation of factors emerged or catalysed in the Peninsula, such as the socio-economic problems sparked by the 1917 crisis, General Primo de Rivera's dictatorship, and the exacerbation of antagonisms during the Second Republic (Ellwood 23–39; Jiménez Campo; Pastor; Payne, *Fascism* 3–65; Peloille; Rodríguez Jiménez, *Historia* 17–118).

2 On the protectorate, see Madariaga, *España* 259–87; Mateo Dieste; Morales Lezcano 278–84; Salas Larrazábal.

3 Detailed information on Spanish colonialism in Morocco in the nineteenth century can be found in Lécuyer and Serrano 229–92; Madariaga, *España* 104–12; Martín Corrales; Martin-Márquez 54–60; Morales Lezcano, *Historia* 181–201; Rodríguez Jiménez, *¡A mí!* 19–50; Villalobos 55–88.

4 The Spanish-Moroccan War has been studied by Lécuyer and Serrano, Madariaga (*España* 67–84), Rodríguez Jiménez (*¡A mí!* 1–50).

5 On the cultural artefacts produced as a result of the war, see Lécuyer and Serrano 35–92, 135–64; López Barranco 39–66; Carrasco González 17–22; García Figueras, *Recuerdos* 7–9, 33–9, 47–52, 73–6; Martin-Márquez 101–60; Palomo xxvii–xxxii.

6 On the foundation and history of geography as an academic discipline in the nineteenth century, see Livingstone 177–214. Livingstone (216–59), Pratt (*Imperial Eyes* 1–85, 146–55, 201–27), Said (*Orientalism* 210–22, *Culture* 3–14), and the contributors to Godlewska and Smith's essay collection have written about the close links between writing, cartography, geography, military conquest, and colonial control.

7 There are few scholarly works devoted to the Spanish literature written on the Rif War: Carrasco González 71–141; López Barranco 94–358; López García; Martin-Márquez 161–219; John C. Miller; Viscarri, "Literatura" 139–57, *Nacionalismo*.

8 Thus in the section titled "Fascismo prefalangista" of the most exhaustive

history of Spanish fascist literature, there is no mention whatsoever of Africanist works (Rodríguez Puértolas, *Historia* 1: 113–19). In other accounts, Africanist literature is consigned to the theoretically problematic category of "precedents." In their chapter on Africanist literature (21–42), Carbajosa and Carbajosa view the Rif War as a formative experience that had an effect on the future ideology of Giménez Caballero, Sánchez Mazas, and Santa Marina (32); such experience led them to a "nationalistic thinking ... translated a few years later into a pre-fascism that would still take some time to find its political opportunity" (41). Likewise, Albert (*Vanguardistas* 166) detects "pre-fascism" in several passages of Tomás Borrás's novel *La pared de tela de araña* (1924), and Viscarri uses the labels *pre-fascism* and *pre-fascist* to describe and group the Africanist literature on the Rif War (*Nacionalismo*; "Literatura prefascista").

9 I use the concept of *heterotopia* as defined and elaborated by Michel Foucault in his influential lecture "Des espaces autres" (*Dits* 2: 1571–81).

10 On "military space," see Virilio and Lotringer, *Pure War* 9–10.

11 The dual space must not be equated with Homi Bhabha's *in-between* (*Location* 1–9, 40–65). To be sure, the dual space is, as happens with in-between places, a locus for the elaboration of strategies of selfhood, new intersubjective relationships and collective experiences, alternative types of contestation and collaboration, as well as cultural and individual hybridity. But unlike the in-between space, the dual space is much more than a field of negotiations between the colonial subjects and the colonized native population's identity. Moreover, it exceeds Bhabha's identification of the in-between space with subversion (62). Within the dual space, "subversion" is only one among other possible manifestations of power structures as expressed in particular localities. In its interstices may arise social identities, cultural artefacts, and habitus whose purpose consists precisely in the elimination of all otherness.

12 See Said, *Culture* 3–109. On the discourse of colonialism, see also Bhabha, *Location* 70–1, 74–84; Pratt, *Imperial Eyes*. An analysis of the rhetoric of imperialism can be found in Spurr. Richards's analysis of the Victorian "imperial archive" is equally interesting.

13 See Santiáñez, "De la tropa."

14 Entrambasaguas (1263–1315) and Albert (*Vanguardistas* 69–76) are two interesting accounts of Borrás's biography.

15 On *La pared de tela de araña*, see Albert, *Vanguardistas*, 160–8; Carrasco González 102–5; López Barranco 137–8, 144–6. Albert is the only scholar who has noticed the fascist constituents of the novel (e.g., expressionistic and vitalist aesthetics of cruelty, a bellicose discourse defending hierarchy and

the army's discipline and will to fight). In keeping with most literary scholarship, Albert prefers to employ the label *prefascism*.

16 This contrast between a lifeless landscape and the Spanish imposition of
an urban structure onto it is in fact one of the most characteristic actualizations of the binomial structure striated space / smooth space: according to
Deleuze and Guattari (474), whereas the city is the striated space par excellence, the desert constitutes a paradigmatic instance of smooth space. Both
spaces coexist not in opposition, but in a process wherein smooth space is
striated, and striated space reverts to smooth space.

17 For Lefebvre, *dominated space* is space transformed and mediated by technology, by practice (*Production* 164). Military architecture, fortifications, and
ramparts offer fine examples of dominated space (164).

18 The view of military camps in Morocco as striations of smooth space can be
seen in other colonialist works. In 1860, Alarcón already had described a
Spanish encampment as the building of a "Spanish colony," as a "city" built
on what it used to be a "silent, thick jungle" (45–6). In the same historical context as *La pared de tela de añara*'s, Asenjo Alonso's 1932 novel on the
Legion depicts the base camp of that unit at Dar Riffien as a "toy city," with
its "casino, garden, and farm," that resembles a "little Andalusian village"
(64–5; see also 175–6).

19 For a comparative approach, see Said, *Orientalism* 49–110. For Spain, see
Martín-Corrales, *La imagen*; Martin-Márquez 101–60.

20 For an overview of the literary treatment of the "Moors" in the 1920s, see
López Barranco 218–33; López García 93–9. Balfour (348–80) has explored
the function that the Moors had as the "other" among the Spaniards in the
first half of the twentieth century.

21 The belief that Spain could modernize and hence civilize Morocco was
– quite predictably – a key component of Spanish Africanism from the
mid-nineteenth century onwards. On the history and ideas of Spanish Africanism in the nineteenth and twentieth centuries, see Lécuyer and Serrano
229–92; Madariaga, *España* 104–12; Martín Corrales; Martin-Márquez; Morales Lezcano 181–201; Rodríguez Jiménez, *¡A mí!* 19–50; Villalobos 55–88.

22 In a book published in 1942, *Marruecos andaluz*, Rodolfo Gil Benumeya
would describe Chaouen in a similar fashion: "[In Chaouen] a traditional
Granada-style house has been built in that citadel. [Chaouen's Granada]
is a simple Granada, almost current, with workshops, small textile mills ...
slopes between walls ... a corner of the Albaicín, with its small roofs"
(48–9).

23 On such alterity, see Martin-Márquez.

24 Foucault claims that one of the functions of heterotopias lies in creating an

"other" real space as perfect, meticulous, and well organized as ours is chaotic, ill constructed, and jumbled. Some colonies have been concrete cases of those "heterotopias of compensation" (*Dits* 2: 1580). Although the Spanish protectorate of Morocco was far from being a well-organized space, one could argue that Morocco was viewed by some as a heterotopia that put into question the political and spiritual disorientation in the Peninsula.

25 On this score, see Martin-Márquez.

26 On the violence in the novel, see Albert, *Vanguardistas* 161–4.

27 See Albert, *Vanguardistas* 161–2.

28 The practical effects of this inversion of the colonial discourse and military practice (e.g., the deadly performance of the Civil Guard against workers and peasants participating in demonstrations, the savage behaviour of the Regulars during the military operations against the miners in Asturias in 1934, the tactics of terror employed by the Nationalists during the civil war) have been studied by Balfour (348–80). Nerín has compiled examples of the perception of the "Reds" as Moors by Africanist officers who participated in the civil war.

29 On the modern colonial wars, see Klein and Schumacher.

30 See Alarcón's *Diario de un testigo de la Guerra de África* (1860), Gaspar Núñez de Arce's *Recuerdos de la campaña de África* (1860), Víctor Balaguer's *Jornadas de gloria, o los españoles en África* (1860), and Antonio Ros de Olano's *Leyendas de África* (1860), all of them written on the Spanish-Moroccan War (1859–60). They initiated a tradition continued by Eugenio Noel (*Notas de un voluntario: Guerra de Melilla, 1909* [1910]), Carmen de Burgos (narratives and chronicles on the 1909 campaign published in *El Heraldo de Madrid*), M. Ciges Aparicio (*Entre la paz y la guerra (Marruecos)* [1912]), and most particularly Isaac Muñoz, who authored essays and countless articles on Morocco, the "Orient," and Spanish colonialism in the Maghreb.

31 In the debacle of Annual, about 9,000 Spanish troops were killed. On the routing of the Spanish army posted on the east sector of the protectorate and its political aftershock, see Balfour 112–67; La Porte; Martínez de Campos y Serrano; Pando; Servicio Histórico Militar.

32 *Notas marruecas de un soldado* has been studied by Carbajosa and Carbajosa (32–3), López Barranco (156–7, 195–6), John C. Miller (13–57), Selva (38–51), and Viscarri (*Nacionalismo* 165–248, 346–63).

33 The poetic and admiring portrayal of the reveille, an obvious index of a militaristic attitude, can be found in other fascist works, such as Luys Santa Marina's *Tras el águila del César* ([1924] 127]), Rafael García Serrano's *La fiel infantería* ([1943] 131), and Ramiro García de Ledesma's memoirs *Encrucijada en la nieve* ([1996] 62).

34 Jünger elaborated this view of combat, which permeates the books he wrote on the Great War, in *Der Kampf als inneres Erlebnis* (1922).

35 In his propagandistic dithyramb of the Legion, Carlos Micó España narrated in similarly enthusiastic terms and militaristic undertone his sorties aboard an army truck: "For those who like us are keen on open-air life, these expeditions have all the charm of a tour in the countryside alongside very good friends who go to cheerfully eat a paella in the city's environs" (*Los Caballeros* 131).

36 Virilio has written an intelligent essay on the interconnections between modern warfare, perception, and cultural artefacts (*War and Cinema*).

37 Cf. Viscarri, *Nacionalismo* 190–1.

38 Cf. Viscarri, *Nacionalismo* 204.

39 This technique can be observed in literary works on the Legion. On the Spanish reconquest of the territory taken by the Moroccans during the Disaster of Annual, the narrator of the anonymous *El contrabando de armas* (circa 1925) tells what the troops found upon arriving at the plain of Garet. Its "desolate appearance" was owed to the Moroccans, whose barbaric behaviour returned that expanse of territory to "those times" in which it was a "sterile land." Previous to the rout, the military occupation and civilian striation had brought "work and money" that transformed the area. The Spanish settlers "had cultivated the land, and the plain had that happy aspect of white farms, whereas the greenness denoted the effort invested in making productive" what until then had produced nothing (5–6). By pointing out the effects of these reversals (smooth-striated-smooth space), the author thus insinuates that only the Spaniards have the right to occupy that land.

40 Cf. Selva 47–9.

41 "A la juventud española," an anonymous article published in the fascist journal *El Fascio* (16 March 1933), argued that the "first Spanish fascists" had been those who in 1923 stood up against a weak state by giving support to or participating in Primo de Rivera's coup d'état.

42 On the concept of *field,* see Bourdieu, *Langage* 213–58, 273–5, 313–19.

43 On the castes and factions in the Spanish armed forces, see Balfour 67–70, 301–47.

44 See Ucelay-Da Cal, "Los orígenes," for an examination of the role played by the military in the forging of a Spanish fascism.

45 On the Legion, see Álvarez; Balfour 121–33, 331–4, 388–98; Galey; Rodríguez Jiménez, *¡A mí!*; Togores 112–257.

46 Other scholars have already pointed out the similarities between the Legion and fascism: Balfour 331–4; Jensen 7–8. Two excellent syntheses of the

identity and values of the legionnaires can be found in Balfour (396–8) and Togores (166–7).

47 The corpus of literature on the Legion has been studied by Carrasco González (136–8) and López Barranco (95–121).

48 On the impact that the Legion had on the press, see Rodríguez Jiménez, *¡A mí!* 184–5. On the films and documentaries related to the Legion, see F[ernández]-Fígares y Romero de la Cruz; Rodríguez Jiménez, *¡A mí!* 188–9.

49 See Rodríguez Jiménez, *¡A mí!* 184–5. The legionnaires' romantic aura constitutes a topos of the French Foreign Legion's mythology as well. A classic romanticized view of the Foreign Legion is Percival Christopher Wren's novel *Beau Geste* (1925).

50 On Millán Astray, see Jensen 140–55 and Togores's otherwise highly favourable biography.

51 The social origins of the volunteers pointed at by Millán Astray would be stressed out by the legionary literature, more often than not with deliberate inaccuracies and falsities added to enhance the romantic image of the Legion (e.g., Carretero 51; Fernández Piñero 88).

52 See also Turner 94–203.

53 Let it be added that the combat experience would consolidate the internalization of the fascist habitus, as underscored by several legionary novels (e.g., Asenjo Alonso 343; Carretero 47–8, 60, 72–6; *El contrabando* 2; Ros Andreu 111, 135, 248). War is the ultimate liminal phase. Thanks to the war, the legionnaires undergo a spiritual transformation. They are no longer mischievous, lovesick, or selfish people, but rather strong men who, purified by combat, have fully assumed as a *modus vivendi* the values learnt in the base camp.

54 See Jensen 149–51; Rodríguez Jiménez, *¡A mí!* 123–6; Togores 183–6.

55 The cult of death and the fallen is one of the most important topoi of legionary literature. See, for instance, Asenjo Alonso, who dedicates his novel to "the dead of the Legion" (13; see also 244–5, 265), or Triviño Valdivia, who likewise offers his book "to the heroes of the THIRD, to the group … that gave its life on the Fatherland's altar, to those who lived and live in their ranks, keeping the sacred fire of valor and discipline, blessed path that leads to the heights of glory, the AUTHOR dedicates this book" (3; Triviño Valdivia's capitalization).

56 Compare with Asenjo Alonso's detailed narration of the devoted procession of the coffin carrying the remains of Lieutenant Colonel Valenzuela through the streets of Melilla to the harbour (265).

57 Millán Astray played a huge role in the inculcation of the creed. Micó España emphasizes that the lieutenant coronel spoke incessantly to his legion-

naires: "This was done in order that our thought would be idle as seldom as possible. The mind of the legionnaire, occupied by virile thoughts, by *ideas macho* … is never at rest, and it creates slowly and gradually a character, with its corresponding tendencies and attitudes" (*Los Caballeros* 56).

58 Historians have argued that beneath Millán Astray's conception of the Legion lay aspects of the Bushido, or code of conduct of the samurai. On this score, see Jensen 149–51; Togores 175–83.

59 In a book written to familiarize readers with the Legion, Carlos Micó España used the language of the avant-garde manifestos to explain the reasons that prompted him to join the Legion: "Because a life without startle is tedious.… Because the literary coteries make me yawn … Because I don't know where the virtues of the race have been gone to, and I want to ascertain if they found shelter in the military's chest" (*Los Caballeros* 22–3).

60 On Franco's *Diario*, see Rodríguez-Puértolas, *Literatura* 1: 613–15; Viscarri, *Nacionalismo* 69–164. For an account of Franco's activities in Morocco, see Preston, *Franco* 32–73.

61 A history of that campaign can be read in Balfour (173–9); Martínez de Campos y Serrano; Servicio Histórico Militar; Villalobos (233–6).

62 For more information on war zones and their literary representation, see Piette.

63 On Luys Santa Marina's life and works, see Carbajosa and Carbajosa 35–41, 145–6, 173–4, 197–201, 266–70; Onrubia Rebuelta, *Escritores* 1: 41–5; Rodríguez Puértolas, *Historia* 1: 142–4, 488, 604–7; Viscarri, *Nacionalismo* 249–52. Compare my reading of *Tras el águila del César* with Carbajosa and Carbajosa's (35–41), López Barranco's (109–10, 120–1), Rodríguez Puértolas's (*Historia* 1: 142–4), Martin-Márquez's (198–202), and Viscarri's (*Nacionalismo* 249–342).

64 On this score, see Viscarri, *Nacionalismo* 255–6.

65 Dawes 74–7, 134–46; Norris 33–57; Sherry, "Great War," *Great War*, compare with Fussell. The cognitive challenge of warfare to human understanding and to modes of representation has been studied many times; see, for instance, Dawes; Hynes; Jameson, "War"; McLouhglin, "War"; Paret.

66 Cf. Viscarri, *Nacionalismo* 270–2.

67 Arendt also explored fascism's evil in her book on Eichmann's trial (*Eichmann*). On this topic see, among other works, Hewitt, "Bad Seed"; Levinas, "Souffrance"; MacCannell; Žižek, *Did Somebody* 61–8, 73–87.

68 The murderous joy felt by the legionnaires in the battlefield is present in other novels on the Legion. Among many other instances, see Asenjo Alonso; *El combate de Sidi-Abrán* 7; Fernández Piñero 10, 16, 18, 32, 35, 88.

69 The legionnaires had a particular liking for bayonet and knife-point as-

saults (Balfour 306), as reflected in legionary fiction. Asenjo Alonso's *¡¡¡Los que fuimos al Tercio!!!* (120–6), López Rienda's *Juan León, legionario* (46–7), Micó España's *Los Caballeros de la Legión* (189), Ros Andreu's *La conquista de Alhucemas* (82–3), and Triviño Valdivia's *Los del Tercio en Tánger* (247–8) narrate with gusto and in morbid detail bloody bayonet assaults joyfully conducted by the legionnaires. On the meaning and function of such assaults in an international context, see Bourke 41–3, 77–80; Grossman 120–6.

70 With the blessing of the minister of war, the high commissioner of Spain in the protectorate, General Felipe Alfau y Mendoza, ordered in 1913 the beheading of prisoners to teach the Moroccans a lesson (Balfour 176). Thereafter, that measure became common currency in the colonial army's dealings with the enemy. In the 1920s, the Legion put it into practice with a vengeance. In a book published by the prestigious publishing house Rivadeneyra, the journalist and legionnaire Micó España described with as much relish as obscene exhibitionism the technique employed by the legionnaires to decapitate two Moroccans shot down by his unit: "And drawing a jackknife the macabre task of beheading the Moor's corpse starts out ... It is more difficult than what it seems, to cut off a head: a laborious job and also one requiring skill. One has to look for the interstices – as when one opens an oyster – of the vertebrae, put the machete through one of them, and then jack up" (*Los Caballeros* 175).

71 Schmitt elaborated his concept of *absolute enmity* in *Theory of the Partisan* (85–95).

72 An excellent account of the Legion's daily life can be found in Balfour (388–98, 427–30).

73 An almost identical scene is to be found in Pedro García Suárez's 1945 fascist war novel *Legión 1936* (9–11).

74 Cf. Viscarri, *Nacionalismo* 306–8.

75 This threat to civil society from soldiers resented by the civilian population is at the core of other coetaneous war novels. In *Le Feu*, the war has awoken in the soldiers – all of them peasants and workers – a class consciousness tinted with revolutionary undertones; in Barbusse's novel, the war may lead to socialist revolutionary action. The main characters of Remarque's *Im Westen nichts Neues* experience a similar political awakening.

76 In his book on the Legion (*Los Caballeros* 47, 250–1), Micó España expresses opinions against leftist attitudes and political organizations that belong to the anti-communist and anti-democratic discourse underlying legionary novels like Asenjo Alonso's and Ros Andreu's.

77 And yet one ought to be careful in the analysis of the fascists' sexuality, as Carroll (147–70) and Mosse (*Fascist* 175–82) have cautioned. The presumed

connection between fascism and homosexuality (see Theweleit) could be interpreted, in Frost's opinion, as a function of anti-fascist propaganda, for it amounted to a denigratory accusation of fascist "sexual degeneracy." The film industry has exploited the image of the fascist as a sexual degenerate: Liliana Cavani's *Il portiere di notte* (1974) and Pier Paolo Pasolini's disturbing *Salò o le 120 giornate di Sodoma* (1975) are two cases in point.

78 Like other fascist intellectuals (e.g., the Italian Futurists) or writers whose literary production has been associated with fascism (e.g., Ernst Jünger, most particularly in his book *Der Kampf als inneres Erlebnis*) defending war, Sánchez Mazas radicalizes in fact a vision of war and conflict born in the political discourse (e.g., the Girondists during the sessions of the National Assembly in the winter of 1791–2) and in the philosophic thinking (Herder, Kant, Fichte, and Hegel in Germany, Joseph de Maistre in France) of the end of the eighteenth century and the first decades of the nineteenth century. Kunisch and Münkler offer a good overview of that "renaissance of war."

79 On language as an instrument of warfare, see Pratt, "Harm's Way" 1515–31.

80 On the brutalization of politics in Germany, see, for instance, Mosse, *Fallen Soldiers* 159–81.

81 Sánchez Mazas offers a view of the armed forces and their function within the state put into practice years later in Nazi Germany and Franco's Spain, and consolidated on a worldwide scale after the Second World War. For Virilio and other thinkers, the post-industrial society has subordinated political life and economic activity to the military. The state, according to Virilio, is presently dominated by a military caste, it is a state-army, and the army constitutes the ultimate representation of the state (Virilio, *L'Insécurité* 75, 89, 91, 92, 122–3, 124, 126–7, 146–8, 152–6; Virilio and Lotringer, *Pure War* 15–17, 27, 31, 92, 164, 171). On this score, see also Santiáñez, *Goya/Clausewitz* 119–29. Sánchez Mazas's uncompromising defence of the military caste belongs, therefore, to the slow, steady, insidious militarization of the world.

82 Sánchez Mazas was certainly not alone in proclaiming this attitude. Articles by Gonzalo Queipo de Llano, Baldomero Argente, and Millán Astray published in the *Revista de Tropas Coloniales* display a habitus whose messianism was addressed at rescuing Spain from its "decadence." In an article published in that journal in February 1924, Queipo de Llano claims that Spain can be regenerated only from the outside, by the army in Morocco, for it is not tainted by the lethargy and corruption of the metropolitan culture (qtd. in Balfour 328; for an analysis of this attitude so common among Africanist officers, see Balfour 65, 237, 303–4, 311–12, 321, 325–8, 331–4, 346–7).

83 See also Virilio, *L'Espace* 157–61, *L'Insécurité* 159, 161, 191–2; Virilio and

Lotringer, *Pure War* 93–6. Focusing on the urban rather than on the processes of decolonization, Lefebvre reaches a similar conclusion (*Urban* 170–1).
Today's "global city," defined as a "political center for the administration,
protection, and operation of a vast territory" (170), is a centre of power that
requires wealth. While in the past the entire metropolitan land sucked up
wealth from its colonies, today "domination is consolidated in a physical
locale, a capital … As a result, control is exercised throughout the national
territory, which is transformed into a semicolony" (171).

3 Spatial Myths

1 On Italian Fascist intellectuals, see Gregor, *Mussolini's Intellectuals*; Hamilton 1–89. The multimedia edition of De Felice's *Mussolini* includes useful
   biographical information of many Fascist intellectuals and politicians. For
   general information on fascist intellectuals, see Hamilton; Mosse, *Fascist*
   95–116.
2 For more information on Sánchez Mazas's stay in Italy, see Carbajosa and
   Carbajosa 43–51; Rodríguez Jiménez, *Historia* 29–35. Some of the articles
   that he published in *ABC* in the 1920s have been included in Sánchez Mazas, *Las terceras*.
3 See *Circuito imperial* 48–9 for Giménez Caballero's exalted remembrance of
   his epiphany in Rome. On this episode and the writer's ideas on Rome, see
   Albert, "'El saetazo'"; Carbajosa and Carbajosa 51–6; Foard 108–32; Rodríguez Jiménez, *Historia* 56–7; Selva 106–7.
4 The rise and consolidation of Fascism in Italy awoke the interest of journalists, intellectuals, and politicians as diverse as Josep Pla, Ramiro de Maeztu,
   Álvaro Alcalá-Galiano, Gabriel Alomar, Carmen de Burgos, and José Ortega
   y Gasset. For a representative collection of texts on Italian Fascism published in Spain between 1922 and 1929, see Peloille.
5 The best work on the "literary court of José Antonio" is Carbajosa and Carbajosa's. On Spanish fascist intellectuals in the context of cultural life in
   Spain during the 1920s and 1930s, see Bécarud and López Campillo 26–31,
   65–73, 76–80, 88–91, 110–14; Caudet; García Queipo de Llano; Payne, *Fascism* 51–65; Peña Sánchez.
6 On La Conquista de Estado, see Ellwood 29–32; Ledesma Ramos, *¿Fascismo?*
   77–94; Payne, *Fascism* 58–61; Rodríguez Jiménez, *Historia* 66–72.
7 Consistent with a pattern characteristic of the scholarship devoted to the
   principal figures of Spanish fascism, little has been written on Redondo
   aside from laudatory works produced by fellow fascists (e.g., Martinell Gifre,
   Martínez de Bedoya, Sánchez). See the more recent and reliable contribu-

tions of Demetrio Ramos (pseud. "Mónico Mélida Monteagudo"), Mínguez Goyanes, Payne (*Fascism* 61–5, 254–5), and Rodríguez Jiménez (*Historia* 87–8).

8 See Ellwood 32–3; Payne, *Fascism* 61–3; Rodríguez Jiménez, *Historia* 87–102.

9 See Ellwood 33–5; Payne, *Fascism* 63–5, 85–6, 77–8, 98–100; Rodríguez Jiménez, *Historia* 102–18.

10 In addition to the already mentioned authoritative histories of Spanish fascism by Ellwood, Payne (*Fascism*), and Rodríguez Jiménez (*Historia*), see also Gallego and Morente Jiménez's collection of essays devoted to the social and cultural origins of Francoism, as well as Jiménez Campo's, Mainer's (*Falange* 16–27), and Pastor's works on the origins of fascism in Spain.

11 See, for instance, Elorza 69–82; Labanyi, *Myth* 35–41; Prill; Rodríguez Puértolas, *Historia* 1: 74–80.

12 Some fascist myths are the Leader, the "people's community," the fatherland, the nation's origins, the nation's "new birth," the "martyrs" of fascism, the fallen in the battlefield, the hero, war as a cleansing activity (and as a "crusade" in the case of the Spanish Civil War as viewed by the Nationalists), the race, and the "new fascist State," considered by Gentile ("Fascism" 244) as the dominant myth. On fascism and myth, see, for instance, Falasca-Zamponi 42–118; Gentile, "Fascism" 229–51, *Sacralization*; Griffin, *Modernism*; Kershaw, *The "Hitler Myth"*; Michaud; Mosse, *Fascist*, passim.

13 The mobilizing function of the myth in fascist politics goes back, as Sternhell (*Birth* 36–91) and other scholars have argued, to Georges Sorel's view of the myth as the best instrument to rally the workers and inspire in them immediate action against the state.

14 For an approach to "mythical space and place" through the lens of human geography, see Tuan's pathbreaking book (85–100).

15 On "becoming a Fascist," see Bosworth 121–49.

16 See Mann for a comparative sociological study of who the fascists and their sympathizers were (their class and cultural origins, their motivations, their rise to power, their ideas, their fears, their hopes) in Italy, Germany, Spain, Austria, Hungary, and Romania.

17 Ledesma Ramos himself wrote an essay, *Discurso a las juventudes de España* (1935), the main objective of which consisted precisely in the indoctrination of Spain's youth (in ¿*Fascismo?* 207–334).

18 Other articles and speeches by Primo de Rivera dealing with the fascist habitus are "Carta a un estudiante" (*Obras* 217–18), "Discurso de proclamación" (*Obras* 189–97), "El ruido y el estilo" (*Obras* 913–16), "Entraña y estilo" (*Obras* 417–19), "España, incómoda" (*Obras* 451–3), "Juventudes a la intemperie" (*Obras* 687–92), "Sentido heroico de la milicia" (*Obras* 615).

19 Blaming his father's downfall on the opposition of the intellectuals to his regime (see his essay "Los intelectuales y la dictadura," in *Obras* 9–13), Primo de Rivera did all his best to attract writers and intellectuals to Falange. In Madrid, the nightly social gatherings at the coffee shops El Café Europeo, El Comercial, Café Lyon, and the snobbish dinners held at the Hotel de París created a lasting good relationship between Primo de Rivera and right-wing young intellectuals (on this issue, see Carbajosa and Carbajosa 99–105).

20 Logically, this habitus entails too the assimilation of the actions needed to lead other men. An interesting fascist approach to this topic is to be found in a lecture read by Emilio R. Tarduchy on 18 May 1942, published shortly afterwards as a pamphlet with the title *Nociones del arte de mandar aplicadas a la Falange.* Not to be overlooked is the double status of the author: colonel of the Army and first-hour Falangist.

21 Compare with the four tablet maps commissioned by the Fascist government and displayed in 1934 on the outer wall of the Basilica of Maxentius overlooking the Via dell'Impero in Rome. By recreating four moments of the Roman Empire, these maps aimed at reinforcing the geopolitics of the Fascist state. Like the maps analysed earlier, the four maps are striking instances of the fascist cartographic imagination as well as its underlying political function. As Minor observes, "As part of public art, the maps on the Via dell'Impero were powerful tools in the forging of connection between classical Roman civilization and that of the empire of the Fascists" (160).

22 Although it would rarely enjoy absolute hegemony within the Franco regime, from the wake of the civil war onwards FET-JONS would lose no opportunity to stamp the fascist habitus on the younger generations. An interesting instance is Julián Pemartín's booklet *Teoría de la Falange* (1941), to a large extent devoted to the Falangist's "style" (25–37), defined by the author as a "way of being" (33). As late as 1974, in a book bearing the revealing title of *Ética y estilo falangistas* Hillers de Luque prescribed a series of fascist norms to the youth.

23 A fascinating literary articulation of the link between fascist habitus and myth is Rafael García Serrano's *opera prima, Eugenio o proclamación de la Primavera* (1938). The thematization of the fascist habitus in novelistic discourse also can be found in classics of fascist literature such as Felipe Ximénez de Sandoval's *Camisa azul (Retrato de un falangista)* (1939), José María Alfaro's *Leoncio Pancorbo* (1942), and Gonzalo Torrente Ballester's *Javier Mariño: Historia de una conversión* (1943).

24 For more information on the myth of Castile in the nineteenth-century Spanish nationalist historiography, see Fox.

25 I borrow this expression from Peter Gay, who explores the "hunger for wholeness" in Weimar culture (70–101). On the sense of cultural crisis and the "culture wars" of the 1920s in Germany, see also Evans's cogent synthesis (*Coming* 118–29).

26 Many pages have been written on the *völkisch* movements and ideals (an "idealism debased," in Stackelberg's apt expression) in Germany and Austria from their inception in the early nineteenth century until the Third Reich. For an excellent introduction to this phenomenon, see Mosse, *Crisis*. More recently, Hamann has published an outstanding historical analysis of the *völkisch* currents in turn-of-the-century Vienna, which had a lasting effect, as she demonstrates, on the young Hitler.

27 See Castillo Cáceres 279–85; Rodríguez Jiménez, *Historia* 92–5. In order to avoid possible misunderstandings, I have restricted the use of the term *völkisch* to the Austro-German world, while to refer to the *völkisch* world view as manifested in other national cultures I have chosen the English word *folkish*.

28 In 1939, Manuel Iribarren would write a whole novel, titled *La ciudad*, based on these folkish views of the city. "Spain," the author argues in the introduction, "has never been a Metropolis"; instead, "it has been and still is Country, Village, Region" (9).

29 For detailed information on fascist anti-Semitism in Spain, see Álvarez Chillida 340–7; Preston, *Spanish Holocaust* 42, 44–7; Martín Gijón; Rodríguez Jiménez, "El discurso."

30 See, for instance, "El peligro judío" (27 June 1931), "El judío internacional: Intervención de los hebreos americanos en la revolución rusa" (28 September 1931), "Las garras del judaísmo" (21 December 1931), "El precursor de los Protocolos" (11 July 1932), "Stawiski el judío" (15 January 1934), all of them published in *Libertad*.

31 On Spanish anti-Semitism since the Second Republic until the Second World War, see Álvarez Chillida 301–420.

32 Catalans were, so to speak, the Jews of Spain. Catalonia's wealth, higher level of modernity, and demands for political autonomy made its citizens the "enemies" of Spain. There is no shortage of fascist essays against Catalonia, one of Spanish fascism's bêtes noires. Ledesma Ramos's obsession with Catalonia is a case in point; see, for instance, some of the articles he published in *La Conquista del Estado* in 1931: "Después de las elecciones: ¡Alerta a las Constituyentes!" (*Escritos* 239–41), "El separatismo de Cataluña" (*Escritos* 271), "España, una e indivisible" (*Escritos* 211–13), "Hay que hacer frente a las procacidades de Maciá" (*Escritos* 228–9), "La peculiaridad y la política de Cataluña" (*Escritos* 124), "La vida política" (*Escritos* 290–3), "Nuestra an-

gustia hispana" (*Escritos* 255–8), "¿Qué pasa en Cataluña?" (*Escritos* 145). In *¿Fascismo?* (77–94) Ledesma Ramos himself elaborated on La Conquista del Estado's "battle" against Catalan "separatism." Present-day anti-Catalanism is often expressed with a language and tone not very different from the fascists' in the 1930s.

33 See also Churruca's "Nuestra misión" (*Libertad* [27 August 1934]), yet another call to Castilians to take up arms.

34 Likewise, during the "years of struggle" the Nazis sought tactical support from the rural areas. Their success caused them "to shift in their propaganda from the urban working class to other sectors of the population" (Evans, *Coming* 209).

35 In a similar vein, the anonymous author of "Hacia la revolución nacional sindicalista" (in *F.E.* [12 July 1934]) asserted, "Any revolution needs a technique, a tactics, and myths." Ledesma Ramos's conception of the function of the myth in politics has its source in Gustave Le Bon's (*Les Lois psychologiques de l'évolution des peuples* [1894], *La Psychologie des foules* [1895]) and Georges Sorel's (*Réflexions sur la violence* [1907]) remarks on the importance of myth in relation to the nature and behaviour of the masses.

36 See also Ledesma Ramos, *¿Fascismo?* 166.

37 On Alfaro and *Leoncio Pancorbo*, see Carbajosa and Carbajosa 137–8, 157–8, 262–6; Castillo Cáceres 366–8; Cueva Puente 373–86; Rodríguez Puértolas, *Historia* 1: 572–3, 2: 644–6.

38 This type of fascist character can be found in Drieu la Rochelle's *Gilles* (Gilles), Brasillach's *Les Sept couleurs* (Patrice), Ledesma Ramos's *El sello de la muerte* (Antonio de Castro), and Torrente Ballester's *Javier Mariño* (Javier Mariño). For an introduction to the fascist hero in Spanish literature, see Gil Casado.

39 See Ucelay-Da Cal, *Llegar a capital,* "Spanish Civil War."

40 See Bailey; Jenkyns.

41 On the reception of Rome in European culture between the French Revolution and the Second World War, see Edwards.

42 In addition to Painter's book on Mussolini's Rome, which covers many issues related to the Fascist reconstruction of Rome (e.g., archeological works, architecture, population, neighbourhoods, housing, urban changes and building constructions made apropos of the sports, education, and celebrations), see Ciucci, *Gli architetti* 77–92; Zalasca-Zamponi 90–5.

43 On the impact of classical antiquity in Germany, see Losemann; Scobie. Spotts has written an interesting analysis of Hitler as "The Master Builder" (311–98), and Speer (part 1, especially 59–98, 122–39, 158–80) has provided us with a detailed, fascinating panorama of Hitler's vision of and obsession with architecture.

44 The *romanità* was a discourse deployed "to cement group cohesion and legitimate action in the name of continuity with ancient Rome" (Wyke 189) that
crystalized during the *Risorgimento*. Italy's expansionism in the early 1900s,
which had its climax in the military expedition to Libya of 1911–12, meant
a shift in the language of *romanità*. From its earlier republicanism, now the
romanità conveyed imperial ambitions. D'Annunzio's bellicose poetry of that
period and pro-imperialist motion pictures like Enrico Guazzoni's *Marcan-
tonio e Cleopatra* (1914) and Giovanni Pastrone's *Cabiria* (1914) were corner-
stones of a reformulation of the *romanità* adopted a few years later by the
Fascists. On the imperialist *romanità* of the 1910s, see Wyke 188–204. The
Fascist cult of the *romanità* has been widely studied; see, for instance, Painter
71–6; Stone; Visser 5–22.

45 Scholarship on the Escuela Romana del Pirineo is extremely scarce. Some
exceptions are Carbajosa and Carbajosa (1–22), De Prada (27), Mainer
(*Falange* 21–3), and Ortega Gallarzagoitia (334–5).

46 Useful introductions to Basterra are Carbajosa and Carbajosa 9–10, 12; Duplá Ansuategui; Mainer, "Para leer" xiii–lviii; Rodríguez Puértolas, *Historia*
1: 93, 103–6.

47 Mussolini himself, let us remember, was considered as the new Augustus.
Works such as Giuseppe Bottai's *L'Italia di Augusto e l'Italia d'oggi* (1937) and
Emilio Balbo's *Protagonisti dei due imperi di Roma: Augusto e Mussolini* (1940)
drew parallels between Augustus and the Duce.

48 On Sánchez Mazas and the Escuela Romana del Pirineo, see Carbajosa and
Carbajosa 4–5, 6–8, 14–16.

49 However, in later fascist discourse – especially from the civil war onwards
– the opposite view would be more common. For instance, in "España en
la opinión romana" (1941) Riber compares the surviving defenders of the
besieged Alcázar of Toledo with the people of Numantia (345–6).

50 In the 1930s and 1940s, other journalistic pieces developed similar views on
the connection between Castile and Rome; see, for instance, Arturo Iglesias
García's "Canto a Castilla" (*Libertad* [11 June 1934]) and Eugenio Monte's
"Castilla en pie" (*F.E.* [7 December 1933]).

51 On the connections between FE-JONS and Italian Fascism, see, for instance,
Payne, *Fascism* 160–2, 88–9, 154–6, 173, 191. Concerning the repercussion
of Fascist culture in Spain, see Peña Sánchez.

52 In a speech read on 12 May 1935 at the Gran Teatro de Córdoba, he reiterates this connection: the most glorious Cordovans, among them Seneca and
Trajan, did not aspire to a small new order for Cordova or Spain; rather
they went to Rome "to take charge of the world. These Cordovans knew that
by ordering the world they were ordering Spain" (*Obras* 549).

53 Compare that series with other articles by Giménez Caballero on Fascist

Rome, especially "Primacía del trabajo" (*El Fascio: Haz Hispano* [16 March 1933]) and "Bohemios, no: cófrades" (*Arriba* [21 March 1935]).

54 Commenting on the fascists' cult of national symbols and myths, as well as their preoccupation with mythical national origins, Mosse reminds us that "Himmler sent an expedition to the Tibet in order to discover Aryan origins … [and] the Italian Fascist Foreign Ministry sponsored archeological expeditions to revive the idea of the Roman Empire" (*Fascist* 35). On the other hand, the search for the mythical origins of the nation cohabited with the fascists' self-perception of being the "men of the future" (35).

55 See Arendt, *Origins* 123–302, for a classic study of the close connection between twentieth-century totalitarianism and imperialism as conceived of and carried out in the nineteenth century by democratic societies like the United Kingdom and France.

56 On the concept of *imperio* in fascist discourse as well as the imperial ambitions of Spain in the early years of the Franco regime, see Blinkhorn 21–3; Cano Ballesta, *Estrategias* 21–55; Caudet 489–92; Chueca 43–51; Gibson 31; González Calleja and Limón Nevado 57–71; Naval 56–60; Payne, *Fascism* 310–62, *Franco* 61–205; Rodríguez Puértolas, *Historia* 1: 64–7, 374–5, 396–8, 439–44, 2: 856–7, 889–90, 893–4, 911–12, 990–1; Saz Campos, *España* 267–97, *Fascismo* 269–71; Tusell, *Franco*, Ucelay-Da Cal, *El imperialismo* 800–79.

57 See, for instance, Payne, *Franco* 61–205; Tusell, *Franco*.

58 A critical review and a taxonomy of the different theories of empire, all of them predicated on that definition, can be found in Doyle (11–47, 123–38).

59 For instance: Bosworth and Romano (on Italian expansionism); Kallis, *Fascist Ideology* (comparative approach to imperialism in Fascist Italy and Nazi Germany); Mazower (on Nazi Germany's expansionism in Europe).

60 Some of the earliest fascist texts propounding an imperial project for Spain are Rafael Sánchez Mazas's chronicles on the Rif War and Ramón de Basterra's poems on his sojourn in Rome as well as his diptych *Virulo: Las Mocedades* (1924) and *Virulo: Mediodía* (1927). The zenith of the fascist discourse of empire came in the 1930s and early 1940s. In addition to the texts selected here, see Esteban Calle Iturrino's *Cantos de guerra y de imperio* (1937), Francisco Fuentenebro's *Poemas imperiales* (1938), José Sigüenza's *Poemas del Imperio* (1938), and Luis Rosales and Luis Felipe Vivanco's anthology *Poesía heroica del Imperio* (1940).

61 Here I follow Wittgenstein's theory of meaning as laid out in his *Philosophical Investigations*: "For a *large* class of cases – though not for all – in which we employ the word *meaning* it can be defined thus: the meaning of a word is its use in the language" (§ 43). *Imperio* and related words form one of those cases in which the meaning of a word consists of its use.

62 See Preston, *Franco* 49.

63 Point 3 of the twenty-five points program adopted in 1920 by the Deutsche
    Arbeiterpartei (as the Nationalsozialistische Deutsche Arbeiterpartei was
    then called) explicitly demands "land and territory (colonies) for the nour-
    ishment of our people and for settling our surplus population" (in Hitler,
    Speeches 1: 103). Most likely borrowing the expression from the hugely suc-
    cessful novel by Hans Grimm *Volk ohne Raum* (1926), the Nazis would later
    characterize the Germans as a "people without space," an expression that
    summarizes perfectly Cordero Torres's ideas on the topic.

64 See also Santiago Montero Díaz's *Idea del Imperio* (1943), a pamphlet in
    which the author lays out his own exo-imperialist project. As was the case
    in Nazi Germany and Fascist Italy, the Spanish educational system fostered
    the view of Spain as an imperial country through textbooks written for the
    youth: L. Ortiz Muñoz's *Glorias imperiales* (1940) constitutes one early ex-
    ample of this phenomenon.

65 Rooted in the construction of a national identity, the need felt by some to
    regenerate a country perceived as being in a process of decadence, a wish
    to re-establish Spain's prestige in the international arena, and a longing for
    empire, the discourse on *Hispanidad* began to develop in the last thirty years
    of the nineteenth century. A means to re-articulate the Spanish hegemony
    in Latin America, it centred on the Spanish legacy in Latin America, the
    cultural unity among the peoples of Spain and Latin America, and the lead-
    ing role that Spain had to assume vis-à-vis the Latin American nations. On
    the *Hispanidad* in Spanish politics and intellectual life since the nineteenth
    century through the 1930s, see Delgado Gómez-Escalonilla 15–70; Loureiro
    65–76; Rama.

66 On *Hispanidad* as a means of cultural and political exo-imperialism in Span-
    ish fascist discourse as well as in the political practice of the Franco regime,
    see García-Moreno Barco; González Calleja and Limón Nevado; Saz Cam-
    pos, *España* 276–81.

67 On this score, see also his *Discurso* 236.

68 See also Solas García 151–4.

4 The City

1 Foucault, who considers politics as the continuation of war through other
    means (*Dits*, 2: 171–2), has pointed out that there are no relations of power
    without resistance (*Dits*, 2: 1060–1). Consequently, the formation of dis-
    courses and the genealogy of knowledge should be analysed by considering
    the tactics and strategies of power, which deploy "through implantations,

distributions, demarcations, control of territories, organizations of domains that could well make up a sort of geopolitics" (*Dits*, 2: 39–40).

2 See also Ledesma Ramos, *Discurso* 233–4.

3 For Virilio, "The masses are not a population ... but the multitude of passers-by. The revolutionary contingent attains its ideal form not in the place of production, but in the street, where for a moment it stops being a cog in the technical machine and itself becomes a motor (machine of attack), in other words, a *producer of speed*" (*Speed* 29; see also 29–48).

4 But once the political goals have been attained, the totalitarian governments hold sway over, by their very nature, the circulation of the masses (Virilio, *Speed* 41).

5 In a novel published in 1939, Manuel Iribarren would refer in very explicit terms to the struggle for hegemony vis-à-vis the conquest of urban space before the outbreak of the civil war: two powerful and conflicting forces, fascism and communism, prepare to fight each other "to attain hegemony in the city" (*La ciudad* 14).

6 According to Mann (313), seventy-five Falangists, 269 anarcho-syndicalists, 275 socialists and communists, and sixty-two rightists were murdered for political reasons during the Second Republic.

7 For a thorough account of the violent activities conducted by or related to FE-JONS, see Payne, *Fascism* 102–14, 122, 187–8, 189–90. For a fascist narrative of those activities, see Ledesma Ramos, *¿Fascismo?* 161–4, 169–73, 175–6, 193; Ramos González. For an introduction to Nazi violence prior to 1933, see Bessel, *Political Violence*; Evans, *Coming* 220–1, 229–30, 266–88; Theweleit. For a historical account of Fascist violence before Mussolini's dictatorship, see Bosworth 93–214. On fascist paramilitarism in Italy, Germany, Austria, Romania, Hungary, and Spain, see Mann.

8 Since objects are constituted as objects of discourse, it is theoretically problematic to differentiate between discursive (linguistic) and non-discursive (behavioural) practices. Hence the expression *discursivity of the social*, borrowed from Laclau and Mouffe.

9 On the city's textuality, see, among other works, de Certeau 91–130; Donald; Frisby; Lefebvre, *Production* 130–40, 142–3, *Urban* 49–53, *Writings* 100–3, 137–8; Lehan; Pike; Sharpe and Wallock, "From" 1–50; Wirth-Nesher. For an account on the link between the urban and the textual in Spanish cities, see Resina's collection of critical essays. In addition, see Sansot's phenomenological approach to the "poetics" of the city.

10 See Mainer, "De Madrid" 181–98, for an excellent content-oriented approach to Madrid as seen by key fascist writers. Information on the fascist literary treatment of Madrid also can be found in Castillo Cáceres (311–17, 404–77), Lacarta (252–67), and Ricci (252–71).

11 *Madrid de corte a checa* has been and still is the fascist novel most favoured by
readers and literary critics alike. On Foxá's novel, see Bertrand de Muñoz,
La guerra 1: 208–9; Carbajosa and Carbajosa 153–7, 248–50 (biographical
information on 27–8, 66–7, 90–1, 139–41, 194–5, 250); Entrambasaguas
891–941 (with biographical information); Hickey 419–35; Lentzen 444–59;
Mainer, "De Madrid" 182–3; Martínez Cachero, "Cuatro" 290–4; Oropesa
221–37; Ricci 252–71; Ríos-Font 129–36, 138–9; Rodríguez Puértolas, *Historia* 1: 296–301; Schmolling 97–121; Umbral 237–40; Varela 95–109.

12 For information on the history of Madrid in the 1930s, see Bravo Morata,
vols 7–9; Juliá [Díaz], *Madrid* 41–92, "Madrid" 393–410; Pla; Tusell Gómez,
La Segunda 9–19.

13 Named after the notorious Soviet secret police agency created by Lenin
in 1917, the chekas in Spain's main cities were detention centres wherein
detainees would be interrogated, sometimes tortured, and judged. On the
origin, nature, organization, and functioning of the chekas in Madrid, see
Cervera 60–8; Montoliú, *Madrid en la guerra civil* 1: 93–7. For "historiographic" accounts on the chekas written from a pro-Franco or fascist perspective,
see Casas de la Vega 75–91, 103–19; Flaquer; and the recent revisionist book
by Vidal.

14 Likewise, in Fernández Arias' *Madrid bajo 'El Terror,' 1936–1937* (1937) the
dialogue or lack thereof constitutes one of the book's main devices. Although the many dialogues inserted in this book involve anti-Republican
individuals only, they generate an urban atmosphere. Here the dialogue
does not reproduce antagonism between hegemonic formations; instead,
it is itself antagonism against the enemy, for it is presented as a form of life
conflicting with the Republic. Accordingly, the narrator closes his narration
of the execution of rebels on the night of 20–1 July 1936 by writing, "That
night, in Madrid there were no dialogues" (50). Thus the Republic implies
lack of dialogue, of significant conversation.

15 See Lefebvre, *Urban* 124, 172–80.

16 A fascist depiction of Madrid's periphery, seen as a morally abhorrent and
physically disgusting area, can be found in Manuel Iribarren's 1939 novel
La ciudad: "The street where he lived, dirty and winding, was inhabited by
cheap whores and louts. That was a poor area ... where the metropolis undesirables shelter their moral and material failure ... Each mole is a pathological case; the whole neighbourhood, a clinic open up to the psychiatrists'
unquenchable curiosity" (230).

17 Guillén Salaya would later become a fascist; for a good introduction to
his literary production vis-à-vis his political ideology, see Mainer, *Literatura*
67–100.

18 On the masses, see the classic interpretations of Gustave Le Bon's seminal

Psychologie des foules (1895), Gabriel Tarde's *L'Opinion et la foule* (1901), Sigmund Freud's *Massenpsychologie und Ich-Analyse* (1921), and Elias Canetti's idiosyncratic *Masse und Macht* (1960). For a contemporary analysis, see Laclau's splendid *On Populist Reason*. Useful information on the masses in modern literature can be found in Lehan (8–9, 71), Pike (110–16), and Williams (*Country* 215–32).

19 Tusell Gómez develops this idea in *La Segunda* 15–19.

20 Reflecting on this phenomenon, the fascist journalist José-Vicente Puente underscored the close link between the masses' use of urban space and hegemony. In Puente's view, the cities initiated the processes that led to the war: "Resentful masses, the people living in the cities' outskirts have set about to crush the ruling minorities … And they have been led, egged on … by failed hicks" who avenge their own failure on the others' success (93–4).

21 A classic psychoanalytic study of the masses as seen by the fascists can be found in Theweleit (1: 229–49, 2: 3–142).

22 This is one of the main topoi articulating the fascist depiction of Madrid. In order to condition the readers' view of the city between 1931 and 1939, fascist authors tended to portray Madrid as a locus reshaped, disciplined, and controlled by the "Russians," a noun by which they referred to those "evil foreigners" whose mission was to destroy Spain. The title of a 1940 novel by Francisco Camba, *Madridgrado*, condenses that component of the fascist tendentious production of a deformed image of the city and the Republicans (see also Fernández Arias's *Madrid bajo 'El Terror'* 100). On this subject, see, for instance, Castillo Cáceres 404–77; Núñez Seixas 180–9, 245–61.

23 The fascist soldier's violent gaze upon Madrid can be found in other works: García Suárez's *Legión 1936* (129–32, 141, 174), Puente's *Madrid recobrado* (39, 221, 237–8), Ximénez de Sandoval's *Camisa azul* (354–5).

24 On this score, see Ucelay-Da Cal, "National Conflict" 38–54. Two outstanding introductions in English to the Spanish Civil War are Preston's (*Spanish Civil War*) and Beevor's (*Battle*).

25 On the different "cities" in wartime Madrid, see Bahamonde Magro 329–43. For a detailed analysis of the organization, activities, and demography of what the author calls "clandestine Madrid," see Cervera. Historical accounts of Madrid during the war can be found in Montoliú (*Madrid en la guerra civil*) and Juliá Díaz ("Madrid" 411–28). Two interesting approaches to Madrid's everyday life in that period are Abella's and Díaz-Plaja's.

26 Equally interesting are the chronicles on wartime Madrid by pro-Franco journalists such as Alberto Martín Fernández, Víctor Ruiz Albéniz, and Manuel Sánchez del Arco, some of which have been compiled by Figueres.

27 The novel would be reedited in 1940, 1944, and 1963. In 1962, Borrás
published a pendant to *Checas de Madrid*: his war diary *Madrid teñido de rojo*.
On *Checas de Madrid*, see Albert, "El tremendismo" 106–8, *Vanguardistas*
375–409; Nora 3: 377–8; Rodríguez Puértolas, *Historia* 2: 635–8; Schmolling
137–54.

28 Much has been written on the violence unleashed by the war; among other
works, see Cervera; Juliá Díaz, *Victimas*; Reig Tapia, *Ideología, Violencia*; and
most particularly, Preston, *Spanish Holocaust*.

29 The narrator of *Madridgrado* writes that the militiamen tear off "with their
paws the damask of the armchairs where the nobility's young ladies had sat
for centuries" (Camba 126).

30 A commonplace in fascist urban writing, the changes imposed on private
clubs or semi-public places belonging to the aristocracy and bourgeoisie
recur also in Ximénez de Sandoval's *Camisa azul* (see, for instance, the narrator's contrast between the Círculo de Bellas Artes before the war and its
wartime function – to host a cheka; in 112–13).

31 A Catholic reading of this matter can be found in Huidobro Pardo's 1940
Escarmentemos (219–26). For the author, not only are the streets paths connecting spaces and places. In addition, they express the connection, or lack
thereof, between the citizens and God. Accordingly, as soon as the people
of Madrid closed out its worship of God, God abandoned the city to its fate.
As always in fascist urban writing, cities are, or ought to be, unidimensional
loci. The law of God must determine the urban grammar as well as its actualization by the citizens. To avoid the horrible consequences of the violation
of said law, the citizens must always abide by the government's dispositions.
Hence the law of God projects itself into another space – the state. "When
in the future some government's regulations are detrimental to us, let us
remember the past horrors and compare them with the detriments. Let us
learn to obey" (258–9).

32 This idea has been elaborated by Albert in *Vanguardistas* (391–400).

33 As soon as the war was over, journalistic articles and stories of all kinds
celebrated the "heroic" activities of the fifth column. This is the case of
Fuertes's four-installment reportage, published in October 1939 in *Arriba*,
and Puente's mention of what he calls "pale heroes" in *Madrid recobrado* (25–
8, 31–4). See Cervera 213–337, an extensive history of the fifth column's
clandestine network.

34 Like the conspirator, the saboteur, or the professional revolutionary, the
spy working to attain revolutionary aims feels at home in geographies of
hegemonic practices like the one we are here discussing. In Pierre Drieu
la Rochelle's literary work are some of the most conspicuous fascist literary

representations of politically motivated personal duplicity and espionage (e.g., *Béloukia* [1936], *Gilles* [1939, 1942], *L'Homme à cheval* [1943]).

35 See Cervera 263–82.

36 See, for instance, Fernández Arias 70–2; Puente, *Madrid recobrado* 49–52.

37 See Thomas 79–81, 87–9.

38 Three weeks after the end of the war, Puente wrote that the socialists, militiamen, and left-wing politicians in general "gave Madrid the appearance of an immense prison" altogether different from the noble and usual atmosphere of the city; those politicians "surrounded the streets with a net of intrigues and denunciations that made life something threatening … and that forgot the good noble people" (*Madrid recobrado* 45). A fascist journalistic narration of the Republican horrors can be read in Fernández Arias. For historical accounts of the repression against enemies, real or otherwise, of the Republic, see Beevor, *La guerra* 81–7; Casas de la Vega 75–91, 103–19; Cervera 53–105; Montoliú, *Madrid en la guerra civil* 1: 97–107; Preston, *Spanish Holocaust* 221–302, 341–80.

39 On this paradox, see Albert, "El tremendismo" 101–8, *Vanguardistas* 375–409.

40 Notwithstanding García Serrano's relative fame and the canonic quality of some of his novels, the scholarship devoted to his life and works is all but abundant. Rodríguez Puértolas gives useful biographic and critical information in his history of Spanish fascist literature (*Historia* 1: 301–4, 652–8); on this score, see also Onrubia Rebuelta 1: 57–69. On *Plaza del Castillo*, see Mainer, *Falange* 123–4; Nora 3: 45–8; Rodríguez Puértolas, *Historia* 1: 301–4.

41 On the presence, function, and meaning of war and the civil war in Spanish literary fascism, see, for instance, Albert, *Vanguardistas* 429–39; Carbajosa and Carbajosa 148–81; Mainer, "La retórica." An excellent collection of essays on representations of the Spanish Civil War in fascist and pro-Republican works alike can be found in Valis, *Teaching*.

42 See Mainer, *Falange* 123–4; Mata Induráin; Nora, 3: 44–8; Rodríguez Puértolas, *Historia* 2: 655–7; Schmolling 257–72.

43 Theweleit argues that the (fascist's) "body armor" attains its final form in the military academy (2: 143–53). Through drill and discipline, the body is estranged from the pleasure principle "and reorganized into a body ruled by the 'pain principle'" (150). In the military academy, cadets join in the military "machine," the antithesis of the desiring-machine, "a totality that maintains every component in appropriate and uninterrupted motion" (150). Interestingly, the man who becomes a component of that "machine" "becomes whole, a whole that is simultaneously subordinate and dominant" (153).

44 For the Nationalists, their rebellion against the Republic was aimed at "re-conquering" Spain. As Fernández Arias exclaimed, "The army has risen up in order to reconquer Spain … so that not even one single 'red' mark remains in our national map!" (79; see also 78, 105, 158–9). Many fascist war poems are devoted to the "reconquest" of Spain's "geography" or "map"; see, for instance, Eugenio d'Ors, "Romance del impaciente ante un mapa mural en color de las operaciones de guerra" (1939); Agustín de Foxá, "La España cautiva" (1937); Federico de Urrutia, "Romance de Castilla en armas" (1938).

45 Compare my analysis of *Camisa azul* with Albert, *Vanguardistas* 179–83, 326–46, 409–29; Mainer, *Falange* 124; Rodríguez Puértolas, *Historia* 1: 315–18, 2: 676–8. For biographic information on the author, see Albert, *Vanguardistas* 76–85; Rodríguez Puértolas, *Historia* 1: 315, 2: 676–7, 918–20.

46 A section of Falange created in 1937, the Servicio Exterior's main task was to expand the party and seek Latin America support for the Nationalists' cause upon two main principles – *Hispanidad* and Empire (Delgado Gómez-Escalonilla 130–42). Payne (*Fascism* 342–6, 376) provides a good overview of the Servicio Exterior.

47 This is said about the successful assault of the Cuartel de la Montaña by armed civilians and loyal troops. Describing the same event, Camba refers to the people as "plebs" ("populacho"): "It is as if all over Madrid the mob that once took the Bastille had resurrected. The ragged and dirty plebs … from Madrid's underworld go through the streets yelling" (40–1).

48 On the siege and liberation of the Alcázar of Toledo, see Beevor, *La guerra* 184–6; Preston, *Spanish Civil War* 128–33.

49 See, for instance, Francisco de Iracheta y Mascort, *Romance del Alcázar: La patria me hace cantar. Versos triunfales* (1940); Alfredo Martínez Leal, *El asedio del Alcázar de Toledo, memorias de un testigo* (1937); Alberto Risco, *La epopeya del Alcázar de Toledo: Relación histórica de los sucesos desde los comienzos del asedio hasta su liberación, 21 julio a 28 septiembre de 1936* (1937); and of course, José Moscardó (commander of the troops defending the Alcázar), *Diario del Alcázar* (1943). On the myth of the Alcázar in fascist and Francoist discourse, see Herreros; Llorente Hernández, "La representación" 61–9; Sánchez-Biosca.

50 On the fascist "poetics of the ruins," see Castillo Cáceres 528–37. Ruins played an important role in the fascist use of space. An excellent summary of the political function of ruins in Nazism can be found in Albert Speer's memoirs (66), where the author sketches some thoughts, already put forth in his 1937 article "Stein statt Eisen," of what he called "law of ruin value" (*Ruinengesetz*).

51 On urban planning in the early Franco regime, see Blanco 17–40; Castillo

Cáceres 583–611; de Terán 141–5, 223–321; Moneo 79–94; Sambricio, "Madrid," "De nuevo," "El Plan," "¡Qué coman!," "La renovación," "La vivienda."

52 On fascist architecture in the Franco regime, see Castillo Cáceres 583–611; Cirici 44–6, 110–50; Doménech Girbau; Flores López; Llorente Hernández, *Arte* 67–85, 275–302; Sambrico, "La arquitetura," "La renovación," "¡Que coman!"; Urrutia 353–85.

53 The full text of the Plan General de Ordenación de Madrid can be found in Sambricio, *Plan Bidagor.* On the Plan, see, for instance, de Terán 238–42; Díaz Nosty; Doménech Girbau 69–71; Moneo 82–4; Sambricio, "De nuevo," "Madrid, 1941" 311–28, *Plan Bidagor.*

54 On the repression carried out by the Franco regime, see Núñez Díaz-Balart; Preston, *Spanish Holocaust* 471–517; Reig Tapia, *Ideología.*

55 For more information on Madrid in the war's aftermath and the changes brought about by the Nationalists on the city, see Bravo Morata 13: 47–55; Montoliú, *Madrid en la posguerra* 13–127; Sueiro and Díaz Nosty 1: 1–21.

56 Fascist accounts described the event as a "return to normality." In *Madridgrado*, for instance, the reader learns that the Paseo de la Castellana "seemed to return to its glory days, when the happy people of Madrid vibrated in it" (Camba 403–4). In an interesting article that appeared on *ABC* the day after the "liberation of Madrid" (comp. Figueres 679–87), the journalist Alberto Martín Fernández (pseud. "Juan Deportista") narrates his walk in Madrid on 28 March as an appropriation of the city.

57 Executive order published in several dailies (e.g., Serrano Suñer, "Una orden," *Arriba* [17 May 1939]: 1). For factual information on the victory parade, see Bravo Morata 13: 63–71; Castillo Cáceres 567–73; Montoliú, *Madrid en la posguerra* 66–70; Platón 12–22; Preston, *Franco* 410–12; Sueiro and Díaz Nosty 1: 1–20.

58 On the different "rites of victory" organized by the new rulers, see Di Febo 145–87.

59 Descriptions of Franco's podium, the platforms for the authorities, press, and foreign representatives, and the triumphal arch placed over the podium can be found in Bravo Morata 13: 65; Montoliú, *Madrid en la posguerra* 68–9; Sueiro and Díaz Nosty 1: 1–12. Other constructions built for the cortège were a bridge on the Plaza de Cibeles and a colonnade on the Plaza Colón.

60 The Orden General del Desfile de la Victoria issued on 1 May by the Army of the Centre's chief of staff, Colonel Antonio Uguet, specifies the place, the itinerary, the number and composition of units, the points of concentration and dispersal of every unit, the itinerary to be followed by each unit af-

ter its dispersal, the order of the units, and the uniform to be worn, among other matters (published in *Arriba* on 18 May 1939).

61 Constituted in Burgos on 31 January 1939, the first Franco cabinet placed its ministries in several cities. After the war they would all begin to move their dependencies to Madrid.

62 The lineality of the victory parade contains a political message. As Marin argues, "A one-way trajectory implies the notion of an irreversible direction…. The point of arrival of the group in motion will always be in some respect the symbolic victory of the forces that the group has conveyed by gathering and parading against those whom its very march has defied or challenged in an equally symbolic antagonism" (43).

63 This contrast relates the victory parade to the fascist marches proper. According to Theweleit, the Nazi ritual of the parading mass transformed the (feminine) "streams" intrinsic to mass demonstrations into (masculine) "columns" (1: 429–35); it meant, in other words, the taming of the "floods," of the "red" masses. "The scenario of the parade," argues Theweleit, "abolished the contradiction between the desiring production of the individual and the demands of social power" (1: 430).

64 Interestingly, some fascist authors added up a spectral parade to the empiric parade on the streets and skies of Madrid. For Salaverría, while the military who survived the war paraded in Madrid, those fallen in battle marched "under the bright stars' light and at the tune of ideal pieces of music" ("El desfile sagrado," in *ABC* [20 May 1939]). On his part, Puente locates that very spectral parade on the streets ("Ayer no desfilaron," *Arriba* [20 May 1939]; in *Madrid recobrado* 48). In either case, the spectre belongs to the "people's community."

65 On 19 May, the Caudillo read a radio speech that laid out some principles of the new regime. For Franco, final victory had not been achieved yet. The Caudillo informed his listeners about "dangers still awaiting our Fatherland" (Franco, "El discurso del Caudillo" 1). War goes on "in another field" (1), and for this reason all Spaniards must be vigilant: "Victory would come to nothing if we didn't carry on the heroic day's tension and concern, if the everlasting dissidents, the resentful ones, the selfish, the defenders of a liberal economy were given leeway" (2). Giménez Caballero had spoken in an identical vein on Radio Nacional one day earlier (speech printed by *Arriba* on 19 May under the title "La unidad de la victoria").

66 Bourdieu has defined the concept of *rite of institution* in *Ce que parler veut dire* (121–34).

67 Writing on Italian Fascism, Berezin concludes likewise that the public political ritual was "the [Fascist] regime's attempt to create temporary fascist

communities of emotional attachment that would create bonds of solidarity" (30).

68 Allusions to the victory would be common currency in the first years after the war. A remarkable instance is *El desfile de la Victoria: Madrid 19–20 de Mayo de 1939, Año de la Victoria* (1944), a book of poems by Pedro A. Gómez Lozano (pseud. "Radug D'Aril"). Preceded by a prologue, the poems are grouped into two parts, "Cumbres de la Cruzada" and "La Parada de la Castellana."

5 Russia: Spectres and Paratopos

1 The Spanish Division of Volunteers is better known as División Azul, or Blue Division, a name originally proposed by José Luis Arrese that would gain popularity due to the Falangist blue shirt worn by the volunteers under their German uniform. For a historiographic account of the Blue Division, see Kleinfeld and Tambs; Moreno Juliá; Payne, *Franco* 146–54; Rodríguez Jiménez, *De héroes*. Caballero Jurado and Ibáñez Hernández's 1989 annotated bibliography on the literature and filmography produced apropos of the Blue Division is an indispensable tool for any scholar working on this topic. The reader must take with a grain of salt veteran Fernando Vadillo's otherwise engaging, exhaustive, well-written, novelized nine-volume history of the Blue Division, the Blue Squadron, the Blue Legion, the Spanish volunteers posted in Wehrmacht or Waffen-SS units, and finally, the Gulag ordeal of the approximately four hundred Spanish POWs. The website of the Fundación División Azul has to be consulted with the same prudence.

2 See also Díaz de Villegas 28, 220; Oroquieta Arbiol and García Sánchez 67. A summary of the vengeful feelings voiced by the crowd and fuelled by the government can be found in Rodríguez Jiménez, *De héroes* 45–9. Interestingly, this myth has survived the demise of the Franco regime and constitutes still a topos of Spanish fascism. In the section titled "¿Qué fue la División Azul?" of the Fundación División Azul's website, we read, for instance, that on 24 June 1941 Spain's youth gathered in Madrid to demand the country's involvement in the "anti-Bolshevik crusade and defence of Europe, and thus return the Soviet's visit of 1936–39." Three additional instances are Morales and Togores's illustrated history of the Division (63), an article by Fernando González de Canales titled "Maldito sea el pueblo que olvida a sus héroes," and the Blue Division veteran Enrique de la Vega Viguera's short history of this expeditionary force (22).

3 On the genesis of the Blue Division, see Kleinfeld and Tambs 17–26; Moreno Juliá 57–115; Rodríguez Jiménez, *De héroes* 40–1, 49–52. For a quick introduction on the Blue Squadron, see Morales and Togores 49–56.

4 On the recruit of volunteers, see Kleinfeld and Tambs 511; Moreno Juliá 83–101; Rodríguez Jiménez, *De héroes* 50–70. The definitive structure of the Blue Division has been studied by Rodríguez Jiménez, *De héroes* 89–92.

5 The members of the Blue Division received their training in the military base near Grafenwöhr. On the military training period in Grafenwöhr, see Kleinfeld and Tambs 49–73; Moreno Juliá 122–34; Rodríguez Jiménez, *De héroes* 87–105.

6 Major Oroquieta Arbiol, the designated representative of the POWs in their journey from Odessa to Barcelona, specifies in his memoirs that out of the 286 men aboard the *Semiramis* there were 248 POWs from the Blue Division, nineteen merchant sailors and twelve Republican airmen stranded in the Soviet Union by the end of the civil war who for no apparent reason had been sent into captivity by the Soviet authorities, four children evacuated during the civil war, and three Spanish workers arrested in Germany by the Red Army at the end of the Second World War (in Oroquieta Arbiol and García Sánchez 599). On the misfortunes of the POWs during their almost thirteen years of captivity in the Gulag, as well as their liberation and life in Spain thereafter, see Moreno Juliá 321–39; Payne, *Franco* 152–3; Rodríguez Jiménez, *De héroes* 371–80; Vadillo, *Los prisioneros*. It must be added that in April 1954 there still remained in the Soviet Union an undetermined number of Spanish POWs, who would be repatriated in seven expeditions between September 1956 and May 1959 (see Moreno Juliá 342–4).

7 A fitting choice indeed: General Muñoz Grandes had been the commander-in-chief of the Blue Division from its inception until his replacement in December 1942 by General Emilio Esteban-Infantes.

8 The Blue Legion (Legión Azul), officially known as Legión Española de Voluntarios, replaced the Blue Division after its dissolution in October 1943; it was created in November 1943 and disbanded in March 1944. For information on the Blue Legion, consult Kleinfeld and Tambs 489–503; Moreno Juliá 191–209, 291–303; Rodríguez Jiménez, *De héroes* 337–57; Vadillo, *Balada final*.

9 According to Moreno Juliá (410–13), at least 130 Spaniards volunteered to fight clandestinely in Wehrmacht or Waffen-SS units; on this "clandestine fight," see Moreno Juliá 204–9, 303–9; Rodríguez Jiménez, *De héroes* 357–70; Vadillo's novelized account *Los irreductibles*. See also *Berlín, a vida o muerte* (Portuguese version 1947; Spanish version 1975), a short autobiographical narrative written by the most famous of these volunteers, Miguel Ezquerra.

10 A compelling, sensitive portrayal of the arrival of the *Semiramis* as well as the feelings and thoughts of the ex-POWs and of their relatives awaiting at the port of Barcelona can be found in Carmen Kurtz's novel *El desconocido* (13–90), awarded with the Premio Planeta in 1956.

11 Compare with the figures given by Payne (*Franco* 152) and by the Fundación División Azul.

12 On the volunteers' social origin and professional occupation, as well as the different reasons behind their decision to enrol in the expeditionary corps, see Payne, *Franco* 148–9; Rodríguez Jiménez, *De héroes* 52–70; Ydígoras 33.

13 The motion pictures are Pedro Lazaga's *La patrulla* (1954), José María Forqué's *Embajadores en el infierno* (1956), Vicente Lluch's *La espera* (1956), and Miguel Iglesias's *Carta a una mujer* (1961). See Alegre for a critical study of these films. In their critical bibliography, Caballero Jurado and Ibáñez Hernández (74–8) list German and Spanish newsreels and documentaries on the Blue Division.

14 On the latter issue, see Payne, *Franco*; Tusell, *Franco*.

15 There are very few exceptions to this silence: Caballero Jurado 9–54; Rodríguez Puértolas, *Historia* 1: 595–600, 616–19, 2: 709–20; Viscarri, "Preserving." On the Second World War and Spanish literature, see Mainer, "La segunda" 171–201.

16 In his novel *Los hombres se matan así* (1961), Eleuterio Paniagua depicts the Volkhov River in a similar vein: "To look at it at nightfall ... produces a feeling of despair and anguish, as if in a shipwreck of the world" (174).

17 Certainly not an uncommon feeling among Spanish veterans; see, for instance, Salvador, *División* 196, 222; Ydígoras 186, 417.

18 Adolf Hitler himself left little room for ambiguity regarding this matter in the pages of *Mein Kampf* (1925–7) devoted to expound his "Eastern policy" as well as his own version of the theory of the *Lebensraum* (642–67). Analogous ideas were sketched around the same time by Joseph Goebbels in his novel *Michael: Ein deutsches Schicksal in Tagebuchblättern* (1929) and elaborated in some detail by the Nazi ideologue Alfred Rosenberg in *Der Zukunftsweg einer deutschen Aussenpolitik* (1927) and *Der Mythos des 20. Jahrhunderts* (1934). For a cogent analysis of the ideological background of this war of extermination in the context of the war-driven nature of Nazism, consult Bessel, *Nazism* 112–20, 130–1, and most specially, Bartov's book on "Hitler's army." The war in the Eastern front has been told many times; two recent authoritative accounts are Evans's (*Third Reich at War* 166–214, 403–23, 483–92) and Bellamy's. For the Nazi vision of war, see Bessel, *Nazism*; Gat 80–103.

19 See Mayer 200–33.

20 Kleinfeld and Tambs 489, 491; Morales and Togores 45; Moreno Juliá 250–2; Rodríguez Jiménez, *De héroes* 207–15, 346–7, 356–7.

21 The *paratopos* must not be confused with the *paratopia*, a concept used in a variety of disciplines, such as semiotics (Greimas and Courtés 226; Lücke 205; Sebeok and Umiker-Sebeok 169–71) and literary studies (Maingueneau).

22 Far from being unmovable essences, places are unstable entities contingent
on individual, ecological, political, and economic processes. They are, to
put it in Harvey's words, "within the processes that create, sustain, and dissolve all regions, places, and spacetimes into complex configurations" (*Cosmopolitanism* 194).

23 Which does not mean that "place" is an obsolete entity. Quoting the 2006
UN *Report on Migration*, De Blij points out that only about 200 million
people (fewer than 3% of the world population) live outside the country
of their birth. "Place," concludes De Blij, "most emphatically place of birth,
but also the constricted space in which the majority of lives are lived, remains the most potent factor shaping the destinies of billions" (136).

24 Compare with Marc Augé's concept of *non-places*.

25 See, for instance, Bourke 335–57.

26 First Word War: Edmund Blunden's *Undertones of War* (1928), Robert
Graves's *Good-bye to All That* (1929), Siegfried Sassoon's *Memories of an Infantry Officer* (1930), Ludwig Maercker's *Vom Kaiserheer zur Reichswehr: Geschichte
des freiwilligen Landesjägerkorps: Ein Beitrag zur Geschichte der deutschen Revolution* (1921), Ernst Röhm's *Die Geschichte eines Hochverräters* (1928), and Peter
von Heydebreck's *Wir Wehr-Wölfe: Erinnerungen eines Freikorps-Führers* (1931).
Rif War: Ramón J. Sender's *Imán* (1930). Vietnam War: Michael Cimino's
The Deer Hunter (1978), Alan Parker's *Birdy* (1984), and Oliver Stone's *Born
on the Fourth of July* (1989).

27 On this *décalage* and the dissidence within FET-JONS of the so-called *falangistas auténticos*, see Ellwood 205–53; Rodríguez Jiménez, *Historia* 457–61,
505–35.

28 In addition, see Ellwood 157–201; Rodríguez Jiménez, *Historia* 467–504.

29 As Carmen Kurtz shows in her novel *El desconocido* (1956), the frustration
also could be caused by other reasons as well, such as the difficulty or impossibility of adjusting to a world (family, friends, hometown) that had
changed, for the veteran, beyond recognition.

30 References to the act of writing and to memory can be found, for instance,
in Hernández Navarro 63, 233, 257, 371–2; Salvador, *División* 6–7, 10, 14,
113–14, 202–6, 330–5; Sánchez Diana, *Cabeza* 16–18, 179, 209; Ydígoras 9,
11, 32, 403, 416.

31 On Tomás Salvador and *División 250*, see Alborg 209–32; Caballero Jurado
and Ibáñez Hernández 125–9; Martínez Cachero, *La novela* 454–5; Nora 3:
194–8; Rodríguez Puértolas, *Historia* 2: 718–19; Sobejano 173–7; Soldevila
Durante 540–2.

32 On the different meanings of *conjuration*, see Derrida, *Specters* 49–50, 58–9.
On *ghost*, *spectre*, and *spectrality*, see Agamben, *Nudities* 37–42, *Stanzas*;

Chambers; Cheah; Derrida, *Specters*; Geldof 325–49; Gordon; Labanyi, "History," introduction; Horkheimer and Adorno 215–16; Laclau, "Time"; Spivak.

33 For instance: Gordon; Derrida, *Specters* 94–7, 220–1; Labanyi, "History" 65–82, introduction 1–14; Laclau, "Time"; Spivak; Sprinker.

34 One example of this ambiguity is the trial of Adolf Eichmann. In her astute analysis of what she calls "Eichmann's ghost" (45–69), Torgovnick claims that even the people who have no recollection of the trial have been shaped by it: "Eichmann's ghost rises whenever facts about the Holocaust become disputed or the world returns to unanswered questions" (46–7). At the same time, out of the trial itself – let alone the clandestine kidnapping of Eichmann from Argentina by Israeli agents – there rose unpleasant questions (e.g., the legality of the trial, the impartiality of the jury, prosecutor, and witnesses, the role played by the Jewish Councils in the Holocaust, the attitude of the Allies vis-à-vis Jewish immigration, and the possible but never carried out bombing of the extermination camps to end the ongoing destruction of human lives), as Hannah Arendt's *Eichmann in Jerusalem* clearly, if provocatively, shows. "Eichmann's ghost," concludes Torgovnick, "remains the undead in our culture. Known, but not known. A cipher rather than a felt reality. The ordinary man, the family man, as war criminal. The war criminal to end all war criminals – except that he wasn't" (69).

35 Compare with Dionisio Ridruejo's poem "Ahora avanzo entre mis muertos, solo" (*Cuadernos* 138–9), which describes the poet's dead comrades as spectres.

36 See also Salvador, *División* 17–19; Ydígoras 42.

37 For instance: Eizaguirre; García de Ledesma; Ridruejo, *Los cuadernos*; Ruiz Ayúcar; Ydígoras.

38 Compare with the elegiac description of Novgorod in Ridruejo (*Los cuadernos* 270–2) and with the empathetic depiction of that city in Ydígoras (150–1).

39 Much has been written on the siege and battle of Leningrad; for a recent account, see Glantz. The description of the besieged city of Leningrad from its outskirts is another topos of the Blue Division culture; see, for instance, Hernández Navarro 341; Vadillo, *Arrabales* vols. 1 and 2; Ydígoras 288–90. García de Ledesma, who spent several weeks in Leningrad as a double agent, provides an interesting description of its streets and the suffering of its inhabitants (141–85); of equal interest is Oroquieta Arbiol's description, in this case because this *divisionario* crossed the city as a POW (Oroquieta Arbiol and García Sánchez 81–2).

40 Sometimes looking through binoculars is not an act of repressed violence,

but just the opposite. Facing the enemy can awaken a sense of brotherhood. In *Algunos no hemos muerto*, the narrator and protagonist of the novel remembers an occasion in which he had been in a static position separated from the Russians by only two hundred metres. There, face to face, the two adversaries seem to have forgotten "our little quarrels" (Ydígoras 261). With the help of binoculars, Spaniards and Russians leisurely gaze and wave at each other: "I raised my hand, and that man … raised his. Afterwards, we smiled at each other," concluding that their world, the enemies' world, was identical to his own (261).

41　See Salvador, *División* 206–11; Hernández Navarro 339–55; Ydígoras 161–78.

42　Very little has been written on Ydígoras and his novel; basic information on both can be found in Caballero Jurado and Ibáñez Hernández 135–8; Rodríguez Puértolas, *Historia* 2: 719; Soldevila Durante 541–2.

43　On this score, see Hynes 1–30.

44　As it happens, there are very few pacifist works in the Blue Division culture. Eleuterio Paniagua's 1961 novel *Los hombres se matan así* is an exception to the norm. Perhaps for this reason it has been considered by the *divisionarios* as the Blue Division's "black book" (Caballero Jurado and Ibáñez Hernández 53).

45　"Ich hatt' einen Kamerad" is a much-loved traditional song of the German armed forces. Its lyrics were written by Ludwig Uhland in 1809, and the text was set to music by Friedrich Silcher in 1825.

46　There is a similar scene in Sánchez Diana's *Cabeza de puente*: the autodiegetic narrator, recovering from war injuries in Königsberg, feels after a while "the nostalgia for the front" mixed up with the pleasure he feels by being with his comrades (183–4).

47　The heroic defence of Posad (12 November–7 December 1942) brought the Blue Division much prestige among the Germans. Many pages have been written on Posad by *divisionarios* (e.g., Ridruejo, *Los cuadernos* 231–43; Salvador, *División* 119–33; Sánchez Diana, *Cabeza* 141–55; Vadillo, *Orillas* 2: 87–207). On the Battle of Posad, see Kleinfeld and Tambs 165–205; Moreno Juliá 166–8; Rodríguez Jiménez, *De héroes* 144–59.

48　For more references to these military cemeteries, see Hernández Navarro 364; Salvador, *División* 250.

49　On *Ida y vuelta*, see Caballero Jurado and Ibáñez Hernández 101–3; Caballero Jurado 9–54; Rodríguez Puértolas, *Historia* 2: 714.

50　For a thorough study on the structure of war, see Scarry.

51　See Friedrich's systematic study of the bombings on Germany between 1940 and 1945. A fascinating history of bombing in Lindqvist.

52　On French fascist literature, see, for instance, Carroll; Kaplan.

53 The connections between modern warfare, destruction, and the literary and artistic avant-garde have been studied, among others, by Virilio (*Art*) and Sloterdijk.

54 For an authoritative historiographic account of this battle, see Beevor, *Fall.*

55 Compare with several articles by a prominent Falangist, the journalist Eugenio Montes: "Sinfonía patética de Alemania," "Meditación ante la Universidad de Berlín," and "El cisne de Heidelberg" (*Elegías europeas* [1949] 199–215). For a detailed, sympathetic, Célinean description of the destruction brought about by the aerial bombings on Berlin, see Montes 202, 208.

56 To this short list could be added Eusebio Calavia Bellosillo's *Enterrados en Rusia* (1956, written in collaboration with Francisco Álvarez Cosmen) and two more recent memoirs: *4045 días cautivo en Rusia, 1943–1954: Memorias* (1987), by Joaquín Poquet Guardiola, and *Esclavos de Stalin: el combate final de la División Azul (memoria histórica de un prisionero en la URSS)* (2002), by Ángel Salamanca Salamanca in collaboration with Francisco Torres García.

57 See Moreno Juliá 321–39; Rodríguez Jiménez, *De héroes* 371–80.

58 To the Battle of Krasny Bor *divisionario* Fernando Vadillo has devoted two volumes, titled *Lucharon en Krasny Bor* (1975), of his massive novelized history of the Blue Division. A scholarly approach to that battle can be found in Kleinfeld and Tambs 347–441; Morales and Togores 44; Moreno Juliá 184–7; Rodríguez Jiménez, *De héroes* 264–78.

59 An outstanding scholarly work on the Gulag is Anne Applebaum's book, the reading of which provides an excellent context to the memoirs here analysed, among other reasons because this book devotes a great deal of attention to covering the lives and deaths of camp inmates.

60 Compare with Rodrigo Royo's 1956 novel *El sol y la nieve* (1956), which centres precisely on one side of this multifaceted clash: two Spanish brothers (a Falangist and a Communist) fighting in Russia, one in the Blue Division, the other with the Soviet partisans.

61 A thesis shared by Rodríguez Jiménez, who claims that the history of the Blue Division ought to be seen as an extension of the civil war (*De héroes* 17, 279–324). Hence the meaning of the otherwise ideologically ambiguous title of his book: on the one hand there are the *divisionarios*, the "heroes," and on the other the "undesirables," a word applied to the Spanish communist exiles assigned to the Red Army or intelligence agencies as well as to the deserters of the Blue Division.

62 On the removal of Primo de Rivera's remains in Alicante and the ritual leading to their reburial in San Lorenzo de El Escorial, see Payne, *Fascism* 307–8; Rodríguez Jiménez, *Historia* 322–33.

63 On 29 March 1959, José Antonio Primo de Rivera's remains were exhumed

from his tomb in El Escorial and transferred to the Valle de los Caídos. See Palomar Baró for an interesting and thorough Francoist description of the event; the author adds to his narrative an equally interesting selection of primary sources related to this third burial (the first having taken place right after his execution in November 1936) of Primo de Rivera.

Works Cited

"A la juventud española. 1921–1931, 1923–1933." *El Fascio. Haz Hispano* 16 Mar. 1933: 1. Print.

Abella, Rafael. *La vida cotidiana durante la guerra civil: La España nacional.* Barcelona: Planeta, 1973. Print.

Adorno, Theodor W. *Critical Moments: Interventions and Catchwords.* Trans. Henry W. Pickford. New York: Columbia UP, 2005. Print.

– *Minima Moralia: Reflexionen aus dem beschädigten Leben.* Frankfurt am Main: Suhrkamp, 2001. Print.

Agamben, Giorgio. *Nudities.* Trans. David Kishik and Stefan Pedatella. Stanford: Stanford UP, 2011. Print.

– *Stanzas: Word and Phantasm in Western Culture.* Trans. Ronald L. Martinez. Minneapolis: U of Minnesota P, 1993. Print.

"Agrarios." *F.E.* 25 Jan. 1934: 1. Print.

Aguado, Emiliano. "Ramiro y sus escritos filosóficos." *Escorial. Revista de cultura y letras.* Nov. 1941: 303–6. Print.

Alarcón, Pedro Antonio de. *Diario de un testigo de la guerra de África.* 1860. Ed. María del Pilar Palomo. Seville: Fundación José Manuel de Lara, 2005. Print.

Albert, Mechthild. Introducción. Albert, *Vencer* 7–10. Print.

– "'El saetazo de Roma': Ernesto Giménez Caballero y la Italia fascista." *Cultura italiana e spagnola a confronto, anni 1918–1939.* Ed. Titus Heydenreich. Tübingen: Stauffenburg, 1992. 95–111. Print.

– "El tremendismo en la novela fascista." Albert, *Vencer* 101–18. Print.

– *Vanguardistas de camisa azul: La trayectoria de los escritores Tomás Borrás, Felipe Ximénez de Sandoval, Samuel Ros y Antonio Obregón entre 1925 y 1940.* Trans. C. Díez Pampliega and J.R. García Ober. Madrid: Visor Libros, 2003. Print.

– ed. *Vencer no es convencer: Literatura e ideología del fascismo español.* Frankfurt am Main, Madrid: Vervuert, Iberoamericana, 1998. Print.

Alborg, Juan Luis. *Hora actual de la novela española.* Madrid: Taurus, 1958. Print.

Alegre, Sergio. *El cine cambia la Historia: Las imágenes de la División Azul.* Barcelona: PPU, 1994.

Alfaro, José María. *Leoncio Pancorbo.* Madrid: Editora Nacional, 1942. Print.

Allardyce, Gilbert. "What Fascism Is Not: Thoughts on the Deflation of a Concept." *American Historical Review* 84.2 (1979): 367–88. Print.

Alonso Baquer, Miguel. "Estrategia (Madrid, 1936-1939)." Alvar Ezquerra 303–26. Print.

Alvar Ezquerra, Alfredo, ed. *Visión histórica de Madrid (siglos XVI al XX).* Madrid: Real Sociedad Económica de Amigos del País, 1991. Print.

Álvarez, José E. *The Betrothed of Death: The Spanish Foreign Legion during the Rif Rebellion, 1920–1927.* Westport, CT: Greenwood, 2001. Print.

Álvarez Chillida, Gonzalo. *El antisemitismo en España: La imagen del judío (1812–2002).* Madrid: Marcial Pons, 2002. Print.

Anderson, James, and Liam O'Dowd. "Borders, Border Regions and Territoriality: Contradictory Meanings, Changing Significance." *Regional Studies* 33 (1999): 593–604. Print.

Antliff, Michael. *Avant-Garde Fascism: The Mobilization of Myth, Art, and Culture in France, 1909–1939.* Durham: Duke UP, 2007. Print.

Applebaum, Anne. *Gulag: A History of the Soviet Camps.* New York: Doubleday, 2003. Print.

The Architecture of Doom [*Undergångens arkitektur*]. Dir. Peter Cohen. Peter Cohen, 1991. Film.

Arconada, César. "La doctrina intelectual del fascismo español." *Octubre* 6 (1934): 22. Print.

Areilza, José María de, and Fernando María Castiella. *Reivindicaciones de España.* 2nd ed. Madrid: Instituto de Estudios Políticos, 1941. Print.

Arendt, Hannah. *Eichmann in Jerusalem: A Report on the Banality of Evil.* Rev., enl. ed. New York: Penguin, 1994. Print.

– *The Origins of Totalitarianism.* 1951. New ed. New York: Harcourt Brace, 1979. Print.

Asenjo Alonso, José. *¡¡¡Los que fuimos al Tercio!!! Novela periodística.* Madrid: Miguel Albero, 1932. Print.

Augé, Marc. *Non-Places: An Introduction to Supermodernity.* 2nd ed. Trans. John Howe. London: Verso, 2008. Print.

Aznar [Zubigaray], Manuel. Introducción. *Marruecos: Diario de una Bandera.* By Francisco Franco. Madrid: Doncel, 1976. 7–31. Print.

Bachelard, Gaston. *La Poétique de l'espace.* 2nd ed. Paris: Presses Universitaires de France, 1958. Print.

Bahamonde Magro, Ángel. "Madrid en la guerra civil española." Alvar Ezquerra 327–43. Print.

Bailey, Cyril, ed. *The Legacy of Rome*. Oxford: Oxford UP, 1923. Print.

Baker, Edward. *Madrid Cosmopolita: La Gran Vía, 1910–1936*. Madrid: Marcial Pons Ediciones de Historia, 2009. Print.

Balfour, Sebastian. *Abrazo mortal: De la guerra colonial a la guerra civil en España y Marruecos (1909–1939)*. Trans. Inés Belaustegui. Barcelona: Península, 2002. Print.

Barbusse, Henri. *Le Feu (Journal d'une Escouade)*. 1916. Paris: Ernest Flammarion, éditeur, 1917. Print.

Bartov, Omer. *Hitler's Army: Soldiers, Nazis, and War in the Third Reich*. Oxford: Oxford UP, 1992

Basterra, Ramón de. "Heros. Llegada a la isla de Capri." *Hermes. Revista del País Vasco* 15 July 1919: 243–4. Print.

— *Llama romance*. Ed. Manuel Asín and José-Carlos Mainer. Vol. 1 of *Poesía*. By Basterra. 2 vols. Madrid: Fundación BSCH, 2001. Print.

— "Paseos romanos." *Hermes. Revista del País Vasco* July 1917: n.p. Print.

— "Paseos romanos." *Hermes. Revista del País Vasco* Dec. 1917: n.p. Print.

— "Paseos romanos." *Hermes. Revista del País Vasco* Feb. 1918: n.p. Print.

— "Paseos romanos. Voces en la fronda." *Hermes. Revista del País Vasco* June 1917: n.p. Print.

— *Poesía*. Ed. Manuel Asín and José-Carlos Mainer. 2 vols. Madrid: Fundación BSCH, 2001. Print.

— *Las ubres luminosas*. 1923. Ed. Manuel Asín and José-Carlos Mainer. Vol. 1 of *Poesía*. By Basterra. 2 vols. Madrid: Fundación BSCH, 2001. Print.

— *Virulo. Mediodía*. 1927. Ed. Manuel Asín and José-Carlos Mainer. Vol. 2 of *Poesía*. By Basterra. 2 vols. Madrid: Fundación BSCH, 2001. Print.

— *Virulo. Poema. I. Las mocedades*. 1924. Ed. Manuel Asin and José-Carlos Mainer. Vol. 2 of *Poesía*. By Basterra. 2 vols. Madrid: Fundación BSCH, 2001. Print.

Bataille, Georges. *La Littérature et le mal*. 1957. Paris: Gallimard, 2002. Print.

Bécarud, Jean, and Evelyne López Campillo. *Los intelectuales españoles durante la II República*. Madrid: Siglo XXI de España Editores, 1978. Print.

Bedoya, Javier M de (*see also* Martínez de Bedoya, Javier). "Miremos hacia el campo." *Libertad* 16 Apr. 1934: 2. Print.

— "Renovación violenta." *Libertad* 26 Feb. 1934: 2. Print.

Beevor, Antony. *The Battle for Spain: The Spanish Civil War 1936–1939*. New York: Penguin, 2001. Print.

— *The Fall of Berlin 1945*. New York: Penguin, 2003. Print.

— *La guerra civil española*. Trans. Gonzalo Pontón. Barcelona: Crítica, 2005. Print.

Bellamy, Chris. *Absolute War: Soviet Russia in the Second World War.* New York: Alfred A. Knopf, 2007. Print.

Ben-Ami, Shlomo. *Fascism from Above: The Dictatorship of Primo de Rivera in Spain, 1923–1930.* Oxford: Oxford UP, 1983. Print.

Beneyto Pérez, Juan. *España y el problema de Europa: Contribución a la historia de la idea de imperio.* Madrid: Editora Nacional, 1942. Print.

Benítez de Castro, Cecilio *Se ha ocupado el Kilómetro seis (Contestación a Remarque).* Barcelona: Maucci, 1939. Print.

Benjamin, Walter. *Illuminations: Essays and Reflections.* Trans. Harry Zohn. Ed. Hannah Arendt. New York: Harcourt Brace Jovanovich, 1968. Print.

Berezin, Mabel. *Making the Fascist Self: The Political Culture of Interwar Italy.* Ithaca: Cornell UP, 1997. Print.

Berghaus, Günter. *Futurism and Politics: Between Anarchist Rebellion and Fascist Reaction, 1909–1944.* Providence: Berghahn, 1996. Print.

– "Futurism and the Technological Imagination Poised between Machine Cult and Machine Angst." *Futurism and the Technological Imagination.* Ed. Günter Berghaus. Amsterdam: Rodopi, 2009. 1–39. Print.

Bertrand de Muñoz, Maryse. *La guerra civil española en la novela: Bibliografía comentada.* 3 vols. Madrid: José Porrúa Turanzas, 1982. Print.

Bessel, Richard. *Nazism and War.* New York: Modern Library, 2004. Print.

– *Political Violence and the Rise of Nazism: The Storm Troopers in Eastern Germany, 1925–1934.* New Haven: Yale UP, 1984. Print.

Bhabha, Homi K. *The Location of Culture.* London: Routledge, 1994. Print.

– ed. *Nation and Narration.* London: Routledge, 1990. Print.

Blanchot, Maurice. *L'Écriture du désastre.* Paris: Gallimard, 1980. Print.

Blanco, Manuel. "España Una." *Arquitectura en regiones devastadas.* Ed. Secretaría General Técnica. Madrid: Centro de Publicaciones del Ministerio de Obras Públicas y Urbanismo, 1987. 17–40. Print.

Blinkhorn, Martin. "The 'Spanish Problem' and the Imperial Myth." *Journal of Contemporary History* 15.1 (1980): 5–25. Print.

Blunden, Edmund. *Undertones of War.* 1928. London: Penguin, 2000. Print.

Böcker, Manfred. *Ideologie und Programmatik im spanischen Faschismus der Zweiten Republik.* Frankfurt am Main: Peter Lang, 1996. Print.

Bohigas, Oriol. *Modernidad en la arquitectura de la España republicana.* Barcelona: Tusquets, 1998. Print.

Borrás, Tomás. *Checas de Madrid.* 1939–40. 5th ed. Madrid: Bullón, 1963. Print.

– *Madrid teñido de rojo.* Madrid: Artes Gráficas, 1962. Print.

– *La pared de tela de araña.* 1924. Madrid: Bullón, 1963. Print.

– *Ramiro Ledesma.* Madrid: Editora Nacional, 1971. Print.

Bosworth, R.J.B. *Mussolini's Italy: Life under the Fascist Dictatorship, 1915–1945.* New York: Penguin, 2007. Print.

Bosworth, R.J.B., and Sergio Romano, ed. *La politica estera italiana.* Bologna: Il Mulino, 1991. Print.

Bourdieu, Pierre. *Ce que parler veut dire: L'économie des échanges linguistiques.* Paris: Librairie Arthème Fayard, 1982. Print.

– "Habitus." *Habitus: A Sense of Place.* Ed. Jean Hillier and Emma Rooksby. Burlington: Ashgate, 2005. 43–9. Print.

– *Langage et pouvoir symbolique.* Paris: Éditions du Seuil, 2001. Print.

– *Le Sens pratique.* Paris: Les Éditions de Minuit, 1980. Print.

Bourke, Joanna. *An Intimate History of Killing: Face-to-Face Killing in Twentieth-Century Warfare.* New York: Basic Books, 1999. Print.

Brasillach, Robert. *Les Sept couleurs.* Paris: Librairie Plon, 1939. Print.

Bravo Morata, Federico. *Historia de Madrid.* 2nd ed. 22 vols. Madrid: Fenicia, 1985–. Print.

Brocà Tela, Salvador de. *Los antecedentes filosóficos del pensamiento de José Antonio Primo de Rivera y de Ramiro Ledesma: Sinopsis del trabajo y conclusiones.* Barcelona: Universidad, Secretariado de Publicaciones, Intercambio científico, 1976. Print.

– *Falange y filosofía.* Salou: UNIEUROP, Editorial universitaria europea, [1976]. Print.

Brown, F.S., M.A. Compitello, V.M. Howard, et al., eds. *Rewriting the Good Fight: Critical Essays on the Literature of the Spanish Civil War.* East Lansing: Michigan State UP, 1989. Print.

Butler, Judith. *Excitable Speech: A Politics of the Performative.* London: Routledge, 1997. Print.

– *Frames of War: When Is Life Grievable?* London: Verso, 2009. Print.

Caballero Jurado, Carlos. Introducción. Hernández Navarro 9–54.

Caballero Jurado, Carlos, and Rafael Ibáñez Hernández. *Escritores en las trincheras: La División Azul en sus libros, publicaciones periódicas y filmografía (1941–1988).* Madrid: Barbarroja, 1989. Print.

Calavia Bellosillo, Eusebio, and Francisco Álvarez Cosmen. *Enterrados en Rusia.* Madrid: Saso, 1956. Print.

Calzada, Luciano de la. "Hacia la nueva España." *Libertad* 27 June 1931: 1. Print.

Camba, Francisco. *Madridgrado: Documental film.* 1939. 2nd ed. Madrid: Ediciones Españolas, 1940. Print.

Canetti, Elias. *Masse und Macht.* Frankfurt am Main: Fischer, 1960. Print.

Cano Ballesta, Juan. *Las estrategias de la imaginación: Utopías literarias y retórica política bajo el franquismo.* Madrid: Siglo XXI, 1994. Print.

– *Literatura y tecnología: Las letras españolas ante la revolución industrial (1890–1940)*. Valencia: Pre-Textos, 1999. Print.

Carbajosa, Mónica, and Pablo Carbajosa. *La corte literaria de José Antonio: La primera generación cultural de la Falange*. Barcelona: Crítica, 2003. Print.

Carrasco González, Antonio M. *La novela colonial hispanoafricana: Las colonias africanas de España a través de la historia de la novela*. Casa de África 7. Madrid: SIAL, 2000. Print.

Carretero, José María [El Caballero Audaz]. *El héroe de la Legión. Novela de la guerra*. Madrid: Publicaciones Prensa Gráfica (primer número extraordinario), [c. 1930]. Print.

Carroll, David. *French Literary Fascism: Nationalism, Anti-Semitism, and the Ideology of Culture*. Princeton: Princeton UP, 1995. Print.

Casas de la Vega, Rafael. *El terror: Madrid 1936. Investigación histórica y catálogo de víctimas identificadas*. Madridejos, Toledo: Fénix, 1994. Print.

Casey, Edward S. *The Fate of Place: A Philosophical History*. Berkeley: U of California P, 1997.

Cassirer, Ernst. *An Essay on Man*. New Haven: Yale UP, 1944. Print.

Castillo Cáceres, Fernando. *Capital aborrecida: La aversión hacia Madrid en la literatura y la sociedad del 98 a la posguerra*. Madrid: Polifemo, 2010. Print.

Caudet, Francisco. *Las cenizas del fénix: La cultura española en los años 30*. Madrid: Ediciones de la Torre, 1993. Print.

Cavell, Stanley. *Philosophy the Day after Tomorrow*. Cambridge: Belknap, 2005. Print.

Céline, Louis-Ferdinand. *D'un château l'autre*. Paris: Gallimard, 1957. Print.

– *Nord*. Paris: Gallimard, 1960. Print.

– *Rigodon*. Paris: Gallimard, 1969. Print.

Cervera, Javier. *Madrid en guerra: La ciudad clandestina, 1936–1939*. Madrid: Alianza, 1998. Print.

Chambers, Samuel A. "Ghostly Rights." *Cultural Critique* 54 (2003): 148–77. Print.

Cheah, Pheng. "Spectral Nationality: The Living on [sur-vie] of the Postcolonial Nation in Neocolonial Globalization." *boundary 2* 26.3 (1999): 225–52. Print.

Chueca, Ricardo. *El fascismo en los comienzos del régimen de Franco: Un estudio sobre FET-JONS*. Madrid: Centro de Investigaciones Sociológicas, 1983. Print.

Churruca. "Nuestra misión." *Libertad* 27 Aug. 1934: 5. Print.

Cirici, Alexandre. *La estética del franquismo*. Barcelona: Gustavo Gili, 1977. Print.

Ciucci, Giorgio. *Gli architetti e il fascismo: Architettura e città, 1922–1944*. Turin: Einaudi, 1989. Print.

– "A Roma con Bottai." *Rassegna* 2.3 (1980): 66–71. Print.

Clausewitz, Carl von. *On War*. Trans. Michael Howard and Peter Paret. Ed. Michael Howard and Peter Paret. Princeton: Princeton UP, 1984. Print.

El combate de Sidi-Abrán. Raúl de Velasco 9. Barcelona: Publicaciones Mundial, c. 1925. Print.

"Compostura y orgullo." *F.E.* 8 Feb. 1934: 1.

"Conjunción y organización. Cómo ha de formarse el núcleo inicial del fascismo." *El Fascio. Haz Hispano* 16 Mar. 1933: 5. Print.

"La conquista del Estado." *Libertad* 20 May 1935: 2. Print.

"Consigna." *F.E.* 7 Dec. 1933: 1. Print.

El contrabando de armas. Raúl de Velasco 14. Barcelona: Publicaciones Mundial, c. 1925. Print.

Copjek, Joan, ed. *Radical Evil*. London: Verso, 1996. Print.

Cordero Torres, José María. *Aspectos de la misión universal de España*. Madrid: Ediciones de la Vicesecretaría de Educación Popular, 1942. Print.

– *La misión africana de España*. Madrid: Ediciones de la Vicesecretaría de Educación Popular, 1941. Print.

– *Tratado elemental de derecho colonial español*. Madrid: Editora Nacional, 1941. Print.

– "Trayectoria y perspectivas de nuestra expansión territorial." *Escorial. Revista de cultura y letras* May 1942: 265–74. Print.

Cresti, Carlo. *Architettura e fascismo*. Florence: Vallecchi, 1986. Print.

Cuadrado Costa, José. *Ramiro Ledesma Ramos, un romanticismo de acero*. Madrid: Barbarroja, 1990. Print.

Cueva Puente, Ángel. "La semiosis de la ideología en la biografía novelada: Leoncio Pancorbo, de José María Alfaro." *Actas del VII Seminario Internacional del Instituto de Semiótica Literaria, Teatral y Nuevas Tecnologías de la UNED*. Ed. Francisco Gutiérrez Carbajo and José Romera Castillo. Madrid: Visor, 1998. 373–86. Print.

"Dar." *F.E.* 8 Feb. 1934: 1. Print.

Dawes, James. *The Language of War: Literature and Culture in the U.S. from the Civil War through World War II*. Cambridge: Harvard UP, 2002. Print.

De Blij, Harm. *The Power of Place: Geography, Destiny, and Globalization's Rough Landscape*. Oxford: Oxford UP, 2009. Print.

"De cara al desfile." *Arriba* 13 May 1939: 5. Print.

de Certeau, Michel. *The Practice of Everyday Life*. Trans. Steven Rendall. Berkeley: U of California P, 1984. Print.

De Felice, Renzo. *Autobiografia del fascismo: Antologia di testi fascisti 1919–1945*. Turin: Einaudi, 2001. Print.

– *Mussolini: Edizione multimediale in 4 cd-rom*. Turin: Einaudi, 2001. CD-ROM. 4 discs.

De Prada, Juan Manuel. "La Escuela Romana del Pirineo: 'Fervor de Bilbao.'" *ABC* 30 July 2000: 27. Print.

de Terán, Fernando. *Historia del urbanismo en España.* Vol. 3. Madrid: Cátedra, 1999. Print.

Deleuze, Gilles, and Félix Guattari. *A Thousand Plateaus: Capitalism and Schizophrenia.* Trans. B. Massumi. London: Continuum, 1992. Print.

Delgado Gómez-Escalonilla, Lorenzo. *Imperio de papel: Acción cultural y política exterior durante el primer franquismo.* Madrid: CSIC, 1992. Print.

Derrida, Jacques. *Of Grammatology.* Trans. Gayatry Chakravorty Spivak. Baltimore: Johns Hopkins UP, 1997. Print.

– *On the Name.* Trans. John P. Leavey, Jr, David Wood, and Ian McLeod. Ed. Thomas Dutoit. Stanford: Stanford UP, 1995. Print.

– *Specters of Marx: The State of Debt, the Work of Mourning and the New International.* Trans. Peggy Kamuf. New York: Routledge, 1994. Print.

"El día de la victoria." *ABC* 20 May 1939: 9–21. Print.

Di Febo, Giuliana. *Ritos de guerra y de victoria en la España franquista.* Bilbao: Desclée de Brouwer, 2002. Print.

Díaz de Villegas, José. *La División Azul en línea.* 1967. Barcelona: Acervo, 2003. Print.

Díaz Nieva, José, and Enrique Uribe Lacalle. *El yugo y las letras: Bibliografía de, desde y sobre el nacionalsindicalismo.* Madrid: Ediciones Reconquista and Ediciones Barbarroja, 2005. Print.

Díaz Nosty, B. "Madrid imperial." In *Madrid: Cuarenta años* 23–36. Print.

Díaz-Plaja, Fernando. *La vida cotidiana en la España de la guerra civil.* Madrid: Edaf, 1994. Print.

Diéguez Patao, Sofía. *La generación del 25: primera arquitectura moderna en Madrid.* Madrid: Cátedra, 1997. Print.

"Disciplina." *F.E.* 18 Jan. 1934: 1. Print.

Doménech Girbau, Luis. "Corrientes de la arquitectura española contemporánea." *Arquitectura en regiones devastadas.* Ed. Secretaría General Técnica. Madrid: Centro de Publicaciones del Ministerio de Obras Públicas y Urbanismo, 1987. 61–77. Print.

Donald, James. *Imagining the Modern City.* Minneapolis: U of Minnesota P, 1999. Print.

Doyle, Michael W. *Empires.* Ithaca: Cornell UP, 1986. Print.

Drieu la Rochelle, Pierre. *Gilles.* 1942. Paris: Gallimard, 1996. Print.

Duplá Ansuategui, Antonio. "El clasicismo en el País Vasco: Ramón de Basterra." *Vasconia* 24 (1996): 81–100. Print.

Eatwell, Roger. *Fascism: A History.* New York: Penguin, 1997. Print.

– "The Nature of 'Generic Fascism': The 'Fascist Minimum' and the 'Fascist Matrix.'" Iordachi, *Comparative Fascist Studies* 134–61.

Edwards, Catharine, ed. *Roman Presences: Receptions of Rome in European Culture, 1789–1945*. Cambridge: Cambridge UP, 1999. Print.

Eizaguirre, Ramón P. *En el abismo rojo: Memorias de un español, once años prisionero en la URSS*. Madrid: Artes Gráficas "Rehyma," 1955. Print.

Ellwood, Sheelagh. *Historia de Falange Española*. Trans. A. Desmonts. Barcelona: Crítica, 2001. Print.

Elorza, Antonio. "El franquismo, un proyecto de religión política." *Fascismo y franquismo, cara a cara: Una perspectiva histórica*. Ed. Javier Tusell, Emilio Gentile, and Giuliana Di Febo. Madrid: Biblioteca Nueva, 2004. 69–82. Print.

"Empire." *Le Grand Robert de la langue française*. 2nd ed. 6 vols. Paris: Dictionnaires Le Robert, 2001.

"Empire." *Oxford English Dictionary*. 2nd ed. Oxford: Oxford UP, 2009. CD-ROM. 1 disc.

Entrambasaguas, Joaquín de. "Tomás Borrás." *Las mejores novelas contemporáneas*. Ed. J. de Entrambasaguas. Vol. 6. Barcelona: Planeta, 1960. 1263–1315. Print.

Espina, Concha. *Retaguardia (imágenes de vivos y muertos)*. 1937. 4th ed. Madrid: Edic. de la Vicesecretaría de Educación Popular, 1939. Print.

"Esquema de una política de aldea." *Arriba* 25 Apr. 1935: 1–2. Print.

"Estado e historia." *F.E.* 25 Jan. 1934: 1–2. Print.

Esteban, José, and Manuel Llusia, eds. *Literatura en la guerra civil: Madrid, 1936–1939*. Madrid: Talasa, 1999. Print.

Estébanez Calderón, Serafín. *Manual del oficial en Marruecos: Cuadro geográfico, estadístico, histórico, político y militar de aquel imperio*. Madrid: Imprenta de D. Ignacio Boix, Editor, 1844. Print.

Etlin, Richard A. *Modernism in Italian Architecture, 1890–1940*. Cambridge: MIT Press, 1991. Print.

Evans, Richard J. *The Coming of the Third Reich*. New York: Penguin, 2005. Print.

– *The Third Reich at War*. New York: Penguin, 2009. Print.

– *The Third Reich in Power*. New York: Penguin, 2005. Print.

Ezquerra, Miguel. *Berlín, a vida o muerte*. 1975. 4th ed. Granada: García Hispan, Editor, 1999. Print.

Falasca-Zamponi, Simonetta. *Fascist Spectacle: The Aesthetics of Power in Mussolini's Italy*. Berkeley: U of California P, 1997. Print.

"¿Un fascismo de Azaña y Prieto?" *No importa. Boletín de los días de persecución* 20 May 1936: 3. Print.

Fernández Arias, Adelardo [El Duende de la Colegiata]. *Madrid bajo "El Terror," 1936–1937 (Impresiones de un evadido, que estuvo a punto de ser fusilado)*. Zaragoza: Librería general, 1937. Print.

Fernández Piñero, Julián [Juan Ferragut]. *Memorias de un legionario*. Madrid: Imprenta artística Sáez Hermanos, 1925. Print.

F[ernández]-Fígares y Romero de la Cruz, María Dolores. *La colonización del imaginario: Imágenes de África*. Granada: Universidad de Granada, Centro de Investigaciones Etnológicas Ángel Ganivet, 2003. Print.

Figueres, Josep Maria. comp. and ed. *Madrid en guerra: Crónica de la batalla de Madrid, 1936–1939*. Barcelona: Destino, 2004. Print.

Flaquer, Alberto. *Checas de Madrid y Barcelona*. Barcelona: Rodegar, 1963. Print.

Flores López, Carlos. "La reconstrucción de Madrid y la arquitectura española (1939–1949)." Alvar Ezquerra 347–60. Print.

Foard, Douglas W. *The Revolt of the Aesthetes: Ernesto Giménez Caballero and the Origins of Spanish Fascism*. New York: Peter Lang, 1989. Print.

Foucault, Michel. *Dits et écrits, 1954–1988*. Quarto. Ed. Daniel Defert and François Ewald. 2 vols. Paris: Gallimard, 2001. Print.

– *Surveiller et punir: Naissance de la prison*. Paris: Gallimard, 1975. Print.

Fox, Edward Inman. *La invención de España*. Madrid: Cátedra, 1998. Print.

Foxá, Agustín de. "Arquitectura hermosa de las ruinas." *Vértice* April 1937: n.p.

– *Madrid de corte a cheka*. 1938. Las mejores novelas contemporáneas. Vol. 9. Ed. Joaquín de Entrambasaguas. Barcelona: Planeta, 1967. Print.

– "Pasa el Ejército." *ABC* 20 May 1939: 7. Print.

Franco, Francisco. "El Caudillo se dirige a los españoles." *ABC* 20 May 1939: 20–1. Print.

– "Discurso de S.E. el Generalísimo en la Radio Nacional." 20 Nov. 1938. Web. 9 Nov. 2010.

– "Discurso de unificación." 19 Apr. 1937. Web. 8 Nov. 2010.

– "El discurso del Caudillo." *Arriba* 20 May 1939: 1–2. Print.

– "Inauguración del Valle de los Caídos." 1 Apr. 1959. Web. 11 Nov. 2011.

– *Marruecos: Diario de una Bandera*. 1922. Madrid: Doncel, 1976. Print.

Frank, Joseph. *The Idea of Spatial Form*. New Brunswick: Rutgers UP, 1991. Print.

Freud, Sigmund. *Massenpsychologie und Ich-Analyse*. 2nd ed. Leipzig: Internationaler Psychoanalitischer Verlag, 1923. Print.

– *The Standard Edition of the Complete Psychological Works of Sigmund Freud*. Trans. James Strachey. Ed. James Strachey, Anna Freud, Alix Strachey, and Alan Tyson. 24 vols. London: Hogarth and Institute of Psycho-Analysis, 1953–74. Print.

Friedländer, Saul. *Nazi Germany and the Jews*. 2 vols. New York: Harper, 1997–2007. Print.

Friedrich, Jörg. *Der Brand: Deutschland im Bombenkrieg 1940–1945*. Munich: Propyläen, 2002. Print.

Frisby, David. *Citiscapes of Modernity: Critical Explorations*. Cambridge: Polity, 2001. Print.

Frost, Laura. *Sex Drives: Fantasies of Fascism in Literary Modernism.* Ithaca: Cornell UP, 2002. Print.

Fuertes, Julio. "'España una,' primer frente nacional en la zona roja, I." *Arriba* 13 Oct. 1939: 3. Print.

– "'España una,' primer frente nacional en la zona roja, II." *Arriba* 15 Oct. 1939: 1. Print.

– "'España una,' primer frente nacional en la zona roja, III." *Arriba* 19 Oct. 1939: 3. Print.

– "'España una,' primer frente nacional en la zona roja, IV." *Arriba* 22 Oct. 1939: 3. Print.

Fundación División Azul. Web. 7 Feb. 2008. <http://www.fundaciondivisionazul.org>.

Fussell, Paul. *The Great War and Modern Memory.* Oxford: Oxford UP, 1975. Print.

Gabola, P. Félix. "Ruinas gloriosas." *Arriba* 11 Aug. 1939: 3. Print.

Galán, Fermín. *La barbarie organizada: Novela del Tercio.* Madrid: Castro, 1931. Print.

Galey, John H. "Bridegrooms of Death: A Profile Study of the Spanish Foreign Legion." *Journal of Contemporary History* 4.2 (1969): 47–64. Print.

Gallego [Margalef], Ferran. *Ramiro Ledesma Ramos y el fascismo español.* Madrid: Síntesis, 2005. Print.

– "La realidad y el deseo." Gallego [Margalef] and Morente 253–447. Print.

Gallego [Margalef], Ferran, and Francisco Morente, eds. *Fascismo en España: Ensayos sobre los orígenes sociales y culturales del franquismo.* N.p.: Ediciones de Intervención Cultural / El Viejo Topo, 2005. Print.

García de Ledesma, Ramiro. *Encrucijada en la nieve: Un servicio de Inteligencia desde la División Azul.* Granada: García Hispán, editor, 1996. Print.

García Figueras, Tomás. *Recuerdos centenarios de una guerra romántica: La guerra de África de nuestros abuelos (1859–60).* Madrid: CSIC, Instituto de Estudios Africanos, 1961. Print.

– *Reivindicaciones de España en el Norte de África.* Madrid: S.I.E.M, 1942. Print.

García Pérez, Nemesio. "Contra la ciudad." *Libertad* 11 Mar. 1935: 5. Print.

García Queipo de Llano, Genoveva. *Los intelectuales y la Dictadura de Primo de Rivera.* Madrid: Alianza, 1988. Print.

García Serrano, Rafael. "A Roma por todo y volver a reír: Memoria de la conferencia de Ernesto Giménez Caballero: Roma en la literatura española." *Jerarquía. La revista negra de la Falange* 1 (1936): 1–30. Print.

– *Eugenio o proclamación de la Primavera.* 1938. Madrid: Fermín Uriarte, 1964. Print.

– *La fiel infantería.* 1943. Madrid: Eskua, 1958. Print.

– *Plaza del Castillo.* 1951. Biblioteca El Mundo, Las mejores novelas en caste-
llano del siglo XX. Madrid: Bibliotex, 2001. Print.

García Suárez, Pedro. *Legión 1936.* Madrid: Sagitario, Ediciones de los Estudian-
tes Españoles, 1945. Print. A

García-Moreno Barco, Francisco. "El ideal imperialista de Falange Española y
su proyección sobre Hispanoamérica a través del concepto de 'Hispanidad.'"
Atenea 14.1–2 (1994): 23–34. Print.

Garzón, Baltasar. "Auto. Diligencias previas proc. abreviado 399/2006. Juzgado
Central de Instrucción número 005. Audiencia Nacional." 16 Oct. 2008. Web.
20 Nov. 2010.

Gat, Azar. *Fascist and Liberal Visions of War: Fuller, Liddell Hart, Douhet, and Other
Modernists.* Oxford: Oxford UP, 1998. Print.

Gay, Peter. *Weimar Culture: The Outsider as Insider.* New York: Norton, 2001.

Gay, Vicente. *Madre Roma.* Barcelona: Bosch, 1935. Print.

Geertz, Clifford. *The Interpretation of Cultures.* 1973. New York: Basic Books,
2000.

Geldof, Koenraad. "The Unbearable Literariness of Literature: Spectral
Marxism and Metaphysical Realism in Charles Taylor's 'Sources of the Self.'"
New Literary History 30.2 (1999): 325–49. Print.

"Generación actual." *F.E.* 19 July 1934: 3. Print.

Gennep, Arnold van. *Les Rites de passage: Étude systématique des rites de la porte et
du seuil, de l'hospitalité, de l'adoption, de la grossesse et de l'accouchement, de la naissance, de l'enfance, de la puberté, de l'initiation, de l'ordination, du couronnement
des fiançailles et du mariage, des funérailles, des saisons, etc.* Paris: É. Nourri, 1909.
Print.

Gentile, Emilio. "Fascism as a Political Religion." *Journal of Contemporary History*
25.2–3 (1990): 229–51. Print.

– *The Sacralization of Politics in Fascist Italy.* Trans. Keith Botsford. Cambridge:
Harvard UP, 1996. Print.

– *The Struggle for Modernity: Nationalism, Futurism, and Fascism.* Westport:
Praeger, 2003. Print.

Gibbs-Smith, Charles H. *Aviation: A Historical Survey from Its Origins to the End of
the Second World War.* 2nd ed. London: Science Museum, 2003. Print.

Gibson, Ian. *En busca de José Antonio.* Barcelona: Planeta, 1980. Print.

Giesler, Hermann. *Ein anderer Hitler: Bericht seines Architekten Hermann Giesler: Er-
lebnisse, Gespräche, Reflexionen.* Leoni am Starnberger See: Druffel, 1977. Print.

Gil Benumeya, Rodolfo. *Marruecos andaluz.* Madrid: Ediciones de la Vicesecretaría de Educación Popular, 1942. Print.

Gil Casado, Pablo. "La novela fascista española: mística del personaje falangista." *España contemporánea* 3.2 (1990): 79–90. Print.

Giménez Caballero, Ernesto. *Arte y Estado*. Madrid: Gráfica Universal, 1935. Print.

– "Bohemios, no: cófrades." *Arriba* 21 Mar. 1935: 4. Print.

– *Circuito imperial*. Madrid: La Gaceta Literaria, 1929. Print.

– "En torno al casticismo de Italia. Carta a un compañero de la joven España." *La Gaceta Literaria* 15 Feb. 1929: 1, 5. Print.

– "España y Roma, I. Introducción. La estirpe de un instinto." *F.E.* 11 Jan. 1934: 10. Print.

– "España y Roma, II. Roma y la España antigua." *F.E.* 18 Jan. 1934: 10–1. Print.

– "España y Roma, III. Séneca o los fundamentos estoicos del fascismo." *F.E.* 25 Jan. 1934: 8–10. Print.

– "España y Roma, IV. Romance andaluz y humorismo aragonés." *F.E.* 1 Feb. 1934: 9. Print.

– "España y Roma, V. Foro y campo." *F.E.* 8 Feb. 1934: 11. Print.

– "España y Roma, VI. Orbe y pueblo." *F.E.* 22 Feb. 1934: 14. Print.

– "España y Roma, VII. La primera Cristiandad." *F.E.* 12 Apr. 1934: 9. Print.

– "España y Roma, VIII. El Poeta español de Cristo." *F.E.* 19 Apr. 1934: 9. Print.

– "España y Roma, IX. La Cristiada Española." *F.E.* 26 Apr. 1934: 9–10. Print.

– "Exaltaciones de Madrid." *Jerarquía. La revista negra de la Falange* 2 (1937): 127–42. Print.

– *Genio de España: Exaltaciones a una resurección nacional. Y del mundo.*. 1932. 2nd ed. Madrid: Ediciones de La Gaceta Literaria, 1934. Print.

– *Hércules jugando a los dados*. Madrid: Ediciones "La Nave," 1928. Print.

– *Julepe de menta*. Madrid: Cuadernos literarios, 1929. Print.

– *Madrid nuestro*. Madrid: Ediciones de la Vicesecretaría de Educación Popular, 1944. Print.

– "Madrid, ya es demócratico." *El robinsón literario de España (o la república de las letras)* 4 (1931): 7. Print.

– "Nota para la tercera edición (1938)." *Genio de España. Exaltaciones a una resurrección nacional. Y del mundo.* By Giménez Caballero. Barcelona: Ediciones "Jerarquía," 1939. xii–xvii.

– *Notas marruecas de un soldado*. 1923. Barcelona: Planeta, 1983. Print.

– "Primacía del trabajo. El sentido social del fascismo." *El Fascio. Haz Hispano* 16 Mar. 1933: 10. Print.

– *Roma madre*. Madrid: Ediciones "Jerarquía," 1939. Print.

– "La unidad de la victoria (Alocución por Radio Nacional)." *Arriba* 19 May 1939: 8. Print.

– *Yo, inspector de alcantarillas (Epiplasmas)*. Madrid: Turner, 1975. Print.

Glantz, David M. *The Battle for Leningrad, 1941–1944*. Lawrence: U of Kansas P, 2002. Print.

Godlewska, Anna, and Neil Smith, eds. *Geography and Empire*. Oxford: Blackwell, 1994. Print.

Goebbels, Joseph. *Kampf um Berlin: Der Anfang*. 20 Aug. 2009. Web. 5 Nov. 2010 <http://www.archive.org/details/KampfUmBerlin-DerAnfang>.

Gómez Lozano, Pedro A. [Radug D'Aril]. *El desfile de la Victoria: Madrid 19–20 de Mayo de 1939, Año de la Victoria*. Madrid: Prensa Española, 1944. Print.

González Calleja, Eduardo, and Fredes Limón Nevado. *La Hispanidad como instrumento de combate: Raza e Imperio en la prensa franquista durante la guerra civil española*. Madrid: CSIC, 1988. Print.

González de Canales, Fernando. "Maldito sea el pueblo que olvida a sus héroes…" 7 Dec. 2008. Web. 7 Feb. 2009. <http://www.generalisimofranco .com/opinion02/100.htm>.

González Ruiz, Nicolás. "Función social de la crítica." *Escorial. Revista de cultura y letras* Nov. 1941: 274–84. Print.

Gordon, Avery F. *Ghostly Matters: Haunting and the Sociological Imagination*. New ed. Minneapolis: U of Minnesota P, 2008. Print.

Gracia, Jordi. *La resistencia silenciosa: Fascismo y cultura en España*. Barcelona: Anagrama, 2004. Print.

Gramsci, Antonio. *Selections from the Prison Notebooks*. Trans. Quentin Hoare and Geoffrey Nowell Smith. Ed. Quentin Hoare and Geoffrey Nowell Smith. New York: International, 1971. Print.

El Gran Desfile de la Victoria en Madrid. Departamento Nacional de Cinematografía, 1939. Noticias en el archivo de RTVE. 26 Jan. 2009. Web. 9 Mar. 2010.

Graves, Robert. *Good-bye to All That*. 1929. 2nd ed. New York: Doubleday Anchor, 1957. Print.

The Great Dictator. Dir. Charlie Chaplin. Perf. Charlie Chaplin, Paulette Goddard, Jack Oakie. Charlie Chaplin, 1940. Film.

Gregor, A. James. *Mussolini's Intellectuals: Fascist Social and Political Thought*. Princeton: Princeton UP, 2005. Print.

– *The Search for Neofascism: The Use and Abuse of Social Science*. Cambridge: Cambridge UP, 2006. Print.

Greimas, A.J., and J. Courtés. *Semiotics and Language: An Analytical Dictionary*. Trans. Larry Crist et al. Bloomington: Indiana UP, 1982. Print.

Griffin, Roger. General Introduction. Griffin, *Fascism* 1–12. Print.

– *Modernism and Fascism: The Sense of a Beginning under Mussolini and Hitler*. Basingstoke: Palgrave Macmillan, 2007. Print.

– *The Nature of Fascism*. New York: St. Martin's, 1991. Print.

– ed. *Fascism*. Oxford: Oxford UP, 1995. Print.

Grossman, Dave. *On Killing: The Psychological Cost of Learning to Kill in War and Society*. Boston: Little, Brown, 1996. Print.

Guillén Salaya, F. *El diálogo de las pistolas.* Madrid: Biblioteca "Atlántico," 1931. Print.

– *Mirador literario: Párabola de la nueva literatura.* Madrid: Biblioteca "Atlántico," 1931. Print.

Gupta, Akhil, and James Ferguson. "'Culture': Space, Identity and the Politics of Difference." *Culture, Power, Place.* Ed. Akhil Gupta and James Ferguson. Durham: Duke UP, 1997. 33–51. Print.

"Hábito y estilo." *F.E.* 18 Jan. 1934: 6–7. Print.

"Hacia la revolución nacional sindicalista." *F.E.* 12 July 1934: 7. Print.

Hamann, Brigitte. *Hitlers Wien: Lehrjahre eines Diktators.* Munich: Piper, 1996. Print.

Hamilton, Alastair. *The Appeal of Fascism: A Study of Intellectuals and Fascism, 1919–1945.* New York: Macmillan, 1971. Print.

Harley, J.B. *The New Nature of Maps: Essays in the History of Cartography.* Ed. Paul Laxton. Baltimore: Johns Hopkins UP, 2001. Print.

Harvey, David. *The Condition of Postmodernity: An Enquiry into the Origins of Cultural Change.* Oxford: Blackwell, 1989. Print.

– *Cosmopolitanism and the Geographies of Freedom.* New York: Columbia UP, 2009. Print.

– *Spaces of Hope.* Berkeley: U of California P, 2000. Print.

– *The Urban Experience.* Baltimore: Johns Hopkins UP, 1989. Print.

Heidegger, Martin. "Building Dwelling Thinking." Trans. A. Hofstadter. *Poetry, Language, Thought.* By Heidegger. New York: Harper, 1971. 145–61. Print.

Hernández Navarro, Antonio José. *Ida y vuelta.* 1946. Ed. Carlos Caballero Jurado. Madrid: Actas, 2004. Print.

Hernando, Miguel Ángel. *Prosa vanguardista en la generación del 27 (Gecé y La Gaceta literaria).* Madrid: Prensa Española, 1975. Print.

Herreros, Isabelo. *El Alcázar de Toledo: Mitología de la cruzada de Franco.* Madrid: Vosa, 1995. Print.

Hewitt, Andrew. "The Bad Seed: 'Auschwitz' and the Physiology of Evil." Copjek 74–104. Print.

– *Fascist Modernism: Aesthetics, Politics, and the Avant-Garde.* Stanford: Stanford UP, 1993. Print.

Heydebreck, Peter. *Wir Wehr-Wölfe: Erinnerung eines Freikorps-Führer.* 3rd ed. Leipzig: Verlag von K.F. Koehler, 1931.

Hickey, Leo. "Presupposition and Implicature in *Madrid, de corte a checa.*" *Bulletin of Hispanic Studies* 73 (1996): 419–35. Print.

Hickman, Miranda B. *The Geometry of Modernism: The Vorticist Idiom in Lewis, Pound, H.D., and Yeats.* Austin: U of Texas P, 2005. Print.

Hillers de Luque, Sigfredo. *Ética y estilo falangistas.* Madrid: Gráficas Lázaro Carrasco, 1974. Print.

Hitler, Adolf. *Hitler's Table Talk, 1941–44: His Private Conversations*. Trans. Norman Cameron and R.H. Stevens. London: Weidenfeld and Nicolson, 1973. Print.

– *Mein Kampf*. Trans. Ralph Manheim. Boston: Houghton Mifflin, 1999. Print.

– *The Speeches of Adolf Hitler, April 1922–August 1939*. Trans. Norman H. Baynes. Ed. Norman H. Baynes. Vol. 1. 2 vols. New York: Fertig, 1969. Print.

Horkheimer, Max, and Theodor W. Adorno. "On the Theory of Ghosts." *Dialectic of Enlightenment*. Trans. John Cumming. London: Verso, 1997. 215–16. Print.

Huidobro Pardo, Enrique. *Escarmentemos Meditaciones de un refugiado con un epílogo de asalto al Consulado*. Madrid: Fax, 1940. Print.

Husserl, Edmund. "The World of the Living Present and the Constitution of the Surrounding World External to the Organism." Trans. Frederick A. Elliston and Lenore Langsdorf. *Husserl: Shorter Works*. Ed. Peter McCormick and Frederick A. Elliston. Notre Dame: U of Notre Dame P, 1981. 238–50. Print.

Hynes, Samuel. *The Soldier's Tale: Bearing Witness to Modern War*. London: Penguin, 1997. Print.

Iglesias García, Arturo. "Canto a Castilla." *Libertad* 11 June 1934: 10. Print.

"Imperio." *Diccionario de la lengua española*. 26th ed. Madrid: Real Academia Española, Espasa-Calpe, 2003. Print.

"El Imperio." *F.E.* 26 Apr. 1934: 3. Print.

Iordachi, Constantin. "Comparative Fascist Studies: An Introduction." Iordachi, *Comparative Fascist Studies* 1–50. Print.

– ed. *Comparative Fascist Studies: New Perspectives*. London: Routledge, 2010. Print.

Iribarren, Manuel. *La ciudad*. Madrid: Ediciones Españolas, 1939. Print.

Jameson, Fredric. *Fables of Aggression: Wyndham Lewis, the Modernist as Fascist*. Berkeley: U of California P, 1979. Print.

– "War and Representation." *PMLA* 124.5 (2009): 1532–47. Print.

Jenkyns, Richard, ed. *The Legacy of Rome: A New Appraisal*. Oxford: Oxford UP, 1992. Print.

Jensen, Geoffrey. *Irrational Triumph: Cultural Despair, Military Nationalism, and the Ideological Origins of Franco's Spain*. Reno: U of Nevada P, 2002. Print.

Jiménez Campo, Javier. *El fascismo en la crisis de la Segunda República española*. Madrid: Centro de Investigaciones Sociológicas, 1979. Print.

Juliá Díaz, Santos. "Madrid, capital del Estado." Juliá [Díaz], Ringrose, and Segura 393-410. Print.

– *Madrid, 1931–1934: De la fiesta popular a la lucha de clases*. Madrid: Siglo XXI, 1984. Print.

– ed. *Víctimas de la guerra civil*. Madrid: Temas de Hoy, 1999. Print.

Juliá [Díaz], Santos, David Ringrose, and Cristina Segura. *Madrid: Historia de una capital.* Madrid: Alianza, 1994. Print.

Jünger, Ernst. *Feuer und Blut: ein kleiner Ausschnitt aus einer grossen Schlacht.* Berlin: Frundsberg, 1929. Print.

– *Der Kampf als inneres Erlebnis.* Berlin: Mitller, 1922. Print.

– *In Stahlgewittern.* Stuttgart: Klett, 1961. Print.

"Justificación de la violencia." *No importa. Boletín de los días de persecución* 6 June 1936: 1. Print.

Kallis, Aristotle A., ed. *The Fascism Reader.* London: Routledge, 2003. Print.

– *Fascist Ideology: Territory and Expansionism in Italy and Germany, 1922–1945.* London: Routledge, 2000. Print.

Kant, Immanuel. *Kritik der reinen Vernunft.* Ed. Raymund Schmidt. Hamburg: Felix Meiner, 1956. Print.

– *Metaphysik der Sitten, erster Teil: Metaphysische Anfangsgründe der Rechtslehre.* Ed. Bern Ludwig. Hamburg: Felix Meiner, 1998. Print.

Kaplan, Alice Yaeger. *Reproductions of Banality: Fascism, Literature, and French Intellectual Life.* Minneapolis: U of Minnesota P, 1986.

Kern, Stephen. *The Culture of Time and Space, 1880–1918.* Cambridge: Harvard UP, 1983. Print.

Kershaw, Ian. *Hitler.* 2 vols. New York: Norton, 2000–1. Print.

– *The "Hitler Myth": Image and Reality in the Third Reich.* Oxford: Clarendon, 1987.

Klein, Thoralf, and Frank Schumacher, eds. *Kolonialkriege: Militärische Gewalt im Zeichen des Imperialismus.* Hamburg: Hamburger Edition, 2006. Print.

Kleinfeld, Gerald R., and Lewis A. Tambs. *La División Española de Hitler: La División Azul en Rusia.* Trans. Roberto López. Madrid: San Martín, 1983. Print.

Klemperer, Victor. *The Language of the Third Reich. LTI-Lingua Tertii Imperii. A Philologist's Notebook.* Trans. M. Brady. London: Continuum, 2002. Print.

Kohn, Margaret. *Radical Space: Building the House of the People.* Ithaca: Cornell UP, 2003. Print.

Kristeva, Julia. *Powers of Horror: An Essay on Abjection.* Trans. Leon S. Roudiez. New York: Columbia UP, 1982. Print.

Kunisch, Johannes, and Herfried Münkler, eds. *Die Wiedergeburt des Krieges aus dem Geist der Revolution: Studien zum bellizistischen Diskurs des ausgehenden 18. und beginnenden 19. Jahrhunderts.* Berlin: Duncker & Humblot, 1999. Print.

Kurtz, Carmen. *El desconocido.* 1956. 16th ed. Barcelona: Planeta, 1976. Print.

La Porte, Pablo. *La atracción del imán: El desastre de Annual y sus repercusiones en la política europea (1921–1923).* Madrid: Biblioteca Nueva, 2001. Print.

Labanyi, Jo. "History and Hauntology; or, What Does One Do with the Ghost of the Past? Reflections on Spanish Film and Fiction of the Post-Franco Period."

Dismembering the Dictatorship: The Politics of Memory in the Spanish Transition to Democracy. Ed. Joan Ramon Resina. Amsterdam: Rodopi, 2000. 65–82. Print.

– "Introduction: Engaging with Ghosts; or, Theorizing Culture in Modern Spain." *Constructing Identity in Contemporary Spain: Theoretical Debates and Cultural Practice.* Ed. Jo Labanyi. Oxford: Oxford UP, 2002. 1–14. Print.

– *Myth and History in the Contemporary Spanish Novel.* Cambridge: Cambridge UP, 1989. Print.

– "Women, Asian Hordes and the Threat to the Self in Giménez Caballero's *Genio de España.*" *Bulletin of Hispanic Studies* 73.4 (1996): 377–87. Print.

Lacarta, Manuel. *Madrid y sus literaturas: Del modernismo y la generación del 98 a nuestros días.* Madrid: Ediciones La Librería, 2002. Print.

Laclau, Ernesto. *On Populist Reason.* London: Verso, 2005. Print.

– "'The Time Is out of Joint.'" *Diacritics* 25.2 (1995): 86–96. Print.

Laclau, Ernesto, and Chantal Mouffe. *Hegemony and Socialist Strategy: Towards a Radical Democratic Politics.* 2nd ed. London: Verso, 2001. Print.

Laín Entralgo, Pedro. "Meditación apasionada de la Falange." *Jerarquía. La revista negra de la Falange* 2 (1937): 164–9. Print.

Laqueur, Walter. *Fascism: Past, Present, and Future.* Oxford: Oxford UP, 1996. Print.

Larsen, Stein Ugelvik, Beatrice Sandberg, and Ronald Speirs, eds. *Faschismus und europäische Literatur.* Bern: Peter Lang, 1991. Print.

Le Bon, Gustave. *Psychologie des foules.* Paris: Alcan, 1895.

Lécuyer, M.C., and C. Serrano. *La Guerre d'Afrique et ses répercusions en Espagne: Idéologies et colonialisme en Espagne, 1859–1904.* Paris: Presses Universitaires de France, 1976. Print.

Ledesma Ramos, Ramiro. *Discurso a las juventudes de España.* Ledesma Ramos, *¿Fascismo?* 209–335. Print.

– *Escritos políticos: La Conquista del Estado. 1931.* Madrid: Trinidad Ledesma Ramos, 1986. Print.

– *¿Fascismo en España? Discurso a las juventudes de España.* Esplugues de Llobregat: Ediciones Ariel, 1968. Print.

– "Movimiento español JONS." *El Fascio. Haz Hispano* 16 Mar. 1933: 14–15. Print.

– "El sello de la muerte: La voluntad al servicio de las ansias de superación: poderío y grandeza intelectual. Web. 15 Sept. 2007.

Lefebvre, Henri. *The Production of Space.* Trans. Donald Nicholson-Smith. Oxford: Blackwell, 1991. Print.

– *State, Space, World: Selected Essays.* Trans. Neil Brenner, Gerald Moore, and Stuart Elden. Ed. Neil Brenner and Stuart Elden. Minneapolis: U of Minnesota P, 2009. Print.

– *The Urban Revolution*. Trans. Robert Bononno. Minneapolis: U of Minnesota P, 2003. Print.

– *Writings on Cities*. Trans. Eleonore Kofman and Elizabeth Lebas. Ed. Eleonore Kofman and Elizabeth Lebas. Oxford: Blackwell, 1996. Print.

Lehan, Richard. *The City in Literature: An Intellectual and Cultural History*. Berkeley: U of California P, 1998. Print.

Leibniz, Gottfried Wilhelm. *Philosophical Essays*. Trans. Roger Ariew and Daniel Garber. Ed. Roger Ariew and Daniel Garber. Indianapolis: Hackett, 1989. Print.

– *Philosophical Papers and Letters*. Trans. Leroy E. Loemker. Ed. Leroy E. Loemker. 2 vols. Chicago: U of Chicago P, 1956. Print.

Lentzen, Manfred. "Eine Fortsetzung der Episodios nacionales. Agustín de Foxás Roman *Madrid de corte a cheka*." *Spanische Literatur. Literatur Europas. Wido Hempel zum 65. Geburstag*. Ed. Frank Baasner. Tübingen: Max Niemeyer, 1996. 444–59. Print.

Levinas, Emmanuel. "La Souffrance inutile." *Giornale di Metafisica* 4 (1982): 13–26. Print.

"Libertad y unidad." *F.E.* 18 Jan. 1934: 1–2. Print.

Lindqvist, Sven. *A History of Bombing*. Trans. Linda Haverty Rugg. New York: New Press, 2001. Print.

Linehan, Thomas. *British Fascism 1918–39: Parties, Ideology and Culture*. Manchester Studies in Modern History. Manchester: Manchester UP, 2000. Print.

Linz, Juan. "Some Notes toward a Comparative Study of Fascism in Sociological Historical Perspective." *Fascism: A Reader's Guide. Analyses, Interpretations, Bibliography*. Ed. Walter Laqueur. Berkeley: U of California P, 1976. 3–123. Print.

Livingstone, David N. *The Geographical Tradition: Episodes in the History of a Contested Enterprise*. London: Blackwell, 1992. Print.

Llorente Hernández, Ángel. *Arte e ideología en el franquismo (1936–1951)*. Madrid: Visor, 1995. Print.

– "La representación en el arte franquista del mito del Alcázar de Toledo (1939–1945)." *Archivos de la filmoteca: Revista de estudios históricos sobre la imagen* 35 (2000): 61–9. Print.

López Barranco, Juan José. *El Rif en armas: La narrativa española sobre la guerra de Marruecos (1859–2005)*. Madrid: Mare Nostrum Comunicación, 2006. Print.

López García, David. *El blocao y el oriente: Una introducción al estudio de la narrativa del siglo XX de tema marroquí*. Murcia: Secretariado de Publicaciones, Universidad de Murcia, 1994. Print.

López Rienda, Rafael. *Juan León, legionario (Los héroes de la Legión). Novela de guerra*. Madrid: Imprenta Zoila Ascasíbar y Cía, 1927. Print.

Losemann, Volker. "The Nazi Concept of Rome." Edwards, *Roman Presences* 221–35. Print.

Loureiro, Ángel. "Spanish Nationalism and the Ghost of Empire." *Journal of Spanish Cultural Studies* 4.1 (2003): 65–76. Print.

Lücke, Bärbel. *Semiotik und Dissemination. Von A.J. Greimas zu Jacques Derrida. Eine erzähltheoretische Analyse anhand von Elfriede Jelineks "Prosa" "Oh Wildnis, oh Schutz von ihr."* Würzburg: Königshausen & Neumann, 2002. Print.

MacCannell, Juliet Flower. "Fascism and the Voice of Conscience." Copjek 46–73. Print.

Macipe López, Antonio. *Ramiro Ledesma Ramos.* Sevilla: Círculo Cultural La Conquista del Estado, 2003. Print.

Madariaga, María Rosa de. *España y el Rif: Crónica de una historia casi olvidada.* La Biblioteca de Melilla. 2nd ed. Melilla: Consejería de Cultura, UNED, Centro Asociado de Melilla, 2000. Print.

– *Los moros que trajo Franco.* Barcelona: RBA, 2006. Print.

"Madrid, preparada para recibir al Caudillo." *Arriba* 18 [May 1939]: 1. Print.

Madrid: Cuarenta años de desarrollo urbano 1940–1980. Vol. 5. Madrid: Ayuntamiento de Madrid, 1981. Print.

Maeztu, Ramiro de. *Defensa de la Hispanidad.* 1934. Buenos Aires: Poblet, 1952. Print.

Mainer, José-Carlos. "*Alma española* (1903–1904): Después del 98." *Miradas sobre España.* Ed. Facundo Tomás, Isabel Justo, and Sofía Barrón. Barcelona: Anthropos, 2011. 291–305.

– "De Madrid a Madridgrado (1936–1939): La capital vista por sus sitiadores." Albert, *Vencer* 181–98. Print.

– ed. *Falange y literatura: Antología.* Barcelona: Labor, 1971. Print.

– *Literatura y pequeña burguesía (Notas 1890–1950).* Madrid: Edicusa, 1972. Print.

– "Para leer a Ramón de Basterra (instrucciones de uso)." Basterra, *Poesía* 1: xiii–lviii. Print.

– "La retórica de la obviedad: Ideología e intimidad en algunas novelas de guerra." *Autour de la guerre d'Espagne, 1936–1939.* Ed. Serge Salaün and Carlos Serrano. Paris: Publications de la Sorbonne Nouvelle, 1989. 69–91. Print.

– "La segunda guerra mundial y la literatura española: algunos libros de 1940–1945." *La corona hecha trizas.* By Mainer. Barcelona: PPU, 1989. 171–201. Print.

Maingueneau, Dominique. *Le Discours littéraire: Paratopie et scène d'énonciation.* Paris: Armand Colin, 2004. Print.

Malaparte, Curzio. *Kaputt.* Trans. Cesare Foligno. New York: New York Review of Books Classics, 2005. Print.

"Manifiesto editorial." *Escorial. Revista de cultura y letras* Nov. 1940: 7–12. Print.

Mann, Michael. *Fascists.* Cambridge: Cambridge UP, 2004. Print.

Marin, Louis. "Establishing a Signification for Social Space: Demonstration, Cortege, Parade, Procession." *On Representation.* By Marin. Trans. Catherine Porter. Stanford: Stanford UP, 2001. 38–53. Print.

Marinetti, F[ilippo] T[ommaso]. *Critical Writings.* Trans. Doug Thomson. Ed. Günter Berghaus. New York: Farrar, Straus and Giroux, 2006. Print.

– *Teoria e invenzione futurista.* Ed. Luciano De Maria. Milan: Arnoldo Mondadori Editore, 1968.

Marquerie, Alfredo. *Cuatro pisos y la portería.* La novela de "Vértice." Madrid: Vértice, 1940. Print.

Martín Corrales, Eloy. *La imagen del magrebí en España: Una perspectiva histórica, siglos XVI–XX.* Barcelona: Ediciones Bellaterra, 2002. Print.

– ed. *Marruecos y el colonialismo español (1859–1912): De la guerra de África a la "penetración pacífica."* Barcelona: Edicions Bellaterra, 2002. Print.

Martín Gijón, Mario. "Nazismo y antisemitismo en la literatura falangista. En torno a *Poemas de la Alemania Eterna* (1940)." *Vanderbilt e-Journal of Luso-Hispanic Studies* 6 (2010). Web.

Martin-Márquez, Susan. *Disorientations: Spanish Colonialism in Africa and the Performance of Identity.* New Haven: Yale UP, 2008. Print.

Martinell Gifre, Francisco. *La política con alas: José Antonio, Ramiro y Onésimo desde una perspectiva actual.* Madrid: Ediciones del Movimiento, 1974. Print.

Martínez Cachero, José María. "Cuatro novelas españolas 'de' y 'en' la guerra civil (1935–1939)." *Bulletin Hispanique* 85.3–4 (1983): 281–98. Print.

– *La novela española entre 1936 y 1980: Historia de una aventura.* Madrid: Castalia, 1985. Print.

Martínez de Bedoya, Javier (*see also* Bedoya, Javier M. de). *Onésimo Redondo, caudillo de Castilla.* Valladolid: Libertad, 1937. Print.

Martínez de Campos y Serrano, Carlos. *España bélica. El siglo XX: Marruecos.* Madrid: Aguilar, 1972. Print.

Martínez Gorriarán, Carlos, and Imanol Agirre Arriaga. *Estética de la diferencia (El arte vasco y el problema de la identidad, 1882–1966).* Irún, Donostia: Alberdania, galleria altxerri, 1995.

Mata, Pedro. *Los moros del Riff o el presidiario de Alhucemas.* Barcelona: Manini Hermanos, 1856. Print.

Mata Induráin, Carlos. "La guerra civil y la ideología falangista en *La fiel infantería,* de R. García Serrano." *Revista anthropos: Huellas del conocimiento* 148 (1993): 83–7. Print.

Mateo Dieste, Josep Lluís. *La "hermandad" hispano-marroquí: Política y religión bajo el protectorado español de Marruecos (1912–1956).* Barcelona: Edicions Bellaterra, 2003. Print.

Mayer, Arno J. *Why Did the Heavens Not Darken? The "Final Solution" in History*. New York: Pantheon, 1988. Print.

Mazower, Mark. *Hitler's Empire: How the Nazis Ruled Europe*. New York: Penguin, 2008. Print.

McLoughlin, Kate, ed. *The Cambridge Companion to War Writing*. Cambridge: Cambridge UP, 2009. Print.

– "War and Words." McLoughlin, *Cambridge Companion* 15–24. Print.

Merino, Eloy E., and H. Rosi Song, eds. *Traces of Contamination: Unearthing the Francoist Legacy in Contemporary Spanish Discourse*. Lewisburg: Bucknell UP, 2005. Print.

Merleau-Ponty, Maurice. *Phénomenologie de la perception*. Paris: Gallimard, 1945. Print.

Mermall, Thomas. "Aesthetics and Politics in Falangist Culture (1935–45)." *Bulletin of Hispanic Studies* 50 (1973): 45–55. Print.

Michaud, Eric. *The Cult of Art in Nazi Germany*. Trans. Janet Lloyd. Stanford: Stanford UP, 2004. Print.

Micó España, Carlos. *Los Caballeros de la Legión (El libro del Tercio de Extranjeros)*. Madrid: Sucesores de Rivadeneyra, 1922. Print.

– *El camillero de la Legión: Novela de la guerra*. La Novela de Hoy 12. Madrid: Sucesores de Rivadeneyra, 1922. Print.

Millán Astray, José. *La Legión*. Madrid: V.H. Sanz Calleja, 1923. Print.

Miller, John C. *Los testimonios literarios de la guerra español-marroquí: Arturo Barea, José Díaz Fernández, Ernesto Giménez Caballero, Ramón Sender*. Ann Arbor: University Microfilms, 1978. Print.

Miller, J. Hillis. *Topographies*. Stanford: Stanford UP, 1993. Print.

Milza, Pierre. *Fascisme français: Passé et présent*. Paris: Flammarion, 1987. Print.

Mínguez Goyanes, José Luis. *Onésimo Redondo (1905–1936): Precursor sindicalista*. Madrid: San Martín, 1990. Print.

Minor, Heather Hyde. "Mapping Mussolini: Ritual and Cartography in Public Art during the Second Roman Empire." *Imago Mundi* 51 (1999): 147–62. Print.

Moneo, Rafael. "Madrid: los últimos veinticinco años (1940–1965)." In *Madrid: Cuarenta años* 79–94. Print.

Montero, Matías. "Universidad e Imperio." *F.E.* 12 July 1934: 7. Print.

Montero Díaz, Santiago. *Idea del Imperio*. Madrid: Escuela de Formación y Capacitación de la Vieja Guardia, 1943. Print.

– *Ramiro Ledesma Ramos*. Madrid: Círculo Cultural Ramiro Ledesma Ramos, 1962. Print.

Montes, Eugenio. "Castilla en pie." *F.E.* 7 Dec. 1933: 9. Print.

– *Elegías europeas*. Madrid: Afrodisio Aguado, 1949. Print.

Montoliú, Pedro. *Madrid en la guerra civil.* 2 vols. Madrid: Sílex, 1998–9. Print.

– *Madrid en la posguerra, 1939–1946: Los años de la represión.* Madrid: Sílex, 2005. Print.

"Moral de la falange clásica." *F.E.* 25 Jan. 1934: 6–7. Print.

Morales, Gustavo, and Luis E. Togores. *La División Azul: Las fotografías de una historia.* Madrid: La Esfera de los Libros, 2008. Print.

Morales Lezcano, Víctor. *Historia de Marruecos: De los orígenes tribales y las poblaciones nómadas a la independencia y la monarquía actual.* Madrid: La Esfera de los Libros, 2006. Print.

Moreno Juliá. Xavier. *La División Azul: Sangre española en Rusia, 1941–1945.* Barcelona: Crítica, 2005. Print.

Morgan, Philip. *Italian Fascism.* New York: St. Martin's, 1995. Print.

Mosse, George L. *The Crisis of German Ideology.* New York: Universal Library, 1964. Print.

– *Fallen Soldiers: Reshaping Memory of the World Wars.* Oxford: Oxford UP, 1990. Print.

– *The Fascist Revolution: Toward a General Theory of Fascism.* New York: Fertig, 1999. Print.

– ed. *International Fascism: New Thoughts and New Approaches.* London: Sage, 1979. Print.

Mumford, Lewis. *The City in History: Its Origins, Its Transformations, and Its Prospects.* New York: Harcourt Brace Jovanovich, 1961. Print.

Naval, María Ángeles. *La novela de Vértice y La novela del sábado.* Madrid: Consejo Superior de Investigaciones Científicas, 2000. Print.

Nerín, Gustau. *La guerra que vino de África.* Barcelona: Crítica, 2005. Print.

Neville, Edgar. *Frente de Madrid. La calle mayor. F.A.I. Don Pedro Hambre. Las muchachas de Brunete.* Madrid: Espasa-Calpe, 1941. Print.

Nietzsche, Friedrich. *Jenseits von Gut und Böse: Vorspiel zu einer Philosophie der Zukunft.* Munich: Goldmann, 1960. Print.

Nolte, Ernst. *Der Faschismus in seiner Epoche. Action française. Italianisher Faschismus. Nationalsozialismus.* Serie Piper 365. Munich: Piper, 1984. Print.

Nora, Eugenio G. de. *La novela española contemporánea (1939–1967).* 2nd ed. Vol. 3. Madrid: Gredos, 1971. Print.

Norris, Margot. *Writing War in the Twentieth Century.* Charlottesville: UP of Virginia, 2000. Print.

"Noticiero de España." *F.E.* 7 Dec. 1933: 4. Print.

Núñez Díaz-Balart, Mirta. *Los años del terror: La estrategia de dominio y represión del general Franco.* Madrid: La Esfera de los Libros, 2004. Print.

Núñez Seixas, Xosé Manoel. *¡Fuera el invasor! Nacionalismos y movilización bélica durante la guerra civil española (1936–1939).* Madrid: Marcial Pons, 2006. Print.

Olivera Tarancón, Manuel. "¿Es lícita la violencia?" *Libertad* 30 July 1934: 1. Print.

Onrubia Rebuelta, Javier. *Bibliografía sobre el Nacional-Sindicalismo.* Madrid: La Hora de España, 1987. Print.

– *Escritores falangistas.* 2nd ed. Vol. 1. Madrid: Fondo de Estudios Sociales, 1982. Print.

Oropesa, Salvador A. "*Madrid de corte a checa* (1938) de Agustín de Foxá: la novela falangista." *Letras peninsulares* 18.1 (2005): 221–37. Print.

Oroquieta Arbiol, Gerardo, and César García Sánchez. *De Leningrado a Odesa.* 2nd ed. Barcelona: AHR, 1958. Print.

Ors, Eugenio d'. *Novísimo glosario.* Madrid: Aguilar, 1946. Print.

– *Nuevo glosario.* 3 vols. Madrid: Aguilar, 1947–9. Print.

Ortega Gallarzagoitia, Elena. "Ramón de Basterra en Sevilla." *Ámbitos: Revista internacional de comunicación* 1 (1998): 333–44. Print.

Ortega y Gasset, José. *El Espectador.* Vol. 6. Madrid: Revista de Occidente, 1927. Print.

Ortiz Mateos, Antonio. "Toponimia franquista de las calles de Madrid." *Nuevatribuna.es.* Web. 13 Jan. 2010.

Ortiz Muñoz, Luis. *Glorias imperiales.* Madrid: Magisterio Español, 1940. Print.

Painter, Borden W., Jr. *Mussolini's Rome: Rebuilding the Eternal City.* New York: Palgrave Macmillan, 2005. Print.

Palacios Cueto, Teodoro, and Torcuato Luca de Tena. *Embajador en el infierno: Memorias del capitán Palacios: once años en los campos de concentración soviéticos.* 1955. 6th ed. Barcelona: Ojeda, 2006. Print.

Palomar Baró, Eduardo. "Traslado de los restos mortales de José Antonio del Monasterio del Escorial al Valle de los Caídos." Web. 24 Nov. 2011. <http://www.generalisimofranco.com>.

Palomo, María del Pilar. Introducción. Alarcón vii–lxxxv. Print.

Pando, Juan. *Historia secreta de Annual.* Madrid: Temas de Hoy, 1999. Print.

Paniagua, Eleuterio. *Los hombres se matan así.* Madrid: Lorenzana, 1961. Print.

Paret, Peter. *The Cognitive Challenge of War: Prussia 1806.* Princeton: Princeton UP, 2009. Print.

Pascual, Ángel María. "Tratado segundo de la Razón de Imperio." *Jerarquía. La revista negra de la Falange* 4 (1938): 33–64. Print.

Pastor, Manuel. *Los orígenes del fascismo en España.* Madrid: Tucar, 1975. Print.

Paxton, Robert O. *The Anatomy of Fascism.* New York: Knopf, 2004. Print.

– *Vichy France: Old Guard and New Order, 1940–1944.* New York: Knopf, 1972. Print.

Payne, Stanley G. "The Concept of Fascism." *Who Were the Fascists? Social Roots of European Fascists.* Ed. Stein Ugelvik Larsen, Bernt Hagtvet, and Jan Petter Myklebust. Bergen: Universitetsförlaget, 1980. 14–25. Print.

– *Fascism in Spain, 1923–1977.* Madison: U of Wisconsin P, 1999. Print.
– *Franco and Hitler: Spain, Germany, and World War II.* New Haven: Yale UP, 2008. Print.
– *A History of Fascism, 1914–1945.* Madison: U of Wisconsin P, 1995. Print.
Peloille, Manuelle. *Fascismo en ciernes: España 1922–1939. Textos recuperados.* Toulouse: Presses Universitaires du Mirail, 2005. Print.
Pemartín, Julián. *Teoría de la Falange.* Madrid: Editora Nacional, 1941. Print.
Peña Sánchez, Victoriano. *Intelectuales y fascismo: La cultura italiana del Ventennio Fascista y su repercusión en España.* Granada: Universidad de Granada, 1995. Print.
Pérez de Tudela, Almudena. "El Escorial como modelo entre la vanguardia y la posguerra: E. Giménez Caballero." *Literatura e imagen en El Escorial [Actas del Simposio, 1/4-IX-1996].* San Lorenzo de El Escorial: Servicio de Publicaciones R.C.U. Escorial-María Cristina, 1996. 1001–13. Print.
Pérez de Urbel, Fray Justo. "El arte y el imperio." *Jerarquía. La revista negra de la Falange* 3 (1938): 71–89. Print.
Pérez Firmat, Gustavo. *Literature and Liminality: Festive Readings in the Hispanic Tradition.* Durham: Duke UP, 1986. Print.
Petsch, Joachim. *Baukunst und Stadtplanung im Dritten Reich: Herleitung, Bestandsaufnahme, Entwicklung, Nachfolge.* Munich: Hanser, 1976. Print.
Piette, Adam. "War Zones." McLoughlin, *Cambridge Companion* 38–46. Print.
Pike, Burton. *The Image of the City in Modern Literature.* Princeton: Princeton UP, 1981. Print.
Piper, Karen. *Cartographic Fictions: Maps, Race, and Identity.* New Brunswick: Rutgers UP, 2002. Print.
Pla, Josep. *Madrid: El advenimiento de la República.* Trans. E. Gallego. Madrid: Alianza, 1986. Print.
Platón, Miguel. *Hablan los militares: Testimonios para la historia (1939–1996).* Barcelona: Planeta, 2001. Print.
Poggi, Christine. *Inventing Futurism: The Art and Politics of Artificial Optimism.* Princeton: Princeton UP, 2009. Print.
Pratt, Mary Louise. "Harm's Way: Language and the Contemporary Arts of War." *PMLA* 124.5 (2009): 1515–31. Print.
– *Imperial Eyes: Travel Writing and Transculturation.* London: Routledge, 1992. Print.
Preston, Paul. *Franco, "Caudillo de España."* Trans. Teresa Camprodón and Diana Falcón. Barcelona: Grijalbo Mondadori, 1994. Print.
– *The Politics of Revenge: Fascism and the Military in 20th-Century Spain.* London: Routledge, 1995. Print.
– *The Spanish Civil War: Reaction, Revolution, and Revenge.* Rev. and enl. ed. New York: Norton, 2007. Print.

– *The Spanish Holocaust: Inquisition and Extermination in Twentieth-Century Spain.* New York: W.W. Norton, 2012. Print.

Prill, Ulrich. "Mitos y mitografía en la literatura fascista." Albert, *Vencer* 167–79. Print.

Primo de Rivera, José Antonio. "Al volver: ¿Moda extranjera el fascismo?" *La Nación* 23 Oct. 1933. Print.

– *Obras de José Antonio Primo de Rivera.* Ed. Agustín del Río Cisneros. Madrid: Almena, 1970. Print.

"El pueblo." *F.E.* 5 July 1934: 3. Print.

"El pueblo y la calle." *Arriba* 30 Mar. 1939: 1. Print.

Puente, José-Vicente. *Madrid recobrado: Crónicas de antes y después del veintiocho de marzo.* Madrid: Imp. Samarán, 1939. Print.

Puente, Moisés. *Yo, muerto en Rusia: Memorias del alférez Ocañas de la División Azul.* 1954. 2nd ed. Madrid: San Martín, 2003. Print.

"Puntos de partida." *El Fascio. Haz Hispano* 16 Mar. 1933: 3. Print.

"Puntos iniciales." *F.E.* 7 Dec. 1933: 6–7. Print.

"¿Qué fue la División Azul?" *Fundación División Azul.* Web. 7 Feb. 2008. Print.

Rama, Carlos M. *Historia de las relaciones culturales entre España y la América Latina. Siglo XIX.* Mexico City: Fondo de Cultura Económica, 1982. Print.

Ramos, Carlos. *Construyendo la modernidad: Escritura y arquitectura en el Madrid moderno (1918–1937).* Lleida: Edicions de la Universitat de Lleida, 2011. Print.

Ramos, Demetrio [Mónico Mélida Monteagudo]. "Los resortes de Onésimo Redondo y los días 'grises' de sus Juntas Castellanas de Actuación Hispánica." *Aportes* 39 (1996): 35–40. Print.

Ramos González, Miguel. *La violencia en Falange Española.* Oviedo: TARFE, 1993. Print.

"Reconquista." *Libertad* 6 May 1935: 6. Print.

Redondo, Onésimo. "A España, por Castilla." *Libertad* 20 Nov. 1933: 3. Print.

– "La agresión socialista a la agricultura." *Libertad* 13 July 1931: 4. Print.

– "¡Castilla, salva a España!" *Libertad* 10 Aug. 1931: 1. Print.

– "Los enemigos de España." *Libertad* 27 June 1931: 1. Print.

– "Justificación de la violencia." *Libertad* 21 Dec. 1931: 5. Print.

– "Lo que somos y lo que queremos." Spec. Issue of *Libertad* 13 June 1932: 1. Print.

– "Manifiesto electoral de Onésimo Redondo." *Libertad* 2 Nov. 1933: 3–4. Print.

– "La misión de Castilla." *Libertad* 3 Aug. 1931: 2. Print.

– "El monopolio de la violencia." *Libertad* 26 Oct. 1931: 1. Print.

– "El peligro comunista." *Libertad* 10 Aug. 1931: 1. Print.

– "El peligro judío." *Libertad* 27 June 1931: 1. Print.

– "La revolución hispánica." *Libertad* 13 July 1931: 1. Print.

– *Textos de doctrina política.* 2 vols. Madrid: Publicaciones españolas, 1954–5. Print.

"Reflexiones sobre la violencia." *F.E.* 19 Apr. 1934: 4. Print.

Reich, Wilhelm. *The Mass Psychology of Fascism.* Trans. Mary Boyd Higgins. Ed. Mary Boyd Higgins and Chester M. Raphael. New York: Farrar, Straus and Giroux, 1970. Print.

Reig Tapia, Alberto. *Ideología e historia (Sobre la represión franquista y la guerra civil).* Madrid: Akal, 1984. Print.

– *Violencia y terror: Estudios sobre la guerra civil española.* Madrid: Akal, 1990. Print.

Remarque, Erich Maria. *Im Westen nichts Neues.* Berlin: Propyläen, 1929. Print.

"Renunciar." *F.E.* 8 Feb. 1934: 1. Print.

Resina, Joan Ramon, ed. *Iberian Cities.* London: Routledge, 2001.

Riber, Lorenzo. "España en la opinión romana." *Escorial. Revista de cultura y letras* Dec. 1941: 323–46. Print.

Ricci, Christián H. *El espacio urbano en la narrativa del Madrid de la Edad de Plata (1900–1938).* Madrid: CSIC, 2009. Print.

Richards, Thomas. *The Imperial Archive: Knowledge and the Fantasy of Empire.* London: Verso, 1993. Print.

Ricœur, Paul. *La Métaphore vive.* Paris: Éditions du Seuil, 1975. Print.

Ridruejo, Dionisio. *Cuadernos de Rusia. En la soledad del tiempo. Cancionero de Ronda. Elegías.* Ed. Manuel A. Penella. Madrid: Castalia, 1981. Print.

– *Los cuadernos de Rusia: Diario.* Ed. Gloria de Ros and César Armando Gómez. Barcelona: Planeta, 1978. Print.

Ríos-Font, Wadda C. *The Canon and the Archive: Configuring Literature in Modern Spain.* Lewisburg: Bucknell UP, 2004. Print.

Rodríguez Jiménez, José Luis. *¡A mí la Legión! De Millán Astray a las misiones de paz.* 5th ed. Barcelona: Planeta, 2005. Print.

– *De héroes e indeseables: La División Azul.* Madrid: Espasa-Calpe, 2007. Print.

– "El discurso antisemita en el fascismo español." *Raíces: Revista judía de cultura* 38 (2000): 27–40. Print.

– *Historia de Falange Española de las JONS.* Madrid: Alianza, 2000. Print.

Rodríguez Puértolas, Julio. *Historia de la literatura fascista española.* 2 vols. Madrid: Akal, 2008. Print.

– *Literatura fascista española.* 2 vols. Madrid: Akal, 1986. Print.

Romero, Luis. *Tudá (Allá).* Barcelona: Acervo, 1957. Print.

Ros, Samuel. *El hombre de los medios abrazos: Novela de lisiados.* Madrid: Biblioteca Nueva, 1995. Print.

– *Meses de esperanza y lentejas (la Embajada de Chile en Madrid).* La novela del sábado 23. Madrid: Ediciones Españolas, 1939. Print.

Rós Andreu, Juan B. *La conquista de Alhucemas o en el Tercio está el amor. Novela histórica (Escenas "crudas" de la famosa retirada de Xauen y del glorioso desembarco de las tropas españolas en Alhucemas).* Las Palmas: Tip. La Provincia, 1932. Print.

Ross, Kristin. *The Emergence of Social Space: Rimbaud and the Paris Commune.* Minneapolis: U of Minnesota P, 1988. Print.

Royo, Rodrigo. *El sol y la nieve.* Madrid: Talleres gráficos CIES, 1956. Print.

Ruiz Albéniz, Víctor. *¡Kelb rumi! (La novela de un español cautivo de los rifeños en 1921).* Madrid: Librería y Editorial Rivadeneyra, 1922. Print.

Ruiz Ayúcar, Ángel. *La Rusia que conocí.* Madrid: Ediciones del Movimiento, 1954. Print.

Ruiz de Alda, Julio. "Tierra." *Arriba* 18 Apr. 1935: 4. Print.

Rykwert, Joseph. *The Seduction of Place: The City in the Twenty-First Century.* New York: Pantheon, 2000. Print.

Sabín Rodríguez, José Manuel, ed. *La dictadura franquista (1936–1975): Textos y documentos.* Madrid: Akal, 1997. Print.

"Sacrificio." *F.E.* 11 Jan. 1934: 1. Print.

Said, Edward W. *Culture and Imperialism.* New York: Vintage, 1994. Print.

– *Orientalism.* New York: Vintage, 1978. Print.

Salas Larrazábal, Ramón. *El Protectorado de España en Marruecos.* Madrid: Mapfre, 1992. Print.

Salaverría, José María. "El desfile sagrado." *ABC* 20 May 1939: 7. Print.

Salvador, Tomás. *Camaradas 74.* Barcelona: Plaza & Janés, 1975. Print.

– *División 250.* 1954. Madrid: Armas Tomar Ediciones, 2006. Print.

Sambricio, Carlos. "La arquitectura española 1936–45: La alternativa falangista." *Cuando se quiso resucitar la arquitectura.* Murcia: Colegio Oficial de Aparejadores y Arquitectos Técnicos, 1983. 173–97. Print.

– "De nuevo sobre el Plan Bidagor." Sambricio, *El Plan Bidagor* 12–18. Print.

– "Madrid, 1941: Tercer año de la Victoria." *Madrid, vivienda y urbanismo: 1900–1960. De la 'normalización de lo vernáculo' al Plan Regional.* By Sambricio. Madrid: Akal, 2004. 289–328. Print.

– ed. *El Plan Bidagor 1941–1946. Plan general de ordenación de Madrid.* Madrid: Nerea, 2003. Print.

– "El Plan Regional del Comité de Reforma, Reconstrucción y Saneamiento de Madrid (CRRSM) de 1939." *Madrid, urbanismo y gestión municipal, 1920–1940.* Ed. Carlos Sambricio et al. Madrid: Area de Urbanismo e Infraestructuras, Gerencia Municipal de Urbanismo, 1984. 115–36. Print.

– "'¡Que coman república!' Introducción a un estudio de la Reconstrucción en la España de la Postguerra." *Cuando se quiso resucitar la arquitectura.* By Sambricio. Murcia: Colegio Oficial de Aparejadores y Arquitectos Técnicos, 1983. 199–243. Print.

– "La renovación arquitectónica en la posguerra." *Barcelona-Madrid 1898–1998: sintonías y distancias*. Ed. Xavier Bru de Sala. Barcelona: Centre de Cultura Contemporània de Barcelona, 1997. 234–9. Print.

– "La vivienda en Madrid, de 1939 al Plan de Vivienda Social, en 1959." *La vivienda en Madrid en la década de los 50: El Plan de Urgencia Social*. Ed. Carlos Sambricio et al. Madrid: Electa, 1999. 13–84. Print.

San Antonio Gómez, Carlos de. *El Madrid del 27: Arquitectura y vanguardia, 1918–1936*. Madrid: Comunidad de Madrid, Consejería de Educación, 2000. Print.

– *20 años de arquitectura en Madrid: La edad de plata, 1918–1936*. Madrid: Comunidad de Madrid, Consejería de Educación y Cultura, Secretaría General Técnica, 1996. Print.

Sánchez, Narciso. *Onésimo Redondo*. Madrid: Publicaciones españolas, 1953. Print.

Sánchez Diana, José María. *Cabeza de puente: Diario de un soldado de Hitler*. Abr. and rev. ed. by Carlos Caballero Jurado. 2nd ed. Alicante: García Hispán, editor, 1990. Print.

– *Ramiro Ledesma Ramos: Biografía*. Madrid: Editora Nacional, 1975. Print.

Sánchez Ferlosio, Rafael. *Sobre la guerra*. Barcelona: Destino, 2007. Print.

Sánchez Mazas, Rafael. "Algunas imágenes de la guerra." *El pueblo vasco* 26 Oct. 1921: 1 Print.

– "Antes de ir a Zeluán." *El pueblo vasco* 28 Sept. 1921: 1. Print.

– "Bajo el cañón de Nador." *El pueblo vasco* 20 Sept. 1921: 1. Print.

– "Bienvenida a los de Garellano." *El pueblo vasco* 4 Oct. 1921: 1. Print.

– "La campaña de África." Series. *El pueblo vasco* 14 Sept.–23 Dec. 1921. Print.

– "El contagio de afeminamiento." *El pueblo vasco* 15 Nov. 1921: 1. Print.

– "Desde Segangan a Zeluan con Garellano." *El pueblo vasco* 19 Oct. 1921: 1. Print.

– "Empezamos o acabamos." *El pueblo vasco* 2 Nov. 1921: 1. Print.

– "En la posición avanzada de El Had. Camino del zoco. La bandera del campamento." *El pueblo vasco* 20 Sept. 1921: 1. Print.

– "Examen de conciencia del cobarde." *El pueblo vasco* 6 Nov. 1921: 1. Print.

– "La excursión por el Gurugú y la excursión por la Historia." *El pueblo vasco* 16 Oct. 1921: 1. Print.

– "La furia de plazuela vista desde Melilla." *El pueblo vasco* 30 Oct. 1921: 1. Print.

– "Hacia Atlaten." *El pueblo vasco* 6 Oct. 1921: 1. Print.

– "Hacia Atlaten, II (continuación y fin)." *El pueblo vasco* 7 Oct. 1921: 1. Print.

– "Hacia Atlaten (III y último)." *El pueblo vasco* 8 Oct. 1921: 1. Print.

– "Haz y yugo." *El Fascio. Haz Hispano* 16 Mar. 1933: 8. Print.

– "Herrera, viviente." *Arriba* 2 July 1939: 1–2. Print.
– "Impresión de Sánchez Mazas." *El pueblo vasco* 18 Sept. 1921: 5. Print.
– "La impresión genuina." *El pueblo vasco* 3 Dec. 1921: 1. Print.
– "Los instantes y las figuras." *El pueblo vasco* 4 Nov. 1921: 1. Print.
– "Intermedio." *El pueblo vasco* 22 Nov. 1921: 1. Print.
– "Interrogaciones ante Berenguer." *El pueblo vasco* 7 Dec. 1921: 1. Print.
– "La Legión de los ilusos y tramposos." *El pueblo vasco* 27 Sept. 1921: 1. Print.
– "Los que se van en un desfile amargo." *El pueblo vasco* 20 Oct. 1921: 1. Print.
– "María de la Corona de Iguerman." *El pueblo vasco* 16 Nov. 1921: 1. Print.
– "Roma la vieja y Castilla la Nueva." *ABC* 21 June 1922: 2–3. Print.
– "La sed de vanagloria." *El pueblo vasco* 21 Sept. 1921: 1. Print.
– "Sensibilidad." *El pueblo vasco* 3 Nov. 1921: 1. Print.
– "Telegrama de nuestro enviado. La visita de Cierva. Los de Garellano." *El pueblo vasco* 12 Oct. 1921: 1. Print.
– *Las terceras de ABC.* Comp. Fernando Ponce. Madrid: Editorial Prensa Española, 1977.
– "Texto taquigráfico del discurso pronunciado por el consejero nacional y miembro de la Junta Política de FET y de las JONS, camarada Sánchez Mazas." *Arriba* 9 Apr. 1939: 8. Print.
– "Textos sobre una política de arte." *Escorial. Revista de cultura y letras* Oct. 1942: 3–21. Print.
– "La toma de Atlaten." *El pueblo vasco* 11 Oct. 1921: 1. Print.
– "La toma del zoco El Arbaa." *El pueblo vasco* 16 Sept. 1921: 1. Print.
– "La tragedia de Monte-Arruit. Impresión de Sánchez Mazas." *El pueblo vasco* 26 Oct. 1921: 1. Print.
– "Una mañana frente a Iguerman, I." *El pueblo vasco* 17 Nov. 1921: 1. Print.
– "Vuelven las mañanas ardientes de fuego. I, Taxuda." *El pueblo vasco* 10 Nov. 1921: 1. Print.
Sánchez-Biosca, Vicente. "Arquitectura, lugar de memoria y mito: El Alcázar de Toledo o la imagen prendida." Web. 1 Feb. 2010.
Sansot, Pierre. *Poétique de la ville*. Paris: Éditions Payot & Rivages, 2004. Print.
Santa Marina, Luys. *Tetramorfos (De las memorias de César Gustavo de Gimeno) / Domus*. Nuevos novelistas españoles. Madrid: Sucesores de Rivadeneyra, 1927. Print.
– *Tras el águila del César: Elegía del Tercio, 1921–1922*. 1924. Barcelona: Planeta, 1980. Print.
Santaló Rodríguez de Viguri, José Luis. *Introducción a la política del Imperio Nuevo*. Valladolid: Imp. Católica F. García Vicente, 1938. Print.
Santiáñez, Nil. "De la tropa al tropo: Colonialismo, escritura de guerra y enunciación metafórica en *Diario de un testigo de la guerra de África*." *Hispanic Review* 76.1 (2008): 71–93. Print.

– *Goya/Clausewitz: Paradigmas de la guerra absoluta*. Barcelona: Alpha Decay, 2009. Print.

Sartre, Jean-Paul. *Situations III*. Paris: Gallimard, 1949. Print.

Saz Campos, Ismael. *España contra España: Los nacionalismos franquistas*. Madrid: Marcial Pons, 2003. Print.

– *Fascismo y franquismo*. Valencia: Universitat de València, 2004. Print.

Scarry, Elaine. *The Body in Pain: The Making and Unmaking of the World*. Oxford: Oxford UP, 1985. Print.

Schmitt, Carl. *The Concept of the Political*. Trans. George Schwab. Expanded ed. Chicago: U of Chicago P, 2007. Print.

– *Theory of the Partisan: Intermediate Commentary on the Concept of the Political*. Trans. G.L. Ulmen. New York: Telos, 1997. Print.

Schmolling, Regine. *Literatur der Sieger: Der spanische Bürgerkriegsroman im gesellschaftlichen Kontext des frühen Franquismus*. Frankfurt am Main: Vervuert, 1990. Print.

Schneider, Michel, and José Cuadrado Costa. *Ramiro Ledesma, Pierre Drieu la Rochelle y Robert Brasillach por la Revolución Nacional*. Molins de Rei: Nueva República, 2002. Print.

Scobie, Alex. *Hitler's State Architecture: The Impact of Classical Antiquity*. University Park: Pennsylvania State UP, 1990. Print.

Sebald, W.G. *Luftkrieg und Literatur. Mit einem Essay zu Alfred Andersch*. 5th ed. Frankfurt am Main: Fischer Taschenbuch, 2005. Print.

Sebeok, Thomas A., and Jean Umiker-Sebeok. *The Semiotic Sphere*. New York: Plenum , 1986. Print.

Selva, Enrique. *Ernesto Giménez Caballero: Entre la vanguardia y el fascismo*. Valencia: Pre-textos, Institució Alfons el Magnànim, 1999. Print.

Serrano Suñer, Ramón "Una orden del ministro de la Gobernación, camarada Serrano Suñer." *Arriba* 17 May 1939: 1. Print.

Servicio Histórico Militar. *Historia de las campañas de Marruecos*. Vol. 4. Madrid: Imprenta Ideal, 1983. Print.

Sharpe, William, and Leonard Wallock. "From 'Great Town' to 'Nonplace Urban Realm': Reading the Modern City." Sharpe and Wallock, *Visions* 1–50. Print.

– eds. *Visions of the Modern City: Essays in History, Art, and Literature*. Baltimore: Johns Hopkins UP, 1987. Print.

Sherry, Vincent, ed. *The Cambridge Companion to the Literature of the First World War*. Cambridge: Cambridge UP, 2005. Print.

– "The Great War and Literary Modernism in England." Sherry, *The Cambridge Companion* 113–37. Print.

– *The Great War and the Language of Modernism*. New York: Oxford UP, 2006. Print.

Shoa. Dir. Claude Lanzmann. Claude Lanzmann, 1985. Film.

Silva, Umberto. *Arte e ideología del fascismo.* Trans. Manuel Aznar. Valencia: Fernando Torres, 1975. Print.

Simón Valdivieso, José. "El campesino de España estará con nosotros." *F.E.* 7 Dec. 1933: 5. Print.

Sloterdijk, Peter. *Terror from the Air.* Trans. Amy Patton and Steve Corcoran. New York: Semiotext(e), 2009. Print.

Smith, Neil. *Uneven Development: Nature, Capital, and the Production of Space.* 3rd ed. Athens: U of Georgia P, 2008. Print.

Sobejano, Gonzalo. *Novela española de nuestro tiempo (en busca del pueblo perdido).* Madrid: Prensa Española, 1970. Print.

"Sobriedad." *F.E.* 8 Feb. 1934: 1. Print.

Soja, Edward W. *Postmodern Geographies: The Reassertion of Space in Critical Social Theory.* London: Verso, 1989. Print.

– *Thirdspace: Journeys to Los Angeles and Other Real-and-Imagined Places.* Oxford: Blackwell, 1996. Print.

Solas García, José. *La Nación en la Filosofía de la Revolución Española.* Madrid: "Fax," 1940. Print.

Soldevila Durante, Ignacio. *Historia de la novela española (1936–2000).* Vol. 1. Madrid: Cátedra, 2001. Print.

Sorel, Georges. *Réflexions sur la violence.* 1907. Paris: Rivière, 1921. Print.

Soucy, Robert. *French Fascism: The First Wave, 1924–1933.* New Haven: Yale UP, 1986. Print.

– *French Fascism: The Second Wave, 1933–1939.* New Haven: Yale UP, 1995. Print.

Southworth, Herbert R. "El imperio ficción de la Falange y el imperio realidad de Castilla." *Cultura, sociedad y política en el mundo actual.* Ed. Ministerio de Educación y Ciencia and Universidad Internacional Menéndez Pelayo. Madrid: Universidad Internacional Menéndez Pelayo, 1981. 199–207. Print.

Spackman, Barbara. *Fascist Virilities: Rhetoric, Ideology, and Social Fantasy in Italy.* Minneapolis: U of Minnesota P, 1996. Print.

Spain. Cortes Generales. "LEY 52/2007, de 26 de diciembre, por la que se reconocen y amplían derechos y se establecen medidas en favor de quienes padecieron persecución o violencia durante la guerra civil y la dictadura." *Boletín Oficial del Estado* 27 Dec 2007: 53410–16. Print.

Speer, Albert. *Inside the Third Reich: Memoirs.* Trans. Richard and Clara Winston. New York: Macmillan, 1970. Print.

Spivak, Gayatri Chakravorty. "Ghostwriting." *Diacritics* 25.2 (1995): 65–84. Print.

Spotts, Frederic. *Hitler and the Power of Aesthetics.* Woodstock: Overlook, 2009. Print.

Sprinker, Michael, ed. *Ghostly Demarcations: A Symposium on Jacques Derrida's Specters of Marx*. London: Verso, 1999. Print.

Spurr, David. *The Rhetoric of Empire: Colonial Discourse in Journalism, Travel Writing, and Imperial Administration*. Durham: Duke UP, 1993. Print.

Stackelberg, Roderick. *Idealism Debased: From Völkisch Ideology to National Socialism*. Kent: Kent State UP, 1981. Print.

Steiner, George. *Language and Silence: Essays on Language, Literature, and the Inhuman*. New Haven: Yale UP, 1998. Print.

Sternhell, Zeev. "Fascism." Iordachi, *Comparative Fascist Studies* 53–9. Print.

– *Neither Right nor Left: Fascist Ideology in France*. Trans. David Maisel. Princeton: Princeton UP, 1986. Print.

Sternhell, Zeev, with Mario Sznajder and Maia Asheri. *The Birth of Fascist Ideology: From Cultural Rebellion to Political Revolution*. Trans. David Maisel. Princeton: Princeton UP, 1994. Print.

Stone, Marla. "A Flexible Rome: Fascism and the Cult of *Romanità*." Edwards, *Roman Presences* 205–20. Print.

Sueiro, Daniel, and Bernardo Díaz Nosty. *Historia del franquismo*. 4 vols. Madrid: Sedmay, 1978. Print.

Tarde, Gabriel de. *L'Opinion et la foule*. 4th ed. Paris: Félix Alcan, 1922. Print.

Tarduchy, Emilio R. *Nociones del arte de mandar aplicadas a la Falange. Conferencia dada por el coronel de infantería camarada Tarduchi*. n.p.: n.p., n.d. Print.

Tasca, Angelo. *Nascita e avvento del fascismo; l'Italia dal 1918 al 1922*. Florence: La Nuova Italia, 1963. Print.

Taylor, Robert R. *The Word in Stone: The Role of Architecture in the National Socialist Ideology*. Berkeley: U of California P, 1974. Print.

Teut, Anna. *Architektur im Dritten Reich, 1933–1945*. Frankfurt am Main: Ullstein, 1967. Print.

Thamer, Hans-Ulrich. "The Orchestration of the National Community: The Nuremberg Party Rallies of the NSDAP." *Fascism and Theatre: Comparative Studies on the Aesthetics and Politics of Performance in Europe, 1925–1945*. Ed. Günter Berghaus. Providence: Berghahn, 1996. 172–90. Print.

Theweleit, Klaus. *Male Fantasies*. Trans. Stephen Conway, Erica Carter, and Chris Turner. 2 vols. Minneapolis: U of Minnesota P, 1987. Print.

Thomas, Gareth. *The Novel of the Spanish Civil War (1936–1975)*. Cambridge: Cambridge UP, 1990. Print.

Thurlow, Richard. *Fascism in Britain: A History, 1918–1985*. Oxford: Blackwell, 1987. Print.

"La tierra." *Libertad* 10 Dec. 1934: 1. Print.

Togores, Luis E. *Millán Astray, legionario*. Madrid: La Esfera de los Libros, 2003. Print.

"Topography." *Oxford English Dictionary.* 2nd ed. Oxford: Oxford UP, 2009. CD-ROM. 1 disc.

Torgovnick, Marianna. *The War Complex: World War II in Our Time.* Chicago: U of Chicago P, 2005. Print.

Torrente Ballester, Gonzalo. *Javier Mariño: Historia de una conversión.* Madrid: Editora Nacional, 1943. Print.

– Prólogo. *José Antonio Primo de Rivera (Antología).* 3rd ed. Madrid: Ediciones Fe, 1942. 9–35. Print.

– "Razón y ser de la dramática futura." *Jerarquía. La revista negra de la Falange* 2 (1937): 50–80. Print.

Tovar, Antonio. *El Imperio de España.* Valladolid: Afrodisio Aguado, Ediciones Libertad, Servicio de Prensa y Propaganda de F.E. de las J.O.N.-S, 1936. Print.

Trapiello, Andrés. *Las armas y las letras: Literatura y guerra civil (1936–1939).* Rev. ed. Barcelona: Península, 2002. Print.

Triviño Valdivia, Francisco. *Los del Tercio en Tánger.* Valencia: Editorial "Arte y Letras," [1926]. Print.

Tuan, Yi-Fu. *Space and Place: The Perspective of Experience.* Minneapolis: U of Minnesota P, 1977. Print.

Turner, Victor. *The Ritual Process: Structure and Anti-Structure.* New Brunswick: Aldine, 1997. Print.

Tusell [Gómez], Javier. *Franco, España y la II Guerra Mundial: entre el Eje y la neutralidad.* Madrid: Temas de hoy, 1995. Print.

– *La Segunda República en Madrid: Elecciones y partidos políticos.* Madrid: Tecnos, 1970. Print.

Ucelay-Da Cal, Enric. *El imperialismo catalán: Prat de la Riba, Cambó, D'Ors y la conquista moral de España.* Barcelona: Edhasa, 2003. Print.

– *Llegar a capital: Rango urbano, rivalidades interurbanas y la imaginación nacionalista en la España del siglo XX.* Papers de la Fundació 137. Barcelona: Fundació Rafael Campalans, 2002. Print.

– "Los orígenes del fascismo en España: el militarismo." *Josep Fontana, història i projecte social: Reconeixement a una trajectòria.* Ed. Josep Fontana. Vol. 1. 2 vols. Barcelona: Crítica, 2004. 1380–410. Print.

– "The Spanish Civil War as a National Conflict." Valis, *Teaching Representations* 33–43. Print.

Uguet, Antonio. "Orden General del Desfile de la Victoria." *Arriba* 18 May 1939: 7. Print.

Umbral, Francisco. "Los prosistas de la Falange." *Las palabras de la tribu (De Rubén Darío a Cela).* By Umbral. Barcelona: Planeta, 1994. 231–71. Print.

"Unidad de destino." *Arriba* 21 Mar. 1935: 1. Print.

Urrutia, Ángel. *Arquitectura española, siglo XX.* Madrid: Cátedra, 1997. Print.

Vadillo, Fernando. *Arrabales de Leningrado.* 1971. 3rd ed. 2 vols. Alicante: García Hespán, editor, 1992–93. Print. Vols. 3 and 4 of *La gran crónica de la División Azul.* 9 vols. 1991–6.

– *Balada final de la División Azul, I. Los legionarios.* Granada: García Hispán, editor, 1984. Print. Vol. 7 of *La gran crónica de la División Azul.* 6 vols. 1967–96.

– *Los irreductibles.* Granada: García Hernán, editor, 1993. Print. Vol. 8 of *La gran crónica de la División Azul.* 9 vols. 1991–6.

– *Lucharon en Krasny Bor.* 1975. 3rd ed. 2 vols. Granada: García Hispán, editor, 1994. Print. Vols. 5 and 6 of *La gran crónica de la División Azul.* 9 vols. 1991–6.

– *Orillas del Voljov.* 1967. 3rd ed. 2 vols. Granada: García Hispán, editor, 1991–2. Print.Vols. 1 and 2 of *La gran crónica de la División Azul.* 9 vols. 1991–6.

– *Los prisioneros.* Madrid: Barbarroja, 1996. Print. Vol. 9 of *La gran crónica de la División Azul.* 9 vols. 1991–6.

Valis, Noël. "Civil War Ghosts Entombed: Lessons of the Valley of the Fallen." Valis, *Teaching Representations* 425–35. Print.

– ed. *Teaching Representations of the Spanish Civil War.* New York: Modern Language Association of America, 2007. Print.

Valls, Fernando. *La enseñanza de la literatura en el franquismo (1936–1951).* Barcelona: Antoni Bosch, 1983. Print.

Varela, Antonio. "Foxá's *Madrid, de corte a checa*: Fascism and Romance." Brown, Compitello, Howard, and Martin 95–109. Print.

Vega Viguera, Enrique de la. *No es culpable: Historia de la División Azul.* Madrid: Barbarroja, 1999. Print.

"Los 27 puntos del Programa de Falange Española de las J.O.N-S." *Doctrina de F.E. de las J.O.N-S. Los 27 puntos del Programa de Falange Española de las J.O.N-S. Discursos de los camaradas jefes José Antonio Primo de Rivera, Raimundo Fernández Cuesta y Onésimo Redondo.* Valladolid: Ediciones "Libertad," n.d. 3–11. Print.

Vidal, César. *Checas de Madrid: Las cárceles republicanas al descubierto.* 2nd ed. Madrid: Random House Mondadori, 2004. Print.

Villalobos, Federico. *El sueño colonial: Las guerras de España en Marruecos.* Barcelona: Ariel, 2004. Print.

Virilio, Paul. *Art and Fear.* Trans. Julie Rose. London: Continuum, 2003. Print.

– *L'Espace critique.* Mesnil-sur-l'Estrée: Christian Bourgois Éditeur, 1984. Print.

– *L'Insécurité du territoire.* 2nd ed. Paris: Galilée, 1993. Print.

– "The Kosovo War Took Place In Orbital Space." Interview by John Armitage. *CTheory.net.* 18 Oct. 2000. Web. 7 Nov. 2010.

– *Speed and Politics.* Trans. Marc Polizzotti. Los Angeles: Semiotext(e), 2006. Print.

– *War and Cinema: The Logistics of Perception.* Trans. P. Camiller. London: Verso, 1989. Print.

Virilio, Paul, and Sylvère Lotringer. *Pure War.* Trans. M. Polizzotti and B. O'Keeffe. New York: Semiotext(e), 1997. Print.

Viscarri, Dionisio. "Literatura prefascista y la guerra de Marruecos." *RILCE: Revista de Filología Hispánica* 12.1 (1996): 139–57. Print.

– *Nacionalismo autoritario y orientalismo: La narrativa prefascista de la guerra de Marruecos (1920–1927).* Bologna: Il Capitello del Sole, 2004. Print.

– "Preserving the Falangist Myth in the Post-Franco Era: The Case of Fernando Vadillo's *Los legionarios* and *Los irreductibles.*" Merino and Rosi Song 70–98. Print.

Visser, Romke. "Fascist Doctrine and the Cult of the *Romanità.*" *Journal of Contemporary History* 27.1 (1992): 5–22. Print.

Vivanco, Luis Felipe. "El arte humano." *Escorial. Revista de cultura y letras* Nov. 1940: 141–50. Print.

Wahnón, Sultana. *La estética literaria de la posguerra: Del fascismo a la vanguardia.* Amsterdam: Rodopi, 1998. Print.

Warf, Barney, and Santa Arias, eds. *The Spatial Turn: Interdisciplinary Perspectives.* London: Routledge, 2009. Print.

Whittam, John. *Fascist Italy.* Manchester: Manchester UP, 1995. Print.

Wilford, John Noble. *The Mapmakers.* 2nd ed. New York: Vintage, 2001. Print.

Williams, Raymond. *The Country and the City.* Oxford: Oxford UP, 1973. Print.

– *Marxism and Literature.* Oxford: Oxford UP, 1977.

Winchester, Clarence, and F.L. Wills. *Aerial Photography: A Comprehensive Survey of Its Practice and Development.* London: Chapman and Hall, 1928. Print.

Wirth-Nesher, Hana. *City Codes: Reading the Modern Urban Novel.* Cambridge: Cambridge UP, 1996. Print.

Wittgenstein, Ludwig. *Philosophical Investigations.* Trans. G.E.M. Anscombe. 2nd ed. Oxford: Blackwell, 1997. Print.

Wyke, Maria. "A Flexible Rome: Fascism and the Cult of *Romanità.*" Edwards, *Roman Presences* 205–20. Print.

Ximénez de Sandoval, Crispin, and Antonio Madera y Vivero. *Memorias sobre la Argelia.* Madrid: Impr. y estereotipia de M. Rivadeneyra, 1853. Print.

Ximénez de Sandoval, Felipe. *Camisa azul (Retrato de un falangista).* Valladolid: Librería Santarén, 1939. Print.

Ydígoras, Carlos María. *Algunos no hemos muerto.* 1957. Barcelona: Noguer y Caralt, 2002. Print.

Žižek, Slavoj. *Did Somebody Say Totalitarianism? Five Interventions in the (Mis)use of a Notion.* London: Verso, 2001. Print.

– *Tarrying with the Negative: Kant, Hegel, and the Critique of Ideology.* Durham: Duke UP, 1993. Print.

– *Violence.* New York: Picador, 2008. Print.

Index

TORONTO IBERIC